The Sources of

Richard R. Nelson

The Sources of
Economic Growth

Harvard University Press
Cambridge, Massachusetts / London, England

Copyright © 1996 by the President and Fellows of Harvard College
All rights reserved
Printed in the United States of America
Second printing, 2000

First Harvard University Press paperback edition, 2000

Library of Congress Cataloging-in-Publication Data

Nelson, Richard R.
  The sources of economic growth / Richard R. Nelson.
      p.   cm.
  Includes bibliographical references and index.
  ISBN 0-674-82145-9 (cloth)
  ISBN 0-674-00172-9 (pbk.)
  1. Economic development.   2. Technological innovations—Economic
aspects.   3. Social institutions.   I. Title.
HD75.N45   1996
338.9—dc20   96-16498

Contents

Introduction   1

Part I   A Perspective on Economic
Growth and Technical Advance   7

1. Research on Productivity Growth and Productivity Differences:
Dead Ends and New Departures   9

2. Capitalism as an Engine of Progress   52

Part II   Schumpeterian Competition   85

3. Schumpeter and Contemporary Research on the Economics
of Innovation   87

4. Why Do Firms Differ, and How Does It Matter?   100

5. On Limiting or Encouraging Rivalry in Technical Progress:
The Effect of Patent-Scope Decisions   120

Part III   Science and Technical Advance   145

6. The Role of Knowledge in R&D Efficiency   147

7. The Link between Science and Invention:
The Case of the Transistor   159

8. American Universities and Technical Advance in Industry   189

Part IV   International Differences and
              International Convergence   231

9. The Rise and Fall of American Technological Leadership:
   The Postwar Era in Historical Perspective   233

10. National Innovation Systems: A Retrospective on a Study   274

   Notes   303

   References   308

The Sources of Economic Growth

Introduction

This volume brings together a collection of essays on economic growth, technical advance as the key driving force behind economic growth, and the social institutions that mold technical advance and in turn are modified as an essential part of the economic growth process. Together, they provide a theory about economic growth that differs in certain important respects from the neoclassical growth theories which have been dominant in the economics profession since the late 1950s. The theory sketched in these essays fits very well, however, with the writings on economic growth of general economic historians and historians of technology, business, and social institutions.

In their emphasis on the primacy of technical advance, some of the "new" neoclassical growth theories developed over the last few years have an affinity with the perspective presented here. Both the new neoclassical growth theories and the theory developed in this book are motivated by the recognition that the older neoclassical growth theories dealt with technical change awkwardly at best. The theory sketched here differs from the new neoclassical growth theories in its attempt to encompass what I believe are the central elements of the historical accounts of technical advance and related activities and institutions. The way I have put the matter implies that I do not believe that the new neoclassical growth theories have yet achieved consistency with the empirical record. To do so will require, I believe, their taking on board some of the elements treated in these essays.

The discrepancy, obvious to anyone who studies both, between neoclassical growth theory, old or new, and the pictures drawn by economic historians should not be regarded as a natural and unproblematic difference between the writings of those concerned with developing formal theories and those concerned with describing what actually has been happening. Certainly in the natural sciences a discordance between "theory" and "observation" is treated as an indication that something is the matter with the theory, or that there are problems with the observations, or some of both. I propose that the differences between economic growth as depicted in neoclassical growth theory and the characterization of economic growth by historians should be treated as an indication that something is amiss with that kind of growth theory. In addition, it needs to be recognized that the historical accounts of economic growth are rife with theory, albeit of a different kind than that in standard growth modeling.

Although much of the theorizing in historical accounts is implicit, the essays on economic growth presented here are expressly theoretical. They focus on certain variables and mechanisms and ignore others. Their arguments are causal. At the same time they are closer to detailed empirical work than most of the extant neoclassical growth models, and their expression is in words not mathematics.

There has been relatively widespread recognition among economists that traditional neoclassical theory has proved an inadequate vehicle for organizing understanding about economic growth. One manifestation of the unrest has been the development of new neoclassical growth theories. But there have been other new developments as well, and some of these fit well with the theoretical positions staked out here. Thus the theory of growth contained in these essays stresses several features that are prominent in some of the new theoretical writings on complex dynamic systems. One is path dependence. What happens to the system today can profoundly influence how the system will behave for a long time into the future. Put another way, history matters. Economic historians always have believed this, and now formal theorists are beginning to understand that the historians likely have a point. The essays in this volume present a picture of strongly path dependent economic growth processes.

A second feature of many of the new models of complex dynamic systems is the possibility of strong interactions among variables. Virtually every one of the essays in this volume takes issue, explicitly or implicitly, with the proclivity of neoclassical growth theory, and the "growth accounting" which was associated with that theory, to try to "divide up the credit" for economic growth among different sources, assigning so much of the credit to technical advance, so much to growing capital intensity, so much to rising educational attainments—to list the sources generally treated as the most important. From the perspective developed here, this "dividing up" exercise is nonsense. On the one hand, the large increases in capital intensity that have been the hallmark of modern economic growth were induced by, and would have been worthless without, the development of new technologies that productively employed more capital per worker. On the other hand, the development of those new technologies would not have borne economic fruit without the physical investments that put them in operation. In turn, since the last part of the nineteenth century the work that has led to the development of new technologies increasingly has been the province of university-trained engineers and applied scientists. Technical advance has been dependent upon the development of certain kinds of human capital. But we would not have had the vast increases in educational attainment that we have seen if education had not given significant economic advantages.

To use a sports analogy, growth accounting is like an attempt to describe the performance of a basketball or football team in terms of the particular performances of the individuals on that team, without taking account of the fact that the performance of any one player often is made possible by what the others are doing, and even that whether a particular action on the part of one of the players helps or hinders team performance has a lot to do with the extent to which it is complementary to what the others are doing.

Perhaps even more than the new neoclassical growth theories, the theory of growth presented in this volume singles out a particular factor as the key driver behind growth—technical advance. This proposition is not in conflict with the one put forth just above—that the various sources of growth need to be understood as mutually reinforcing one another. The argument is that technical advance is both the principal driver and the key catalyst in calling forth and supporting the investments in new physical capital and human capital that are needed as accompaniments. Behind the scenes are a set of institutions that demark modern capitalism and support and channel the major components of the economic growth process, a matter to which I shall return shortly.

I noted that some of the new neoclassical growth models have taken on board the notion of the centrality of technological advance. However, these new models have not as yet come to grips with the fact that technical advance must be understood as an evolutionary process. It involves the generation and testing of a variety of new alternatives in competition with one another and with prevailing practice, with ex post selection determining the winners and losers. This is a different view of technical advance from that contained in the old neoclassical growth theories or, as yet, in any of the new, which presume that technical change and economic growth are processes involving moving equilibria, whose paths can be and are foreseen (except for random events) by the involved actors. A few of the new neoclassical growth models have built in some of the uncertainty that surrounds technical advance, but none of them recognizes that in a regime of continuing technical advance, the economy as a whole is in a continuing state of disequilibrium. While there may be forces at work at any time to move the system toward equilibrium given the prevailing state of technology, advances in technology and other jolts keep offsetting these equilibrating forces. Thus the regularity and the order that the analyst sees in economic growth may be analogous to the "spontaneous order" highlighted by the new work on dynamic systems rather than an order that can be explained as a moving general equilibrium of a traditional sort.

The view presented in these essays of the economic institutions that have grown up to generate and support technical advance and the other activities and investments associated with economic growth also diverges significantly from the presently standard picture in economics. Conventional economic theory stresses the primacy of for-profit firms, in competition with one another, operating in markets in which supply and demand are balanced so as to determine equilibrium prices and quantities. Other economic actors, for example, government agencies and regulatory bodies, are recognized almost as an afterthought and treated as "responses to market failures." Entities such as universities, or scientific and technical societies or industry associations, are not placed in the picture, at least when it is drawn theoretically as contrasted with being described historically.

The essays in this volume present a different picture, one in which technical advance and economic growth are seen as proceeding through the operation of a complex set of institutions: some for-profit, some private but not-for-profit, and some governmental. Even among private for-profit entities, there is some sharing and openness about technology and other matters as well as proprietary rivalry. The "nonmarket" elements of the system of institutions are not seen as coming about as the result of responses to "market failure" any more than market institutions can be explained by "public sector failure." Rather, the prevailing set of institutions—private and public, rivalrous and cooperative—are seen as having evolved through a complex set of processes that involve both individual and collective action. Institutional change, like technological change, must be understood as an evolutionary process.

The result is that modern capitalism is a very complex system. While there are certain similarities among the modern major capitalist nations, there are also major differences. The complexity of modern capitalist systems was shamefully overlooked by many Western economists in the advice given to the economies that used to be in the socialist camp, and that are now struggling to develop reliable capitalist alternatives. While these countries now are learning that there is much more to modern capitalism than privatization and markets, it is devoutly to be hoped that their lag in learning about the complexity of modern capitalism, in part because few people told them, will not badly set back the reform endeavor.

My original plan was to include several essays in a more mathematical mode to illustrate the continuum I want to argue exists in economics between theory expressed verbally and theory expressed more mathematically. Constraints on space, however, ruled this out. And my editor persuaded me of the advantages of a volume that, while expressly theoretical, did not employ mathematics.

Economists need to recognize that until recently (measured against the history of our discipline) the standard mode of economic theorizing was verbal. Adam Smith, David Ricardo, Alfred Marshall, Frank Knight, Joseph Schumpeter, John Maynard Keynes—to list only some of the figures that have dominated the history of economic thought—used words not mathematics as their dominant theoretical media. Only recently has the term "theory" come to mean theoretical argument expressed mathematically.

I want to argue that the present conventional thinking in economics, which accepts as "theory" only something that is presented mathematically, and draws a relatively sharp line between theorizing and empirical exploration or description, is unfortunate and misguided. I strongly believe that what Sidney Winter and I have called "appreciative" and "formal" theorizing both are important parts of the intellectual enterprise in economics, and that when that enterprise is going well, these two elements work together.

By appreciative theorizing, I mean the descriptions and explanations of what is going on that economists put forth when they are paying considerable attention to the details of the subject matter. While less abstract than formal theorizing, this attempted description of what is going on certainly is a form of theorizing, albeit theorizing relatively close to the empirical subject matter. Formal theorizing is more abstract or more distanced from the empirical subject matter. Formal theorizing can sharpen up, correct, and lead appreciative theorizing. In recent years most formal theorizing has been mathematical. Earlier it was mostly verbal. But whether expressed mathematically or verbally, when formal theorizing does not pay attention to or has little contact with appreciative theorizing, that is a sign of trouble. The formal theoretical enterprise then becomes self-referential and loses much of its contact with the subject matter it purports to be about.

Here I think that the divide between formal growth theory and the appreciative theorizing in economic history writing has been particularly unfortunate. Most of formal growth theorizing has proceeded in awareness of the numbers that provide some measures of economic growth and the associated variables. Only a small portion of what empirical researchers have learned about economic growth, however, has been described in the form of "numbers." Put another way, the quantitative record of growth contained in gross national product statistics, time series of national labor and capital inputs, industry output and input series, numerical price indices, trade flows, and the like accounts for only a relatively small portion of what economists know empirically about growth. And while it is important that growth theories square with the quantitative record, that alone is not an adequate check of a theory. I would like to argue that economists doing formal growth theory have, for the most part, paid far too little attention to the qualitative historical record.

I believe that the areas of economic analysis with which I am concerned in this volume have been, over the past quarter century, suffering badly from a disconnection between formal and appreciative theorizing. Those doing formal growth theory, or reflecting theoretically on the nature of institutions of modern capitalism, have not paid enough attention to the closer-to-the-ground theorizing by economists who have been studying the matter empirically. Those doing detailed empirical work and, in the course of that work, presenting a causal story have in general not seen fit to call attention to the often major differences between their account and what is presumed in formal growth theory. As I think back on it, much of my own work during this period can be understood as the result of my growing awareness of the disjunction between formal theoretical work and the empirical studies of the subject matter, and reflects my attempts to bring these two parts of the intellectual enterprise closer together. The essays in this volume are intended to form such a bridge.

A Perspective on Economic Growth and Technical Advance

From the beginnings of modern economics as a field of study, economic growth has often been a central area of inquiry, but on and off. Much of Adam Smith's *Wealth of Nations* was about economic growth. Karl Marx was very much a growth theorist. Although the formal theory Alfred Marshall developed was concerned with "statics," much of what he wrote was concerned with patterns of long-run economic development.

But in the early decades of the twentieth century concern for long-run economic growth waned. Undoubtedly one of the reasons was that the formal theory being developed, to which Marshall had contributed, was focusing on market equilibria. The concern was with what lay behind demand and supply curves, and how these jointly determined the observed configuration of outputs, inputs, and prices. The troubled economic times after World War I and, in particular, the Great Depression also tended to pull the attention of economists toward analyzing shorter-run phenomena such as balance of payments disequilibria, inflation, and unemployment.

There was a renaissance of interest in long-run economic growth after World War II. One reason was the new National Product data, available first for the United States, and later for the other advanced industrial nations, which for the first time allowed economists to measure economic growth at a national level. Prior to the availability of these series, which owed their origins largely to the conceptual and empirical work of Simon Kuznets, economists concerned with growth had to rely on piecemeal statistics on the output of coal, or steel output per person employed in steel, and so forth. Now they had measures of economywide output and its changes over time. And with this new data, economists began to comprehend quantitatively what they had long known qualitatively—that the era they were in had been seeing dramatic increases in output per worker and per capita income. In the early 1950s, empirical work using these data made it clear that "growth of total factor productivity" was accounting for the lion's share of the measured increases in output per worker. Technological advance was proposed as a major force behind growth in total factor productivity.

For the most part, this empirical research proceeded without any elaborate theoretical structuring. In the late 1950s neoclassical growth theory was formulated and, in a sense, rationalized many of the calculations made by the empirical workers, but otherwise did not add much to the empirical research enterprise. In any case, during this period there was a considerable amount of research on the sources of growth. What was learned then has by and large stood the test of time. In the Introduction, however, I indicated at least three respects where I believe that analysis was problematic. One was its proclivity to "divide up the sources of growth," when in fact there was powerful evidence that they were strong complements. A second was a tendency to treat economic growth as a process involving moving, but continuing, equilibrium, whereas evidence of continuing disequilibrium was very powerful. Third, much of the institutional complexity of modern capitalism was repressed.

With the advantage of hindsight, we now can recognize that the 1950s and 1960s were an era of unusually rapid growth in the United States and even more so in Europe and Japan. The very rapidity of growth over that period naturally turned attention to the question of what lay behind rapid productivity and income increases. The early 1970s saw a significant decline in growth rates in the United States and the other high-income countries. With this development, the salient issues changed. Economists turned to the question of why growth rates had slowed down. The slowdown in growth and the largely unsuccessful attempts by economists to understand it brought the weaknesses of their analytic approach to growth closer to the surface.

The two essays which follow provide a natural start to this volume. Chapter 1 elaborates the history of research on economic growth that has been sketched above and provides a relatively detailed critique of the underlying prevailing theory, and it also outlines an alternative theory of economic growth, which is fleshed out in the essays that follow. At the heart of that theory is an evolutionary theory of technical change. Chapter 2 lays out its essentials.

1

Research on Productivity Growth
and Productivity Differences:
Dead Ends and New Departures

There surely isn't any excuse for another review of mainline economic research on the sources of productivity growth, and this isn't one. There is a real need for an essay that convincingly explains the recent productivity growth slowdown so that one can see the basic causes, whether they be persistent or transitory, and the policy options. This, however, is not an essay about the slowdown either, although it is motivated by the inconclusiveness of studies on that topic. The premise behind this essay is that the theoretical model underlying most research by economists on productivity growth over time, and across countries, is superficial and to some degree even misleading regarding the following matters: the determinants of productivity at the level of the firm and of interfirm differences; the processes that generate, screen, and spread new technologies; the influence of macroeconomic conditions and economic institutions on productivity growth. Sections 2 through 4 will deal with these topics, considering heterodox as well as orthodox literature bearing on them. In section 5, I review recent efforts to develop evolutionary models of productivity growth. But first, section 1 briefly takes up the current state of the art regarding productivity studies. I suggest that there is evident unrest about the prevailing theoretical formulation. While some empirical research sticks quite close to it, a substantial body of research proceeds along lines that deviate in important ways from the tenets of that theory.

1. The Schizophrenia of Contemporary Research on Productivity Growth and Related Phenomena

To begin, a bit of intellectual history is in order. While the conceptual apparatus used today is relatively new, the interest of economists in pro-

Originally published in the *Journal of Economic Literature* (September 1981): 1029–1064.

ductivity growth is venerable. Chapter I of the *Wealth of Nations* is mostly about technological advance and productivity growth, as it is called today. John Stuart Mill, like Karl Marx, was a growth theorist. Alfred Marshall was much interested in long-run economic change. In classical growth theory, as in neoclassical growth theory, firms were viewed as profit-seeking and industries as competitive. But the connotation was more flexible than that of contemporary orthodox price theory. In the verbal discussion, if not in the formal analysis, growth was viewed as an evolutionary process. A nation's institutions were regarded as stimulating or blocking, fruitfully channeling or diverting that process.

It is worth noting that, during the early postwar era, the microeconomic conceptions underlying empirical analyses of productivity growth seem closer to the older theoretical tradition than to the newer one. In his 1952 review article, Moses Abramovitz stressed the links of then current empirical research to classical thinking, and remarked upon the absence of many recent theoretical developments. Yet despite the absence of the modern framework for thinking about productivity growth, the papers by Jacob Schmookler (1952), Theodore Schultz (1953), Solomon Fabricant (1954), John Kendrick (1956), and Abramovitz (1956) are remarkable in foreshadowing the central conclusion of studies done somewhat later within the neoclassical framework—that the growth of output experienced in the United States has been significantly greater than reasonably can be ascribed to input growth. Technological advance, changing composition of the work force, investments in human capital, reallocation of resources from lower to higher productivity activities, economies of scale, all were recognized as parts of the explanation. But no attempt was made to divide up the credit. The possibility of significant interaction was recognized. In these studies factor prices were used to weight the various inputs in order to get a measure of total input growth; however, there was no elaborate justification of this as a means of tracking movements along a production function, nor did the authors postulate that the economic growth path being followed was one of moving competitive equilibrium. Schmookler refers to Joseph Schumpeter, and Abramovitz to Simon Kuznets, both of whom had stressed that growth was a disequilibrium process.

It is also interesting that the early postwar theoretical discussion about economic growth did not proceed using the language and concepts of microeconomic theory, but involved the extensions of Keynesian theory by Roy Harrod and Evsey Domar. These models employed neither the assumption of profit maximization, nor the presumption of competitive equilibrium, nor even full employment. Indeed, the models were designed to explore the conditions under which aggregate demand and full employment output could grow at the same rate. Given the assumptions, the required conditions were extremely stringent.

1.1 The Neoclassical Art Form and Its Elaboration

Robert Solow's 1956 theoretical article was largely addressed to the pessimism about full employment growth built into the Harrod-Domar model. Solow pointed out that the razor's edge property of that model was due largely to the assumption of fixed coefficients. With flexible factor coefficients the capital-labor ratio could adjust so that, for any savings (investment) rate, demand for and supply of labor could grow at the same rate. He went on to develop what has come to be called the (stripped down) neoclassical model of economic growth. (Trevor Swan published a similar, if less influential, analysis in 1956.) In that model he admitted the possibility of technological advance which shifted the production function. In his 1957 empirical article, Solow showed how to attribute growth to various sources and how to measure technological advance, consistent with his theoretical formulation. Let me review here the basic ideas to call attention to certain features that by now are so familiar they seldom are reflected upon.

Firms are the key productive actors, transforming inputs into outputs according to a production function. The production function, which defines the maximum output achievable with any given quantity of inputs, is determined by the state of technological knowledge. Technological knowledge is assumed to be public or at least this is implicit in models based on an industry or an economy-wide production function. Firms choose a point on their production function to maximize profits, given product demand and factor supply conditions. Generally these markets are assumed to be perfectly competitive so that a firm treats prices as parameters. Assuming factor prices adjust, and no Keynesian difficulties exist, the model is consistent with full employment and usually this condition is assumed. Over time, output grows as inputs increase and firms move along their production functions, and as technology advances. Assuming differentiability of the production function, profit maximization, and factor price taking on the part of the firms, the elasticity of output with respect to any input equals its share of total factor returns, at least for small increments to inputs. Proportional output growth due to input growth along the production function equals the sum of share-weighted proportional input growths. The residual (if any) is a measure of production function shift, or technological advance.

There clearly are some strong presumptions here. The view of firms and markets is very stylized—not much room for incompetent management, labor-management strife, or oligopolistic rivalry. Technological advance, while acknowledged as a central feature of growth, is treated in a very simple way, and the Schumpeterian proposition that technological advance (via entrepreneurial innovation) and competitive equilibrium cannot coexist is ignored. Full employment is simply presumed; the model contains no specific mechanism to ensure this condition. The sources of growth are viewed as operating independently and additively. While in part this reflects the mathematical analysis of small changes, in growth accounting this view is carried over to analysis of the sources of growth over relatively long periods of time. The institutional environment is very simple—there is no particular place in the structure for labor unions, banking systems, schools, or regulatory regimes.

The purpose of any theoretical formulation is to provide a particular focus and interpretation. Reality inevitably is much richer than any theory. Empirical scholars in economics recognize that theory is abstraction, and try to take into account important factors omitted by prevailing theory. Further, a simple theory, initially formulated, is amenable to later widening, deepening, and to modifications that deal with anomalies. The fruitfulness of a broad theoretical structure has to be judged in terms of the energy it lends to research, and the power of the knowledge won through that research. By these criteria the neoclassical art form clearly must be judged as having been very fruitful. It has given life, direction, and a considerable degree of coherency to research done by a large number of economists over a considerable period of time. That research has greatly enhanced our knowledge of the factors behind productivity growth.

But while sensible scholars treat formal theoretical frameworks pragmatically, still these frameworks constrain as well as focus, blind as well as illuminate, the empirical research endeavor. Prevailing formal theory influences profoundly what empirical data are ignored, and how attended empirical data are interpreted. Where empirical scholars consider phenomena beyond those that have a theoretical place, analysis tends to be ad hoc.

It is my belief that research, guided by the neoclassical paradigm, has reached a stage of sharply diminishing returns, with many important questions still not resolved adequately. Further, a sizable portion of research on productivity growth, while perhaps initially undertaken to widen and deepen the simple neoclassical model, has identified phenomena and relationships not treated adequately, or even denied, by that theory. It is not my purpose to review in any detail all of the research under discussion; there have been a plethora of such reviews. But to establish my point, it is useful to review some of that literature, organized under two headings. The first consists of research that appears, at first glance, to follow the neoclassical line rather closely. The second has clearly deviated in certain important ways.

1.1.1 *Growth Theory and Growth Accounting.* Since the mid-1950s, considerable research has proceeded closely guided by the neoclassical formulation. Some of this work has been theoretical. Various forms of the production function have been invented. Models have been developed which assume that technological advance must be embodied in new capital. Technological advance has been made endogenous to the theory through linking it to an increasing R&D capital stock. In some models technological advance is assumed to be steered toward saving on labor or on capital by factor prices. Many of these models were reviewed in Solow (1970), and by Hans Binswanger and Vernon Ruttan (1978).

Much of the work has been empirical and guided by the growth accounting framework implicit in the neoclassical model. Edward Denison (1962, 1967, 1974), Kendrick (1961 and 1973), Zvi Griliches (1960), and Dale W. Jorgenson and Griliches (1967) made especially important early contributions to this literature. A good portion of this work has been concerned with squeezing down the size of the residual. While Solow's interpretation gave particular economic meaning to it, *viz.,* technological advance, in most economists' eyes the residual had much weaker analytic standing than that part of growth that could be explained by movements along a production function. There certainly was reason for economists to try to assure themselves that any change in productivity that could be accounted for by movements along the production function in fact were so treated. Labor input was disaggregated and attention paid to the education, sex, and age composition of workers. Capital input was disaggregated into machinery and structures, and its "vintage" considered. Some scholars attempted to account for natural resource input. In recent years energy has been counted as a separate input. For good surveys of the earlier work, see M. I. Nadiri (1970), and F. H. Hahn and R. C. O. Matthews (1967). Denison (1979) and Kendrick and E. Grossman (1980) provide more recent, if less sweeping, reviews, along with analyses of more contemporary trends.

Several empirical scholars have incorporated depreciated R&D in a "meta" production function, and attempt to measure the contribution of R&D spending to growth of productivity. See Edwin Mansfield (1968, chap. 3), Griliches (1980), and Nadiri (1980). These approaches preserve the potential importance of technological advance as part of the neoclassical growth story, but remove or soften the association of technological advance with the residual.

An important recent methodological development in production function fitting and growth accounting has been the exploitation of duality relations implicit in the theory of the profit-maximizing cost-minimizing firm. The solution to a firm's profit-maximization problem simultaneously determines output and input, costs and profits, as a function of product and factor prices. Duality theory points to ways to calculate production function shape and shift indirectly through estimation, for example, of the shape and shift of factor demand curves, or of the cost function. These methods permit greater use to be made of price data in estimating production relations. Jorgenson and his colleagues (see particularly Christensen and Jorgenson, 1971) have been prominent in developing these methods.

The research briefly described above varies considerably in the extent of adherence to the basic neoclassical model of economic growth. The work of Jorgenson and his colleagues, and of Griliches, stays quite close to the theoretical line. The growth accounting work of Kendrick, and particularly of Denison, demonstrates vividly, however, a point made earlier. Sensible empirical researchers often will add variables that the formal theoretical models do not contain and, more generally, interpret the background theory very flexibly. Thus Denison explicitly considers inefficiencies in resource allocation, and institutional obstacles to the adoption or spread of best practice technology. In his recent studies of the productivity growth slowdown, Denison has included variables like the extent of regulation, and the cost of crime. It is important to note, however, that where relatively formal theoretical arguments are used in growth accounting studies, these are drawn from the neoclassical model. The non-neoclassical variables are, simply, just added on, in an ad hoc way. But variables take on meaning only in the context of a theoretical framework, formal or informal. If these kinds of variables, or processes, are important, we need to revise our conceptualization of the growth process. I review below certain bodies of research which, even more than the growth accounting studies, suggest a need for reconceptualization, and which point in certain interesting directions.

1.1.2 *Eclectic Research on Productivity Growth.* The neoclassical picture of the firm is stark and simple. While many economists were using this basic theory of the firm, other scholars were studying a variety of factors bearing on the productivity and productivity growth of firms while entertaining different and more complex views of their nature. Such variables as the style of decision making, background of the managers, and the character of labor management relations were considered. See Charles Perrow (1979). Still other scholars focused their attention on differences in productivity among firms in the same industry. An early classic study is by László Rostas

(1948); more recent examinations of U.S.-U.K. differences are reported in Richard Caves (1980). While this research has not definitively established any robust correlations, it has provided evidence that neoclassical variables do not account for all of the differences among firms in productivity and related variables.

At the same time that some scholars were including R&D in a neoclassical production function, others (sometimes the same scholars in a different guise) were exploring more pragmatically the microeconomics of technological advance. The research of Edwin Mansfield and his colleagues (1968, 1971, 1977) has been especially fruitful. Two key findings should be highlighted here. One is the substantial uncertainty that surrounds efforts to create, or evaluate, new technologies. The other is the considerable variation among firms in the technologies they create and adopt, particularly in industries where technology is advancing rapidly; this fact is partly the consequence of uncertainty, but stems in part from the fact that much of technological knowledge is proprietary. More generally, the assumptions built into the simple form of the neoclassical model—that technological knowledge is a public good and that growth is an equilibrium process—would appear to be inconsistent with the mechanisms that draw forth new technologies in capitalist economies.

Other scholars refocused attention on resource reallocation from low to high productivity sectors (see, for example, Kindleberger, 1964; Kuznets, 1966, and Cornwall, 1977)—a phenomenon highlighted in earlier writings, but repressed in the macro-neoclassical formulation. Various multisector neoclassical models were developed and techniques developed to estimate the contribution of resource shifts to growth within a growth accounting framework (Denison, 1962 and later volumes). But resource reallocation surely reflects and involves discrepancies between factor returns in different sectors. While it is simple to extend the neoclassical model to include many sectors, the basic logic of that model is committed to continuing equilibrium, not resource reallocation driven by prevailing disequilibrium.

That model also is committed to relatively sustained full employment, and indeed relatively full employment and considerable macroeconomic stability marked the heyday of rapid growth during the late 1950s and 1960s. Angus Maddison (1967) and Andrew Schonfield (1965), among others, ascribed a good share of the credit for rapid productivity growth to sustained full employment, and inquired into the conditions responsible for that state of affairs which contrasted so sharply with the Depression years. Both gave part of the credit to adoption by governments of Keynesian policies. Many scholars have noted that the post-1973 productivity growth slowdown has been accompanied by higher average unemployment and inflation rates, and stop and start economic policies. Economists divide on the explanation, but Maddison (1980) and James Tobin (1980) seem not to doubt that inadequate policies are at least in part responsible for macroeconomic instability and slow growth.

Other scholars focused their attention on social, political, and economic institutions. Abramovitz (1979), among others, has stressed that international trade in goods, capital movements, and flows of technology proceeded much more rapidly in the post–World War II era than earlier. Various scholars contrasted the educational systems in various countries, noting the longstanding weakness of British training of engineers compared with the German and American (Pavitt, 1980). It was observed that the United States, Canada, and Britain were marked by significantly more strike activity than Germany, Sweden, or Japan. During the 1970s, when productivity growth rates began to decline, scholars began to focus on changing institutional structures as a possible cause. The rise of regulatory environments was one such possibility (Denison, 1979; MacAvoy, 1979; and Kendrick and Grossman, 1980). Other scholars focused on the institutions of the welfare state (Bacon and Eltis, 1976; Lindbeck, 1974).

One might consider that these lines of analysis are not inconsistent with the neoclassical growth accounting formulation, but are attempts to widen or deepen it. Still, the questions being asked, the variables being considered, and the relationships explored, are different from those out of which the standard model is built. At the least, their consideration poses the analytic problem somewhat differently. But it is also possible that the canonical neoclassical formulation not merely oversimplifies but obscures some of the central features of productivity growth. If so, it might be worthwhile to consider some significantly different theoretical formulations.

1.2 Limitations and Tensions

The main reason for entertaining more eclectic or even radically novel approaches to understanding productivity and productivity growth is that research within the orthodox framework is not answering certain questions adequately, and where answers are provided, these raise still further questions. This is so for each of the three roughly separable kinds of questions that have been explored. What lies behind a particular country's growth rate and its variation over time? What explains differences in levels and rates of change of productivity among countries? Why do certain industries experience much faster productivity growth than others?

The first kind of question probably has received the most attention. It is noteworthy, therefore, that despite all the effort to make the "residual" go away it still is very much with us: see, for example, Denison (1962, 1974, 1979). And despite all the effort to give substance to its interpretation as "technological advance," or "advance of knowledge," that interpretation is far from persuasive. Everybody knows that the residual accounts for a hodge-podge of factors, but these are difficult to sort out. If this "measure of our ignorance" is not completely mysterious, it certainly is not well understood.

If anything, the research attempting to explain cross-country differences in productivity levels, and in productivity growth rates, has been even less conclusive. Differences in capital-labor ratios, and in educational attainments, may explain a portion of the macro-productivity level differences, but a "residual" plays a large role in the cross-country analysis. Again, Denison's work (1967) is representative. Differences across countries in their post–World War II productivity growth rates are not correlated with inter-country R&D spending differences. They are, however, strongly connected with two other variables—their initial productivity levels (or distance from the U.S. productivity level) and the rates of growth of their physical capital stock. As a general rule, countries that started with low productivity levels closed some of the gap, and the gap was closed faster by countries that had high investment rates. See, for example, John Stein and Allen Lee (1977) and Abramovitz (1979). But there are some nagging exceptions. The considerable difference in initial productivity levels itself is something which is not well explained by neoclassical growth theory. While the different experiences during World War II explain part of the U.S. productivity advantage in the 1950s, Maddison's data (1979) show that the United States was the productivity leader by 1913. Why? Britain's productivity growth record has been poor relative to other countries since World War I. Why?

The research on cross-industry differences in productivity growth focuses on a phenomenon repressed in the macroscopic models—that very significant interindustry differences in fact exist. R&D spending is an important explanatory variable in cross-industry analysis. For a review see Richard Nelson and Sidney Winter (1977). By and large the industries with rapid measured "technological advance" are heavy R&D spenders themselves, or their suppliers of inputs and capital equipment are heavy R&D spenders, or both. But how does one explain why certain industries are so much more R&D intensive than others?

As recounted above, scholars not bound by the details of the neoclassical perspective have put forth a somewhat richer one, and one which diverges from neoclassical assumptions in certain important respects. The remainder of this paper reviews and examines in more depth heterodox literature bearing on three different but related topics touched on in the earlier discussion.

The first is the nature of the variables affecting productivity at the level of the individual firm, and the sources of differences in productivity among firms. As suggested, there is a substantial body of literature which does not see a firm simply as a profit seeking "chooser" of inputs and technology operating within a framework of widely available technological knowledge, and known factor prices. Rather, it sees a firm as a "social system," which motivates its members in greater or lesser degree, and which influences how managerial decisions are carried out, and how alternatives are perceived and evaluated. Several studies of interfirm productivity differences have found social systems related variables, as well as neoclassical ones, to be important. In addition, these studies document significant differences in technologies employed by different firms, differences not readily explained on neoclassical grounds. These topics are explored in section 2.

The second is the character of technological advance. Standard theory sees it either as an exogenous datum—a set of publicly available new opportunities that firms exploit, having regard to factor prices—or as the result of an accumulation of knowledge gained by investment in R&D guided by prospective returns. Uncertainty and the particular incentives provided by patent rights are ignored in most treatments of the connection between R&D and productivity growth. Research on the microeconomics of technological advance has, however, highlighted that the effort devoted to the discovery and exploitation of new technology is strongly influenced by uncertainty, and also is a function of the property rights that invention creates. Also, there is an interaction between exploitation of knowledge and learning itself. Government, universities and many other agents, besides user firms, play a part in technological advance. This literature is reviewed in section 3.

The third is the connections among and the factors behind the proximate sources of growth treated in growth accounting. It is apparent that these sources interact strongly. Capital accumulation and education support technological progress. At the same time, the returns to physical investment and increased education depend on technological progress. This suggests that, in deepening analysis of growth, we ought to consider not only forces that affect the proximate sources singularly, but also more general features of the economic environment and of political and social institutions that support all three sources and the growth they promote. We are, therefore, led to a concern with international differences and intertemporal changes in the economic environment and institutions—tentative forays into which are the subject of section 4.

Some of the features stressed in the heterodox literature are easily incorporated in an extended neoclassical theory, others are most difficult to assimilate. However, while the heterodox view is more complex than the neoclassical one and differs in certain fundamental respects, it is amenable to its own simplifications and abstractions. To the extent that innovation involves considerable randomness, and to the degree that the processes that screen and select new technologies take time to work out, evolutionary models of productivity growth may be more appropriate than neoclassical ones. The essay concludes by sketching some recent attempts at evolutionary modeling.

2. The Determinants of Productivity at the Level of the Firm

Economists have not engaged in much empirical research on the determinants of productivity of individual firms. Interest in productivity differences among firms has been mostly focused on intercountry differences in industry averages. In part, this neglect is due to the fact that economists, generally, are interested in data aggregated at least to the level of an industry. In part it reflects the fact that, from the neoclassical perspective, there are few interesting empirical questions that can be explored or resolved by studying particular firms or by considering differences among individual firms in similar market conditions.

From the neoclassical perspective the productivity of a firm at any time is simply determined by available technology, and market conditions (primarily factor prices). There may be reason, however, to back off from the strong presumptions contained in this analysis. In the first place, large business firms are complex organizations. If this fact is recognized, certain difficulties with the simple neoclassical theory of productivity emerge. In the second place, the assumption that technological knowledge is public, to be obtained and exploited freely, which is implicit in this analysis, is suspect even as a simple first approximation; indeed, the presumption of public technological knowledge may preclude effective analysis of the processes by which new technologies are generated, screened, and spread. In this section I consider, first, some of the literature on the relationships between firm organization and productivity. I then turn to some of the studies of interfirm productivity differences.

2.1 The Firm as an Organization

The neoclassical theory of the firm contains two strong presumptions. The first is that "technological knowledge" is the basic determinant of the input-output possibilities available to a firm. The second is that management "choice" among clearly defined options determines what a firm does. The implicit image is of a firm as a machine, with some human parts, with management controlling the action by making choices which are implemented through direct command, perhaps mediated by a tight hierarchical structure. These presumptions may be useful as first approximations, or they may not.

To begin with, recognize that most firms contain many people, and generally have a management group distinct from the individuals who actually carry out production. This calls attention to complications repressed in the neoclassical theory of production. One is the need for mechanism to coordinate action. Given division of labor, jobs must be compatibly designed and appropriately meshed. A network of information flow is needed so that the whole job gets done smoothly. This problem of organization would exist even if all individuals shared the goals of top management. But, in general, the employees of firms do not automatically share the same objectives as managers. So there is a requirement for motivation and monitoring. The literature on organization in its relation to productivity, mostly outside of economics, contains both these themes.

James March and Herbert Simon (1958) distinguish two broad lines of development of what they call "classical" organization theory. One, deriving from the work of F. W. Taylor (1911), is concerned with physical activities involved in production. Its hallmark is concern for "scientific management" which means, largely, the design of a particular task, the flow of material among stations, etc. A second, flowing from the work of L. H. Gulick and L. Urwick (1937) and Max Weber (1947) is focused on problems of organizational structure—on such questions as whether certain widely used services should be organized under one service department, or decentralized to the various using departments. Both traditions are concerned immediately with coordination (although in different ways), and also with motivation schemes. Thus Taylor wrote about incentive pay schemes. Weber discussed the advantages of career ladders. But both pictured the organization as a machine with human elements, and saw the management problem as one of designing a machine so that it worked well.

Something like this image of organization lies behind the standard theory of the firm. The human actors are classified as "labor," but consideration of problems of coordination and control is repressed. In certain more complex models, the organizational aspects of production may be admitted by recognizing that resources are involved in coordinating and controlling, in addition to those involved in "producing." The state of coordination and control "technology" may even be admitted as a variable, like production technology. But given these constraints, management is still viewed as *choosing* what is to be done. This characterization is in the spirit of the Jacob Marschak–Roy Radner theory of teams (1972) and is consistent with recent work on agency. See Steven Ross (1973).

But few contemporary scholars of organization now view behavior in organizations as did the classical organization theorists. The famous Hawthorne works experiment (Roethlisberger and Dickson, 1939), conducted over fifty years ago, led organization theorists to abandon the notion that an organization was like a "machine" that could be programmed and tightly controlled by top management, and to recognize explicitly that an organization is a social system which may be resistant or unresponsive to management commands. Scholars like George Homans (1950) and Charles Perrow (1979) have outlined such a view on organizational behavior.

Technology, in the sense of well-articulated blueprints, defines what is to be done only within broad limits; there is considerable room for variation in effort, attention, and cooperation. Careful "work design" can narrow the range, but not eliminate it. Similarly, management cannot effectively "choose" what is to be done in any detailed way, and has only broad control over what is done, and how well. Only a small portion of what people actually do on a job can be monitored in detail.

Given the perhaps considerable range of flexibility left by technology and managerial instructions and overview, the social system of work sets norms, enforces them, and resists pressures or commands from management that are inconsistent with those norms. The lower levels of representatives of management, such as foremen whose function is to monitor and discipline performance, are at least partially coopted into the social system. Consistent with classical organization theory, certain ways of doing things and certain performance levels will be established and adhered to, but contrary to the teaching of classical theory, these will be influenced as much by the social structure as by management directions and pressures. On the other hand, these procedures and norms can be influenced by the sentiments and attitudes of the workers, and by the tone of the organization more generally. Management may have a good deal to do with what that tone is. How workers feel about their job, about their fellow workers, about management, and about the organization, may be more important in influencing productivity than is the particular way they are instructed to do their work, the formal organizational structure, or even financial incentives.

It is natural that, given this view of things, the variables stressed by Taylor and Gulick and their followers would appear to be relatively uninteresting and unpromising as management tools. Scholars of organization who accepted the new "social system" view looked in other directions. A number of different research traditions developed.

Chester Barnard (1938), and later Simon (1957), stressed that top management is limited in the number of things it can control or attend to in any detail, and explored the functions of management in a more constrained setting. Three broad functions were identified: to fix long-term firm strategies that provide guidance to lower-level decision making; to establish a social context and incentive schemes so that lower-level decision makers act in the firm's interests; and to deal with exceptional cases and problems that cannot be handled routinely or delegated.

Other scholars—Christopher Argyris (1962) is an important example—concerned themselves with decision-making styles and procedures. The key questions they asked were whether better information was developed, whether better decisions were made, whether implementation was more effective, under participatory modes of decision making or in a hierarchical regime in which decisions are made at the top, with little participation from below.

Other traditions were concerned with worker morale and loyalty to the organization. One group of scholars focused on the fact that workers brought to their work feelings and problems from outside their jobs, and proposed that, by neglecting these, management caused alienation. Various forms of grievance procedures were studied to understand how these affected how workers felt about their jobs and how this, in turn, influenced their absentee rates, strike rates, and productivity. Other scholars studied the way the design of work influenced worker satisfaction and interest. Richard Hackman and Greg Oldham (1980) provide an excellent review of these lines of research.

This sample of questions explored by students of organization is not meant to be exhaustive. However, the questions are illustrative of the wide range of topics opened when a firm is recognized as having a social system, which influences how "technologies" in fact are operated, and how "managerial decisions" are translated into action.

It would be an impressive and rewarding accomplishment if students of the human relations and social organization of firms were able to identify

and document well-defined stable relations between variables under management control and the effectiveness of workers' performance. But my
reading of the results of fifty years of research, one consistent with the evaluation of several review articles by scholars in these fields, is that few such
stable relations have yet been found. See Hackman and Oldham (1980), and
Victor Vroom (1976) for critical reviews. The newer research tradition has
been persuasive, I believe, in casting doubt on the machine model of firm
organization. But it has not been able as yet to identify and measure the key
organizational variables and their influence.

In some experiments, greater worker participation in making decisions
increases productivity, and in others it decreases productivity, and in others
it doesn't matter. In some experiments, "job enrichment" makes workers
more content and productive, in others more content but not more productive, and in still others less content but not less productive. It could be that
such variables, omitted in the standard economic model, should simply be
treated as introducing a random element. Or it could be that there are stable
relations to be found but that these are more complicated than those who
initially did the experiments contemplated. For example, the desire of
workers to participate in decisions may depend on the extent to which the
issues involved are viewed as scientific and technical, and not particularly
relevant to their well-being, as contrasted with being germane to their well-
being and within their ken (Gouldner, 1954). Job enrichment may be preferred by workers if it doesn't involve working harder, but not if it does
(R. B. Goldmann, 1975).

It may be that the bearing of such considerations is more limited in some
contexts than in others. Thus some technologies may impose rather tight
control of the pace of work—for example, chemical process technology is
embodied in equipment which to a considerable extent controls the flow of
materials. In contrast, in many mechanical operations, technologies lend
themselves to a degree of worker control (Woodward, 1965). Some market
environments are loose enough to permit slack performance; others are
strongly competitive and force both management and labor to toe the mark
(Lupton, 1963). Organization theorists are now coming to recognize these
complexities. In any case, economists who have themselves neglected these
kinds of questions bearing on productivity can hardly complain about the
slow advance of knowledge regarding them.

In recent years a number of economists have begun to design models of
firms where people reside as individuals, not as automatons. The behavioral
theory of Richard Cyert and James March (1963) obviously fits this mold.
So do the analyses of Oliver Williamson. Williamson (1970) has shown how

the organization of a multiproduct firm influences the decisions reached by management just below the top. He suggests that the multidivisional form leads to better decisions (and higher productivity?) than the older unitary structure. More recently (1975), he has been concerned with the effect on profitability (productivity?) of a firm's decisions regarding what is to be done "inside" the firm and what is to be done through market arrangements. Harvey Leibenstein (1966, 1976, and 1979) has proceeded from the proposition that human beings do not automatically work their hardest or think fruitfully about what they are doing (both of these themes are recognizable in Taylor). He has been particularly concerned with the role of competition and pressure on the firm to keep what he calls "X inefficiency" under control.

Peter Doeringer and Michael Piore (1971), and more recently Richard Freeman and James Medoff (1979) have drawn attention to the way internal labor markets shape the workings of intrafirm society, and to the role of the union (along with management) in defining internal labor markets and other aspects of the firm's internal society.

In the last few years, there has been increasing recognition among economists and other scholars, and lay persons, of the significant differences in organization and decision-making styles among firms in different countries. Thus, Ronald Dore (1973) has contrasted the structure of large post–World War II Japanese firms with that of British firms, noting significant differences in hiring policies, tenure provisions, decision-making style, and social characteristics. Spurred by Japan's continuing rapid growth, American scholars have recently turned to consider differences between American and Japanese firms. The aim seems to be to encourage American firms to move closer to the Japanese model: see, for example, Vogel (1979).

But the relations are complex and poorly understood. It is worth noting that Japanese productivity grew very rapidly prior to World War II, and that "lifetime employment," and the related cultural characteristics of modern Japanese firms, were not the norm prior to World War II, but are largely a development of the 1950s. It also might be recalled that, only a few years ago, scholars were touting the flexibility of the American system, the ability of scientists and engineers to set up small new firms, the movement of engineers from firm to firm, as the reason for our technological leadership in such fields as semiconductors (Charles River Associates, 1980).

2.2 Intra-Industry Productivity Differences among Firms

As stated above, the interest of economists in productivity differences among firms (in the same industry) has mostly been focused on international differences, and most of the empirical research has been concerned with data at the industry level. However, there has been some research based on data for individual firms. Some of this research has compared firms in different countries, some has compared firms in the same country. Not surprisingly, the international comparisons show considerable differences in productivity. It may be more surprising that there is considerable variation in productivity among firms in the same industry in the same country.

Neoclassical theory would explain international productivity differences by differences in factor intensities associated with dissimilar factor prices, and might admit, as well, possible capital vintage effects. Intranational differences would have to be explained largely in terms of vintages, although local variations in market conditions also might play a role. While the firm by firm comparisons do generally show these variables to be significant, studies suggest that differences in internal organization are also important, and knowledge about and access to technologies as well.

Of the studies of differences in productivity levels of firms in different countries, a sizeable fraction has been concerned with the low productivity of British firms relative to firms in other countries. There have been two waves of such studies: one, just after World War II, focused on United Kingdom and United States comparisons; the second, more recent, was concerned with Britain's lagging productivity relative to Europe as well as the United States.

Rostas's study (1948) is perhaps the best known of the earlier wave. Written prior to the theoretical developments that came to dominate economic thinking about productivity (and growth) after the 1950s, Rostas's examination of the factors behind measured productivity differences is relatively undisciplined theoretically, but is pragmatic, sensible, and sensitive. He identifies the variables that later come to dominate thinking—differences in capital intensity (which he measures by horsepower) and in the quality and vintage of the equipment employed. Perhaps because American plants are so much larger than British plants in most industries, Rostas is concerned with possible scale economies, and with the relationship between the ability to exploit scale economies and the size of the market. But he also considers Taylor-like variables such as the layout of work in the factory and the general quality of management. Rostas also lists a variable which increasingly came to attract attention in studies trying to explain the low productivity of plants in Britain—the attitudes and work practices of labor.

C. F. Pratten's studies are representative of the second wave. In one (1976a) he compared plants of the same international company producing similar products, but in different countries, and observed that there was a general rank order, invariant with respect to industry, of output per worker in the different plants. American plants were at the top, mostly followed by German plants; French and British plants were toward the middle, and Spanish plants last. His quest was for the reasons behind the relatively poor performance of the British plants.

When managers of the companies were asked for their explanation of the differences, they sometimes said that their more productive plants had better (newer?) machines than British plants. But they said as well that the British plants were "overmanned." This overmanning extended to both overhead activities, like office work, and to physical production lines. The managers attributed this in part to restrictive union practices and in part to a combination of general union pressure and lack of effective management response. Several respondents remarked on the greater difficulty in getting British labor to accept changes proposed by management, compared with the situation in America or Germany.

In a companion study, Pratten (1976b) examined differences in output per worker in Swedish plants and closely matched British plants. This study also showed systematic country differences. Swedish plants had higher output per worker in virtually every industry where a paired plant comparison was made. The reasons put forth by Pratten include greater mechanization in Sweden, better labor relations, and more technically sophisticated management.

D. T. Jones and S. J. Prais (1978), in their study of productivity differences among U.S., German, and U.K. auto plants, come up with a similar list of factors. The authors emphasize overmanning in British plants. They also report more "downtime" owing to machine breakdown plus union-imposed constraints on repair manning, work slowdowns, and strikes. The authors stress as well that British plants tend to be smaller and to have shorter production runs than West German or American plants, and that this is costly in terms of productivity. They propose that the small size of the British plant is not unrelated to the variables mentioned above. Labor-management relations tend to be worse in a variety of dimensions in larger British plants than in the smaller ones, job slowdowns are more common and more difficult to deal with, strikes occur more often, etc. Jones and Prais suggest that these troubles make British managers loath to set up large plants.

Several of the studies discussed above mention that technology in British firms was not as "up-to-date" as in American or Swedish firms. There are various possible reasons. One is quite compatible with the neoclassical formulation. If technological knowledge were public and new capital always embodied the best available new technology, then newer plants would be inherently advantaged relative to older plants. These are the assumptions built into "vintage" models such as those by W. E. G. Salter (1966), Solow, Tobin, C. Von Weizacker, and M. Yaari (1966), and L. Johansen (1972). In some of the comparisons it appears that machinery in the British firm was older than that in its foreign counterpart. But technological knowledge is not completely public. Some is proprietary. Even where not proprietary, information about new technology is not costless to acquire and may require considerable sophistication, and luck, to evaluate properly. More, the technology chosen by a firm in many cases is not determined by management preference alone. The choice may be constrained by legal restrictions to buy from nationals or by other forms of governmental influence. In many cases, technological change is the subject of labor-management bargaining.

The case studies of British industry, contained in the volume edited by Pavitt (1980), indicate that the technological backwardness of British industry has less to do with the age of British machinery, than with the low level of technological training of British management and the lack of strong organized R&D in many British firms. This conclusion is consistent with that reached two decades earlier by Carter and Williams (1957).

Studies of productivity differences among firms in different countries often seem written as if firms in the same country had roughly similar productivity levels. However, there are now a number of studies that reveal much intracountry variation.

For more than a half century the U.S. Bureau of Labor Statistics (BLS) has been engaged sporadically in studies of productivity differences among U.S. firms. During the 1920s and 1930s, studies of industries, ranging from garments (1939) to automobile tires (1933), from shoe making (1923) to blast furnaces (1929) were made. While these differed slightly in format, invariably they contained the following elements. The overall production processes of the industry were broken down into a large number of detailed subprocesses, and "best practice" was identified. Evolution of best practice over time was described and changes in labor productivity using "best practice" tabulated. In general, the BLS studies also presented data on productivity levels of firms not using best practice. There was considerable dispersion at any time, and a large gap between average practice and best practice. Quite often a number of firms operated at productivity levels less than half of best practice.

Not all the studies attempted to explain this variation, but a number did. Many of the variables mentioned are the same as in the studies focused on international differences—differences in degree of mechanization, vintage of the equipment and technologies employed, differences in the layout of work. Differences in labor-management relations were not mentioned.

By contrast, Freeman and Medoff and their colleagues have recently considered the effect of unionization on productivity in several American industries (1979). Unionization would appear to be a variable different in kind from those conventionally treated by economists, and the exploration of its effect amounts to an hypothesis that internal organization matters. The authors consider whether a firm is unionized or not as a dichotomous variable in a regression that also contains a firm's capital-labor ratio and other more conventional factors. They interpret their regressions as showing that unionized firms are more productive than nonunionized firms in the furniture and cement industries, but less productive in the underground bituminous coal industry. They identify the cases where unionization increases productivity with situations where there is room for a mutually advantageous deal between management and labor and where the presence of a union facilitates the making of that deal. They identify the negative cases with situations where the conflict is more basic and unionization simply strengthens labor's hand. The questions raised by Freeman and Medoff are important, even if the answers presently put forth are not particularly compelling.

Salter's study (1966) is one of the few that explicitly recognizes the productivity dispersion revealed by the BLS data. He focuses on differences in technology associated with different ages of plants. Lars Wohlin (1970) analyzed productivity dispersion and productivity growth in the Swedish pulp and paper industry, using Salter's model. Since the main interest of both authors was in productivity growth in the industry as a whole, not interfirm productivity differences per se, neither author tested to see the extent to which vintage differences explain productivity differences. Griliches and Vidar Ringstadt (1971) attempted to explain differences in productivity among Norwegian firms on the basis of (regional) factor price differences (they did not consider vintage differences). Not much of the productivity dispersion was so explained.

Neoclassical models of course ignore organizational variation of the sort considered by Freeman and Medoff. As stated above, they ignore as well differences among firms in access to and knowledge about new technologies, and the complex values and processes often involved in making decisions about what technologies to adopt. While intracountry differences regarding technological access and choice might be expected to be smaller than intercountry differences, they still might be considerable. The only direct test, that I know about, of the extent to which new capital systematically embodies better technology than older capital is by R. G. Gregory and Denis

W. James (1973). They found that, in Australian industry, firms with new capital on average did have higher productivity than firms with older capital. There was considerable productivity variation, however, among firms with new capital.

2.3 What Explains Productivity Differentials?

While augmentation of the production function framework to recognize capital of different vintages has brought within the compass of neoclassical theory a significant portion of the factors behind productivity differences among firms, there certainly is more to the story. Cross-firm variation in productivity at any moment of time is an interesting phenomenon in itself. But is there any reason why such variation ought to be recognized in analysis of productivity growth, at an industry level, over time? I think the answer is yes, and for two reasons. First, to the extent that firm structures and decision-making style are important variables influencing productivity, this fact in itself cautions against thinking of the determinants of labor productivity simply in terms of the quantity of complementary inputs, and technology. A richer set of variables is involved. These variables may, and likely do, influence productivity in the average firm, as well as the extent of inter-firm dispersion. While some of the added set may reasonably be treated as constant, others may not. Second, to the extent that differences across firms reflect differences in the technological bets they have made, or differences in access to certain technologies, this fact may reflect important aspects of the process of technological advance. Since virtually all scholars now agree on the central role of technological advance and productivity growth, it clearly is important to have an adequate conceptualization of the way the technological advance occurs and of what determines its rate.

2.3.1 *Organizational Aspects.* It is clear that variables relating to the differences in individual or organization capabilities enter prominently in many of the above-mentioned studies. The two such variables most often cited are the character of labor-management relations, and the skills of management. Were this survey widened to include comparisons of firms in developed and less developed countries, worker skills and experience would also show up as important variables. See R. Nelson, P. Schultz, and R. Slighton (1971). While in principle the production function framework can be stretched to count any input that is differentiated from another in any way as a different input, differences in skills and organizational effectiveness would appear to have a different logical standing than, say, differences in the amount of machinery of a given type. They can be best interpreted in terms of what is accomplished by given inputs with a given "technique," not in terms of different quantities of inputs employed in that technique.

While not absent within a country, differences in labor-management relations, and managerial and worker skills enter most prominently in the comparison between firms in different countries. One is tempted to argue that relatively systematic and durable national differences in institutions and general socioeconomic climate lie behind these differences. The studies of British productivity certainly are consistent with the proposition that fractious labor-management relations and management deficiencies in technical training have been the rule, not the exception, in Britain for a long time. On the former, see Caves (1980); on the latter, C. F. Carter and B. R. Williams (1957) and Pavitt (1980). These variables certainly need to be considered in analyzing productivity differences. To the extent that they influence innovativeness, they may also be important for understanding productivity growth rates. This, of course, raises the question of how durable these characteristics are. At least some scholars who have pointed to these variables have done so with the hope that, if their costs were better comprehended, they might be changed. I return to the question of institutional change in section 4.

2.3.2 *Technological Competence.*   While vintage models do capture certain features of the processes of technological advance, they repress others. Vintage models assume that, in their decisions regarding new technologies, all firms face and know about the same set of alternatives. Differences in choice then reflect differences in factor prices and other market conditions. The proprietary nature of many new technologies, and the time and cost involved in learning about them and in learning to use them, are assumed away.

Accept the proposition built into vintage models that today's distribution of productivity levels among firms is in part at least the cross-sectional consequences of technological advance, where today's best new technology is not adopted instantly and completely by everybody. But change (or augment) somewhat the assumptions of the vintage model to admit that some firms today are not aware of, make wrong bets about, and maybe even are blocked off from access to today's new technology. Recognize that, if innovation is at all risky or costly (because of R&D or other resources involved) it is imitation lag that yields the return to the innovator. If all firms were fully informed about and had full access to new technology created by one firm in an industry, that firm would have far less incentive to develop and introduce new products or processes.

Then today's cross-sectional dispersion, its width and its expected durability, should be recognized as an essential element of the productivity growth process, even if there were no strict "embodiment" requirement. One would not expect that all firms would be on the same production function, vintage effects included or not. Some of the variation, not explained by orthodox variables, could be treated as random noise. But part surely reflects that some firms have systematically gained a head start over their competitors. The internal organization, or the R&D spending, of a firm might then be systematically related to its average technological lead, or lag, compared with the pack. This part of the variation surely should not be treated as random noise. It is what drives the growth process. I turn now to survey some literature on the process of technological advance.

3. The Dynamics of Technological Advance

Virtually all scholars of productivity growth now agree on the central role of technological advance. Over the past two decades, a considerable amount of research has been done on the processes involved. Much of that work has been within the intellectual framework provided by neoclassical growth theory, but some has proceeded along other lines. These alternative lines of research have revealed some serious difficulties with the treatment of technological advance within the orthodox framework.

The neoclassical model oversimplifies the connections between an industry's R&D spending and technological advance, and its implicit view of the links between market conditions and profit opportunities for R&D spending contains an internal contradiction. The model also oversimplifies the way that new technology is spread throughout an economic sector. Intersectoral and interindustry differences, which are considerable and important, are repressed. I consider these topics in turn.

3.1 The Generation of New Technology

As recounted in section 1, the neoclassical formulation has progressed from treating technological advance as an unexplained residual, to consideration of technological advance as the result of an accumulating R&D capital stock. In turn, R&D investments by firms have been treated as subject to the same profit maximizing calculations as other investments. Most such models relate profits opportunities for R&D investments directly to the market conditions facing an industry, in particular to product demand (price or quantity) and factor prices.

This model of R&D and technological advance is consistent with certain observations. In cross-industry analysis, differences in R&D spending by industries and their suppliers are associated with differences in measured rates of technological advance, in the manner that the model would lead one to expect. There are a large number of studies showing that R&D funding, and patenting, are sensitive to economic variables that plausibly influence the profitability of R&D. Schmookler (1966) and others have accumulated a great deal of evidence that shifts in the pattern of demand for goods and services lead to parallel shifts in inventing. The predictions of induced innovation models regarding the effects of changes in factor input conditions on inventing are, by and large, borne out. See Binswanger and Ruttan (1978).

There are, however, four aspects of the processes by which new technology is generated that are repressed or ignored in these models: (1) there is considerable uncertainty involved; (2) there usually are multiple undertakers of R&D; (3) when R&D is done competitively, the regime of property rights in technologies significantly influences, and warps, R&D incentives; and (4) in many technologies, learning by doing is an important complement, or substitute, for R&D.

(1) Virtually all case studies of R&D aiming to create a technology significantly different from established practice reveal considerable uncertainty at the start of the endeavor. For a discussion of some of the implications, see Burton Klein (1962). Firms are unsure how much expense and time will be needed to achieve a satisfactory new design; they do not know the exact form that design will take, or how the technology will perform. In recent years, some investigators have attempted to quantify these uncertainties by measuring the accuracy of forecasts of R&D costs and time required to complete a project (Mansfield, 1968, 1971, 1977). But these studies do not focus on perhaps the most significant form of R&D uncertainty—uncertainty about which of a vast set of potential designs or solutions will prove the best. Uncertainty may be the wrong word. Humans engaged in inventive efforts simply do not, and in the nature of the case cannot, comprehend the set of alternatives that they face. The set is fundamentally vague. This is an essential feature of R&D and technological advance. Any model that attempts to relate productivity growth to past R&D, or to predict how R&D allocation will shift as a result of changed market conditions, ought to recognize that the generation and selection of ideas for investigation involves a major element of chance. This random element in the execution of individual projects by single firms takes on special significance in a context of multiple R&D decision makers.

(2) In general, a large number of independent R&D decision-making units are involved in exploring opportunities for technological advance in an industry. The number may include firms in the industry in question, other firms that supply materials and capital equipment, users of products, private inventors, potential entrants to the industry, sometimes governmental laboratories and universities. This pluralistic R&D system generates a portfolio of projects. Generally, there will be some duplication or near duplication within that portfolio but also considerable diversity.

This diversity is socially valuable. The batting average of scientists and engineers, economists, government officials, and businessmen in predicting the most important future technological developments has been abysmal. Experts very often are wrong both in what they predict will happen, and in what they predict won't happen. It is fortunate that there are many different experts who lay their bets in different ways. But the diversity also means that there will be winners and losers in the R&D game.

(3) In an optimal portfolio there will be individual winners and losers. There is no reason to believe, however, that the pluralistic portfolio is likely to be optimal or even efficient, either in terms of maximizing expected industry profits, or social welfare. In many sectors, pluralism is associated with competition among profit-seeking business firms. In such a setting, the R&D that is profitable, and unprofitable, is strongly influenced by the existing regime of property rights. There are several different kinds of "market failure" associated with an industry structure, involving a number of competing firms, each doing R&D, in which the firm that achieves an invention first receives a patent that prevents direct copying (Nelson, 1980).

First, there is a simple positive externality problem. If patents prevent direct copying, but there is a "neighborhood" illuminated by an invention that is not foreclosed to other firms by patents, some of the returns to innovation leak away. Second, there are a set of problems akin to those occurring when there are multiple independent tappers of an "oil field." If patents are strong and wide, a competitive race to get there first may waste R&D inputs. And, given that one firm gets there first, there are incentives for another firm to develop a substitute technology even if it is worse than the best one, provided it is better than the one it has and the best is blocked by patents. The imitation threat deters R&D spending. The competition race and blocking problem may spur R&D spending, but toward socially inefficient allocations.

The unlikelihood of social optimality of course carries implications, if subtle ones, regarding government R&D policy. But it carries predictive modeling implications as well. While it may generate relationships that square qualitatively with some empirical evidence, a model which assumes that industry R&D is determined so as to maximize industry (expected) profit, or social (expected) value, is fundamentally misspecified.

(4) In many industries learning-by-doing, or by using, is an important part of the process by which new technology gets created, modified, and broken in. Learning-by-doing is in part a substitute for, and in part a complement to, learning through R&D, and is the source of certain important phenomena repressed in the orthodox formulation.

The learning-by-doing aspects of a technology tend to be difficult to articulate in a manner that can be "transferred" easily. Thus, even in a non-proprietary context, there is a certain "privateness" to technological knowledge. Where such tacit knowledge is important, one firm can learn from another, but such technology transfer usually involves personnel exchange, example setting, and teaching. See W. H. Gruber and D. G. Marquis (1969), G. R. Hall and R. E. Johnson (1970), and David Teece (1976, 1977). The costs and time involved can be considerable.

Industries and technologies apparently differ significantly in the importance of learning by doing (or operating experience more generally) and, relatedly, in the limits of what can be learned in distinct deliberate R&D activity. In some technologies, deliberate R&D is very important—pharmaceuticals, aircraft, and electronics are good examples of industries where R&D, as a specialized activity separate from production, is very powerful. In some activities, it would appear that very little can be done in R&D that goes beyond learning-by-doing or using—violin making and education are cases in point. It is noteworthy that technological advance—both as measured by growth theorists and as recounted by historians and technologists—has been much more rapid where R&D is effective than where learning-by-doing is dominant. This is one reason for the correlation between an industry's R&D spending and its technological progress. But, it is a reason that does not imply that more R&D would significantly increase productivity growth in industries where, presently, such growth is slow. In some of these, at least, R&D is low because it is not particularly fruitful.

Why might this be? A number of scholars have pointed to the great difference in strength of the underlying sciences or of engineering in the former technologies as contrasted with the latter (Rosenberg, 1976). An inference might be drawn that a reasonably strong science or engineering base is required to make separate R&D—staffed by people with special training—more fruitful than the simple natural experimentation and learning that occurs in the course of production itself. The issues here are important and clearly in need of further exploration.

Even where R&D is an important source of technological progress, there appears often to be strong interaction between learning through experience, and through R&D. Learning curves, reflecting reductions in unit production cost as experience accumulates, are steep in the production of aircraft and semiconductors. See Harold Asher (1956) and Charles River Associates (1980). This partly reflects growing practical experience that leads to smoother, better coordinated action on the part of labor, better management understanding, and more effective work design and job layout. But part involves experience feeding back to generate redesign of certain aspects of product and process. The study by Samuel Hollander (1965) of productivity growth in Du Pont's rayon plants, and by Carl Dahlman (1979) of a new Brazilian steel plant, show intricate connections between learning by doing and R&D. Eric Von Hippel (1976) and Nathan Rosenberg (1980) have pointed to the role of user learning and feedback to R&D in the evolution of certain products.

R&D itself is an activity that involves learning through experience. Thus in many industries, technological advance is characterized by an occasional major technological breakthrough involving a significant change in operating principles, followed by a series of improvements and variegations. These follow-on advances may, in cumulative impact, be as important as the original breakthrough. John Enos (1962) has described this phenomenon for petroleum technologies, Ronald Miller and David Sawers (1968) for aircraft, and Devendra Sahal (1981) for tractors and other items of mechanical machinery.

In these cases, it makes sense to think of accumulating "knowledge capital." The knowledge capital builds up within a particular technological regime, and becomes obsolete when a radically new technology is introduced and comes to dominate. But the variables and relations involved are not well pictured by the simple neoclassical formulation.

3.2 The Screening and Spread of Technology

In the original neoclassical formulation, new technology instantly diffuses across total capital. In the later vintage formulation, technology is associated with the capital that embodies it and thus adoption of a new technique is limited by the rate of investment. But in this latter formulation, as in the original one, uncertainty and the proprietary nature of some new technologies are repressed. Once uncertainty is recognized, the trial in actual practice of new technology can be seen as an extension of the research and development process, another stage in the progressive winnowing and refining of ideas spawned by dreamers and inventors. Somewhat peculiarly, however, almost all research on the screening and spreading of new technology has been concerned with new technology that turned out to be productive. The mistakes and aborts, of which there are plenty, have been neglected.

These are two conceptually distinct kinds of mechanisms by which the use of a profitable new technology is spread. One is the diffusion of a new technology from firm to firm. The other is the growth of firms that use a superior technology relative to those that do not. The relative weights on these different mechanisms differ from sector to sector, and from technology to technology.

There is a large literature on the diffusion of (generally nonproprietary) new technology among potential users. Among economists, Griliches's work on the diffusion of hybrid corn was pathbreaking (1957). Mansfield has conducted extensive studies of diffusion of new technology in industry (1968, 1971, 1977). Scholars from other disciplines also have studied diffusion. Griliches's work on hybrid corn followed on a longstanding tradition of research on diffusion by rural sociologists. See, for example, Ryan and Gross (1943). The sociologists Coleman, Katz, and Menzel were early students of diffusion of new practice among physicians (1957).

More recent research has amply confirmed a central result of these early studies. When a technology is new, there is considerable uncertainty among potential users as to its merits. There is some disagreement among economists about the sophistication of users' judgments. Contrast Griliches (1957), who assumes that farmers in general judge competently the merits of hybrid corn, with Ray (1974), who reports that the calculations made by firms often are quite haphazard or arbitrary. But it is clear enough that firms (managers) differ in the speed with which they evaluate new options, the judgments they arrive at, and even the range of options of which they are aware.

Information about a new technology grows as more firms employ it and as their experience accumulates. Firms may rationally decide to delay adoption of a new technique until they have information about the experiences of other firms. Several scholars have noted that, under such conditions, a "contagion" model might apply to diffusion. See, for example, Griliches and Mansfield, above. Such a model, even were there no requirement for new capital to embody new technology at any time, would lead one to expect a significant gap between average and best practice of the sort we have observed in the preceding section. Further, there is no guarantee that new capital will embody the best new technology. See Gregory and James (1973).

In most of the diffusion studies, the source of the new technology lies outside the industry or sector where its use is spreading. Thus hybrid corn was developed by government laboratories and seed companies, not farmers. Mansfield's studies were of the spread of new equipment, produced by a supplying firm, among using firms. The mechanism for spread of an innovation clearly is different when one of the firms in the industry is itself the source of the innovation. In such a setting, the innovative firm may have incentive to restrict its use by other firms.

When innovative firms are able to expand their capacity and market share at the expense of their rivals, this competitive mechanism, rather than (or along with) diffusion may be a principal one by which a new technology comes to replace an older one. Indeed, the ability to shield a new technology from one's rivals (at least temporarily) and to expand one's market share, provide strong incentive for a firm to undertake research and development. The extension of use of a new technology so developed tends to involve the growth of the capital and market share of the innovating firm. There have been only a few studies explicitly concerned with the relation between a firm's innovative successes, and its growth or decline. One is by Mansfield (1968). He found that innovating firms do, in fact, tend to grow more rapidly than the laggers. Almarin Phillips, studying innovation in the civil aircraft industry, also found that the market share of an innovating firm tended to grow rapidly (1971). Studies of competition in the pharmaceutical industry (David Schwartzman, 1976) and in the semiconductor industry (Charles River Associates, 1980) show that the market share of different companies is closely connected to their innovative successes.

Even in industries where an innovating firm can significantly expand its market share at the expense of its rivals, diffusion also plays a role in the spread of new technologies. In the first place, innovating firms are seldom able to shield their technologies from their rivals completely, at least not for very long. Patented innovations can be copied, or the protected process bypassed by some substitute. A study by Mansfield et al. (1980) shows that these costs may be considerable, but not insuperable. In the second place, capital goods and material suppliers often are important sources of new technologies, and these sources have an interest, not in the restriction of their new technologies, but in their rapid spread among the potential users in the industry.

Diffusion is the dominant mechanism for the spread of a new technology in sectors where the firms are small compared with the market as a whole and where for a variety of reasons, they are unable to expand their market shares rapidly. Farming is the archetypical example. Residential construction, and many service industries, are other examples. Physicians' services fit this mold. Many public sector activities have this characteristic; education, firefighting, and refuse collecting are examples. In such activities, firms are not rivals, and there are no strong disincentives to sharing technological knowledge. In these circumstances a network of information exchange about technology develops. Journals that publicize relevant information appear. Professional societies and conferences play important roles in disseminating information, and managers consult with their fellows.

These also are industries and activities where firms have little or no incentive to engage in R&D on their own. These sectors, therefore, are dependent for their technology upon suppliers, upon cooperative R&D mechanisms, or upon government financed R&D. Thus, while doctors and nonteaching hospitals rarely do R&D on their own account, pharmaceutical companies do and the government supports significant medical R&D largely through the medical schools. Farmers do not engage in research but seed and equipment suppliers do, and the government funds agricultural R&D at the land grant colleges.

I have written as if the spread of a new technology, and its development, were separate processes; in many cases they interact strongly. As stated, one reason why potential users wait before adopting is lack of adequate information to form a judgment. As use spreads, information feeds back not only to potential users, but to the designers of the product and their competitors. The learning phenomena described in the preceding section proceed along with diffusion, the product is redesigned to improve its performance, and production costs drop. Some potential users may choose to wait for the second or third generation of a new technology to appear before the plunge. As the product improves, and versions better suited for particular classes of users appear, more and more potential users find it profitable to adopt. See Paul David (1975). Then a significantly different, new design may come along. The product cycle begins again.

3.3 Differences among Sectors

The discussion above has identified important structural differences among economic sectors which determine who does the R&D, the relative roles of R&D and learning by experience, and the mechanisms by which new technology is carried into widespread use. The system that generates and spreads new technology in agriculture differs from the system in pharmaceuticals. The aircraft industry is not the same as firefighting. For some industries, Schumpeterian competition would appear to be a good model: for others, cooperation.

It would be interesting if one could associate certain industry character-istics with rapid technical change and productivity growth, and others with slow technical change and productivity growth. But the causal connections would not appear to be simple.

The progressive industries are all characterized by significant R&D ac-tivity either by firms in the industry, by supplying firms, or by government funded programs. In technically progressive industries marked by oligopo-listic competition, firms in the industry generally are major sources of in-novation. In technically progressive atomistic industries, technological pro-gress is dependent upon the work of outsiders. But it remains something of a puzzle as to why certain oligopolistic industries are actively engaged in R&D and others not, and why government has developed programs of R&D support for some industries but not for others. One reason why R&D has not become an established feature in some industries may be that the sci-entific and engineering basis of a technology is weak and R&D is not pro-ductive. Another reason may be that the policies and institutions that sup-port R&D have not formed.

An extensive literature has developed about the structural conditions needed for an industry to support considerable R&D, and to conduct it efficiently. See Nelson, Peck, and Kalachek (1967) and Morten Kamien and Nancy Schwartz (1975). Much of the analysis has been concerned with the Schumpeterian hypothesis that, in general, relatively concentrated oligopo-lies generate more technological progress than less concentrated industries. It now is apparent that this hypothesis is too simple and, as stated, not generally valid. Particularly in new industries, or in industries where the existing technology is relatively new, small firms and often new entrants are important sources of new technology. See John Jewkes, David Sawers, and Richard Stillerman (1969) and Charles River Associates (1980). In such a context, small scale R&D is often productive. The ability of a new firm to enter the industry and to grow then may be vital to rapid innovation. As a technology matures, experience begins to count more and the effort needed to make further improvements often becomes more expensive. See Dennis Mueller and John Tilton (1970), and William Abernathy (1978). Entry be-comes more difficult. Large size becomes a requirement for the support of efficient R&D.

But even where the structure of an industry is appropriate to support the relevant kind of R&D, successful innovation is far from an automatic result. The risks that surround R&D, and the uncertainty about the ap-propriability of results, mean that it may not be at all obvious to a firm whether it is more profitable to try to forge ahead or merely to try to stay abreast of the technological developments of competitors. If all firms make conservative judgments, an industry may be marked by very little R&D. Even where R&D is potentially fruitful, a firm which decides to innovate may be a failure if new markets are hard to crack, or if imitation is relatively easy. Even where innovation pays, the market positions of established firms may be relatively sheltered and it may take a long time before it becomes clear that the nature of competition in the industry has changed, and that the requirements of economic success and viability have been modified. This appears to be the case in several industries where British firms have been slow to realize, or act upon the realization, that a strong R&D effort now is essential for survival. See Pavitt (1980). Hayes and Abernathy (1980) believe that, during the 1970s, in many industries American management shortened their time horizons and cut back on innovative R&D. They suggest that this is one reason why the American technological lead over Germany and Japan has eroded. It may take time for this managerial mistake (if it is one) to be recognized widely and remedied. The efficacy of governmental R&D support programs is difficult to assess ex ante, or even after considerable experience has accumulated. Nor are the conditions for political support of government R&D programs well understood. While there are several good histories of the evolution of government support for basic science (see, for example, Price, 1954) no good history of governmental industry R&D assistance exists.

Thus, for analysis of the determinants of industry R&D spending, just as for analysis of the determinants of the kinds of inventions that will be made, the presumption that profitability shapes outcomes takes us one step forward. But there are many other considerations that influence R&D spending, and only a few of these are well understood. There are probably significant elements of historical chance that are unlikely to be reduced to predetermined events even within a sophisticated analysis. Over time, economic forces stimulate and guide the evolution of particular technologies. Similarly, over time economic competition molds the evolution of private and public R&D policies and institutions. But economic forces here are unlikely to be sharply defining in the short run, and considerable time may elapse before they bring about major changes.

This suggests the importance of the general economic climate of a country and its institutions, which broadly support, or hinder, innovative activity, and other sources of productivity growth. I turn now to this topic.

4. The Sources of Growth Reconsidered

In growth accounting a number of different sources of growth are identified and their contributions estimated separately. It is well recognized that such an explanation of growth has limited causal depth. The analysis can be deepened by exploring the factors determining the magnitude and character of the various sources of growth—for example, the investment rate—and their variation over time and across nations.

But the intellectual route that proceeds most naturally from the growth accounting starting place is not the only one for gaining deeper understanding. It is apparent that the sources of growth are strongly interdependent. In addition to deepening the analysis by looking for variables that impinge on each of the sources of growth, one might also try to discern broad factors or conditions that foster or hinder a generally stimulating growth environment. Intellectual exploration along this route leads naturally to consideration of macroeconomic conditions and economic institutions as the basic factors molding economic growth, and to examination of institutional inertia and institutional change.

4.1 The Attribution Problem

4.1.1 *The Adding Up Problem.* Economists like to take derivatives and to analyse the effect of small changes. The instinct is particularly strong when the focus is on the contribution of different factors of production to output. But when the changes in question are large, marginal analysis may be misleading.

Thus, factor prices measure the contribution to output of a factor at the margin. However, growth accounting usually has been concerned with changes over a considerable interval of time. The fact that the yearly percentage increases in labor, capital, and gross national product are typically quite small should not obscure the fact that, even over a period as short as a decade, the percentage changes are substantial. If there is any curvature to isoquants, the marginal productivity of any factor toward the end of a decade is influenced by the relative growths of the different factors over the decade. This is a well-known difficulty with analyses of growth based on a factor-price weighted input index.

The growth accounting procedure implicit in Solow's analysis seems to get around the problem. Factor shares are employed to estimate output elasticities rather than factor prices to estimate marginal products, and input and output indexes are defined logarithmically. Even though the marginal productivity of a factor may fall as it increases relative to other factors along a production function, its share need not. In the special case of a Cobb-Douglas production function, shares are invariant to factor proportions. Aside from the Cobb-Douglas case, factor shares are not invariant to factor proportions and will change over finite time if factors grow at different rates. The Divisia index, in which for each period the then obtaining factor shares are used as weights for a logarithmic input index, has been proposed to cope with the possible empirical problems. See, for example, M. Richter (1966). In fact, this is what Solow employed in his 1957 formulation. But while the Solow proposal recognizes curvature, it doesn't obviate the implications of curvature. If factors are complements, growth is super-additive in the sense that the increase in output from growth of inputs is greater than the sum of the increases in output attributable to input growth, calculated one by one, holding other inputs constant at their base level in each subcalculation. The growth of one input augments the marginal contribution of others. Where complementarity is important, it makes little sense to try to divide up the credit for growth, treating the factors as if they were not complements. See Nelson (1973).

The problem here is the same one that bothered economists at the turn of the century as some tried to extend the evolving marginal productivity theory of factor remuneration to a discussion of "just shares" in the sense of some sort of "average" contribution. One can analyze the contribution to output of a worker, or a machine, at the margin. It does not make sense, however, to try to calculate the contribution to output of all of labor, or all the machines. Or, to take another example, consider the sources of a well made cake. It is possible to list a number of inputs—flour, sugar, milk, and so on. It is even possible to analyze the effects upon the cake of having a little bit more or less of one ingredient, holding the other ingredients constant. But it makes no sense to try dividing up the credit for a good cake to various inputs.

It may be fruitful to consider the several sources of growth as being like the inputs to a cake. All are needed. There are two evident kinds of interaction among the three "sources" that have dominated most analyses of productivity growth—technological advance, capital growth, and rising educational attainments. First, they appear to be complementary, in the sense that increase of any one raises the marginal contributions of the others. Second, because of this, forces that lead to the augmentation of any one are likely to stimulate an increase in the others.

4.1.2 *Growth Fueled by Technological Advance.* In a context of strong interaction among factors, if analysis is to proceed it is necessary to focus on the key processes involved and try to see the role of the various factors in these processes. It is useful, I think, to view technological advance as the central driving force. I propose, also, that reallocation of resources ought to be seen as a key process in productivity growth which governs the pace at which potentialities opened by new technology can be exploited. In part, resource reallocation simply reflects differences in income elasticities of demand among products. But it reflects, even more than this, the fact that technological advance destroys the economic viability of certain industries, firms, and jobs, as it creates new ones. Within this context of growth driven by technological advance, and involving significant resource reallocation, capital and education play key supporting roles.

In the simplest of the neoclassical models, new physical capital is treated like any other factor of production; its augmentation relative to labor increases labor productivity according to the logic of linear homogeneous production functions. Within vintage models, and in the view expressed here, a more important role of new capital is as a carrier of new technology. Carrying the logic of interaction farther, to the extent that new capital carries new technology, new investment ought to increase the returns to and stimulate R&D spending. New capital-embodying technologies just out of the R&D laboratory also would appear to be the locus of much learning-by-doing, and using, which in turn feeds back to stimulate more R&D (Rosenberg, 1980). Investment in new physical capital also enables firms with advanced technologies to expand their market shares at the expense of lagging firms. More generally, as Abramovitz (1979) has stressed, physical investment and disinvestment is a principal vehicle by which resources in general are transferred from declining to growing activities and sectors.

In orthodox theory, a better-educated worker is treated as simply "more productive" than a less well educated one. From the viewpoint sketched here, this is oversimplified to the point of being misleading. Increasingly, highly trained engineers and scientists have become essential for carrying on R&D. See, for example, Pavitt (1980). A central task of management is to make decisions regarding R&D allocation, and judgments regarding what new technologies to adopt; various of the studies discussed in section 2 propose that technical sophistication on the part of managers is a prerequisite for doing these jobs well. There is evidence (Ryan and Gross, 1943; Welch, 1970) that better-educated farmers have an advantage in accessing new technological developments relevant to their practices. Better-educated and more recently educated doctors are the early adopters of new pharmaceuticals (Coleman, Katz, and Menzel, 1957). Workers with relatively high educational attainment often are found in the work forces of firms employing new technology; in this context a strong educational background might be viewed as facilitating quick understanding of what is required for learning by doing. To the extent that a broad based education makes a worker flexible and able to learn a variety of different jobs, education may facilitate the shifting of workers between old jobs and new ones, from declining industries to expanding ones. Also, the knowledge and confidence generated by this flexibility may dampen resistance on the part of the work force to technological change.

Just as a high rate of capital formation and a well-educated work force stimulate and facilitate technological advance, so technological advance stimulates a high rate of capital formation and motivates young people to acquire formal education. If technological advance were slower, diminishing returns to capital deepening would have less of an offset, and the returns to investment or the investment rate or both would be lower. If technological advance were slower, there would be less demand for scientists and engineers to enable firms to stay competitive with their technological rivals. There would be less need for managers and workers to deal with new situations and to learn new skills.

From this perspective, it would be surprising if one observed many countries where technological advance was rapid, but where investment rates and educational attainments were low. Nor would one expect to find many instances where capital formation maintained a rapid rate, but new technologies were not being introduced and spread through the economy. Societies might find it hard to sustain high educational attainments on the part of young people entering the work force, and not at the same time be moderately progressive scientifically and technologically. In short, there are not neatly separable sources of growth, but rather a package of elements all of which need to be there.

4.2 The Economic Environment and Economic Institutions

One way to deepen analysis of growth is to study the forces influencing the various proximate sources. The strong interactions among the proximate sources suggest that another route is to try to identify certain features of the economic environment that have a generally supportive or retarding influence on growth. A significant fraction of recent research on growth might be recognized as following this latter path.

This certainly is so regarding the recent work which tries to link productivity growth to macroeconomic conditions—particularly unemployment, inflation, and stability. As stated in section 1, the neoclassical theory of economic growth was born of an effort to identify reasons for the pessimistic conclusions about balanced growth built into the Harrod-Domar models. The key modeling assumption identified—fixed coefficients in production— and modified (through the assumption of variable proportions with input mix presumed sensitive to relative-factor prices), balanced growth was henceforth simply assumed in most of the neoclassical growth models. But nothing in the simple neoclassical growth model guarantees that prevailing factor prices will actually be those consistent with full employment of a nation's prevailing stocks of both capital and labor (or other inputs). Nothing in the model guarantees that aggregate demand will always equal aggregate potential supply of goods and services. These conditions define an equilibrium, but to my knowledge at least, no powerful argument, much less empirical evidence, exists that the macro time path is automatically tightly bound to its equilibrium track. Maddison, and other analysts of the rapid growth of the 1950s and 1960s, argued that, with sophisticated application of monetary and fiscal policies, balanced growth was achievable and was achieved. The post-1973 experience calls that belief into question.

Economists clearly are not in agreement about how much of the current productivity growth slowdown stems from the higher unemployment and inflation rates, and from the wide fluctuations that have been experienced, and it can be argued that slow productivity growth is itself one of the causes of the poor employment and price performance of the economies. In my eyes at least, research on the connections among long-run growth of economic potential and shorter-run macroeconomic performance still has not yet clearly identified, much less quantified, the key mechanisms involved. In part this is because there are so many different and interconnected mechanisms. From an orthodox point of view, the macroeconomic climate has a direct effect on productivity growth through its influence on investment. To the extent that economic slack involves excess capacity, investment is deterred, the growth of the capital-labor ratio is slowed, and so is the introduction of best practice. A decline in investment may also slow down the pace of ad-vance of technological knowledge, and not merely the rate of which best practice is absorbed into use.

Whether the losses of an economic recession are made up in recovery, or are lost forever, is an open question. When a high rate of capacity utilization is achieved again, will growth of physical capital accelerate sufficiently to make up for trough losses (as implied by some models)? Or will the invest-ment in new plant and in R&D lost because of the recession never be made up (as would be implied by a model in which investment is always a fixed fraction of GNP)?

In any case, it is important to look behind the scenes to identify the reasons why governments have had so much difficulty coping with the macroeconomic problems of the 1970s compared with the 1960s. The surge in oil prices is part of the answer, but why have societies found it so difficult to accept the (temporarily) lower living standards that economists have argued are necessary? Why has it proved impossible to implement the kinds of "income" policies many economists have proposed? Does slow productivity growth, or rather a slower productivity growth than previously experienced, tend to cause an inflationary gap between income growth expectations that people regard as reasonable and just, and what the economy can yield? Why have some countries found it easier to meet these problems than others? Such questions may possibly be the most important ones for economists to answer if they are to understand the forces behind the post-1973 slowdown of growth. But they are not the questions addressed in the growth theory tradition.

The search for answers inevitably will lead to consideration of the bases of conflict in a society, and the mechanisms which contain and resolve, or inflame, these conflicts. Is it happenstance that Britain is marked by both fractious labor relations and stop-and-start economic policies and that until recently at least Sweden had neither? How much of the British problem stems from the particular form of her unions? To what extent is that form deeply rooted, or malleable?

The same kind of questions can be asked about a nation's educational system. Several analyses of Britain's poor performance ascribe a good share of the blame to its schools which, until recently, have lagged in the training of engineers relative to the systems in Germany, the United States, and Japan (Austin Albu, 1980). Such analyses posit that the influences of a nation's educational system are not readily studied in terms of human capital, conventionally defined, but rather are atmospheric, influencing management style, hence innovation, capital formation, and the nature of competition. To some extent differences in educational systems reflect underlying differences in culture and social structure. Until recently at least, academically trained engineers had a hard time finding jobs in British industry. The land grant college system of the United States surely reflects an interest in practical mass education that was evident in this land even before the Republic was established. But, during the late 1960s and through most of the 1970s, engineering enrollments fell significantly in the United States (recently they have come up again). Britain has begun to enlarge and improve its system of engineering education. Why? Differences and changes in rates of return on different educational investments are part of the answer, but not all of it. And these returns themselves reflect institutions, attitudes and government policies.

The greatly enlarged regimes of regulation and the growth of the welfare state also have been identified with developments strongly influencing productivity growth. While some analyses of the effects of these new institutions have focused strictly on their resource absorbing or diverting aspects, other scholars have recognized that their effects are atmospheric, like the microeconomic climate, the state of labor relations, and the character of a society's educational system. Businessmen, discussing their concerns about the regulatory environment, stress the uncertainties involved and their fears that anything they try to do that is new will be prohibited. This fear influences decision making regarding R&D and physical investment. Similarly, it has been argued that the most pernicious effect of the rise of the welfare state is that some young people no longer feel that they should or must work very hard for a living. No persuasive evidence as yet supports any of these contentions. I mention them only to call attention to the fact that they have no place in orthodox analysis.

Social scientists (other than economists) and historians long have believed that variables like those discussed above are important. They have tried to explain them and their effects. Economists, working within an intellectual tradition that values formal theoretical and quantitative precision have tended to view work by other scholars on economic growth as lacking in rigor and in amenability to quantification. Undoubtedly it would prove difficult to make questions and answers, such as those above, rigorous and quantitative—far more difficult than to continue elaborating the orthodox framework. However, can we afford to follow only that familiar path?

4.3 The Evolution of Economic Institutions

The durability, and the mechanisms for change, of economic institutions are amenable to study. Increasingly, economists are joining other social scientists in doing so. Research has proceeded both with respect to the evolution of private organizations—in particular the organization of business firms—and of public or society-wide institutional structures.

Perhaps the most interesting examples of such work on the evolution of the business firm have been by Alfred B. Chandler and by Oliver Williamson. Chandler, as the preeminent historian of the evolution of the modern corporation, has argued that, prior to the transportation and communication revolutions of the mid-nineteenth century, constraints on information flow and the ability to control operations located at some distance virtually foreclosed the development of firms with geographically dispersed branch operations (1962, 1977). The exceptions were branches run by members of an extended family. The nineteenth-century technological revolutions reduced information and control problems and permitted firms to encompass geographically dispersed branch operations, if they could develop appropriate managerial structures. The modern line and staff form of organization then took shape, with lower-tier managers in charge of the dispersed operations and reporting to the center. Chandler also has described the later development by corporations of the independent profit-center idea in response to the increased proliferation of geographical branches or product lines, and the resulting overload on peak management within a traditional hierarchical structure.

Williamson, the theorist, building on Chandler's historical work, has developed an argument, based on transaction cost considerations, to show the economic advantage of these newer arrangements over the earlier structures (1970, 1975). Williamson's general theoretical posture is to consider the transaction cost advantages and disadvantages of different modes of organization under different circumstances, and to postulate that the mode that is adopted is the most efficient one for governing those transactions in the particular context. In recent work he has extended this line of thought to consider organizational innovation more generally (1980). Among the organizational innovations that he has attempted to explain by this class of argument are the rise of wholesaling in the late eighteenth century, and that of chain stores in the twentieth. Lance Davis and Douglas North (1971) attempt to explain the long-run evolution of land policy, labor organization, and financial institutions, in the United States, in terms similar to those of Williamson.

Some of the work on institutional change implicitly or explicitly presumes a mixed economy, in which governmental actors play a key role in facilitating, or blocking, privately desired changes. The organizational changes described by Davis and North required public as well as private action. Ruttan (in Binswanger and Ruttan, 1978) has described the way governmental programs in support of agricultural education, research, and extension, evolved in response to changing economic conditions, and to changes in what farmers wanted.

Other scholars have painted with an even broader brush. Years ago, Joseph Schumpeter (1950) predicted that rising capitalist affluence would lead to growing distaste for capitalistic competition, and that some form of socialism would emerge. It is unclear whether he forecast the modern welfare state. Yet that institution clearly is designed to shield individuals and families from the risk and pressures of economic life. More recently, Mancur Olsen (1976) has proposed that the peaceful evolution of a political democracy supports the growth of special interest groups and that interest group politics leads to legislation that protects group interests and inhibits resource reallocation. While Schumpeter held that the safer, more tranquil system, which he foresaw, would be quite capable of sustaining reasonably rapid technological progress, Olsen has proposed that sheltering special interests makes economic change costly and difficult.

With the vision of hindsight it seems that Schumpeter overestimated the extent to which innovation can be "routinized" and made compatible with democratic consensus politics. On the other hand, Olsen's hypothesis cannot easily explain a number of recent political developments which have torn down, or significantly reduced, the levels of protection carefully raised over the years by various interest groups to shield themselves. Simple theories are interesting, and serve to focus attention on certain variables and relationships. But perhaps by now we have had enough experience with simple theories to be ready to entertain a struggle with more complicated ones. There is the story about the drunk who lost his watch at night by the side of the road, who looked under a lamppost where he knew he had not dropped it because there, at least, it was light.

5. Toward Evolutionary Modeling of Economic Growth

The view on productivity growth that one can gather from the literature reviewed in the previous three sections is considerably more complex than that of neoclassical theory. However, it is not merely more complex; it is different. At least certain features of growth that the heterodox view identifies as fundamental are difficult, and perhaps impossible, to treat within a conceptual framework that builds from neoclassical footings.

Neoclassical growth theory clearly shows its origins in the neoclassical theory of firm and industry behavior, at rest. One can accept the value of the simplifying assumptions of that theory to address the kind of questions conventionally associated with standard price theory—namely, the response of a firm to an increase in the demand for its product, or to an increase in the price of one of its factors of production relative to that of another—although even in these applications there are alternative models that view the response somewhat differently. But one might be skeptical about the extent to which a simple augmentation of that theory to admit shifts in the production function would lead to a framework capable of illuminating the key features of long-run economic growth, fueled by technological advance.

The heterodox literature explored in this essay dispenses with, or casts doubt on, the two canonical assumptions of neoclassical theory—that firms literally maximize (expected) profit, and that the industry and economy as a whole are in (moving) equilibrium. The problem with the maximization assumption is not that it connotes a profit motive and intelligent effort to achieve profits, but that it connotes, as well, ability beyond human capabilities to perceive alternative courses of action and compare the consequences of exploring different parts of a previously unexplored terrain. In such a context, human behavior may be purposive, sensible, and even creative, but different people will inevitably focus on different parts of the choice spectrum, and make different evaluations about what is promising and what is not. Similarly, if equilibrium meant only a tendency for the better economic technique, the more effective organization, the more profitable firm, to drive out competitors or to force their reform, there would be no particular difficulty with this concept as a tool for analyzing long-run economic change. The equilibrium concept, however, as it is conventionally employed in economics, does not depict such a dynamic process; it presumes the process is (always) complete. This presumption makes it extremely difficult to analyze such phenomena as diffusion, Schumpeterian competition, and resource reallocation driven by differences in returns to factors and firms.

There has been a long tradition in economics of thinking about economic growth as an evolutionary process. Darwin credits Malthus with having provided him with several key ideas. In turn, Marshall was much influenced by evolutionary theory in biology. In the post–World War II era, the idea that models styled on evolutionary theory might be appropriate in economics has lingered mainly around the fringe of our discipline, but occasionally has been articulated in a mainline journal. Armen Alchian's 1950 article is a well-known example. Tjalling Koopmans (1957) expressed interest in evolutionary modeling in his third essay.

More recent forays in evolutionary modeling have been published by Sidney Winter (1964), Michael Farrell (1970), Richard Day and Theodore Groves (1975), Day and Inderjit Singh (1977) and Gunnar Eliasson and colleagues (1977). Burton Klein (1977) has presented a less formal and more sweeping essay in the Schumpeterian spirit.

In a number of recent papers, Sidney Winter and I have put forth an evolutionary theory of productivity growth (1974, 1977, 1982). In our models, discovery or creation of a new technology is recognized as an uncertain as well as a costly business. Potentially, R&D can be profitable for a firm if that R&D results in a better technology, and if competitors are not able to imitate quickly and easily. Different firms make different technological bets; some turn out to be better bets than others. Over time, productivity grows as new technologies are discovered and applied, as better technologies discovered by some firms are imitated by others, and as profitable firms grow relative to unprofitable ones. The ability of firms to imitate the technologies of other firms and the extent to which profitability of the firm induces its expansion are variables within our model. So also is the relationship between R&D spending and the new technologies that are found or invented.

These models generate dispersion of productivity levels among firms at any time, of the sort that the BLS studies display. They are capable of generating diffusion patterns for particular new technologies that are consonant with the literature on diffusion. The time paths of industry productivity growth are qualitatively consonant with observed time series of real data.

These and the other recent evolutionary models do not address the complexities of internal firm organization or of individual or social psychology. Nor do they treat economic institutions or political processes in a manner much more sophisticated than does neoclassical theory. They provide no good definition of economic climate. They do, however, provide an account of productivity growth that is consistent with what is known about the processes of technological change. This at least would be one step forward, theoretically.

The current state of evolutionary modeling is primitive relative to the advanced state of neoclassical modeling. But enough has been done to demonstrate the feasibility of such models. They are admittedly more complex than those economists studying productivity growth are accustomed to employ, but no more complex than many of the existing large macroeconomic models. Perhaps the most important present limitation on the use of such models in empirical investigation is scarcity of data suitable for use within a model that treats differences across firms at any time, and different growth rates among firms, as essential aspects of productivity growth. Existing data sets do not enable many of the relevant connections among a firm's R&D spending, invention and imitation performance, profitability, and growth to be made. Yet these connections are the heart of an evolutionary model. Were adequate data available, there undoubtedly would be some difficult questions regarding appropriate estimation techniques. And, as stated, present evolutionary models are only one step forward from prevailing theory in dealing with the apparent complexities of productivity growth.

Economists have every temptation to turn aside from trying to develop more complex models and empirical research methods for studying productivity growth. Let me remind you again, however, about the drunk and his watch.

2

Capitalism as an Engine of Progress

1. The Strengths and Weaknesses of the Schumpeterian Model

Virtually all contemporary general accounts of the capitalist engine are based on Joseph Schumpeter in his *Capitalism, Socialism, and Democracy* (1950). For-profit firms, in rivalrous competition, are the featured actors. The context within which they operate is set, on the one side, by the laws and ethos of capitalism which enable firms to keep proprietary, at least for a while, the new technology they create, and on the other, by public scientific knowledge. The latter lends problem-solving power to industrial R&D. The former enables firms to profit when their R&D creates something the market values. Indeed, given that its rivals are induced by this context to invest in R&D, a firm may have no choice but to do likewise. The result is significant corporate investment in R&D, generating a bountiful flow of new products and processes. It is left to the market to select ex-post on the innovations offered by different firms, and on the firms themselves.

Given the striking impact that Schumpeter has had on subsequent analysis, it is worth noting that Chapter 7, where the basic picture is presented, contains only six pages.[1] While Schumpeter discussed technical advance elsewhere in that book and in other places, his overall treatment is still very sketchy. It also is worth noting that *Capitalism, Socialism, and Democracy* was written over fifty years ago. At that time there was little solid scholarship on technical change. Now there is a lot.[2] Thus it is now possible to evaluate Schumpeter's model in the light of the evidence, to fill in the essential fine structure, and to amend or modify as needed, so as to capture analytically the essential system as of his time, and now.

The way I have put the matter suggests that, in the light of what is now

Originally published in *Research Policy* (1990): 193–214.

known, I still regard Schumpeter as a useful analytic starting place. I do. In particular, I believe his insistence that the system he described sets up technical advance as an evolutionary process is exactly the right foundation premise. However, Schumpeter never really developed that point and modern scholarship suggests a great deal of useful development.

Also, many of the details of the modern capitalist engine revealed by recent scholarship are not even hinted at in Schumpeter's coarse-grained picture. In particular, neither Schumpeter's model nor more modern ones at that same level of abstraction adequately comprehend the complex intertwining of modern technology and science, or the rich and variegated set of institutions involved in their advance, that existed even when Schumpeter was writing. And of course Schumpeter could not have foreseen the changes in the nature of technologies and in the institutional landscape that have occurred since his time.

Both of these matters need elaboration. In the remainder of section 1, I pursue these tasks.

1.1 Technical Advance as a Cultural Evolutionary Process

Schumpeter said it emphatically. "The essential point to grasp is that in dealing with capitalism we are dealing with an evolutionary process." Empirical research on just how technical advance occurs amply supports this proposition. Technical advance inevitably proceeds through the generation of a variety of new departures in competition with each other and with prevailing practice. The winners and losers are determined in an actual contest. Many contemporary modelers ignore this, treating technical advance as if it proceeded with much more accurate ex-ante calculation and before the contest agreement on winners than is the case. Nelson and Winter (1982) have argued that such models not merely oversimplify, but fundamentally misstate, how technical advance proceeds under capitalism, which is through an evolutionary process in the sense above.

Evolutionary processes have demonstrated remarkable power to advance the capabilities of a species, or a technology, and to create effective new ones. However, evolutionary processes are inherently wasteful, and technical advance in capitalist economies is no exception. There are wastes of both commission and omission. Looking backwards one can see a little of redundant inventive efforts that never would have been undertaken had there been overall monitoring. On the other hand, economies of scale and scope that might be achieved through R&D coordination tend to be missed, and certain kinds of R&D that would have high expected social value may not be done, because individual firms do not see it as profitable for them to do it, and no one is minding the overall portfolio. Also, because technology is to a considerable extent proprietary, one can see enterprises operating inefficiently, even failing, for want of access to the best technology. These firms may be induced to respond by basically reinventing what already has been invented.

Of course the process through which technical advance proceeds in capitalist economies differs in various obvious respects from evolutionary processes in biology. On reflection, some of the apparent differences may be more apparent than real. Thus technology occasionally makes "big jumps." This is inconsistent with traditional concepts of evolution in biology, but not with more modern notions of punctuated equilibria. Also, it is clear that innovation is far from a strictly random process; rather, efforts to advance technology are carefully pointed in directions innovators believe to be feasible and potentially profitable. However, here again the difference with biological evolution may not be sharp if one recognizes the possibility (as do some contemporary biologists) that selection has operated on genes to make viable mutations more likely than would be the case were mutation strictly random.

I propose that the feature that most sharply distinguishes the evolutionary process through which technology advances from biological evolution is that new findings, understandings, generally useful ways of doing things, do not adhere strictly to their finder or creator but are shared, at least to some extent. In many cases the sharing is intentional, in others despite efforts to keep findings privy. But in any case, that the new technology ultimately goes public means that technology advances through a "cultural" evolutionary process. The capabilities of all are advanced by the creation or discovery of one. This is fundamentally different from biological evolution.

Schumpeter recognized this clearly. While in his model of technical advance, the lure and reward for corporate innovative efforts resides in the temporary monopoly over the new product or process, he stressed that in the general run of things the monopoly is temporary. Sooner or later competitors will catch on. And he recognized the powerful role played by public science and understood that this made technical advance more efficient. But this is a far cry from arguing that technical advance under capitalism is not associated with considerable waste, at least as can be seen with the vision of hindsight.

It is something of a puzzle, therefore, why the capitalist innovation system has performed so well. There certainly is nothing like the twin theorems of welfare economics around to support an argument that capitalism "can't be beat."[3] But of course this key question is: what are the alternatives? Compared with what? Various socialist scholars have observed the wastefulness of capitalism and proposed that a centrally planned and coordinated system, which treated technology as a public good, ought to be able to do better at generating and using new technology. The troubles socialist economies have been having with their innovation systems suggests that this is easier said than done (see Hanson and Pavitt, 1987). The generally poor experience capitalist countries have had when they have tried to tightly plan major technical advances—for example, in civil aircraft and nuclear power—reinforces the point (Nelson, 1982).

What is it about technical change that makes effective central planning so difficult, or perhaps impossible? Certainly one important factor is uncertainty about where R&D resources should be allocated in a field where technology is fluid.[4] There generally are a wide variety of ways in which existing technology could be improved, and several alternative paths toward achieving any of these. And almost always uncertainty about where the bets ought to be laid is accompanied by disagreement on this matter among experts. Further, studies done by highly qualified people attempting to assess which would be the best route have commonly after the fact been found to be badly off the mark on one or another respect. Under such circumstances, attempts to get ex-ante consensus are likely to be futile, and appropriately so, because in such a context exploration of a variety of possibilities is called for.

While in principle there are better ways to provide for this, the capitalist innovation engine does define one viable way of assuring multiple sources of initiative, with real competition among those who place their bets on different ideas. And it does so in a context where there is widespread access to the basic generic knowledge one needs to consider intelligently the possibilities, strong incentives to heed market signals, and to cut losses when it is clear one is a loser. One should not confuse the portfolio of efforts thus generated with any kind of optimal portfolio, or presume that the processes through which winners and losers are determined are efficient in any meaningful sense. But this engine of progress has over the years generated remarkable results.

It is not apparent how clearly Schumpeter understood the sources of strength of the capitalist engine, or its inefficiencies. He certainly did recognize the creativity, energy, and even stubbornness that went into successful innovation, and the uncertainties involved in breaking new ground. But on the other hand, toward the close of part II of his *Capitalism, Socialism, and*

Democracy, Schumpeter predicted an erosion of the importance of actual rivalry in technical advance as science became more powerful and innovation "is reduced to routine." I shall argue later that this was a bad call.

Regarding the inefficiencies of the engine, Schumpeter clearly recognized that the kaleidoscope of temporary monopolies that are a consequence of rivalrous innovation is incompatible with efficiency of resource allocation in a static sense, but argued that this matters little. Recall his famous salvo, "this kind of competition [innovation] is as much more effective than the other [price] as a bombardment is in comparison with forcing a door, and so much more important that it becomes a matter of comparative indifference whether competition in the ordinary sense functions more or less promptly." He also understood that innovation under the system he described was wasteful, but this too did not seem to bother him much.

There is no question that attempts since Schumpeter to formalize his model have sharpened awareness of these matters. The alleged trade-off between static efficiency and dynamic energy has been modelled by several scholars. We now have models of the costs of "patent races," and recent work has called attention to the fact that the myopia built into evolutionary systems can sometimes lead technology down roads that are far from the best.[5]

However, the point I want to begin making here is that, while Schumpeter's model provides a good starting place, it is too coarse-grained to enable serious examination of the strengths and weaknesses of the modern capitalist engine. A closer look at how technical advance actually proceeds provides not only a more complex picture, but one that is different in important respects.

1.2 The Complex Capitalist Engine

The limitations of the simple Schumpeterian formulation come into view when one studies the advent and evolution of modern technologies like airframes and engines, computers, semiconductors, synthetic materials, or pharmaceuticals.[6] The stark Schumpeterian model fails to recognize the variegated nature of modern technological knowledge and the complex and often subtle relationships between technology and science that are essential parts of these histories. Schumpeter recognized that as science grows stronger R&D would become more professionalized. Yet he missed some of the key consequences. A central one I shall argue is not that technological advance has become more routine, which it has not, but that the generic aspects of new technology quickly become common knowledge among the interested professional community. This phenomenon has been an important part of all these histories.

Schumpeter never was explicit about just what he thought science and technology were, or about the nature of their connections, or about the institutional division of labor. However, it is highly likely that he adhered to the conventional wisdom on these matters of his day and ours. Science is a body of understanding, technology of practice. New science is created by university researchers, seeking knowledge with little heed to practice. Industrial scientists use that understanding to work on what will enhance their company's profits, with little heed to advancing general knowledge. But students of technological advance now understand that matters are much more complex and mixed up than this.

In the first place, technology is not adequately characterized as simply a body of practice. It includes that but it involves, as well, a body of generic understanding about how things work, key variables affecting performance, the nature of major opportunities and currently binding constraints, and promising approaches to pushing these back.[7]

Now this analytic distinction sounds, at first hearing, like the division between technology and science according to the conventional wisdom. And, indeed, in certain technological fields, like the design and manufacture of semiconductors, a good portion of the understanding rests on fundamental sciences like physics and chemistry. However, in almost all technologies a sizable share of generic knowledge stems from operating and design experience with products and machines and their components, and analytic generalizations reflecting on these. This understanding may have only limited grounding in any fundamental science, standing, as it were, largely on its own bottom. This is not quite what philosophers of science tend to mean when they talk of a "science."

But a number of observers have noted that many modern fields of inquiry that call themselves sciences do not fit the classic mold. Thus fields like computer science, chemical engineering, metallurgy and pathology are basically about this kind of understanding, and reflect attempts to make it more "scientific."[8]

Economists often have put forth the theoretical premise that technology is a latent public good, in the sense of being widely applicable, and inexpensive (if not literally costless) to teach and learn compared with the cost of invention or discovery in the first place. On the other hand, some empirical students of technical advance, especially Pavitt (1987a), have argued strongly that this premise is basically wrong, with industrial technology being very largely firm-specific and costly if not impossible to use elsewhere.

The issue here is not trivial. It is important both analytically and institutionally. I wish to argue that both positions are half right. It matters which aspect of technology one is talking about.

The notion that technology is a latent public good is a reasonable first approximation, if the focus is on generic knowledge. Generic knowledge tends to be germane to a variety of uses and users. Indeed mastery of such knowledge may be essential if one is to advance or modify prevailing practice with any efficiency. Relatedly, such knowledge is the stock in trade of professionals in a field, and there tends to grow up a systematic way of describing and communicating such knowledge. It is to the advantage of business firms that the young scientists and engineers they hire come equipped with such mastery, so there is a natural harmony of interests between companies and schools regarding its codification.

Moreover, generic knowledge not only has strong latent public good properties. As the applied sciences and engineering disciplines have grown up directly oriented toward such knowledge in particular fields, and dedicated to its advance and codification, generic technological knowledge has become more and more manifestly a public good among professionals. An electrical engineer or a materials scientist working at the forefront of his or her field has a keen professional interest in news of developments. It is well recognized that the academic parts of these disciplines are by their nature open, with strong individual and institutional incentives to tell the news. What is less adequately recognized is that new generic knowledge created in industrial laboratories also is relatively open to outsiders knowledgeable of the field. As I shall discuss later in some detail, scientists and engineers in rival firms have a variety of ways to ferret out the generic aspects of a competitor's new technology, even if the specific details of products and processes may remain beyond their ken.

Regarding publicness or privateness, the body of particular extant technique is more of a mixed bag. Some practiced technique is widely applicable and easily learned by someone skilled in the art, if access were open. But students like Pavitt (1987a) and Nathan Rosenberg (1976, 1985) have argued persuasively that much of prevailing industrial technique is of little use outside the firms employing it, involving fine tuning to their particular products or processes. And many industrial techniques that operate effectively in a given establishment can be transferred to another only with considerable cost, even if the original operator is open and helpful. Efficient operation of complex techniques in many cases is as much a matter of experience with particular products, machinery, and organization, and practice fine-tuned to these through a large number of tacit adjustments, as it is of general understanding plus access to "blueprints" and other documentation. In such cases "technology transfer" may be as expensive and time consuming as independent R&D.[9]

While I have written as if there were a sharp distinction between generic knowledge and particular technique, of course the line is blurry. The locus of the line, and how blurred it is, is partly determined by how patents are drawn up in a field and their effectiveness, matters to which we will return shortly. But to a considerable extent what is generic and public depends on the extent to which the scientific and engineering disciplines have built up a body of general understanding that transcends the specific applications. In no technology is "what works and why" perfectly understood. This is why inventive work is inherently uncertain, or perhaps it is better to regard inventive work as always being uncertain because of a human proclivity to strive beyond what is known scientifically. On the other hand, my argument is that, because of the development of these disciplines, technologies today are much better understood scientifically than they used to be.

The blurry line between generic knowledge and specific application flags attention to the fact that the division of labor between industrial labs and universities is neither sharp nor innate. University laboratories have worked in fields of basic science like physics and molecular biology, but they also have played a significant role in research in the applied sciences—fields like metallurgy, electrical engineering, and animal husbandry—which should be understood as disciplines expressly concerned with the generic aspects of certain technologies. And in a number of fields university laboratories have been an important source of pioneer versions of new technology. One cannot recount the history of fields like computers or the new biotechnologies without noting the major seminal roles played by people at universities.

Yet few accounts of industrial R&D recognize clearly enough that some companies themselves engage in generic research in these applied fields and that the general findings often are published in scholarly journals.[10] Most of this work is undertaken in a focused search for solutions to technical problems arising in particular design and development efforts. But, as Rosenberg (1988) and Cohen and Levinthal (1989) have argued, companies in fields where the underlying sciences are advancing rapidly often do research on those sciences in order to stay up with them and to have the capability to exploit developments in a timely manner, from wherever they may come; that is, they join in the community advancing the relevant sciences.

This observation underlines two aspects of the modern capitalist engine that are absent from many accounts. First, while new generic knowledge has public good properties, one must invest one's own work in a field to know what to make of the news. Second, those who are in on the news together tend to be active members of a research community. And as members of a community, scientists and engineers are expected to share knowledge. Research communities often are institutionalized as scientific or engineering societies, which hold formal meetings, to which members come to hear the news. And these societies also serve as fora for discussions of research agendas, of where the field is going, who is doing what, and so forth.

And government agencies are an important part of the modern system. They were moderately important when Schumpeter wrote, and since that time have become much more so. Since World War II they have become the principal funders of university research. In some fields, government agencies are major actors in the development of new products and processes. Where a government agency holds a strong interest in a technology, it may try to coordinate private efforts as well as fund them.

Once one sees the differentiated nature of technology and its overlap with science, the wide range of institutions that can be and have been involved in the scientific and technological enterprise, and the major supporting and shaping role played by government, it becomes clear that the simple Schumpeterian sketch misses large parts of the modern capitalist engine, and misspecifies others. When the modern engine is looked at in more detail, one can see features that make it more efficient, more capable of being steered, than the simple Schumpeterian model recognizes. I am not arguing here that the capitalist engine is efficient in the standard sense of that term, or that the wastes and proclivities toward myopia highlighted by simple models are really not there. Rather my point is that the engine is of a much more sophisticated and effective design than simply drawn accounts of it.

2. Institutions Supporting Technical Advance in Modern Capitalism

In this section I hazard an analytic description of the modern capitalist engine as of the late twentieth century. The level of abstraction will be considerably lower than in the preceding section, and I draw extensively on a number of recent studies of how parts of the system work. I focus almost exclusively on the United States. While I would and will argue that the systems of the other major capitalist nations are of basically similar design, there are some interesting differences. Some of these will be treated in section 3.

I begin my sketch with the proprietary and rivalrous part of the system, the part stressed in most accounts. I shall be concerned with two questions.

Why the dominant role of R&D laboratories attached to firms who basically make their money by selling products? And how do they get proprietary advantage from the R&D they do? I then examine an aspect of the system conventionally ignored or underplayed—mechanisms through which firms learn from one another and cooperate on some matters. These processes and arrangements distinguish a cultural evolutionary process from a biological evolutionary one. My next topic is the role of universities, which I argue is much more complex and variegated than standard views of what universities do. In particular I stress the role of the applied sciences and engineering disciplines as public repositories of generic technological knowledge, and of university research in these fields.

Finally, I turn to different kinds of government R&D support programs, which are an extremely important part of the modern capitalist engine.

2.1 The Proprietary Domain

2.1.1 *The Key Role of the Industrial R&D Laboratory.* Schumpeter highlighted industrial R&D as the heart of the capitalist engine: organized inventive efforts undertaken by university-trained scientists and engineers, working in special facilities, tied to particular business firms, and focused on advancing their product and process technologies. Many scholars— Christopher Freeman (1982), Nathan Rosenberg (1974), David Mowery (1983), Lawrence Reich (1985), David Nobel (1977) and David Landis (1970) to name a few—have told of the rise of this institutional structure, first in the chemical and electrical industries, and then more widely.

This arrangement now is so familiar that analysts seldom reflect on it. Some of its aspects are relatively easy to understand, and hold in socialist systems as well as capitalist. The key role played by university training clearly reflects the general power the sciences of chemistry and physics had achieved by the late nineteenth century, and the successful development of the new applied sciences and engineering disciplines based on them which were directly oriented to generate knowledge and technique useful in advancing technology. Training in these was largely a job of the universities. The use of people whose training set them apart from on-line workers, the need for special equipment and, sometimes, teamwork, lies behind the widespread use of facilities and management specially dedicated to the R&D enterprise. The desire to shield R&D from pressures to troubleshoot and to permit a longer-run orientation called for a certain distancing from on-line work.[11]

It is the tying of the labs to particular companies that make their money selling products or services (other than R&D) that differentiates capitalist systems from most socialist ones, and this aspect is well worth reflecting on. Why doesn't inventing mostly proceed in organizations that specialize in R&D, like independent or university-affiliated laboratories, who do work on contract or sell their inventions to production firms? The fact that these mechanisms are operative to a certain degree affirms that the question is not specious.

The reasons reveal a lot about the capitalist engine. One is that the two factors stressed above—the power of university training in doing industrial R&D, and the ability to advance technology in separated dedicated facilities—have limits. To do effective industrial R&D generally requires knowledge about the technology of an industry that is not taught in school. It also often requires a certain amount of close and not preprogrammable interaction between lab and client firm or firms, and complementary work and investment on their part. Thus to be effective, industrial R&D must have close industry links.

In many cases the R&D a firm wants done is closely tailored to its own product and process technologies, its strategy for getting ahead or staying up, and its most pressing needs as it sees them. Thus effective lab work requires not only industry-specific but firm-specific knowledge, and sensitivity of the lab to the needs of its client firm. As stressed earlier it seldom is possible to specify in advance exactly how an R&D project will turn out, and often it is necessary to rethink and respecify objectives along the way. Williamson (1975, 1985), Teece (1980), and others argue cogently that such relationships are difficult to govern by contract. Indeed in cases where process engineering is important, or tailoring products to customer demands, technical work may need to be closely integrated with production and marketing and not sharply separated institutionally, much less contracted out.

And in many cases tomorrow's high-priority R&D projects tend to grow out of today's and of what is learned in operating experience. A laboratory that did today's work and with whom mechanisms for interaction already are in place has a natural start on tomorrow's work. Thus there are advantages to a firm of durable as well as close bonds with a lab serving it.

These factors calling for close lab-production links are relevant in socialist economies as well as capitalist ones. They explain why the free-standing research institute system of socialist countries has proved such an unsatisfactory vehicle for industrial research, and why socialist economies now are moving R&D into the enterprise. In capitalist economies there also are proprietary reasons for tying lab to enterprise.

Much of the firm-specific information that motivates an R&D project as well as the content of the project will be regarded by the firm as proprietary, and thus the sponsor may want to ensure that the lab does not consort with its rivals. As we shall see shortly, in many industries the principal way a firm gains profit from R&D is through exploiting a head start. This requires not only that the details of R&D be kept privy until ripe for practice. To reap returns a firm also must be able to identify and marshal in a timely manner the production and marketing capabilities, what Teece (1986) calls cospecialized assets, needed to move rapidly and strongly into the latent market before its rivals can get aboard. Integration of R&D into the firm facilitates such needed coordination.

Of course this is not to say that firms never use laboratories not tied to them, or that independent labs never are important sources of invention. A firm may choose to contract out for relatively routine work or exploratory studies to a lab that has expertise in the field, particularly if that work can proceed with little access to information the firm regards as proprietary. Also, a lab closely tied to a firm may become myopic, leaving room for outsiders to do the real innovating. New firms, or old firms coming into a new business, are a common phenomenon when prevailing firms get conservative. And in circumstances when a new technology is coming into being, and thus there is little relevant specialized knowledge within any industry as of yet, independent or university-affiliated laboratories may be the center of relevant expertise. The current situation in the new biotechnologies is a good example. However, these complications broaden and qualify but do not negate the proposition that the industrial research laboratory is the heart of the modern capitalist engine.

2.1.2 *Mechanisms for Appropriation and Their Domain.* Above I suggested that one of the reasons firms get their R&D done largely in in-house labs is that this facilitates their appropriating the returns. In this section I turn to means of appropriation more generally.

Schumpeter was never explicit about just how a firm that invested in R&D established and protected a proprietary edge. Economists and historians of technology writing since his time have recognized a variety of means, and their work suggests that different ones are operative in different industries. However, until my colleagues and I designed the Yale survey, there was no systematic map of the terrain. Since the details of the questionnaire and the broad results of our probes about appropriability have been reported in several other places (in particular, see Levin et al. [1987]) here I will simply summarize those of our findings that are most relevant to the topic of this section. Some of what I recount will be general, but much of the analysis will be of interindustry differences. The modern capitalist engine is not just more complex than simple pictures of it, but highly variegated.[12]

To oversimplify somewhat, we distinguished three broad classes of means through which firms can appropriate returns to their innovations—through the patent system, through secrecy, and through various advantages associated with exploiting a first-mover advantage—and asked our respondents in different lines of business to score on a scale from 1 to 7 the effectiveness of these means for profiting from product innovation, and from process innovation.

There were significant cross-industry differences regarding the means rated most effective for appropriating returns to product innovation. However, contrary to popular beliefs that stress intellectual property rights, in most industries the gains to an innovator apparently come largely from getting there first and exploiting that advantage, rather than by using the shield of a patent or actively keeping things secret. Included herein are many of the industries generally regarded as among the most technologically progressive, as semiconductors, computers, telecommunication, airframes, and aircraft engines.

An interesting characteristic of most of the above industries is that imitation is expensive even if the new product is not protected by a patent. In some, products take the form of complex systems. Our respondents from the industries producing aircraft and complete guided missile systems—canonical complex systems—reported that it would cost a competent imitator more than three-quarters what it cost the innovator to come up with something comparable, even if there were no patent protection at all. Producing complex systems involves many components and many details that need to be got right; much of this learning proceeds on-line rather than in the lab, and is costly and time consuming to do even if one has a model to take apart or blueprints in hand. These industries and others, like semiconductors, also involve complex production processes with equipment finely tuned to product design. Getting the production equipment in place and learning to run it right is time consuming and costly and by itself can yield an innovator a large and durable advantage over followers.

In these kinds of industries, firms tend to develop differentiated areas of special competence. These particular competencies may be difficult to "transfer" to another firm, even when the former is an active partner in the effort, as when a mother firm tries to enhance the capabilities of a branch abroad, or in a licensing and technology transfer contract. Also, in fields like these, tomorrow's technology often grows out of experience creating and working with today's.[13] Thus an advantage gained by a firm in a particular nook of today's technology is likely to lead to an advantage tomorrow in the same or adjacent nooks. This, rather than durable control over a particular isolated invention, is why the returns to a company of a major initial technical advance may be long term. But to reap those returns requires that it not rest on its laurels.

While I want to emphasize that patents play a much smaller role in enabling innovators to reap returns under modern capitalism than commonly believed, there are certain industries where patent protection is important, perhaps essential, for innovation incentive. Our questionnaire revealed two groups of industries of this sort. One consists of industries where chemical composition is a central aspect of design: pharmaceuticals, industrial organic chemicals, plastic materials, synthetic fibers, glass. The other consists of industries producing products that one might call devices: air and gas compressors, scientific instruments, power-driven hand tools, and so on.[14] In both cases the composition of the product is relatively easy to define and limit. These conditions seem to be conducive to the ability to draw patents that can be enforced. They also describe a context where, in contrast with the more complex systems technologies discussed earlier, imitation is relatively easy for a competent firm. Thus without patent protection an innovator would gain very little from its investments.

The reports regarding means of appropriating returns from process innovation were different in interesting ways from those about product innovation. First-mover advantages and patent protection were rated less effective in protecting process innovation than product innovation in almost all industries. However, most industries rated secrecy more effective. The lesser effectiveness of patents and the greater of secrecy are probably opposite sides of the same coin. Processes are easier than products to hide from competitors; on the other hand mimicking by a competitor is easier to detect and prove for a new product than a new process.

The lesser effectiveness of first-mover advantages in enabling returns to be reaped from process innovation probably reflects that reduced cost tends to be translated into significantly enhanced market share more slowly than a significant improvement in product design. If market share is relatively insensitive in the short run to cost and price, this suggests that incentives for process innovation should be associated with prevailing firm size.

This conjecture squares with the evidence. The bulk of industrial R&D is directed toward new or improved products. Some of the industries marked by high product R&D intensity are highly concentrated—aircraft, for example—others not so, for example, scientific instruments. However, in all of the industries where firms spent substantially on product R&D, at least one of the means of appropriation listed in the questionnaire was reported highly effective. In contrast, few industries spend much on process R&D. In those that do, firms tend to be large and the industry highly concentrated.

Of course, the fact that firms in an industry spend little on process R&D by no means implies that no attention is being given to process innovation. In many industries, the bulk of such work is done by upstream firms, material and equipment suppliers. The respondents to the Yale survey reported that upstream firms were an important source of new technology particularly when the industry in question was not concentrated.

This finding is consistent with a proposition put forth by Eric von Hippel (1982, 1988) that the locus of inventive activity is determined, in part at least, by where the ability to appropriate returns is greatest. When an industry is fragmented, if a process innovation is made by a firm in that industry, its level of use is likely to be quite limited, given the relative insensitivity of market share to process innovation. But if process innovations come in the form of new materials and equipment produced by upstream firms, the market is the industry as a whole. It should be noted here that the incentives that locate process innovation upstream reflect real efficiency gains to the economy as a whole. That under capitalism much of process innovation is done by equipment and materials suppliers makes process technology more public for firms in the using industry.

Of course it is not one way or another. In many industries firms do some work on their production processes and equipment, and their upstream suppliers also do some work. As argued above, the relative balance seems quite sensitive to the degree of concentration of the upstream industry. It also seems sensitive to the extent to which the needs of equipment users are specialized. Thus von Hippel (1988) has shown that the users who do significant invention and design work on equipment tend to have more exacting needs than others in their industry who rely more on suppliers to do the work.

The analysis above is quite consistent with the "taxonomy" of sectoral patterns of technical advance that has been developed by Keith Pavitt and his colleagues (1984). In particular, in his "supplier-dominated" set of industries, firms are small and apparently not idiosyncratic regarding equipment needs, and rely on upstream suppliers for new equipment. In contrast, in his "scale-intensive" industries firms are large and do considerable R&D on their own. They may also draw from the work of specialized equipment suppliers.

2.2 Technology Taking, Sharing, and Interfirm Cooperation

Corporate R&D and innovation yield proprietary capabilities, initially. But generally not completely or for long. Sooner or later other firms ferret it out. Often of course the original innovator will strongly resist competitors' getting in the act, but sometimes the innovator is an active party to dissemination.[15]

2.2.1 *How Proprietary Technology Becomes Public.* An industrial R&D laboratory looks two ways: toward the firm it serves, and toward the external world to monitor developments that yield opportunities or which threaten the mother firm. As Wesley Cohen and Daniel Levinthal (1989) have stressed, monitoring is an active process and involves spending resources.

Technical developments of significance to a firm can come from a variety of different places. Technical change in downstream industries can shift the nature of the demands a firm faces. New equipment and materials developed upstream can profoundly influence what a firm can produce and at what cost. Customers and suppliers generally will help a firm stay up with relevant developments, but if a firm is simply a passive receptor of such information it is unlikely to appreciate its significance or be able to respond rapidly and effectively. An important part of many firms' R&D efforts involves active monitoring of upstream and downstream technologies.

And of course a firm must stay up with what its competitors are doing. While new generic knowledge is accessible to someone who knows the field well and follows it closely, to stay current in a rapidly moving field generally requires that one have a hand in on the research. And to master the details of new product or process technology created elsewhere may be time consuming and costly, even for a company that has considerable experience with the technology.

In the Yale survey, firms were asked about the effectiveness of various means of acquiring knowledge about new products and processes developed by competitors. These included doing independent R&D or reverse engineering, trying to get information from employees of the innovating firm and perhaps hiring them away, patent disclosures, publications of various sort, and open technical meetings. As in our other probes, we asked separately about product innovations and process innovations. Below I concentrate on the product innovation responses.

Highlighting that monitoring outside technological developments generally is an active and costly business; in most industries the means of monitoring judged most effective was either doing independent R&D (presumably while attending to clues about what one's competitors are doing) or reverse engineering. The industries that gave these means low scores almost invariably were those that do little R&D themselves, and hence do not have the capabilities to employ them. Conversely, virtually all R&D-intensive industries rated one or both very effective as a means of learning about (and presumably mastering something comparable to) competitors' innovations. It is apparent that in these industries the fact that viable firms have active R&D efforts serves to bind them together technologically as well as to advance the frontiers.

Those industries that reported reverse engineering to be effective also tended to report that they often learned from conversations with scientists and engineers of the innovating firm. Some reported that hiring away competitors' engineers and scientists was common practice. It is apparent that in the United States in many industries exchange of information among professionals and interfirm flow of R&D personnel serve as mechanisms that keep generic knowledge public.

Patents are intended to disclose information, and many of our industry respondents reported they learned a lot from that information. The industries that rated patent disclosures as effective tended to be the same as those who rated patents effective in protecting product innovations—drugs, industrial organic chemicals, synthetic fibers, and also a collection of industries producing devices of various sorts. In many of these industries scrutinizing patents was apparently a prelude to taking out a license, but in some not.

Publications and open technical meetings were deemed effective sources of information in a number of industries. The industries rating these sources highest tended to be of two sorts. Some were connected with health, or with agricultural processing; in these two areas there is a dense web of information dissemination services, largely supported by governments. In others, engineering societies were strong; the metal and metal-processing industries and electronics are good examples.

It is thus apparent that in most industries companies are not able to block information flow to competitors. As noted earlier, Schumpeter understood this well. What may be more surprising, it appears that in many cases they do not try to block information flow, and in others actively support it by encouraging employees to publish, to talk at technical society meetings, and so on. Why?

In the first place, the very staking of claims involves the release of information. That is one of the intents of the patent system, and where patents are effective in protecting an innovation they also reveal it. Companies in industries where aggressive use of a head-start advantage is important to reaping returns have a strong incentive to stake their claim through advertising, open meetings, and a wide variety of other ways, in addition to patenting. They need to attract customers. To do this they need to tell them about their new wares, and this means telling something to their competitors too.

Claim staking and the associated information release is needed not simply to establish legal property rights and lure customers, but also to make stockholders happy and to attract new capital. It is also often important to let suppliers know of one's new technology, so that they may adjust their own designs and R&D efforts better to serve it.

It is also desirable to enhance the company's reputation in the scientific and technical world. A reputation for doing first-class work enhances a company's ability to compete for newly minted scientists and engineers, to hire away more experienced ones, and to hold on to its own. More basically, it gets the company, or the key scientists and engineers working there, into the relevant networks. In the pharmaceutical industry, company scientists are major contributors to scientific literature. Scientists and engineers working at IBM, Bell Labs, and General Electric have won Nobel prizes for their work. Corporate managers of some firms clearly believe that encouraging their scientists and engineers to be linked-in respected members of the relevant communities is an important investment in corporate prowess to stay ahead of the competition.

It is also important to understand that the divulging of certain kinds of information does not significantly undermine a company's real proprietary edge. Where new products are patentable and patents are effective, as in pharmaceuticals, it does not hurt a company to publish generic information, if it gets the patent. Letting articulated generic information won in R&D go free does not handicap a firm from reaping handsomely from its product innovation, if it has a significant head start on production and marketing of the product in question, and the capacity to take advantage of that lead.

Finally, there are industrywide efficiency gains to be had by sharing technology. Everyone would be better off if everyone shared. Of course the fact that sharing enhances group welfare does not mean that individual firms have incentive to share. The factors discussed earlier provide some incentive for voluntary sharing of certain information by firms, even if these were not associated with reciprocity. But sharing of information that is important to proprietary interests tends to require something in exchange.

2.2.2 *Technology Selling, Trading, and Sharing.* Licensing a patent for money is the simplest such mechanism. Surprisingly little is known about

patterns and characteristics of licensing, although the last several years have
seen several good studies (see Caves et al., 1983). The limited evidence is
that much of patent licensing is between a firm and its affiliates or subsidiaries. In a large share of these and other cases, the licensee's plant is located
in a different country from the licensor's. And terms often restrict the market
of the licensee.

More generally, the evidence seems to be that firms are loath to explicitly
license direct competitors, and, other things equal, would rather export or
have a plant in a foreign market than license a separate firm in that market.
License fees extract only a small portion of the value of the technology to
the user. Caves and colleagues adduce a number of reasons. Two important
ones are: first, that in many cases the licensee has the option of inventing
around the patent or simply violating it and risking suit; and second, that
the decision by the licensor to license generally reflects a judgment that the
licensee's market cannot be easily tapped by export or branch plant operation.

This is not to say that there are not situations where firms license their
direct market competitors. However, these seem to be in industries where
licensees do independent R&D, proprietary gains come largely from a head
start in any case, and there is an implicit or explicit reciprocity about licensing certain kinds of technology.[16]

I have little hard data to support this proposition, but I suspect that patent
licensing among rivalrous firms, where it occurs, is basically the tip of an
iceberg of technology trading and sharing, most of which does not involve
explicit licensing. In a number of industries there seems to be a general implicit agreement not to license patents explicitly, but not to enforce them
either, even when experience indicates that they can be. The firms apparently
recognize that they are better off as a group if these implicitly make a
common pool of their technological knowledge, rather than keep their individual pools strictly private, and if they all refrain from costly litigation.
There is the free rider problem. But I note that these industries, as those
where there is explicit patent licensing reciprocity, tend to be ones where a
head start is the principal mechanism assuring returns to innovation, and
significant R&D is required of any firm for it to keep competitive, even if
other firms do not enforce their patents. A company's patent portfolio is
largely protection against potential suits of other companies using similar
technology, posing the threat of counter-suit. As recent litigation in the semiconductor industry suggests, the agreement not to enforce patents may be
dependent upon firms whose technology is being taken thinking they get
something in return.

Eric von Hippel (1988) has studied several industries in which explicit "technology swapping" is prevalent. When a firm faces a technological problem, an engineer in that firm is likely to call up an engineer he knows in another firm, who often gives help. I noted earlier that in a number of industries conversation with employees of innovating firms was an important source of information about those innovations. Von Hippel argues that when help is given by one engineer to another, an obligation is established wherein the latter implicitly agrees to provide information to the former when the former asks, and the information is at hand to be given. Von Hippel observes that this type of information swapping tends to be most prevalent when the information involved is not of major proprietary importance to the informing firm, in the sense that it would lose a significant advantage over its rivals by divulging that information. But within the limits set by that constraint, voluntary exchange acts to keep down the costs of a proprietary system.[17]

The voluntary divulgence of information in technical society meetings is a matter that warrants careful study, but has received little. My impression is that three things are going on. First, there is communication between upstream and downstream firms, which willy nilly informs competitors. Data from the Yale survey suggest that where upstream suppliers make significant contributions to technical advance in an industry, technical societies also are rated as important. Second, participants share generic findings, partly to enhance individual and company reputation, and partly to keep in relevant networks. Third, the technical society meetings set up the contacts for the kind of exchange von Hippel describes. But to date there has been very little study of these matters.

2.2.3 *Interfirm R&D Cooperation.*   Firms buy, trade, and share technological information. To a limited extent they also cooperate in R&D. There are several conceptually separate arenas where R&D cooperation seems quite common.

One is R&D cooperation between a firm and its suppliers or customers. Earlier I noted the role of upstream firms in process innovation in many industries. Often this comes in the form of standardized equipment or materials, but in many cases new equipment needs to be tailored to the particular idiosyncratic needs of the user. In these cases, downstream and upstream firms may each possess different expertise and capabilities relevant to the design of new process equipment that need to be combined for work to go forward effectively.[18]

Cooperative R&D arrangements between a company and an upstream firm, often an equipment supplier, are widespread. There are clearly some proprietary knowledge leakage problems about these arrangements. In particular the downstream partner may not be able to control the manner in which the upstream partner deals with the downstream firm's competitors. The conditions in which these vertical arrangements thrive thus probably involve either strongly idiosyncratic process needs on the part of the downstream firm, or long-term near-exclusive pairing, or acceptance by the downstream firm that the kind of process technology being worked on will not be a competitive item strongly differentiating firms in that industry.

Upstream-downstream interaction is just one example of situations where two or more companies produce goods that are strong complements, or have different but strongly complementary expertise or other capabilities, or both. Thus airframe manufacturers cooperate with electronics and engine manufacturers in the design and development of new aircraft. Computer and semiconductor manufacturers often work together. A semiconductor producer that is strong on product design may share information and work together with another company whose process technology is stronger. A new biotech firm with a strong scientific staff but little production and marketing experience, and an established pharmaceutical company with limited in-house R&D expertise in a field where the new firm is strong, may get together on a project or group of projects.[19]

The latter are examples of R&D cooperation between firms broadly in the same line of business. These kinds of arrangements tend to be easier to work out when the firms in question are not in strong direct rivalry, producing for example products that appeal to somewhat different customers. As noted earlier, there has long been a tradition of exchange of technological information, and licensing, between firms in the same line of business, but operating in quite different geographical markets.

Yet even where firms are strongly rivalrous, they may try to forge agreements to get done cooperatively certain kinds of research where the results are difficult to keep proprietary, or where certain objectives are recognized as shared. There may be industrywide problems like inadequate procedures for testing raw materials, the solution to which might give little durable advantage to a particular firm, but would significantly benefit the industry as a whole. In many instances an industry can collectively benefit by devising and adopting certain common standards. Setting and advertising these may be useful, for example, in inducing greater efficiency and competition in industries providing inputs, or products that are part of the same system, such as light bulbs and lamps, or television sets and signals provided by television stations. Customers may value highly the ability to use a product of one company together with the product of another, as presently in the case with PCs. As the examples illustrate, there may be serious conflict among companies about whether there should be any standards, as for example when a dominant company like IBM is resistant to other companies making compatible products, or about what the standards should be. But in many cases there is sufficient shared interest to engender a cooperative standard-setting effort. For a good discussion see Besen and Saloner (1988).

In recent years there has been a sharp increase in industry interest in mechanisms for cooperative funding of generic research. While this partly reflects a rather mechanical imitation of what is believed to have been fruitful in Japan, it is also the result of a more considered appreciation of some points that I have stressed above. The applied sciences and engineering disciplines have become more powerful. A company that is not linked into their advance is disadvantaged relative to a company that is. And the best way to get linked in is to be in on the research. On the other hand, the public good properties of what is learned in generic research suggest that much is to be gained by sharing expenses.

In 1984 amendments to the antitrust laws of the United States were made expressly to facilitate such intercompany agreements. A few such organizations have been formed that stand on their own—for example, the Microelectronics and Computer Technology Corporation, until recently the best known (see Peck, 1986), and just recently Sematech. However, by far the greater number of recently created industry-oriented generic research centers have been connected with universities.

2.3 The Role of Universities

Universities are an important part of the modern capitalist engine. They are a recognized repository of public scientific and technological knowledge. They draw on it in their teaching. They add to it through their research.

Within the United States, university science and engineering and our science-based industries grew up together. Chemistry took hold as an academic field at about the same time that chemists began to play an important role in industry. The rise of university research and teaching in the field of electricity occurred as the electrical equipment industry began to grow up in the United States. In both cases the universities provided the industry with its technical people, and many of its ideas about product and process innovation.[20]

Contrary to notions that academic science and scientists stand at some distance from industry, save to provide the latter with people and published papers, in many fields the links between academic science and industrial science traditionally have been close. Consulting by academic scientists and engineers is not a new phenomenon. And industry scientists have long played a role as advisors to academic science and engineering departments, and as trustees at universities, like MIT, who were training people and doing research of relevance to industry.

Academic science departments can be important to technical change for two quite different reasons: because of the training they provide young scientists and engineers who go into industry, and because of the research they do. To be effective in industrial research, a young scientist needs to know basic principles and research techniques, and these can be taught by academics. The research they do, while almost always good exercise for young scientists, may or may not be directly relevant to industry.

The situation is dynamic, not static. Academic research was very important to technological developments in the early days of the semiconductor industry, but as time went by R&D in industry increasingly separated itself from what the academics were doing. As I will document in a moment, at the current time academic biology and computer science are very important sources of new ideas and techniques for industry. The latter is a new field, and the former is experiencing a renaissance. On the other hand, technologies associated with complex product systems or production processes, like aircraft and aircraft engines, telecommunications and semiconductor production, involve much that the academics do not do and mostly do not know in any detail.

In our survey, my colleagues and I asked our respondents to score, on a scale from 1 to 7, the relevance of various fields of basic and applied science to technical change in their line of business. We also asked them to score, on the same scale, the relevance of university research. I propose that a high score for a science on the first question signals the importance of university training in that field, and a high score on the second the relevance of what academic researchers are doing.

On the first question, every field of science received a score of 6 or higher from at least a few industries. As one might have expected, some scientific fields were of importance to only a few industries. However, four broad fields—chemistry, material science, computer science and metallurgy—received scores of 6 or higher from over 30 industries (out of 130).

The fact that an industry rated a field of science as highly relevant by no means implies that it rated university research in that field so. Thus while 73 industries rated the relevance of chemistry as a field of 5 or greater, only 19 industries rated university research in chemistry that highly. Forty-four industries rated the relevance of physics at 5 or greater, but only four gave that high a score to university research in physics. This does not mean that academic research in physics is unimportant over the long run to technical advance in industry. However, the impact will probably be stretched out and indirect, operating through influences on the applied sciences and the engineering disciplines, with the ultimate impact on industrial R&D occurring through these.

What fields of university research have widespread reported relevance to industry, in the sense that a number of industries credited university research in that field with a relevance score of 5 or more? Basically, the applied sciences. Computer science and material science head the list, each with more than 25 industries giving such a score, followed by metallurgy and chemistry, with 21 and 19 industries, respectively. University research in the engineering disciplines also received a high relevance score from a number of industries. Industries for which these fields are important look to universities for new knowledge and techniques, as well as training.

Biology, and the applied biological sciences (medical and agricultural science), appear somewhat special today. While these fields are deemed relevant by only a narrow range of industries, those industries that scored these fields at 5 or higher almost always rated university research in these fields at 5 or higher too. Thus at the present time those industries whose technologies rest on the basic and applied biological sciences seem to be closely tied to the universities for research as well as training.

It appears that there are two different ways in which academic research feeds into technical advance in industry. In some cases academic research provides the original "inventions" or pilot versions of designs that industry subsequently develops and commercializes. This often happens in the engineering disciplines, where research in many cases directly involves building and testing new devices of designs. But in most fields what academic research provides is not pilot inventions but understandings and techniques that industry can later employ for a variety of different purposes. Thus academic research on cancer may provide clues to pharmaceutical companies regarding what to look for, but does not yield an embryonic new design in itself.[21] Of course there are mixed cases. Work in materials science increases knowledge about how to find or create materials for superconductivity. At the same time some academic groups are now in on the hunt for superconductive materials.

In industries where technological advance is being fed significantly by academic research, firms naturally look for close links with university scientists and laboratories where that work is being done. Traditionally, academia has been quite open to those linkages. However, these tend to be located outside the liberal arts and sciences part of the university, in the agricultural experimentation stations, the engineering schools and the medical schools.

In recent years there has been an explosion of new arrangements whereby a single firm or a group of firms funds research at a university laboratory, and receives some sort of advantaged access to that research or its findings. Not surprisingly, the industries most engaged in these activities are ones where firms are large, and who rate academic research as highly important to technological change of interest to them. The major such industries are pharmaceuticals, agricultural chemicals, and electronics. And the fields of university science being tapped by those arrangements tend to be those where academic research was judged highly relevant to technological advance in those industries: certain of the biological sciences, and computer science.

Both the federal and state governments have been actively encouraging these arrangements. The National Science Foundation has been supporting Engineering Research Centers which link university research to industry. There is a raft of new state programs that do this. In these arrangements corporate support is often mingled with public support.

My conjecture is that these kinds of new arrangements for greater industry contact with generic research will prove more durable in the United States than the self-standing industry cooperatives. The same free rider problems and technology transfer problems are there, and this limits the magnitude of industry funding. But there are also other parties interested in sustaining these programs—the universities themselves, for one; these arrangements are becoming an important part of academic research and teaching in the affected fields—federal and state governments for another. Fostering technical progress has become increasingly an articulated rationale for public support of university research.

2.4 Government R&D Support

Particularly since World War II, government R&D support programs have been an important part of the capitalist engine. A variety of government agencies support R&D for different purposes and in different manners, and any attempt at classification hazards oversimplification. However, I find it analytically useful to distinguish among three different kinds of programs.[22]

In one, the guiding purpose is to advance knowledge in certain fields of science. The sponsoring agency may see such advances as salient to its own operational interests, or to its client constituency, but the time horizon is long run and the coupling of projects with pressing practical objectives relatively loose. In a second, the government agency in question has a recognized operational responsibility and an associated need for new or better equipment, and R&D is rather closely tied to meeting those needs. In a third, the objective is to meet the relatively short-run needs of an industry or other client population.

These categories should of course be understood as ideal types or models. In fact many government agencies pursue programs that span two or even all of these types. But I would argue that in such cases it is analytically useful to recognize that several different kinds of things are going on.

Thus, let us return to university research. Since World War II the United States government has been the dominant source of funding for research at universities. Many people think of the National Science Foundation as the canonical agency for university research support. The mission and program of the National Science Foundation is a relatively clear example of the first kind of program listed above. But significantly before the advent of the NSF, government agencies funded research at universities. The Hatch Act of 1887 provided for federal funding of agricultural research, much of it at universities. Clearly this program involved a blend of the first and the third described above.

And at the present time, despite the widespread impression that the NSF is the principal governmental source of funds for academic research in the United States, a significantly greater amount of money comes from government agencies with particular applied missions, who are seeking to advance scientific understanding relevant to those missions. Thus the National Institutes of Health are the dominant source of funding of academic research in the biomedical sciences, the Department of Defense the principal supporter of university science in fields like materials science and computer science, the Atomic Energy Commission and its successor the Department of Energy in high-energy physics and nuclear engineering, and so on. I noted above the growing importance of programs that fund university research deemed particularly promising to industry.

Of course government funding of basic and generic research is small-scale relative to procurement-tied R&D, where an agency is funding work associated with its attempts to get made and delivered particular kinds of equipment, or to solve particular problems of concern to it. While the DoD is by far the largest spender on procurement-related R&D, many other agencies spend some when they want equipment different from or more advanced than is available on the market. Thus the Census Bureau, the Post Office, and the Veterans Administration have on occasion invested in R&D on equipment tailored to their needs.

While there is overlap between the basic or generic research support programs of mission-oriented government agencies and their procurement-tied R&D programs, I distinguish these on several counts. One is the breadth of the objectives. Another is the way the programs are governed. In research-support programs scientists and engineers from outside government as well as in tend to play a major role in setting broad directions and in making allocation decisions. Universities generally are the locus of work, although government and industry labs may be involved as well. In procurement-oriented programs an office in the government agency makes the decisions and monitors the effort closely. The work is usually done in an industrial or government laboratory.

The massive defense procurement-related R&D programs of the last quarter century are so familiar to contemporary observers that it is seldom recognized that this phenomenon, like broad government support of university research, dates from World War II. Prior to then, less R&D went specifically into the design of military equipment, and a large share of what did was financed by companies themselves as an investment in possible future government sales. There are several reasons why the Pentagon shifted from the earlier policy of letting companies invest in R&D to a policy of government finance of R&D on systems and components that it intended to procure when they were ready. One is simply that during the war the armed services worked with companies in this mode, and the habit became natural. A second is that, largely because their demands became more ambitious, the armed services wanted greater control over the R&D on the systems they wanted. As it turned out, in the post–World War II era, both aspects of the military R&D programs, the broad research support aspect and the particular development and procurement aspect, have pulled into place a number of technologies of enormous civilian significance, including modern semiconductors, the electronic computer, and jet aircraft. Various observers have remarked on this, and have gone on to argue that DoD R&D has been the key to United States technological supremacy in commercial products during the 1960s and 1970s. However, this clearly was not a principal intent of the DoD.

Which brings me to the third type of program I listed—R&D support expressly to enhance the capabilities and competitiveness of an industry. This is where much of the current discussion of appropriate government R&D support policies is focused. And despite the cluckings of some who should know better that the United States never has and never should engage in such "industrial policies," it is apparent that the United States certainly has, and will continue to do so.

I noted earlier that support of agricultural research dates back now over a century. While much of that work has been located at universities, it has been specifically aimed to help farmers and, in some instances, farm product processing industries. And much of the work has been aimed at solving particular practical problems.

In a number of instances, the procurement interests of a government agency, particularly the armed forces, have been used to argue for policies to help an industry commercially. Thus RCA was formed at the explicit urging of the U.S. government to ensure that the United States had a strong indigenous radio industry, a matter deemed important for national security. The NACA was organized through government to help the U.S. airframe industry compete internationally so as to ensure a procurement base. The recent formation of Sematech was justified by the argument that a commercially competitive semiconductor industry is essential to national security. The U.S. program in support of civilian nuclear power also grew out of national security concerns, and the desire to exploit spillover.

This is quite a mixed bag. Recent policies that move further in this area include Sematech and the collection of university-based industry-oriented centers mentioned earlier. However, perhaps the most interesting aspect of the current policy discussion has been the proposal that the government take responsibility for coordinating both academic and industry work in emerging fields like superconductivity and high-definition television. What to make of this idea?

3. Toward a Socialization of R&D? The Evolving Roles of Government

The modern capitalist engine is always in the process of being redesigned and rebuilt. I began this essay with Schumpeter's characterization of the American engine, circa 1942. At the time he wrote, several of the important pieces of the contemporary system described in Section 2 were not yet in place. The strong publicly supported university research system and the massive military R&D programs were components added only after World War II. And even the part of the system he highlighted—large companies with large attached laboratories—was relatively new then and nowhere near as prevalent as it became after the war.

Schumpeter well understood that the capitalist engine was always being redesigned. And he had some strong notions regarding where the redesign ultimately would go.

While most scholars of technical advance fasten on those few pages of

Chapter 7, in fact the central argument of *Capitalism, Socialism, and De-mocracy* was that the capitalist system he was describing would sooner or later be transformed into a socialist one. He put forth a number of reasons. One he deemed as particularly important was that it was increasingly be-coming possible to achieve major technical advances without the wastes associated with the capitalist way: "[I]nnovation itself is being reduced to a routine. Technological progress is increasingly becoming the business of teams of trained specialists who turn out what is required and make it work in predictable ways. The romance of earlier commercial advantage is rapidly wearing away, because so many more things can be strictly calculated that had of old to be visualized in a flash of genius."[23] Thus the arguments for capitalism were eroding.

How right was this call? Are we indeed seeing a replacement of the cap-italist engine with one of basically different design?

I have argued throughout this essay that the modern capitalist engine is a much more complex mechanism than Schumpeter's famous sketch sug-gests. It is, indeed, a much more socialized system.

I have stressed the rise of the applied sciences and engineering disciplines, the codification of generic technological knowledge, and the professionali-zation of R&D and related activities, as important forces for the socializa-tion of technological knowledge, and to some extent of R&D. Here Schum-peter's call clearly was on the money.

Certainly government's role in the system has expanded since Schumpeter wrote, not only in the United States but in the other major capitalist nations. Everywhere governments have taken responsibility for the funding of uni-versity research and for a good portion of higher education in science and engineering. In other countries, as well as the United States, government agencies dependent upon the advance of certain fields of science and tech-nology for the success of these missions have made large investments in the advancement of these fields. Everywhere bodies exist to do at least a mod-icum of coordination of national efforts in fields judged strategic.

However, if by socialization one means explicitly planned and coordi-nated action across a broad field of activity, then socialization is still quite limited. There does indeed seem to have been a significant increase in R&D cooperation in some industries, in part as a result of government policies encouraging this and in part as a result of the firms' own volition. But in the United States and elsewhere the vast bulk of civilian-oriented industrial R&D is funded by the companies that expect to benefit from it. Among firms in the same line of business, while there is increased cooperation on some matters, rivalry is still the general rule.

What about Japan? A number of analysts have highlighted features of the Japanese R&D system that differentiate it from the American and European: the role that MITI plays in helping industry chart out appropriate broad directions, the coordination of public and private actions, close interaction between companies and their component and equipment suppliers and occasionally among competitors in precompetitive research. A strong case can and has been made that these features add power and efficiency to the Japanese system.[24]

I would argue, however, that the Japanese system is not of fundamentally different design from the American, but rather is a different and perhaps more effective model in the same broad class. One distinctive part of the present Japanese system is concerned with cooperative precompetitive research. As the name implies, the results of this kind of work are difficult to make proprietary, at least immediately and directly. And as generic knowledge has grown stronger, it has become increasingly important to industry that it keep a hand in on its advance. The Japanese accomplish this in their particular way. But as I argued above, U.S. companies are being drawn down into similar kinds of work too, if through different mechanisms, generally in association with universities. There are differences and changes going on in this arena, but they don't seem to involve a radical system redesign.

Many observers have pointed to the mechanisms orchestrated through MITI by which technologists in Japan get together and share knowledge and judgments about where technology is going and attempt to map out coordinated action. But I have above mentioned that mechanisms for sharing and coordination are not unique to Japan, and recent policies in the United States and in Europe are concerned with strengthening these. Again, the differences and changes would appear to be of degree, not of kind.

And in Japan, as elsewhere, the vast bulk of industrial R&D continues to be work done privately, and companies compete fiercely. Attempts by MITI to guide and coordinate R&D have been resisted when companies felt they encroached on proprietary turf.

And Schumpeter's prognostication that as science grew stronger technical innovation would become predictable and routine has turned out to be a bad call. Since Schumpeter's time a number of large-scale and far-reaching R&D programs have been predicated on that belief, almost always with bad results. While the problems of cost overruns and far off-target performance that have marked American military procurement have been interpreted by many as symptoms of weak management, greedy contractors, and undue and perhaps somewhat corrupt cronyism, it is evident that in most cases both the DoD and the contractor vastly underestimated the uncertainty and the difficulty of the far-reaching task they agreed to take on. And since there was no real competition or alternatives, pressures to cut losses were weak. The problem the United States had with its nuclear reactor programs, the ill-fated SST, and now with the space shuttle tell a similar story. The European record with large-scale ambitious and sheltered projects is no better. While MITI has tried to guide and coordinate industrial efforts, the focus has tended to be on precompetitive R&D, and there certainly has not been tight planning of new product development. In the United States, while the discussion has been particularly sharp, it would appear that the proposals that a government agency coordinate work on superconductivity and high-definition TV are aimed at precompetitive research. Indeed it is highly unlikely that the companies involved would tolerate efforts to coordinate their product design work.

But then, for product and process innovation, the old messy process of letting a number of different parties make their own bets using their own money and relying on ex-post evaluation to decide what course was the right one still has a lot to argue for it over a policy of ex-ante technology-wide planning and administered coordination. It, appropriately, stimulates a variety of approaches in circumstances where it is a mistake to narrow down exploration to a very few. And it serves as a guard against technological hubris of an organization that would be czar.

So I return to my starting place. Schumpeter's quick characterization remains a good first cut at understanding the capitalist engine and its workings. It is a much more complex machine than he described and over the years it has grown even more so. Over the years we have learned to do many things to make the original engine run more efficiently, with more power and less waste, and have learned to steer it at least broadly. We share knowledge, and coordinate action in certain situations. Public funding and government leadership have been used to make generic knowledge more readily public, and to guide and spur the system when this has seemed appropriate.

The structures Japan has developed over the last fifteen years are further steps in these directions. However, rather than changing the basic nature of the engine, the new elements are better seen as cutting down some of its roughness, reducing some of its inefficiencies, enhancing its effectiveness, without significantly diminishing the role played by pluralism, rivalry, and ex-post selection. Technical advance under capitalism still needs to be understood as proceeding through an evolutionary process.

And so too the change in the nature of the capitalist engine itself. At the present time a wide variety of new kinds of organizations, new ways of doing things, new patterns of interorganization interaction, are coming into being in the United States and elsewhere. As with the advance of technology, many different actors are involved in these changes in the system, with very little in the way of overall planning and coordination. And like technical advance, institutional change is very much a cultural evolutionary process. Firms watch other firms and try to learn from their experience. When technical advance appears to be going better in one country than another, a variety of new departures are induced in the latter with the aim of emulating elements of the former's system. For years the United States was the world's model; now obviously Japan is.

But as with technological innovation, these new departures regarding the way of going about doing technological advance must be understood as changes that may or may not succeed. Probably some will, and will become entrenched, and some will not, and will disappear after a while. This openness of the engine to experimental tinkering is one of its greatest design virtues.

Schumpeterian Competition

As I argued in Chapter 2, much of contemporary theorizing about technical advance by economists starts out from Schumpeter, or at least the authors say it does. I noted that, in fact, Schumpeter had only a small bit to say about technical advance, and that what he said was badly incomplete. But in addition economists reading Schumpeter, or reading other economists writing about Schumpeter, have distorted his basic argument, or at least that is the burden of Chapter 3.

Economists tend to read the Schumpeter of *Capitalism, Socialism, and Democracy* as presenting a theory vastly different from that which he presented in his *Theory of Economic Development*. The stress in the former is on entrepreneurs, and in the latter on large established corporations with attached research and development laboratories. The *Theory of Economic Development* was written just shortly after the turn of the twentieth century when Schumpeter was living in Vienna, and *Capitalism, Socialism, and Democracy* was written nearly half a century later when he was living in the United States. Differences in the featured innovating actors clearly reflect these differences in time and place.

However, while the key actors indeed are different, in both books Schumpeter stressed the uncertainties associated with technical advance, and the central role of competition among products, processes, firms, and ways of doing business more generally, in that process. In short, though he was shy about using the term, he argued that technical advance had to be understood as an evolutionary process. Although economists reading *Capitalism, Socialism, and Democracy,* or reading about that book, picked up Schumpeter's argument that, by the mid-twentieth century, large firms operating in oligopolistic markets were the key sources of technological innovation, they tended to miss his continuing stress on the role of competition.

Competition among firms through innovation—Schumpeterian competition—is the theme of the three essays in Part II. Chapter 3 reflects on what Schumpeter actually had to say, and the ways in which he was misinterpreted by many economists. Chapter 4 explores why contemporary economic analyses tend to underplay the role of firm differences which, according to the theory presented there, are an essential part of the evolutionary process. Chapter 5 develops this argument further, in the particular context of the ongoing debate about how broad intellectual property rights ought to be.

Schumpeter and Contemporary
Research on the Economics of Innovation

Over the past thirty years a number of economists have dedicated themselves to studying technical change, or innovation more broadly, its sources, and its economic consequences. Their empirical findings and their theories have had a significant influence on how economists now understand economic growth, on analysis and argument in the field of industrial organization, and recently have been a significant factor behind the rise of what has come to be called "the new trade theory." In all these branches of economics, as well as among scholars directly concerned with technical advance, Schumpeter is widely cited as an inspiration. Some of the recent work even calls itself "neo-Schumpeterian."

This essay is about the influence Schumpeter has had on the research and thinking by contemporary economists about innovation. To anticipate my conclusions, by flagging attention to innovation in the way he did, Schumpeter clearly became a source of inspiration, even legitimacy, for economists turning to that subject. On the other hand, the specific areas of research in this field most closely identified as drawing from or testing specific Schumpeterian propositions have, I believe, been based on a misreading of Schumpeter, or at least a failure to think through what was basic in Schumpeter's arguments and what was not. More, it can be argued that, with few exceptions, economists studying innovation have ignored or repressed Schumpeter's most consistent and elaborated argument about innovation, that it fundamentally involves disequilibrium and that standard equilibrium theory in economics cannot cope with it and its economic consequences. Schumpeter himself clearly harbored the same hang-ups about abandoning equilibrium theories, but he was far clearer than most contemporary economists

Originally published in *Innovative Competition in Medicine*, edited by George Teeling Smith, Office of Health Economics (London: White Crescent Press, 1992), pp. 1–12.

regarding what their problems are. My discussion will most draw from his *Theory of Economic Development* (first published 1911) and his *Capitalism, Socialism, and Democracy* (first published 1942), but in places I also will refer to *Business Cycles* (first published 1939) and his posthumous *History of Economic Analysis* (1954).

Both the *Theory of Economic Development* and *Capitalism, Socialism, and Democracy* clearly lay out the argument that innovation, and the economic development innovation drives, are the really important economic phenomena, and that economists should wake up to that fact. The wake up call is rather gentle in the *Theory*, perhaps reflecting the fact that, while formal theorizing then was fastening on equilibrium concepts, much of the less formal analysis of contemporary economists was recognizing innovation. Indeed a good case can be made that Schumpeter's writings then were in the mainstream of the history of economic thought which from Smith through Marx through Marshall was very much concerned with economic development.

However a case also can be made that the way formal theory in economics was developing around the turn of the century was fore-ordained to drive interest in innovation and economic development outside the mainstream of economics. Thus in a well-known passage Marshall attempted to explain why, while his central interests were in change, his formal analytics would be static:

> The Mecca of economics lies in economic biology rather than economic mechanics. But biological conceptions are more complex than those in mechanics; a volume on foundations must therefore give a relatively large place to mechanical analogies, and frequent use is made of the term equilibrium which suggests something of a static analogy. (Marshall, 1948, p. xiv)

In the *Theory of Economic Development* (1911) Schumpeter both indicates his admiration for general equilibrium theory, and states clearly that in his view such theory could not cope with innovation.

> But static analysis is not only unable to predict the consequences of discretionary changes in the traditional ways of doing things; it can neither explain the occurrence of such productive revolutions nor the phenomena which accompany them. It can only investigate the new equilibrium position after the changes have occurred. (p. 62, 63)

There is scarcely a hint then, however, that Schumpeter was aware that intellectual structures like those put forth by Walras, which clearly was an inspiration for his analysis of the circular flow of economic activity in equilibrium, might actually interfere with the ability to theorize about innovation and, indeed, might drive concern for innovation to the outlands of the discipline.

By the time he was writing *Capitalism, Socialism, and Democracy* (1942), Schumpeter had seen the thrust of mainline economic analysis turn away from development and innovation and toward matters that could be treated with equilibrium concepts, and toward the treatment with equilibrium concepts of economic activity and phenomena for which, in Schumpeter's view, equilibrium theorizing was completely inappropriate. Thus the famous Chapter 7 must be understood as a clarion call, with a strong undertone of scorn, that the way economists were coming to look at competition, and large firms, and market power, and indeed what capitalism is all about, was rooted in a totally misleading statical equilibrium theory. Read again his famous statements on the competition that matters:

> But in the capitalist reality as distinguished from its textbook picture, it is not that kind of competition (read competition through low price-cost margins) which counts, but the competition from the new commodity, the new technology . . . This kind of competition is as much more effective than the other as a bombardment is in comparison with forcing a door. (p. 84)

And

> It is hardly necessary to point out that competition of the kind we now have in mind acts not only when in being but also when it is merely an ever-present threat. It disciplines before it attacks. The businessman feels himself to be in a competitive situation even if he is alone in his field or if, although not alone, he holds a position such that investigating government experts fail to see any effective competition between him and any other firms in the same or neighbouring field, and in consequence conclude that his talk, under examination, about his competitive sorrows is all make believe. (p. 85)

Note that Schumpeter here is, at once, railing at the then (and still largely now) tendency of economists to pose the economic problem in static equilibrium terms, and trying to get economists to focus on innovation and competition through innovation. Here he is again:

> In other words the problem that is usually being visualized is how capitalism administers existing structures, whereas the relevant problem is how it creates and destroys them. As long as this is not recognized, the investigator does a meaningless job. As soon as it is recognized his outlook on capitalist practice and its social results changes considerably. (p. 84)

This message really is not much changed from the message he presented thirty years earlier in the *Theory of Economic Development*. What did change in a major way between the two books was his treatment of the sources of innovation.

In the *Theory of Economic Development* his orientation is toward entrepreneurship and new firms.

> In the first place, it is not essential to the matter—although it may happen—that new combinations (innovations) be carried out by the same people who control the productive or commercial process that is displaced by the new. On the contrary, new combinations are as a rule embodied, as it were, in new firms . . . (p. 66)

In his *Theory*, Schumpeter is curiously uninterested in where the basic ideas for innovations, be they technological or organizational, come from. The "entrepreneur" is not viewed by Schumpeter as having anything to do with their generation:

> It is no part of his function to "find" or "create" new possibilities. They are always present, abundantly accumulated by all sorts of people. Often they are also generally known and being discussed by scientific or literary writers. In other cases there is nothing to discuss about them, because they are quite obvious. (p. 88)

It would appear that it is this passage that lies at the root of the argument, often made, that Schumpeter considered invention and innovation very different acts.

By the time he was writing *Capitalism, Socialism, and Democracy* that sharp separation is gone, as is the notion that the "new possibilities" are lying around for anyone to take up. The venue of innovation is the large firm with attached R&D laboratory that creates the new products the firm introduces. He clearly had firms like General Electric and Du Pont in mind when he wrote:

> The first thing a modern concern does as soon as it feels it can afford it is to establish a research department every member of which knows that his bread and butter depends on his success in devising improvements. (p. 96)

The difference between the two books in viewpoints on the sources of innovation certainly is not surprising, given that the earlier was written in the Austro-Hungarian empire shortly after the turn of the century, and the latter in the United States in the late 1930s.

Schumpeter's argument in Chapter 7, and elsewhere in *Capitalism, So-*

cialism, and Democracy, however, came to be interpreted by economists not simply as stating that large firms with affiliated laboratories had by mid-century become the principal source of technical innovation. Rather, it became the conventional wisdom in economics that Schumpeter had argued that for innovation "the bigger the firm the better." His argument that a firm may feel great competitive pressure even when it appears to be alone in a field came to be interpreted as "monopoly power is conducive for innovation." There are a few places in *Capitalism, Socialism, and Democracy* that Schumpeter came close to saying that. Thus in Chapter 8 he writes:

> Actually however there are superior methods available to the monopolist which either are not available to a crowd of competitors or are not available to them so readily: for there are advantages which although not strictly unattainable at the competitive level of enterprise and as a matter of fact are secured only on the monopoly level, for example because monopolization may increase the sphere of influence of the better or decrease the sphere of influence of inferior, brains, or because the monopoly enjoys a disproportionately higher financial standing. (p. 101)

However, a reading of quotes I earlier gave from Chapter 7 should suffice to persuade that Schumpeter never had in mind what came to be called the "Schumpeterian hypothesis." He certainly had in mind a different kind of competition than that modeled in the price theory texts, but the competition he had in mind was fierce. He warned against using numbers like four-firm concentration ratios as indicators of the strength of competition in a field, but stressed how insecure the footings were of firms that, by the static statistics, looked as if they held great market power.

Nonetheless, casual reading of *Capitalism, Socialism, and Democracy,* or as time went by, more likely mostly reading of the statements of other economists about the "Schumpeterian hypothesis" without reading Schumpeter, led to the rise of a little industry of economists exploring that hypothesis econometrically and theoretically. Throughout the endeavor there were some economists arguing that Schumpeter never said it, and also that the issues of the connections between firm size and market structure and innovation were far more complex than the relationships being tested. In any case, the evidence is now clear that the "Schumpeterian hypothesis" doesn't square with much of the data, and that things are indeed much more complex than that. (For a good up-to-date statement, see Cohen and Levin, 1989).

Was it all a wild goose chase? In some ways yes, but the blame should not be on Schumpeter. And in other ways the pursuit has been fruitful in that finally, it seems to have led economists (or at least some of them) to a much more sophisticated vision of the relationships between market structure and innovation than contained in the simple arguments of twenty years ago.

The 'Schumpeterian hypothesis' undoubtedly is the specific argument about innovation most often tagged to Schumpeter, if wrongly. The second most commonly tagged argument probably is about "long waves," and here too I would argue that the economists following the trail basically missed or forgot what Schumpeter had foremost in his mind.

Business Cycles is a long complex book. Its organizing theme is that patterns of economic activity display the interaction of several different kinds of cyclical movements, each associated with a different kind of economic force. It was Schumpeter's treatment of "long waves" that has attracted the most subsequent attention. The presence of long waves of economic activity, of approximately fifty years' cycle length, had been suggested by several economists prior to Schumpeter's treatment of them, and Schumpeter gives considerable credit to the Russian economist Kondratieff for mapping them out. A good portion of *Business Cycles* is dedicated to examining data bearing on the presence, duration and regularity of long waves. Schumpeter came out strongly, arguing for their existence, and their regularity (about fifty-six years).

Much of the subsequent research stimulated by *Business Cycles* has been concerned with two issues. One is whether the "fifty year" Schumpeterian long cycle clock (or calendar) scheme can explain the rapid growth of many countries for the quarter century after World War II, and the slowdown that has occurred around 1970, and whether the scheme suggests that rapid growth will be renewed in the 1990s. The other is more general assessment of the argument that long cycles are "regular." Many sophisticated economists take the position that, while there certainly are eras of rapid growth, followed by periods of slower growth, the pattern is so irregular that the very term "cycle" is inappropriate.

However, it is not clear how much stock Schumpeter himself put in the "regularity" argument. He thought he saw it in the data, but nothing in his broad theoretical arguments would imply regularity, or explain it. Indeed his verbal discussion of the historical distinctiveness of each "long wave" indicates he wouldn't have been shattered if the evidential case for "regularity" fell apart.

In my view the genuinely interesting and provocative part of Schumpeter's discussion of "long waves" was his explanation for them. His basic explanation was that different economic eras are marked by different clusters of technologies and associated industries. A long "upswing" is stimulated when a new set of technologies and industries comes into existence, stimulating investment and an expansion of economic activity. Thus the long "upswing" of the early nineteenth century was associated with the rise of textiles, iron and coal, and steam engines. The upswing which began in the mid-nineteenth century was associated with the rise of railroads and steel making. The boom of the early twentieth century was driven by automobiles, electric power and associated systems and products, and the modern chemical industries. Schumpeter proposes that each of these long booms ultimately petered out as technical advance in the key sectors slowed, and investment opportunities got saturated. Thus each long upswing was followed by a long period of slower expansion and decline. Then a wave of new innovations would set the stage for the next long upswing.

The argument here is provocative, but not at all associated with any case for regularity. It hinges on whether or not there are forces at work so that basic new industry generating innovations tend to cluster, with on average some considerable time between the clusters, so that they can be considered the basic cause of a subsequent more general boom in economic activity. Contemporary economists are not yet in agreement as to whether this is right. To say that different eras are marked by different clusters of strategic technologies and industries is one thing, and many economists would agree on that. If that is accepted, one must accept as well that the key technologies had to be around, at least in embryonic form, before the surge of development employing them could begin.

But if one is to buy into Schumpeter's theory one must argue that the advent of these technologies, the key inventions or innovations that made them possible, were bunched together at a time shortly before the upswing. However, in some cases it can be argued that the key inventions occurred at different times, with many of them significantly before the upswing that exploited them, even though their development occurred together. They developed together, at the time they did, as a result of forces impinging on the economy that had little to do with the timing of the basic technological breakthroughs. The jury is still out on this one, but at least this is an interesting set of questions (for a good discussion, see Rosenberg and Frischtak 1984).

I want to concentrate now on Schumpeter's argument, articulated both in the *Theory of Economic Development* and in *Capitalism, Socialism, and Democracy*, that one cannot understand, or model, innovation using equilibrium concepts. Earlier I gave Schumpeter's clear direct statement of this in the *Theory*. Here he is again on the problem:

> In the accustomed circular flow every individual can act promptly and ration-
> ally because he is sure of his ground and is supported by the conduct, as
> adjusted to the circular flow, of all other individuals, who in turn expect the
> accustomed activity from him . . . [But] while in the accustomed channels his
> own ability and experience suffice for the normal individual, when confronted
> with innovations he needs guidance. While he swims with the stream in the
> circular flow which is familiar to him, he swims against the stream if he wishes
> to change its channel. (p. 80)

Now while Schumpeter's insistence that competition through innovation
is the most important kind of competition has gradually taken hold in
models in industrial organization and international trends, almost without
exception these models assume that firms are able to "see through" the competition generated by rivalry in innovation, and have as solutions equilibrium conditions. But Schumpeter's views on human cognitive capacity are
far closer to those Herbert Simon later associated with the term "bounded
rationality" than with the exquisite rationality of modern game theory. One
must

> bear in mind the impossibility of surveying exhaustively all the effects and
> counter-effects of the projected enterprise . . . In economic life action must be
> taken without working out the details of what is to be done. (p. 85)

Twenty years later Baumol stated very clearly the reason why the by then
standard models of the firm that assumed firms maximize profits could not
deal with entrepreneurship, laying out an argument with which Schumpeter
almost surely would have agreed.

> In all these [maximizing models] automaton maximizers the businessmen are
> and automaton maximizers they remain. And this shows why our body of
> theory, as it has developed, offers us no promise of being able to deal effectively
> with the description and analysis of the entrepreneurial function. (Baumol,
> 1968, p. 68)

What is most catching about Baumol's remarks is that he recognizes, as
did Schumpeter, that maximization models actually imply a sort of autom-
aton quality to human decision making. They assume a context which is
sufficiently simple so that it can be seen through, or so familiar that old
habits don't just satisfice but maximize, which is exactly how Schumpeter
characterized the circular flow. To model decision making that aims to break
new ground, one must model with other stuff.
But what kind of a "model" of innovation and economic development
driven by innovation would Schumpeter have advocated, had he been in-

clined to formal modelling? I believe some clues are provided by the following much-quoted passage:

> The essential point to grasp is that in dealing with capitalism we are dealing with an evolutionary process. (*Capitalism, Socialism, and Democracy*, p. 82)

But what did he mean by that? It is not sure, but it is clear that he would not have approved of the modeling of innovation in modern game theory. It also is clear that he did not have in mind a simple biological analogy. Thus he argues in the *Theory of Economic Development*:

> But the evolutionary idea (that drawing from Darwin) is now discredited in our field especially with historians and ethnologists for another reason. To the reproach of extra-scientific mysticism that now surrounds the "evolutionary" ideas, is added that of dilettantism. With all the hasty generalization with which the word "evolution" plays a part, many of us have lost patience. (p. 58)

He did use the "e" word, however, in *Capitalism, Socialism, and Democracy*, and his language about "creative destruction" gives us some hints of what he meant. But he never got beyond the hints.

Geoffrey Hodgson, in his recent manuscript on evolutionary theorizing in economics, suggests that while, ultimately, Schumpeter used the word, he made no substantive contribution to the serious development of an evolutionary alternative to neoclassical theory. Partly Hodgson's argument is Schumpeter's failure to spell out the idea. Partly it is that, until the end, Schumpeter remained strongly attracted to Walras, and general equilibrium, as the basic formal conceptualization in economics.

However, Sidney Winter and I thought we saw more than simply a few hints and a metaphor in Schumpeter. As I have pointed out, in both the *Theory of Economic Development*, and in *Capitalism, Socialism, and Democracy*, competitive innovation is always described as a highly uncertain business, one in which the innovator cannot clearly foresee the consequences. Schumpeter is clear in both the *Theory of Economic Development*, and *Capitalism, Socialism, and Democracy*, that the economic context in which innovation is going on is one of disequilibrium, even turbulence. And *Capitalism, Socialism, and Democracy* certainly stresses the competitive aspects of innovation. There are going to be winners, and there also are going to be losers. In our *An Evolutionary Theory of Economic Change* (1982) Winter and I tried to develop formal models, in the spirit of Schumpeter. While we cannot be sure that Schumpeter would have approved of them, we believe that they are much more consonant with how Schumpeter thought of competition through innovation than the innovation models using modern game theory.

While a few other economists have followed along the same road as we have, there is scarcely a crowd. Indeed, until recently at least there has been strong resistance among economists to treating competition and economic change as "an evolutionary process" in the sense that that process is described in Schumpeter's words and in our models.

Why should this be? I noted above the strong hold that the concept of a circular flow had on Schumpeter. In his *Theory of Economic Development* his innovation concept is defined in terms of a circular flow—innovation is a break from that flow. He defined his *Business Cycles* as deviations from an economic (general) equilibrium. More, in various passages where the matter comes up, it appears that Schumpeter thought that there always were natural economic forces pulling the economic system toward an equilibrium. To the extent that this is so, and to the extent that innovation is not so powerful, or so frequent, as to keep kicking the economy far away from equilibrium, a theory that focuses on equilibrium configurations may be a powerful analytic and predictive tool. It is not clear whether Schumpeter was attracted to it because he believed this, or because of aesthetic considerations.

However, Chapter 7 of *Capitalism, Socialism, and Democracy* appears to depict innovation as being sufficiently common and powerful that "equilibrium" is not a particularly relevant concept, even if it could be assumed that, if innovation stopped, the system would quickly get to equilibrium. Winter and I interpreted the message of that chapter, and our own reading of competition through innovation in industries like semiconductors and pharmaceuticals, as indicating that economic modeling of competition through innovation could make little use of "equilibrium analysis" but rather had to treat disequilibrium dynamics explicitly.

The point of view that one ought to model the dynamics explicitly, and treat equilibrium as a special case of "rest," represents a rather radical departure from the modes of economic modeling that have grown up as developments of the basic Walrasian idea of general equilibrium. The standard mode in economics has been to center the analysis on equilibrium configurations, and then to worry about whether those configurations are "stable" in the face of perturbations. Economists working within this orthodox theoretical framework long have recognized that there might be multiple equilibria, and that a particular equilibrium (or equilibria) might not be stable. But these possibilities have rightly been seen as fundamentally threatening to the basic intellectual enterprise, and as matters to be put aside unless there were compelling reasons to attend to them.

For a variety of reasons, mostly having nothing to do with the influence of Schumpeter, over the past few years economists have begun to pick up the analytic stick by the other end. Once one starts with express models of dynamic process, one discovers that the conditions under which there is a unique equilibrium (in the sense of rest) are rather stringent, that in any case the system may be close to an equilibrium only a small portion of time, and that disequilibrium dynamics are analyzable and interesting. This is leading to a surge of new interest among economists in "evolutionary models." I do not know whether or not Schumpeter would have approved of all this. However, I believe he should have, while cautioning about the potential hype.

In my view Schumpeter's argument that one must understand economic development fueled by innovation as an evolutionary process is exactly right. However, it would seem that Schumpeter viewed this as a matter of contemporary circumstance, rather than something fundamental. Thus Part III of his *Capitalism, Socialism, and Democracy* is oriented around the proposition that, as science becomes stronger, innovation will become plannable. The consequences for capitalism would be profound, in his view:

> This social function [entrepreneurship] is already losing importance and is bound to lose it at an accelerating rate in the future even if the economic process itself of which entrepreneurship was the prime mover went on unabated. For, on the one hand, it is much easier now than it has been in the past to do things which lie outside familiar routine—innovation itself is being reduced to routine. Technological progress is increasingly becoming the business of teams of trained specialists who turn out what is required and make it work in predictable ways. (p. 132)

As a result the ideological support for capitalism was doomed to fall away, and socialism would emerge.

This leads directly into Schumpeter's forecast about viable socialism:

> Can socialism work? Of course it can. No doubt is possible about that once we assume, first, that the requisite stage of industrial development has been reached . . . but if we accept these assumptions and discard these doubts the answer to the remaining questions is clearly yes. (p. 167)

Recall that *Capitalism, Socialism, and Democracy* was written during a period of time when capitalism throughout the world was in deep trouble. It was written during a period of time that the Soviet planning system was still taking form, and well before it proved its economic bankruptcy.

Actually, some aspects of the Schumpeterian prediction about the socialization of capitalism look pretty good. He was writing before the widespread development of "welfare states" but his analysis of the ideological resistance to capitalism clearly is consistent with the strength that socialists (and modern liberals) had after the war in putting in place fundamental reforms.

However, a strong case can be made that he is just wrong in arguing that socialism can work, and that a central reason why socialism didn't was exactly that innovation wasn't reduced to a "routine." Peter Murrell (1990) has written a fascinating book arguing the inadequacy of the socialist innovation system, and he is not alone in arguing that what brought down the Soviet economy, and its Eastern European satellites, was the ineffectiveness of socialism as an engine of progress. The socialist economies set themselves up organizationally on the presumption that innovation could be reduced to a routine. It couldn't be.

Of course one must recognize the importance of Schumpeter's caveat that socialism would work if "the requisite stage of industrial development has been reached." Russia clearly was a very backward nation when socialism was put in place, and so also were a number of the countries of Eastern Europe. But socialism also failed in East Germany, and Czechoslovakia, which were pretty advanced industrial nations at the time of takeover. What is remarkable about the innovative performance (to use Schumpeter's broad concept) of the Soviet Union and the Eastern European countries from 1960 until their collapse is that they were in the innovative forefront of practically nothing. Almost all of their technical progress came about by copying developments that had been made earlier in capitalist countries.

A strong argument can be put forth that the socialist economies did not collapse because their economic performance was miserable on absolute terms. In virtually all of them the bulk of citizens experienced very major improvements during the postwar era in their standard of living, compared with what it had been before the war. However, by 1980 or so it had become evident that these economies were incapable of closing the gap in economic and technological performance with the advanced industrial nations. For a system whose legitimacy depended on claims that it was innately superior economically and technologically, this failure was fatal.

Schumpeter was right—the technical change he saw around him was proceeding through an evolutionary process. He was wrong in thinking that this was just a stage that would pass when science got stronger.

Let me conclude this essay by returning to the basic question I was asked to address. What has been Schumpeter's influence on economic research on innovation? I think his main influence has been to stimulate economists, and I believe that there have been more and more of us, to understand that innovation is a central aspect of economic activity, not a peripheral one, and that economic progress is what counts over the long run, rather than static economic efficiency. Schumpeter more than any other economist has been influential on this point. But he has yet to persuade the bulk of the economics profession.

Pick up any introductory economics text, and look to see what fraction of it is concerned with innovation. You will find that precious little is. Pick up a text in microeconomic theory and explore the same question. The way most of them are written, Schumpeter might never have lived. Or pick up a text on industrial organization. You will find that the treatment of innovation tends to be quite limited, and confined largely to description of studies that have chased after the "Schumpeterian hypothesis," and to models that purport to be "Schumpeterian" but which I have argued are not. Economists indeed have become very interested in economic growth, and in their models "technical advance" usually is the driving force. However, virtually all of these models assume continuing economic equilibrium. Economists by and large continue to adhere to the equilibrium models that Schumpeter rightly argued could not deal with innovation, and the economic change caused by continuing rapid innovation, although as I have noted there are now some signs of new developments on this front.

Capitalism, Socialism, and Democracy, which was Schumpeter's next to last great statement, not only about economics but about the state of economic thinking, was an impatient book about the latter. His posthumous *History of Economic Analysis* paints influential economic theorists in a kinder light, but perhaps that was because he was mainly looking backwards toward the great economists of an earlier era. I suspect if he were around today looking at contemporary economic analysis, he would be very impatient.

Why Do Firms Differ,
and How Does It Matter?

Introduction

This essay is concerned with the sources and significance of interfirm differences, from the viewpoint of an economist. How might an economist's perspective on this differ, say, from that of a student of business management? I would argue that the most important difference is that economists tend to see firms as players in a multi-actor economic game, and their interest is in the game and its outcomes, rather than in the particular play or performance of individual firms. That is, economists are interested in how the automobile industry works, and its performance in various dimensions, and not in General Motors or Toyota per se, but only insofar as the particularities of these firms influence the industry more broadly. This perspective is quite different, it seems to me, than that of a student of management who is concerned with the behavior and performance of individual firms in their own right.

My objective in this essay is to make a strong case for the economic significance, in the sense above, of discretionary firm differences. My position certainly has been influenced by the work of scholars of firm management who have persuasively documented significant differences among firms in an industry in behavior and performance, and proposed that these differences largely reflect different choices made by firms. However, because the interests of those authors have differed from the interests of economists, almost no attention has been paid to the industry- or economy-wide implications of such different choices. Thus while the management literature provides a start for my argument, there is much that I need to build myself, in cooperation with like-thinking friends.

Originally published in *Strategic Management Journal* (Winter 1991): 61–74. © 1991 by John Wiley & Sons, Ltd. Reprinted by permission of John Wiley & Sons, Ltd.

It should be recognized that, in trying to make a case for the economic significance of discretionary firm differences, I and my coarguers are fighting against a strong tide in economics, particularly in theoretical economics, that downplays or even denies the importance of such differences. The argument in economics is not that firms are all alike; economists recognize that computer firms differ from textile firms, and in both industries, German firms almost certainly differ from Taiwanese firms. Rather, the position is that the differences aren't discretionary, but instead reflect differences in the contexts in which firms operate: computer design and production technology and the computer market differ from the situation in textiles. Factor prices and availabilities and product markets in Germany differ from those in Taiwan. Thus firms are forced to be different.

The tendency to ignore discretionary firm differences in part reflects that economists are interested not in behavior and performance at the level of firms but, rather, in broader aggregates—industry- or economy-wide performance. It reflects, as well, some strong theoretical views held by most mainline economists about what economic activity is all about, and about the role and nature of firms in economic activity. My argument that discretionary firm differences within an industry exist and do matter significantly is part and parcel of my broader argument that neoclassical economic theory is badly limited.

Let me flag here, for future elaboration, what I do and don't mean by the term 'discretionary'. I do mean to imply a certain looseness of constraints, both in the short and long run, that gives room so that firms that differ in certain important respects can be viable in the same economic environment. I do mean that to some extent these differences are the result of different strategies that are used to guide decision making at various levels in firms. On the other hand, I do not mean that what a firm is and does is under the tight control of high-level decision makers. And I certainly do not mean that what makes a firm strong or weak at any time is well understood, even within the firms themselves, although there well may be an articulated point of view on this. More on these matters later.

The remainder of this essay is structured as follows. In the following section I shall flesh out my above remarks about the very significant differences in perspective between scholars trained or inclined to see discretionary firm level variables as important, and economists who see firm differences as determined largely by more aggregative economic forces. Then I focus on the basic theoretical preconceptions of neoclassical economic theory that lead to this position, and which make it very difficult to move any distance from it. I follow with an exploration of evolutionary economic theory which provides a very different view of what economic activity is all about and within which firm differences are central, and go on to consider the role of firm differences in the evolution of technology and modes of organizing economic activity. Finally, a reprise.

The Divergent Literatures on "Competitiveness"

The differences in perspective can be seen clearly in the divergent literatures concerned with what now popularly is called the "competitiveness" issue—the recent weakness of American firms, particularly vis-à-vis Japanese ones, in industries where not so long ago U.S. firms were doing very well. There is a sharp split between studies that focus on the differences between American and Japanese firms, and studies by economists that are focused on more aggregated variables.

Made in America, a publication put out in the summer of 1989 by the MIT Commission on Industrial Productivity (Dertouzos et al., 1989), is a good example, and summary, of the former line of research. While the staff of the Commission undertook considerable research on its own, the multi-faceted diagnosis it presents is quite consistent with that presented in a number of prior studies concerned with why American firms have been losing out.

American firms are hooked on old-style mass production methods, in an era where flexible manufacturing has become a more effective mode of operation. Similarly, our hierarchical mode of organization and custom of specifying job assignments narrowly, while perhaps appropriate in an earlier era, now are sources of weakness. Research and product design and development stand too distant from manufacturing and production engineering; thus it takes American companies much longer than the Japanese to go from conception to production, and our production costs and quality often are inferior. American firms are myopic, both in the sense of their failure to look at world rather than national markets and in the sense that time horizons are short. The latter partly has to do with the high cost of capital in the United States, but also with the way our managers think and the tools of analysis they are taught in business schools. Compared with the Japanese and Germans, our blue-collar work force comes to the workplace poorly trained by the public education system. This is compounded by a weakness of in-company training and retraining programs. Together, this puts American firms at a significant disadvantage regarding labor skills. American firms are less willing to cooperate with one another on matters where cooperation would yield pay-off, partly because of the attitudes of managers, but also partly because government looks on cooperation with suspicion or hostility. More generally, business and government seldom work together and often are at odds.

Others might summarize the central arguments somewhat differently, but I believe the above does represent fairly the kinds of propositions about firm differences made in the report. The arguments are plausible and provocative, and may provide important guidance to American management, and for public policy.

However, there are two important issues one can raise about the conclusions of the study. First, one can question the confidence one should place in the causal connections asserted in studies like *Made in America*. Second, one also can question whether the variables treated there as basic really are so, as contrasted with themselves being determined by broader forces.

At this stage I want only to flag the former issue. However, there really is a big question about just what Japanese firms in the automobile industry, or the semiconductor industry, are doing that lies behind their evident stronger performance, in various dimensions, than American or European firms. Later in this essay I shall focus on this uncertainty, and some of its implications.

For the present I want to focus on the latter question, because it gets sharply into view the contrast between analyses like *Made in America*, and the standard views of economists about the determinants of "competitiveness." There is some discussion in *Made in America* of macro- or national-level variables, like the exchange rate, the cost of capital, or more generally the system of corporate finance, the effectiveness of the public education system, government policies, and so on. However, this is not where the focus is. It is firm-level variables that receive the top billing, and it is presumed that these are discretionary to a considerable degree. In contrast, the inclination of economists is to focus on macro-, or environmental-level variables, and to play down or ignore the role of firm discretion.

The same year that *Made in America* was published, three economists, Baumol, Blackman, and Wolff (1989), published their interpretation and diagnosis of lagging American productivity growth rates, and the convergence of productivity and living standards among the major industrial nations. The focus of *Productivity and American Leadership: The Long View* (1989) is usually at the level of the national economy, and sometimes at the level of the sector or industry. The variables considered are national savings and investment rates, investments in education, processes through which technology flows from creators to followers, and the like. There is scarcely a word about discretionary behavior at the level of firms.

It is strongly tempting, and I think right headed, to propose that each of the studies has described part of the elephant. The argument in the MIT study, that many of the difficulties American firms are having are self-inflicted, is quite persuasive. At the same time the economist's proposition, that to a considerable extent firms are molded by the broader economic conditions surrounding them, is compelling. What seems sorely needed is an analysis that sees both of these matters, in a coherent way.

While the authors of *Made in America* never quite got into serious analyses of environmental variables, it does not seem difficult to augment an analysis that starts at the firm level to consider the environments that firms are in. Two new books are exemplary in that they do just this. Both recognize explicitly that national or environmental variables strongly influence firm strategy and structure, and that firms have considerable range of choice about these variables. Chandler's *Scale and Scope* (1990) describes in considerable depth how the different economic conditions, institutions, and cultures of the United States, Great Britain, and Germany molded the nature of the modern manufacturing firms that grew up in these different countries in the first decade of the twentieth century, and influenced the industries in which the nations developed special strength. However, there is nothing deterministic about Chandler's description of how the environment shapes firms and influences their performance.

Porter's *The Competitive Advantage of Nations* (1990) presents a similar perspective in which environmental influences matter greatly, but the firms have a considerable range of freedom regarding whether, or just how, they will take advantage of the opportunities the environment affords. Indeed both authors see the firms as to some extent molding their own environment as, for example, in calling forth significant public investments in education in the United States and Germany.

Chandler is a historian by training. Porter's formal training is in economics, but his career has been at a business school and his research focus has been on management. It should be recognized that the orientation of these authors to "firms" is quite different than that in most of economics. Indeed it is apparent that for both authors the center of attention is the firms, and the central questions are "how are they doing" and "what makes them strong or weak." They are drawn to wider economic mechanisms and institutions in the search for answers to these questions. Now firm performance clearly is related to broader economic performance, but I have argued above they are not the same thing. Since neither Chandler nor Porter presents a coherent statement of the economy-wide problem, their analyses stop considerably short of providing an answer that would satisfy economists to the question of "why do firms differ and how does it matter?"

Firms in Neoclassical Economic Theory

To get at that question from an economist's perspective, one needs to start with a broad understanding of what economic activity is all about, and what constitutes good economic performance or poor. Neoclassical theory, which provides the current conventional wisdom on these matters for economists, militates against paying attention to firm differences as an important variable affecting economic performance for several reasons.

The first is the perception of what economic activity is all about. Since the formulation of general equilibrium theory almost a century ago, the focus has largely been on how well an economy allocates resources, given preferences and technologies. This position is far from universal. Empirically oriented economists have been interested in things like technical change, and recently there has been a rash of work on economic institutions and how and why these change over time. Schumpeter some time ago put forth a strong general theoretical challenge to the effect that innovation ought to be the center of economic analysis. But it is hard to overestimate the degree to which economists continue to see the central economic problem as that of meeting preferences as well as possible, given resources and prevailing technologies and institutions. This perspective implies a rather limited view of what firms are about.

Second, partly reflecting this general orientation, but not the only possible formulation of firms' decision processes consistent with it, economists became wedded to a theory of firm behavior that posited that firms face given and known choice sets (constrained for example by available technologies) and have no difficulty in choosing the action within those sets that is the best for them, given their objectives (generally assumed to be as much profit as possible). Thus the "economic problem" is basically about getting private incentives right, not about identifying the best things to be doing, which is assumed to be no problem.

The perspective on the economic problem and the theory of firm behavior described above do not invite a careful inquiry into what goes on in firms. However, the tradition in economics of treating firms as "black boxes" was not inevitable either. The fact that until recently, at least, this has been the norm deserves recognition in its own right.

The overall result is a view that what firms do is determined by the conditions they face, and (possibly) by certain unique attributes (say a choice location, or a proprietary technology) they possess. Firms facing different markets will behave and perform differently, but if the market conditions were reversed so would be firm behaviors. Where the theory admits product differentiation, different firms will produce different products but, in the theoretical literature, any firm can choose any niche. Thus there are firm differences but there is no essential autonomous quality to them.

The theoretical orientation in economics thus leans strongly against the proposition that discretionary firm differences matter. Of course economists studying empirical or policy questions have a proclivity to wander away from the tethers of theory when the facts of the matter compel them to do so. Thus in doing industry studies, economists often have been forced to recognize, even highlight, firm differences, and differences that matter. One cannot study the computer industry sensitively without paying attention to the peculiarities of IBM. The recent history of the automobile industry cannot be understood without understanding Toyota and GM. But as the Baumol, Blackman, and Wolff book testifies, the theoretical preconceptions shared by most economists lead them to ignore firm differences, unless compelled to attend to them.

Several recent developments in theoretical economics would appear to be changing this somewhat. Thus the same summer that *Made in America* and *Productivity and American Leadership* were published, the long-awaited *Handbook of Industrial Organization* (1989) was also. Included in the chapters were several that survey theoretical work that does recognize firm differences.

There are, first of all, the essays by Ordover and Saloner, and by Gilbert, which are expressly concerned with theoretical work that aims to explain firm differences, or at least some consequences of firm differences. In the models reported, there usually is an incumbent in the industry, or in the production of a particular product, who has certain advantages over firms who might think of joining the action. The presence of these advantages, or threats of action should a newcomer try to encroach, is enough to make the advantages durable. Gilbert deals more generally with models where there are costs to firms of changing their market positions. However, with few exceptions the models surveyed in these chapters do not consider in much depth or detail original sources of firm differences.

Reinganum's chapter, which surveys modern neoclassical models of technological innovation, is focused on what certainly is an important source of such differences—industrial R&D and the innovation R&D makes possible.

In the models she surveys, a firm's technology may differ from a rival's because of the luck of an R&D draw, with the advantages made durable by patent protection or subsequent learning curve advantages. Given an initial difference, firms may face different incentives and thus find different courses of action most profitable. However, while these models may rationalize the observation that firms possess different technologies, the answers as to why certainly aren't very deep. And one comes away from them, or at least I do, with very little theoretical insight into why IBM is different, or Toyota, and so what.

There has been a certain amount of recent theoretical work by economists that looks inside of firms, at their structure, and thus seems to give promise of a theoretical window for a deeper look into why firms differ. The chapters by Holmstrom and Tirole, and by Williamson, report on such work. The questions explored in the surveyed work include what determines, through make or buy decisions, the boundaries of a firm, how it is organized, the relative bargaining power of owners, managers, and workers, and so forth. But again, the ultimate reason for why firms differ is rather superficial. Implicitly they differ because some chance event, or some initial condition, made different choices profitable.

In my view, recent theoretical developments in neoclassical theory have loosened two of the theoretical constraints, making it difficult if not impossible to see firm differences as important. Economists are getting away from the theoretical tethers of static general equilibrium theory and are treating technology as a variable not a given. And they are trying to look inside the black box of the firm. However, for the most part there has been failure to get away from the third tether—taking a firm's choice sets as obvious to it and the best choice similarly clear and obvious. And because of that, the reasons for firm differences, in technology or organization, are ultimately driven back to differences in initial conditions, or to the luck of a draw, which may make choice sets different. Given the same conditions, all firms will do the same thing.

As I indicated above, I certainly do not want to play down the role of environment in constraining and molding what firms do. And I do not want to play down the role of chance in causing large and durable subsequent differences among firms. But in my view the models most economists keep playing with do not effectively come to grips with what lies behind the firm differences highlighted in *Made in America*, or the implications of those differences.

The reason, I want to argue, is that while the surveyed work purports to be concerned with "innovation," with the introduction of something new to the economy in the form of new technology or a new way of organizing a firm, the models in question completely miss what is involved in innovation. Thus nowhere in the models Reinganum describes is the fundamental uncertainty, the differences of opinion, the differences in perceptions about the feasible paths, that tend to stand out in any detailed study of technical advance, even recognized, much less analyzed in any detail. Williamson's own work on the determinants of firm organization has been much influenced by Chandler, and he dedicates a certain space in his chapter to a transactions cost interpretation of Chandler's account of the rise of the modern corporation. But nowhere does he recognize explicitly the halting, trial and feedback, often reactive rather than thought-through process that led to the new ways of organizing that Chandler describes.

Put compactly, the treatment of technological and organizational "innovation" described in these chapters simply takes the given "choice set" and "maximizing over it" presumptions of standard neoclassical theory and applies them to "innovation." That is, innovation is treated as basically like any other choice. Investment costs may need to be incurred before the new product or organizational design is ready to be employed, but in neoclassical theory this is true of other capital goods like a bridge or a machine. There may be high risks involved in doing something new, in a formal sense of that term, but this is treated as statistical uncertainty with the correct probability distribution known to all as is standard in microeconomic theory. The innovation may yield a new latent or manifest public good, and this raises theoretical problems of "market failure," but this is no different than investment in, say, public health.

But what if effective treatment of innovation (and perhaps other activities) requires breaking away from the assumptions of clear and obvious choice sets and correct understanding of the consequences of making various choices? Does it really make sense to work with a model that presumes that the transistor, or the M form of organization, were always possible choices out there and known to all relevant parties, and that they simply were chosen and thus came into existence and use when conditions made profitable the relevant investments? Does the assumption that "actors maximize" help one to analyze situations where some actors are not even aware of a possibility being considered by others?

If one reflects on these issues, one may be moved to adopt a very different view of the economic problem. Within this view, which I will call evolutionary, firm differences play an essential role.

Innovation and Firms in Evolutionary Theory

The models of technological innovation surveyed by Reinganum show economists interested in the theory of the firm struggling to break away from the orientation of general equilibrium theory, which sees the economic problem as allocating resources efficiently, given technologies. So too the new literature on organizational innovation. Here economists seem to be basically interested in how new ways of doing things—technologies, and ways of organizing and governing work—are introduced, winnowed, and where proved useful, spread, as contrasted with how familiar technologies and organizational modes are employed. Many years ago Schumpeter insisted that the focus of general equilibrium theory was on questions that, over the long run, were of minor importance compared with the question of how capitalist economies develop, screen, and selectively adopt new and better ways of doing things. Many of the writers surveyed by Reinganum call themselves "neo-Schumpeterians."

However, the dynamic processes Schumpeter described are not captured by the new neoclassical models. As he put it "in dealing with Capitalism, you are dealing with an evolutionary process." He clearly had in mind a context in which people, and organizations, had quite different views about what kinds of innovations would be possible, and desirable, and would lay their bets differently. There are winners and losers in Schumpeter's "process of creative destruction," and these are not determined mainly in ex-ante calculation, but largely in ex-post actual contest.

In his 1911 *Theory of Economic Development*, Schumpeter saw the key innovative actors as "entrepreneurs." His "firms" were basically the vessels used by entrepreneurs, and other decision makers forced to adapt to the changes wrought by entrepreneurial innovators or to go under. By the time (1942) he wrote *Capitalism, Socialism, and Democracy,* Schumpeter's view of the sources of innovation had changed, or rather it might be better to say that there had been a transformation of the principal sources of innovation from an earlier era, and Schumpeter's views reflected this transformation. Modern firms, equipped with research and development laboratories, became the central innovative actors in Schumpeter's theory. The chapter by Cohen and Levin in the *Handbook* admirably surveys the wide range of empirical research that has been inspired by Schumpeter, particularly the research concerned with the relationships among innovation, firm size and other characteristics, and market structure.

In our book, *An Evolutionary Theory of Economic Change* (1982),

Winter and I spent quite a bit of space presenting a "theory of the firm" which is consistent with, and motivates, a Schumpeterian or evolutionary theoretic view of economic process and economic change. Our formulation drew significantly on Simon (1957), on Cyert and March (1963), and on Penrose (1959), as well as on Schumpeter. With the vision of hindsight, it is clear that our writing then was handicapped by insufficient study of the writings of Chandler, particularly his *Scale and Scope* (1962).

Since the time we wrote, there have been a number of theoretical papers on firm capabilities and behavior that draw both on Chandler and on our early formulation, and which add significantly to the picture. Papers by Teece (1980, 1982), Rumelt (1984), Cohen and Levinthal (1989), Dosi, Teece, and Winter (1989), Prahalad and Hamel (1990), Pavitt (1987, 1990), Cantwell (1989, 1990), Kogut (1987), Henderson (1990), Burgelman and Rosenbloom (1989), Langlois (1991), and Lazonick (1990), all present a similar or at least a conformable theoretical view, although with differences in stress. The recent paper by Teece, Pisano, and Shuen (1990) provides an overview of many of these works, and I believe correctly states that the common element is a focus on firm-specific dynamic capabilities.

This emerging theory of dynamic firm capabilities can be presented in different ways. Here it is convenient to focus on three different if strongly related features of a firm that must be recognized if one is to describe it adequately: its strategy, its structure, and its core capabilities. While each has a certain malleability, major changes in at least the latter two involve considerable cost. Thus they define a relatively stable firm character.

The concept of strategy in this theory of the firm is basically what business historians and scholars of management mean, as contrasted with game theorists. It connotes a set of broad commitments made by a firm that define and rationalize its objectives and how it intends to pursue them. Some of this may be written down, some may not be but is in the management culture of the firm. Many economists would be wont to propose that the strategy represents a firm's solution of its profit maximization problem, but this seems misconceived to me. In the first place, the commitments contained in a strategy often are as much a matter of faith of top management, and company tradition, as they are of calculation. Second, firm strategies seldom determine the details of firm actions, but usually at most the broad contours. Third, and of vital importance, there is no reason to argue *a priori* that these commitments are in fact optimal or even not self-destructive. If it is proposed that competition and selection force surviving strategies to be relatively profitable, this should be a theorem not an assumption.

The concept of firm structure in this literature also is in the spirit of Chandler, as is the presumption that strategy tends to define a desired firm structure in a general way, but not the details. Structure involves how a firm is organized and governed, and how decisions actually are made and carried out, and thus largely determines what it actually does, given the broad strategy. A firm whose strategy calls for being a technological leader that does not have a sizable R&D operation, or whose R&D director has little input into firm decision making, clearly has a structure out of tune with its strategy. However, the high-level strategy may be mute about links between its R&D lab and universities, whether to have a special biotech group, and so on.

Change in strategy may require a change in management as well as a change in articulation; indeed for the latter to be serious may require the former. However, within this theory of the firm structure is far more difficult to change effectively than is strategy. While changing formal organization, or at least the organization chart, is easy, and selloffs and buyups are possible, significantly changing the way a firm actually goes about making operating-level decisions and carries them out is time consuming and costly to do. Or rather, while it may not be too difficult to destroy an old structure or its effectiveness, it is a major task to get a new structure in shape and operating smoothly. Thus to the extent that a major change in strategy calls for a major change in structure, effecting the needed changes may take a long time.

The reason for changing structure, of course, is to change, possibly to augment, the things a firm is capable of doing well. Which brings the discussion to the concept of core capabilities. Strategy and structure call forth and mold organizational capabilities, but what an organization can do well has something of a life of its own.

Winter and I have proposed that well-working firms can be understood in terms of a hierarchy of practiced organizational routines, which define lower-order organizational skills, and how these are coordinated, and higher-order decision procedures for choosing what is to be done at lower levels. The notion of a hierarchy of organizational routines is the key building block under our concept of core organizational capabilities. At any time the practiced routines that are built into an organization define a set of things the organization is capable of doing confidently. If the lower-order routines are not there for doing various tasks, or if they are but there is no practiced higher-order routine for invoking them in the particular combination needed to accomplish a particular job, then the capability to do that job lies outside the organization's extant core capabilities.

The developing theory of dynamic firm capabilities I am discussing here starts from the premise that, in the industries of interest to the authors, firms are in a Schumpeterian or evolutionary context. Simply producing a given set of products with a given set of processes well will not enable a firm to survive for long. To be successful for any length of time a firm must innovate. The capabilities on which this group of scholars focus are capabilities for innovation and to take economic advantage of innovation.

In industries where technological innovation is important, a firm needs a set of core capabilities in R&D. These capabilities will be defined and constrained by the skills, experience, and knowledge of the personnel in the R&D department, the nature of the extant teams and procedures for forming new ones, the character of the decision-making processes, the links between R&D and production and marketing, and so on. This means that at any time there will be certain kinds of R&D projects that a firm can carry out with some confidence and success, and a wide range of other projects that, while other firms might be able to do them, this particular firm cannot, with any real confidence.

R&D capabilities may be the lead ones in defining the dynamic capabilities of a firm. However, in a well-tuned firm, its production, procurement, marketing, and legal organizations must have built into them the capabilities to support and complement the new product and process technologies emanating from R&D. In Teece's terms, the firm's capabilities must include control over or access to the complementary assets and activities needed to enable it to profit from innovation. And in an environment of Schumpeterian competition, this means the capability to innovate, and to make that innovation profitable, again and again.

The concept of organizational capabilities, and the theory that Winter and I proposed as to what determines and limits them, does not directly imply any coherency to the set of things a firm can do. However, Dosi and colleagues (1989) argue that, in effective firms, there is a certain coherency. There would appear to be several reasons. The ones stressed by Dosi et al. basically are associated with localized learning in a dynamic context, and follow on the arguments that Winter and I made some time ago that, to be under control, a routine needs to be practiced. Firms need to learn to get good at certain kinds of innovation, and at the things needed to take advantage of these, and this requires concentration or at least coherency, rather than random spreading of efforts. Further, in many technologies one innovation points more or less directly to a set of following ones, and the learning and complementary strengths developed in the former effort provide a base for the next round.

But I think it also is the case that to be effective a firm needs a reasonably coherent strategy, that defines and legitimatizes, at least loosely, the way the firm is organized and governed, enables it to see organizational gaps or anomalies given the strategy, and sets the ground for bargaining about the resource needs for the core capabilities a firm must have to take its next step forward. Absent a reasonably coherent and accepted strategy, decision making about rival claims on resources has no legitimate basis. Decisions from above have no supportive rationale, and there is no way to hold back log-rolling bargaining among claimants other than arbitrary high-level decisions. There is no real guidance regarding the capabilities a firm needs to protect, enhance, or add in order to be effective in the next round of innovative competition.

But I think I simply am restating what Chandler, Lazonick, Williamson, and other scholars of the modern corporation have been saying for some time. To be successful in a world that requires that firms innovate and change, a firm must have a coherent strategy that enables it to decide what new ventures to go into and what to stay out of. And it needs a structure, in the sense of mode of organization and governance, that guides and supports the building and sustaining of the core capabilities needed to carry out that strategy effectively.

If one thinks within the frame of evolutionary theory, it is nonsense to presume that a firm can calculate an actual "best" strategy. A basic premise of evolutionary theory is that the world is too complicated for a firm to comprehend, in the sense that a firm understands its world in neoclassical theory. There are certain characteristics of a firm's strategy, and of its associated structure, that management can have confidence will enhance the chances that it will develop the capabilities it needs to succeed. There are other characteristics that seem a prescription for failure. However, there is a lot of room in between, where a firm (or its management) simply has to lay its bets knowing that it does not know how they will turn out.

Thus diversity of firms is just what one would expect under evolutionary theory. It is virtually inevitable that firms will choose somewhat different strategies. These, in turn, will lead to firms having different structures and different core capabilities, including their R&D capabilities. Inevitably firms will pursue somewhat different paths. Some will prove profitable, given what other firms are doing and the way markets evolve, others not. Firms that systematically lose money will have to change their strategy and structure and develop new core capabilities, or operate the ones they have more effectively, or drop out of the contest.

The Evolution of Technology

In real capitalist economies, in contrast with the neoclassical models, technical advance proceeds through an evolutionary process, with new products and processes competing with one another and with prevailing technology in real time, rather than solely in ex-ante calculation. Some of the innovations will be winners, others losers. With the vision of hindsight the whole process looks messy and wasteful, and a more coherent planning approach to technological advance appears attractive.

However, it is striking how inefficient and misguided efforts to plan and control significant technical advance have been. Where, for one reason or another, society has been denied the advantages of multiple independent approaches to advance technology, which flows naturally from a basis of independent rivalrous firms, almost always the approach chosen has turned out, after the fact, to have major limitations. And since alternatives had not been developed to a point where they could be tried in comparison, there has been lock-in. A number of U.S. military R&D efforts since 1960 are striking examples. Nuclear power programs are another. The fact is that in virtually every field where we have had rapid technical advance that has met a market test or its equivalent, we have had multiple rivalrous sources of new technology.

While Winter and I formally modeled company R&D programs as generating results through a random draw, in fact in the industries that I know well there has tended to be a certain consistency in the R&D efforts of particular companies. This consistency reflects a basically stable company "strategy" and the core R&D and other dynamic capabilities it has put in place to carry it out. Where company strategies and associated capabilities differ significantly, their patterns of innovation are likely to differ significantly as well.

This has an important consequence often overlooked in the literature on technological imitation. When one firm comes up with a successful innovation, its competitors may differ significantly among themselves in their ability effectively to imitate or develop something comparable. Contrary to many economic models, effective technological imitation very often requires the imitating firm to go through many of the same design and development activities as did the innovator, and to implement similar production and other supporting activities. Thus firms with similar strategies and core capabilities are in a much better position to imitate or learn and build from each other's work than firms with different strategies and capabilities.

Thus to an extent the market is selecting on strategies and companies, as well as new technologies. This suggests that in some circumstances strategic diversity may get extinguished.

There is something to this argument. A number of analysts, some working in the tradition of economic research, some in a business school research tradition, have suggested that there is a natural industry life cycle. When an industry or a broad technology is new, a wide variety of approaches to technological innovation—strategies—is taken by different firms. As experience grows, certain of the approaches begin to look significantly better than others. Firms who have made the right bets do well. Those who have not, need to switch over or drop out. A number of studies have shown that, as an industry or technology matures, there is a significant reduction in the number of firms, and in some cases the emergence of a "dominant design," with all surviving firms producing some variety of that tuned to the niche they have found.

One fascinating question is what happens in a relatively mature industry when a new and potentially superior technology comes into existence. The evidence suggests that it matters whether the new technology is conformable with the core capabilities of extant firms, or requires very different kinds of capabilities. Tushman and Anderson (1986) call these two kinds of developments "competence enhancing" and "competence destroying." Under the latter circumstances, new firms are likely to be the innovators, and old firms often are unable to respond effectively. Tushman and Anderson note that a change in management and, presumably, a major change in strategy often are necessary if the old firm is to survive in the new environment. But it may not be sufficient. Structure and core capabilities are far more difficult to change than management and articulated strategies.

For a student of business management the question of what enables a firm to change directions effectively, and be a viable competitor in the new regime, is of central interest in its own right. For an economist what matters is that pharmaceutical R&D take advantage of the new possibilities opened by new biotechnology, and not whether the old pharmaceutical firms do it, or whether they fail, so long as new ones take up the torch.

However, the fact that the leading-edge companies in a field often change is a fascinating matter. It is consistent with the theory of focused and constrained core capabilities presented above. And it is a central reason why, for an economist interested in technological advance, firm differences matter importantly.

The Evolution of Firm Organization

There has been far more study of the way technology advances than there has been of the way firm organization changes. By organization I mean what I think Chandler (1962) means by strategy and structure, those aspects of a firm that are wider and more durable than the particular technologies and other routines it employs at any moment, or even its extant core capabilities, and which in effect guide the internal evolution of these. It is apparent that change in organization in this broad sense, as well as advance in technology, has been an essential feature of the enormous economic progress that has been experienced over the last century and a half.

Some writers clearly would like to give organizational change separate and equal billing with technical advance as a source of economic progress. I would like to argue here, however, that one needs to understand organizational change as usually a handmaiden to technological advance, and not a separate force behind economic progress.

If I understand him correctly, this would be Chandler's position. The new technology of the railroads required, for its effective implementation, the development of organizational capabilities far beyond that possessed by traditional owner-managed firms. Line and staff organizational form, along with the development of the position of hired manager, enabled the railroads to be effectively "governed," to use Williamson's term. Later, new technologies which promised economies of scale and scope in manufacturing called for large firms operating in several different product fields, or market areas. The M form of managerial structure evolved to govern effectively this kind of business operation.

Over the long run what has mattered most has been organizational changes needed to enhance dynamic innovative capabilities. Reich (1985), Hounshell and Smith (1988), and other writers have described how the organizational device of the industrial research and development laboratory came into existence, to permit firms to shield a portion of their scientific and technical personnel from the pressures of day-to-day problem solving so that they could work on the development of new products and processes. This development was preconditioned by the rise of a new "technology" for product and process development, one employing the understandings and techniques of the sciences and engineering disciplines in a systematic way. One can read Chandler's and Lazonick's account of the rise of other aspects of the modern corporation in terms of Teece's arguments about needed complementary assets or capabilities.

As I read the case study evidence, devising and learning to use effectively a significant new organizational form involves much the same kind of uncertainty, experimental groping, and learning by making mistakes and correcting them that marks technological invention and innovation. New modes of organization aren't simply "chosen" when circumstances make them appropriate. They, like technologies, evolve in a manner that is foreseen only dimly. And even when a firm makes a conscious decision to change organization, it may take a long time before it is comfortable and effective in its new suit of clothes.

I want to return here to a point I made at the start of this essay. I suspect that the uncertainties about new organization are even greater than those surrounding technological innovations. This is especially so regarding organization which molds effective dynamic innovative capabilities and the abilities to profit from innovation. At the present time there is little in the way of tested and proved theory (let me use the less pretentious word—knowledge) that enables confident prediction of the best way of organizing a particular activity, or what will be the consequences of adopting a different mode of organization. If the "rationally choosing" view of technological advance is misguided, the "rationally choosing" view of organizational change is even more so.

Just as important, it is common, not infrequent, for a particular mode of organization put in place for one reason to turn out to have advantages, or disadvantages, in arenas that were not considered at the time the original move was contemplated and made. It also is common, not infrequent, that there be considerable dispute about just what features of a firm's organization are responsible for certain successes or failures.

Thus, as I understand it, large Japanese firms adopted "lifetime employment" for their skilled workers in the early postwar era to try to deal with a problem of skill shortages and labor unrest. It is quite unclear how many Japanese managers foresaw advantages associated with worker loyalty, and ability of a firm to do in-house training without fear of losing the investment through worker defection. Just-in-time was, I understand, largely a response to scarce space, high inventory costs, and input shortages. It is not clear how many saw that it would facilitate quality control.

American companies looking at their Japanese competitors often have been uncertain about just why the Japanese are better in some respects, and just what they can effectively transplant. They only will be able to learn by trying some things, seeing what happens, and having the good luck to see it right.

The evidence is very limited, but there is reason to believe that firms have greater ability to replicate themselves in another setting in a way that preserves their strength, than to comprehend and adopt what gives their rivals strength. Thus as Womack, Jones, and Roos (1991) and Clark and Fujimoto (1991) document convincingly, American automobile manufacturers still are struggling to catch up with the Japanese in terms of productivity and quality of production. Where they are coming close it seems to be in cases where the Japanese are serving as partners. This does not look accidental. Florida and Kenney (1991) report that Japanese-owned automobile assembly plants in the United States have rather quickly been able to establish practices—strategies and structures—similar to their home operations, and with comparable outcomes.

I want to put forth the argument that it is organizational differences, especially differences in abilities to generate and gain from innovation, rather than differences in command over particular technologies, that are the source of durable, not easily imitable, differences among firms. Particular technologies are much easier to understand, and imitate, than broader firm dynamic capabilities.

From one point of view it is technological advance that has been the key force that has driven economic growth over the past two centuries, with organizational change a handmaiden. But from another perspective, we would not have got that technological advance without development of new ways of organization that can guide and support R&D and enable firms to profit from these investments.

I have been concentrating on firm organization. However, it is clear that the organizational changes that have enabled nations to support the modern R&D system and the technological advance it generates go far beyond those of firm organization. Universities had to change. New scientific disciplines and societies had to come into being. In many cases new bodies of law were needed. Some technologies required major new public infrastructure for their effective development.

The coevolution of technology and institutions is a fascinating subject. Chandler, and a few other scholars such as Hughes (1983) and Freeman (1989), have begun to address it. There clearly have been major national differences in how the institutions needed to support particular evolving technologies themselves evolved. Perhaps in the study of the coevolution of technology and institutions we will begin to develop a serious theory of how national comparative advantage comes into being, or is lost. But I now am far beyond the scope of this essay.

Reprise

Students of firm management, in particular those working in the strategy field, treat discretionary firm differences as their bread and butter. Economists have tended to play down these differences, or to argue that they are the result not the cause of general economic differences. In good part the difference in viewpoints is due to differences in basic interests—the student of firm management concerned with the fate of individual firms, and the economist interested in general economic performance of an industry or nation. But I have argued that the lack of interest by economists in discretionary firm differences stems as well from a particular theoretical view of economic activity and the role and behavior of firms.

If one takes an evolutionary rather than a neoclassical view of what economic activity is about, then firm differences matter importantly regarding issues that traditionally have been the central concern of economists. Competition can be seen as not merely about incentives and pressures to keep prices in line with minimal feasible costs, and to keep firms operating at low costs, but, much more important, about exploring new, potentially better, ways of doing things. Long ago Schumpeter remarked that the former function was trivial compared with the latter, if the measure was contribution to the economic well-being of humankind.

From the perspective of evolutionary theory, firm diversity is an essential aspect of the processes that create economic progress. Monopoly, or tight oligopoly with strong barriers to entry, can be seen as a serious economic problem, not so much because such structures permit a large gap between price and cost, but because they are unlikely to generate the variety of new routines, and the attendant shifts in resource allocation on which economic progress depends. One is suspicious of arguments to "rationalize" production and innovation for the same reasons, particularly when the winds of change are blowing from uncertain angles.

Thus the "dynamic capabilities" view of firms being developed by scholars in the strategy field can be seen to be important not only as a guide to management, but also as the basis for a serious theory of the firm in economics. It, when embedded in an evolutionary theory of economic change, instructs us regarding "Why do firms differ, and how does it matter?"

On Limiting or Encouraging
Rivalry in Technical Progress:
The Effect of Patent-Scope Decisions

1. Introduction

The scope of the claims of a patent determines the ability of competitors to produce substitutes without fear of infringement suits, and hence the real "monopoly power" of the patent holder. Several recent studies, for example, McFetridge and Rafiquzzan (1986), Gilbert and Shapiro (1990), and Klemperer (1990), have considered the economic policy issues bearing on optimum patent scope in terms of a trade-off between incentives for invention and deadweight losses due to monopoly, an analysis in the spirit of the older literature in economics concerned with optimum patent duration.

The issue considered in these studies is an important one. We wish to argue, however, that these analyses consider only one part of the problem, and the part they do not consider probably is of much greater importance.

In many industries and technologies technical advance is a sequential, connected process. Today's inventions provide not simply the capability to produce new or better products or to produce them more effectively today, but also concepts and starting places for inventive efforts tomorrow. In such cases, the allowed scope of patents on today's inventions strongly influences the incentives today's inventors, and their potential competitors, have in engaging in subsequent inventive efforts. Scotchmer (1991) is one of the few economists who has recognized this. As a general rule, if allowed patent scope is broad, today's inventors may proceed into the next stage of inventing without fear of encroachment by outsiders; outsiders are deterred

By Robert Merges and Richard R. Nelson; originally published in the *Journal of Economic Behavior and Organization* 25 (1994): 1–24. Reprinted with kind permission from Elsevier Science B.V., Amsterdam, The Netherlands.

from participating because of the likelihood that their invention will be held infringing. In contrast, if allowed scope is narrow, outsiders are less deterred from competing in the next round of inventing.

What is the preferable economic context? Does technical change proceed more effectively when there are multiple rivalrous sources of invention, or under the control of one or a few parties who in principle can shape and coordinate the work? While this is an empirical question, different theories of invention predispose one to different answers. To tip our hand, the theory of invention and technical advance in which we believe strongly disposes us to distrust central control, and we think the empirical evidence bears us out. This leads us to argue that, within the bounds provided by the law, patent scope ought to be kept fairly tight in situations where an invention opens up a relatively broad future "prospect," to use Edmund Kitch's term (1977).

In our *Columbia Law Review* paper "The Complex Economics of Patent Scope" (1990), we developed our argument mainly empirically, drawing our case from the actual experiences in a number of industries. Here we want to highlight the theory behind our argument, a theory that we believe is supported by the empirical evidence. This we do in section 2. We then turn to the legal doctrines that guide patent scope rulings at the Patent Office and in the courts, and the room for discretion that they leave. This latitude has permitted considerable variation in the allowed scope of key patents and has, therefore, generated a good deal of experience that can be used to examine the effect of allowing broad, versus narrow, scope. We consider this experience in section 4. We believe the evidence amply supports our theoretical stance. Section 5 presents our conclusions regarding what patent scope policy ought to be.

2. Theoretical Perspectives on Inventing and the Topography of Technical Advance

In this section we do two things. First, we discuss how different presumptions about human and organizational cognition and behavior might lead one to take different views on whether competition or more concentrated control is a better setting for technical advance. The answer to this might well depend not only on behavioral assumptions but also on how different inventions relate to one another, and the second part of this section is concerned with different invention topographies.

2.1. Cognitive and Behavioral Assumptions in Different Theories of Innovation

Most of the formal models of inventing and technical advance drawn up by economists employ the standard assumptions about human cognition and behavior of neoclassical economic theory in general. The actors, in this case the inventors, are assumed to comprehend the full range of choices in fact available to them, and to have an accurate understanding of the consequences of choosing one course of action or another. In recognition of the uncertainties well known to reside in inventive activity, the mapping from choices to outcome may be specified probabilistically. The inventor, or the corporate research laboratory, is presumed to pick the course of action that maximizes (expected) profits. In some models that course may involve a quite complicated sequential strategy.

In most of the models of inventive activity it is presumed that there are a large number of inventors in competition with one another, or at least this is one of the structures considered. In contrast with many other arenas of neoclassical modeling, however, where competition can be shown to lead to Pareto optimal outcomes, in virtually all neoclassical models of invention the actions chosen by rivalrous actors almost invariably will not be the social optimum.

This class contains a variety of models. They are unified by the assumptions about cognition and behavior stated above, and by something built into them that under competitive conditions generates "market failure." Often this has to do with a nonconvex cost structure, such as up-front R&D costs that need to be incurred before a technology can be made operative, which implies that if two firms were to do the same thing (and split the market) the costs would be higher than if just one did. Often it has to do with the presumption that technological knowledge, once generated through R&D, is a latent public good, but the model has something built into it to make technological knowledge to some degree proprietary. Beyond these core features, the models may differ significantly.

Thus some models assume that a completely effective patent goes to the first to make an invention. In one subclass there are a lot of different potential inventions out there, and inventing is like fishing in a common pool (see, for example, Barzel, 1968). Enough inventors will join in the fishing to drive expected returns to zero. The dense concentration of fishermen (inventors) leads to both higher costs per fish caught (invention) and more total resources allocated to fishing (inventing) than is socially optimal. Another subclass posits not a pool of potential inventions but a single one out there.

Competitive invention then is like a race with the first to achieve the goal getting the prize (see, for example, Dasgupta and Stiglitz, 1980). Again, competition leads to more resources invested than need be to get the result. Still other models presume that patent protection is imperfect. Thus to some extent firms can "free ride" on the inventions of their competitors. The result is underinvestment in R&D. But while the models differ, invariably they are marked by a market failure of one kind or another.

Several of these models explore the solution under monopoly. Under monopoly the wastes of competition are avoided, but the monopoly solution generally is not optimal either, because of the incentive to "restrict" supply (in this case of inventive effort, as well as output) that a monopolist has. Within these models, invention under rivalry and monopoly can be compared. If the distortions of rivalry are great enough, and if the monopoly is constrained enough, as by the presence of other firms producing close substitutes, within this kind of model monopoly control of invention, while not optimal, may appear a more socially desirable regime than rivalry.

The discussion so far has been quite general. As noted earlier, the focus of this essay is invention activity where there are strong connections between inventions, in particular on contexts in which today's inventions open up prospects for follow-on inventions tomorrow.

This was exactly the focus of Edward Kitch, in his famous 1977 article. On the basis of reasoning in the spirit of the models already described, Kitch argued that, for inventions that have a potential for significant subsequent improvement and variegation, there is a strong case for granting the inventor a patent of broad scope to enable him or her to develop the field in an orderly fashion, without fear of external encroachment. The basic model he had in mind likely is akin to the fishing model, but differs from the conventional version in that the first to find and catch a fish in the pool can be given exclusive control of future fishing rights. Actually, the particular analogy Kitch uses is that of a mining claim which defines a "prospect" for future development. Kitch's argument is that the prospect will be developed more effectively and efficiently if it is under control of a single party than it would under rivalry. Kitch obviously recognizes the "monopoly problem" and undoubtedly has in mind a context in which there are reasonably close substitute products produced by other parties.

Kitch understands that different individuals or firms may have different interests, and perhaps different capabilities. He presumes, however, that these differences can be accommodated through contracting to give different parties different areas of the prospect to explore. As best we can tell, Scotchmer (1991) would buy into much of this argument. However, she is more concerned than Kitch with the possibility that contracts dividing up the prospect might be difficult to write and enforce. Scotchmer clearly is also worried about the effects of prospect owner control over the basic patent on the likelihood that outsiders can be drawn into agreed contracts, given that their ability to exploit what they have created can be blocked by the holder of the basic patent. Although Scotchmer does not cite Williamson, it would appear that she has Williamson-type issues on her mind. Williamson's theory (1985) surely would lead one to suspect that it would be very difficult to work out licensing arrangements regarding rights to what may be found or created prior to knowing just what the inventions or discoveries will turn out to be.

Williamson's argument assumes bounded rationality, in that he stresses the inability of the parties to foresee all the things that might happen, and to write down a contract that deals with all contingencies. Thus in complex settings, particularly ones that have strong elements of novelty, events are almost sure to arise that are not dealt with explicitly in the contract. Who has the most power will then influence what happens. And recognizing this, potential parties to a contract may be reluctant to engage in it if they fear events may leave them vulnerable.

Williamson has applied the presumption of bounded rationality to analyses of contractual and other relational governance arrangements. Evolutionary theory has applied the presumption of bounded rationality to the theory of invention and technical advance.

Viewing human rationality as bounded, not unbounded, leads one to pull away from some of the basic assumptions of the invention models we discussed earlier, and to focus on phenomena that these models tend to ignore or downplay. In particular, under an evolutionary theory of technical advance, the inventors are presumed unable to see clearly all the alternatives actually available to them, and are assumed to focus on only a small subset of these. Beliefs about the consequences of choosing one path or another are presumed to be influenced as much by the past experience of an individual or organization and theories formed on the basis of that experience as on objective information about a particular new situation.

In some evolutionary models, actors learn through experience. If they face the same situation often enough, they sooner or later come to see and choose the choice within the model that actually is best for them, and thus to behave "as if" they maximized over their actual full choice set, and had in mind the actual mapping between choices and consequences built into the model. But within evolutionary theory this is a theorem about learning and convergence, not an assumption about behavior in any setting (see Nelson and Winter, 1982, chap. 6).

Indeed, in contexts that are new to them, evolutionary theory would predict not only that actors are unlikely to figure out the choice that actually is best for them. It also would predict that different actors would do different things. They would see opportunities differently. They would rank differently those they all saw.

Exploring new terrain, a new "prospect," is exactly this kind of problem. If there are many explorers, though there would be some duplication of efforts, by and large different ones would do different things. Some would choose better things (invention allocations), others worse, some would win in the competition, others lose. This clearly is wasteful, and it clearly would be more socially efficient if the best allocation could simply be imposed. This conclusion is similar to that of neoclassical theory, but the reasoning leading to it is different.

Evolutionary theory also sees in a different light the consequences of avoiding these wastes by establishing unitary control over a prospect. If one eliminates rivalry one would, within this theory, not only remove the spur of competition and establish the socially adverse incentives of monopoly. One also would substitute one myopic decision maker for a plurality of them. For that reason, and because the incentives of a monopoly position generally act to limit search, inventive efforts would be much more confined under unified control than under pluralistic rivalry.

Thus under evolutionary theory the attended choice set will be different, smaller, under unified control than under rivalry, which is a potentially serious counterweight to the proposition that, within the attended set, the exploring can be more orderly. (For a similar argument, see Cohen and Klepper, 1991.)

The perspective of evolutionary theory also inclines one to see the issue of contracting with others for exploration of various parts of the prospect, a possibility held up by Kitch with apparent optimism, in a much less optimistic light. Under evolutionary theory, all the transaction cost problems associated with Williamson's analysis of contracting are highlighted, but still others come into view. In particular, evolutionary theory would lead one to expect strong differences of opinion among persons and firms, in this case between the principal owner and potential explorers of parts of the prospect, about the promise of different parts of the prospect, about the significance of the prospect holder's accomplishments, and about what that initial patent legitimately covers.

2.2. The Topography of Prospects

In the technological histories we shall explore in section 4, prospect-defining inventions play a prominent role. Before getting to the actual cases, however, we consider more generally prospect-defining inventions in terms of the different topographies of the prospects they open up.

A useful way to get into the discussion is to recognize that virtually all inventions define prospects. However, many inventions are what one might call "discrete." While the original version naturally defines a class or prospect, that prospect is quite confined, and the topography relatively simple, involving possible variations that can be made for different uses, and a variety of possible general improvements. Thus the prospect itself is naturally relatively closely bounded. Gillette's safety razor, a case we shall look at shortly, fits this model. So too do many other devices built to meet particular needs.

As we shall see, a patent generally allows claims beyond the particular manifestation of an invention the inventor actually has achieved, and necessarily so if the patent is to provide protection against obvious simple modifications. When the overall potential for modifications and improvements based on the original achievement is relatively clear and bounded, the original inventor is likely to be well positioned and motivated to develop the prospect. Having done the original work, the inventor is likely to be better positioned than anyone else to see certain of the developmental opportunities and the solutions. For some, users or customers may be better positioned, but in such cases the relationships between those that see the needs or opportunities and the prospect owner are likely to be cooperative, not rivalrous. And while some outsiders may have better ideas, since the scope of possible improvements is reasonably tightly bounded, deterring outside involvement in exploring the prospect is not likely to block truly important efforts. While all this doesn't make the case for allowing broad claims, if these are naturally bounded and do not cover potential developments outside the ken of the original inventor, the case against it from evolutionary theory is not strong.

It turns out, however, that the topography of a prospect is highly dependent upon the technological field. In some the prospects are "discrete" in the sense above. But in others they are quite complex. We consider below the particular shape of prospects that can be defined by broad patents first in industries that have what we call "cumulative systems" technologies. Then we turn to prospects defined by patents on organic chemical products.

By a cumulative technology we mean one in which today's advances lay the basis for tomorrow's, which in turn lay the basis for a next round, and so on, with the sequence often progressing very far from the original invention starting place. Yet as we will show, the claims on the original patent may be defined broadly enough to control large portions of the sequence, which traverses much more than a simple well-defined neighborhood. So-called pioneer patents may define for the patent holder claims over the future development of a very large and lucrative prospect, often involving technologies far removed from the original invention and far beyond the ken of the original inventor. And the original inventor and the one who sees a major improvement may well be market rivals.

By a systems technology we mean a technology in which a useful product is made out of many different components, each of which might be invented independently. In systems technologies a new component invention may open up a broad prospect of subsequent inventions that employ it and other components. But in systems technologies, unlike those apparently envisaged by Kitch, prospects may be at odds. If a patent on one component that is key to a variety of systems is defined broadly, the holder of that patent may be able to block others from commercializing those systems without license, but on the other hand the holder of a broad patent on another essential component may be able to block the holder of the former patent from building a state of the art system.

The dynamics of technical advance in many industries involves elements of both the "cumulative" technology model and the "systems" technology model. Automobiles, aircraft, radio, computers, all fields we will consider subsequently, have this hybrid quality. It should be noted that the recent writings about "network externalities" mostly have had as their examples cumulative systems technologies. (See, for example, Katz and Shapiro, 1985, and David, 1992.)

We turn now to an entirely different area of technology, that associated with organic chemical products. There are two different kinds of prospects defined by broad patents in this field that we want to describe. The first is a prospect defined by a patent which includes among its claims a "principle" used to create the product in question, but which has the potential of also being useful in the creation of a wide range of other products. The second is a prospect defined by a patent on a product achieved in a particular way, but which claims the product regardless of how it is achieved.

The "invention" of a new organic chemical product in many cases proceeds through the creation and use of a process that is new in important respects. In such instances it is not uncommon to include in the patent claims the method, or principle, itself which, even at the time of patent application, can be seen to be potentially applicable in one variant or another for producing a wide class of other new products. The claims then are posed not simply in terms of the original product and plausible variants, but include the class that can be created through the principle.

In many cases the kinds of products that can be created using a particular principle may be highly varied, and the arenas of use very different from one to another. Hence the original inventor may not be able to see the value of certain products that can be developed through the principle. Others who can see these possible applications or uses will have to bargain with the patent holder for permission to use the principle, or they unwittingly may get sued for patent violation on their new product by the patent holder who claims that their product was included under his claims.

On a somewhat more narrow front, patent law in the field of chemical products has allowed claims to be drawn on a natural substance produced by an inventor, if the produced substance is of purity significantly greater than can be found in nature. Such a product claim in principle encompasses all conceivable ways of producing the product in question. There well may be ways superior to the first one found. If one or more of these is very different from the original one, there is no reason to believe that the original inventor is well positioned to find or create it. And it is quite likely that the best-positioned firm is a market rival.

Our discussion thus far has been concerned with the topography of a prospect, and not with how the prospect-opening invention came about. However, we think this latter issue is important. The classical argument for a patent to reward effort and creativity presumes an invention marked by considerable originality on the part of the inventor, rather than one that mainly represents taking a speedy path down a trail that was obvious to many. In a number of technologies, however, which we will call "science based," the efforts of "inventors" are strongly guided by the evolution of an underlying science. In such fields, prospect-defining inventions often need to be understood as the first "bringing to practice" of new understandings published in the scientific literature or, more generally, widely known in the relevant scientific community. Earlier we noted the "race" model sometimes employed by economists in analyzing invention. As evolutionary theorists, we think "races," where many people see virtually the same goal and the same means, are not very common. They are common, however, in science-based technologies. We believe that where technical advance largely is led by recent advances in science, there are some special issues regarding patent scope policy.

3. Patent Law Doctrine

Within extant patent law, there is considerable room for discretion regarding how wide allowed claims ought to be. There are several doctrines that can be and often are used by the Patent Office and the courts to bound or prune back claims in the first instance, or to limit what is ruled infringing under them. This section is concerned with these doctrines and their somewhat inconsistent use.

3.1. Specifications and Claims

A patent application has two main parts. The first is a specification of the invention, which is written like a brief science or engineering article describing the problem the inventor faced and the steps taken to solve it. It also must provide a precise characterization of the "best mode" of solving the problem. The second part of the patent application is a set of claims, which usually encompass much more than the best mode(s) described in the specification. Claims define what the inventor considers to be the scope of the invention, the technological territory claimed for control through right to sue for infringement.

The specification and claims serve different functions. The specification is used by the Patent Office to determine whether the inventor has made a patentable invention and, if the patent is issued, has brought the invention into the public domain by enabling others to re-create it. This fundamental principle—that legal protection is premised on an adequate disclosure by the inventor—is built deep into the history of patent law. The patent claims serve a different function. Analogous to the metes and bounds of a real property deed, they distinguish the inventor's intellectual property from the surrounding terrain. The issue being addressed in this essay is how broad allowed claims ought to be.

The Patent Office and the courts have been inconsistent on this question. However, one can discern two bodies of doctrine that have been applied frequently. One of these ties allowed claims to what the patent disclosure enables. The other body of doctrine ties infringement rulings to a notion of equivalents. We consider each in turn.

3.2. Doctrines of Disclosure and Enablement

One important issue in patent law is how broad the patent claims can be, in the light of the description and explanation of the invention contained in the disclosure. Under the law, the disclosure must be sufficient to enable "any person skilled in the art to make and use" the invention claimed in the patent (U.S. Code, 1988, Section 112). But this requirement often is applied rather loosely; a specification that contains detail on the "central core" and the "best mode" of an invention may be accompanied by claims that go far beyond what is described.

However, under the principle of disclosure in exchange for legal protection, one might argue that what is disclosed ought to provide illumination to someone skilled in the art about the full range of variants encompassed within the claims as a matter of quid pro quo. Also, if the claims go significantly beyond the specification, what evidence is there that the inventor actually invented all that is claimed? If one follows out the logic of this question, one is drawn to the conclusion that claims ought to be bounded to a significant degree by what the disclosure enables, over and beyond prior art. The courts often but not always have been attracted to this doctrine. However the issue of boundaries is subtle.

Earlier we mentioned King Gillette's safety razor as an example of a "discrete" invention. It scarcely opened up a wide range of subsequent developments. Yet the invention was very profitable, and there were, and are, a large variety of workable variations of the razor described in Gillette's specifications. Very soon after his invention began to be marketed, competitors arose, selling razors with separate blades like Gillette's, but different from his in one way or another. Gillette sued, claiming they basically were the same.

And he won. In the case of *Gillette Safety Razor Co. v. Clarke Blade and Razor Co.* (1911) the court ruled explicitly that the patentee's justifiable claims need not be limited to the particular method(s) described in the specification. Rather they could extend to cover all designs that followed the principle illuminated by the patent specifications. Gillette claimed any razor with "a detachable razor blade of such thinness as to require external support to give rigidity to its cutting edge" (*Gillette*, 1911, at 156), and this claim was held to cover the competitor's design.

But in general, how does one draw a line around a set defined by a design principle? How far does the set extend?

A case brought by Edison challenging a broad patent held by Sawyer and Mann for material used in light bulb filaments shows that the courts do draw lines based on what the disclosure enables. The patentees had found that carbonized paper worked as an effective light-emitting conductor in light bulbs. Based on this invention, they filed a patent claiming the right to use all carbonized fibrous or textile material as an incandescing conductor.

Edison challenged Sawyer and Mann contending that the claim was too broad: the patent disclosure did not indicate which of the thousands of "fibrous or textile materials" would work as conductors in light bulbs, since most do not. Edison pointed to his own painstaking experimentation with a wide variety of materials, arguing that his discovery that a particular part of a particular bamboo plant performed well as a filament was not made any easier by Sawyer and Mann's disclosure. The court agreed, stating that "if the description be so vague and uncertain that no one can tell, except by independent experiments, how to construct the patented device, the patent is void" in the sense that the claims are excessive (*The Incandescent Lamp Patent*, 1895, at 474).

However, there obviously is the question of just where to draw the line. As we shall see, the Patent Office and the courts have been quite inconsistent on this. And often claims have been allowed that go far beyond the specification, and far beyond what the inventor had in fact achieved. We shall, in section 4, give a number of examples, and argue that when this occurred the result was often trouble.

3.3. Infringement Doctrines and the Interpretation of Equivalents

After the Patent Office issues a patent, the question of allowable patent scope moves to the courts. In some cases, as those just described, the dispute is about whether or not the allegedly infringed claims are valid. In other cases the heart of the dispute is not about that but about whether the accused device actually is infringing. This can be a delicate judgment. The court can rule that the claims are valid, that the accused device does fall within the letter of the allowed claims, and that it infringes. Or the court may even rule that, while not literally covered by the claims, the accused device is infringing because it is an "equivalent."

The doctrine of equivalents developed because of the frequency of cases where, even though the accused product or process does not literally infringe a claim, it may be considered essentially the same device as was patented. What is the meaning of "essentially the same"? The Supreme Court wrote in 1950, quoting from an earlier case: "If two devices do the same work in substantially the same way, and accomplish substantially the same result, they are the same, even though they differ in name, form, or shape" (*Graver Tank*, 1950, at 688).

A good application of the doctrine of equivalents is *International Nickel Company, Inc. v. Ford Motor Company* (1958). International Nickel had obtained a patent which "covers a cast ferrous alloy" called "nodular iron." The patent described and claimed the addition to molten iron of a "small but effective" quantity of magnesium, fixed by the patent as "about 0.04%" as a minimum, as a way to achieve iron with certain desirable properties. Ford's iron contained under .02 percent magnesium—less than half the minimum specified in International Nickel's patent. However, it was judged to be an equivalent substance, and thus to infringe the patent.

As this example illustrates, the doctrine of enablement and the doctrine of equivalents work together, often in harmony. In the nodular iron case the original patent was, in effect, judged to have taught the infringer, even though the drafted claims did not explicitly encompass the infringing substance.

3.4. The Doctrine of "Reverse Equivalents"

There are three ways in which an accused device may be ruled not to infringe. Two we have covered. The claims may be judged invalid. The device may be judged to fall outside the claims and not to be an "equivalent." But there is a third way that is particularly applicable to the defense of inventions that represent major advances over the original. This defense falls under what has come to be called the doctrine of reverse equivalents.

But before describing how the courts have dealt with infringement suits of this class, we should make clear that an accused device that improved upon the original might well have been awarded its own patent, but a "subservient" one. In such a case, the holder of the subservient patent cannot use it without a license from the holder of the dominant patent. At the same time, the holder of the dominant patent cannot practice the particular improvement without obtaining a license.

Cases exist, however, where the accused device has involved mechanisms so different, or has achieved performance so much greater, than the original patent that the courts have ruled it not infringing, as contrasted with subservient.

A recent case involving Texas Instruments' long-standing pioneer patent on the hand-held calculator is a good example. In the years since the original patent was issued, there have been a large number of improvements and changes made, and the question was whether or not one of these vastly improved modern calculators, produced by another manufacturer, still infringed the basic TI patent. The Federal Circuit held that major improvements in all the essential elements of hand-held calculators rendered the improved device noninfringing. The court concluded "that the total of the technological changes beyond what the inventors disclosed transcends . . . equitable limits . . . and propels the accused devices beyond a just scope for the [Texas Instrument] patent" (*Texas Instruments*, 1986, at 1570).

Decisions along these lines would appear consistent with and justifiable under the "enablement" doctrine, but to take it one stage further. In the TI case and related cases, one can see clearly that the original invention, as described, stimulated a wide range of improvement inventions which resulted in patents, but many of them subservient ones. Cases like that of TI show the court's lifting the hold of the original patent once cumulative improvements have radically reshaped the technology to a point clearly not envisaged under the original patent.

The question as we see it is how the enablement, equivalents, and reverse equivalents doctrines should be employed in cases where inventions do seem to open up broad prospects. These doctrines can be employed to give considerable control over the prospect to the original inventor, or they can be used to keep control limited and the prospect open to competitive invention.

4. Fragments of Evidence from the Historical Record

We see no way of providing completely conclusive evidence on whether, considering both benefits and costs, a policy of deliberately using the enablement and equivalents doctrines to rein in allowed patent scope is a better economic policy than that of deliberately defining broad prospects for individual control. For one thing, there is a wide range of industries and technologies where, at least from time to time, inventions open up significant prospects, and there is no way to cover all of them or even to sample systematically. For another, it is inevitable that the evidence will be mixed, some episodes pointing one way, some another. Finally, in view of the real-life complexity of even particular technological histories, different observers may see the same evidence somewhat differently. However, we think our case for keeping the prospect open is persuasive.

In what follows we will examine a number of snippets of technological and economic history. Following the ordering we used at the close of section 2, we begin by examining some interesting cases of the development of cumulative systems technologies, in the sense discussed earlier. We next turn to prospect-defining patents associated with the creation of new organic chemical products. Finally, we pick up some special issues that arise when a prospect-defining invention is "science based."

4.1. Cumulative Systems Technologies

There are two major questions about the effects of broad patents on cumulative systems technologies. We wish first to explore whether there is any evidence that the granting of broad pioneer patents makes subsequent invention and development more orderly and productive, or whether, rather, they seem to complicate and block development. We also want to explore how the presence of broad patents on different components of a cumulative systems technology held by different parties affects subsequent development.

We begin by considering two infamous cases regarding pioneer patents: the role of the Selden patent in the development of automobile technology, and the influence of the Wright brothers' patent on the growth of aircraft technology in the United States. In both of these cases, the holders of a very broad pioneer patent engaged in extensive litigation against others trying to invent in the field without taking out a license. Our question is how this activity affected the evolution of the technologies.

The Selden patent was issued before the turn of the century, and had as its key claim the use of a light gasoline using an internal combustion engine to power an automobile. This claim clearly covered a very broad prospect, and the one within which much of subsequent automobile development in fact proceeded. When brought to court, lawyers for the defense argued that the claim was "obvious," and that the disclosure didn't "enable" anything that wasn't already common understanding of those "skilled in the art." At that time the key constraint in building such a car was not want of the basic idea, but absence of an available light powerful gasoline engine. Selden himself never was able to build a working vehicle; the development of a usable automobile based on this "principle" came somewhat later and was achieved by other inventors.

Nonetheless, the Patent Office granted his claim, and it was twice upheld by the courts. Selden viewed his patent merely as a way of collecting royalties; he had little intention of becoming a serious participant in the automobile production business. The patent certainly was not used by Selden to orchestrate the efficient improvement of automobile technology. He stood willing, at least initially, to license anyone who would acknowledge the validity of his patent and pay his fees. Later, the Association of Licensed Automobile Manufacturers was formed to control licensing of the patent; the apparent principal purpose of this group was to regulate who was in the automobile design and production business, that is, to control competition in the industry, rather than to facilitate orderly technological development

(Flink, 1978). Thus Kitch's proposed strategy of orderly development of the "prospect," though available, was not even tried.

Did the presence of the Selden patent hinder technological progress in the industry? Lawsuits based on it surely absorbed considerable time and attention of people like Henry Ford, whose production methods revolutionized the industry, and who refused to recognize that the Selden patent could block what they were doing. The Selden patent did not stop Ford, but it certainly did slow him down.

Automobiles clearly are complex systems, and even with the broad shadow cast by the Selden patent, inventions and patents proliferated, compounding the licensing problems for anyone who wanted to design and produce an automobile. In the face of the problem, the association, while originally established as a way of policing the industry under the Selden patent, came to serve the more useful function of low transaction cost automatic cross-licensing of patents for its members. Although formal agreements to cross-license all new patents no longer exist, the practice of relatively automatic cross-licensing has endured to the present.

The Wright brothers' patent is somewhat different in a number of regards. First of all, the achievement described in the patent—an efficient stabilizing and steering system—was in fact a major one, and it did enable a multiplicity of future flying machines. Second, the Wright brothers were very interested in producing aircraft, and in improving their design, and they did so actively. Other creative people and companies, however, wanted to enter the aircraft design and manufacture business. They had their own ideas about how to advance the design of aircraft, and they strongly resisted being blocked by the Wright patent. The early attempts by the Wright brothers and Glen Curtiss, who was the most prominent such potential competitor, to reach an agreement came to naught. Litigation followed.

There is good reason to believe that the Wright patent significantly held back the pace of aircraft development in the United States by absorbing the energies and diverting the efforts of people like Curtiss. The aircraft case also is similar to that of automobiles in that the problems caused by the initial pioneer patent were compounded as improvement and complementary patents, owned by different companies, came into existence. The situation was so serious that, during World War I, at the insistence of the secretary of the navy, an arrangement was worked out to enable automatic cross-licensing. This arrangement, like the licensing of automobile patents, turned out to be a durable institution. The cross-licensing system greatly reduced transaction costs, but these costs would not have existed absent the broad patents on the various components.

The case of Edison's basic lamp patent also tells a cautionary tale regarding the effects of a broad, strongly enforced pioneer patent. Edison's patent, issued in 1880, was for a time ignored by many competitors, until it was upheld in court in 1891. General Electric then quickly obtained a series of injunctions and shut down a number of competitors. From that time, until the patent lapsed, GE did control the "prospect." According to Bright (1949), who looked into the history in considerable depth, over that period filament development and lamp development more generally virtually stagnated. GE, protected by the patent, basically sat on its monopoly position, as contrasted with developing its "prospect" in an orderly way. Only when the patent was close to lapsing did GE step up its efforts in lamp technology. Shortly after, of course, technical advance in the field became competitive again.

All these cases speak negatively to the idea that, in cumulative technologies, broadly enforced pioneer patents are socially desirable. But what happens when there are no such patents or, if there are, they are not enforced?

There are two cases, both post–World War II technological developments, where this occurred. One is the case of semiconductor development. There are two instances in the history of this technology where a broad-gauged patent could have given its holder control over a large "prospect," but in fact did not. One was on the initial transistor patents held by AT&T. Because of an antitrust consent decree, AT&T was foreclosed from the commercial transistor business. Some have argued that AT&T would not have gone into the merchant transistor business even had there not been a consent decree. In any case, given that it was not going to do so, AT&T had every incentive to encourage other companies to advance transistor technology, because of the value of better transistors to the phone system. AT&T quickly entered into a large number of license agreements at low royalty rates. Many companies ultimately contributed to the advance of transistor technology, because the pioneer patents were freely licensed instead of being used to block access (Levin, 1982).

The second instance involved the parallel inventions of the integrated circuit (by Texas Instruments) and the Planar process for producing it cheaply (by Fairchild Instruments). Both of these companies obtained patents on their own inventions, which meant that each had to get a license from the other in order to effectively produce integrated circuits. The Department of Defense, which for some time had provided the lion's share of the market for semiconductors, traditionally has tried to avoid being at the mercy of a firm or a small number of firms with key patents. Through a variety of maneuvers it has encouraged general cross-licensing, and this set the tone for deliberations to resolve the problem created by the two patents. Faced with an impasse regarding integrated circuit technology, general cross-licensing was continued. It is hard to argue that this has slowed down the development of integrated circuits.

Another case in which a cumulative systems technology developed without strong, broad patents is electronic computers. The original computer inventors, Eckert and Mauchley, did file for and receive a patent on their basic ENIAC design, which ultimately was ruled invalid because of a judgment that the prior art included much of what they claimed. But even during the period before the Eckert-Mauchley patent was invalidated, a number of other computer inventors went ahead without licensing and received patents on their own contributions. As in the semiconductor case, the Armed Services were the principal purchasers of the technology, and were ill disposed toward being held up by a dominant patent. As a result, cross-licensing became the norm in this industry as well, and again the pace of technical change has been rapid (Flamm, 1987).

The cases we have discussed certainly are not a random sample, nor do they tell a completely uniform story. However, though others may read the evidence differently, we believe that the granting and enforcing of broad pioneer patents is dangerous social policy. It can, and has, hurt in a number of ways. It has made the entry of creative and energetic newcomers difficult. In "systems" technologies, interference has proved to be especially problematic. Resolution has required some sort of institutionalized cross-licensing system. And there are many cases in which technical advance has been very rapid under a regime where intellectual property rights were weak or not stringently enforced. We think the latter regime is the better social bet.

4.2. Prospects Defined by New Organic Chemical Products

We proposed in Section 2 that the nature of "prospects" differs significantly depending on the field of technology. Two particular kinds of prospects defined by patents on organic chemical products were identified.

One is a patent on a new product, in which the "principle" for producing the product is included as one of the claims, and the principle has the promise of wide application. Although there are several interesting cases involving older "principles" for creating products, the advent of biotechnology has brought this kind of prospect-defining patent to the fore.

A most important example is Genentech's broad patent on the use of gene expression techniques using bacterium to achieve the production of human proteins. The techniques in question, or at least their general character, had in fact been well known among scientists in the field for some time. Genentech, however, was the first to be able to use those techniques in particular ways to produce human proteins, or at least two particular ones. There are two questions about this accomplishment that we will consider later—whether the patent ought to cover these natural products achieved through other processes, and how the fact that Genentech's accomplishment was largely based on "public" science ought to be treated.

Here we want to focus on the fact that Genentech's claims go far beyond the two polypeptides described in the specification, to encompass all products that can be created through a broad class of microbial gene expression techniques. The "principle" claimed by the patent and employed successfully by Genentech undoubtedly extends beyond the examples in the specification, but how far? What of an important human protein produced by a technique nominally under the "principle," but whose particular development required much hard research and experimentation? Should this be ruled as infringing under the patent? Or does evidence of major creative problem solving indicate that the route to the new protein was not illuminated by the disclosure and hence the invention should be ruled beyond the legitimate claims by enablement doctrine?

The patent awarded to Leder and Stewart of Harvard University on the basis of their achievement of a genetically engineered mouse is another example. The gene-altered mouse almost certainly will be a boon to cancer research, and the accomplishment of the inventors certainly warrants a patent. The inventors in this case, however, like those in the Genentech case, claimed not just the product they had achieved but the class of products that could be produced through their "principle," in this case "all transgenic non-human mammals" (Leder and Stewart, 1988).

Given that the Patent Office has granted these broad claims, the courts will have to deal with the litigation that almost certainly will arise unless the patents are liberally licensed. Their holders are certain to be beaten out by others on various parts of the prospect that they didn't see, or undervalued, or saw no way to effectively develop. This is just what we have seen in all of the cases considered in the preceding section.

In section 2 we identified another particular kind of a "prospect" sometimes defined by a patent on an organic chemical product. This kind of prospect is created through the practice of granting a product patent to an inventor who devises a way to manufacture a natural substance, generally one found in humans or animals, at high levels of purity or at low cost. The precedent goes back to 1911 when Judge Learned Hand upheld a product, rather than a process, patent on purified human adrenalin made by a new process. The advent of biotechnology has, however, brought the issue to wider attention and posed some new problems.

The legal problem we see with this practice is that it goes strongly against the doctrines of enablement and equivalents. The same product produced by a radically different process would be held infringing, despite the fact that the new process was not enabled by the original patent disclosure, and certainly was not equivalent. The "product" might be equivalent, but the original invention was not the product but rather a way of producing it. The economic problem we see with such practice is that it deters competition in invention and, in some cases, may block superior technology.

A recent case involving another Genentech invention shows just these features. Genentech had invented a recombinant DNA method for producing quite pure human blood clotting factor VIII:C, which had major advantages over a process of purifying the substance from natural blood, invented earlier by Scripps. Scripps sued. Although Genentech won the case, it did so on the legal technicality that the Scripps patent did not adequately disclose the process that Scripps judged best. The court did not retreat from the position that a product patent was legitimate. Recently, the patent appeals court sent the case back to the lower court to explore whether the doctrine of "reverse equivalents" ought to apply. But again, there was no backing off from the notion that a product patent is appropriate.

We are persuaded that granting a product patent on what is basically a process invention is a bad idea, and that it is a mistake to allow the first to find a process that works to block the use of competing processes that might be invented later. Patents should not control inventions they do not enable, especially if the original inventor is not strongly positioned and motivated to make them.

4.3. Patents on "Science-Based" Inventions

Several of the examples above are of inventions that, while representing considerable work and creativity on the part of the inventors, clearly were based on recent advances in public scientific knowledge. It is not happenstance that in these cases, others were also trying to take advantage of the scientific breakthroughs, often working along paths that were virtually identical to that followed by the winner. The patent went to the one who happened to cross the line first. Advances in science that point clearly to likely applications generate "races." We believe that these situations, and they are likely to be increasingly common, raise important issues of patent policy. In the first place, they suggest that in setting the bounds of the patent claims, thoughtful attention must be given to the inclusion of the teachings of public science in defining "prior art," and "nonobvious." Second, in these cases the argument for giving a patent that extends much beyond what the inventor actually achieved is very weak.

Modern biotechnology is rife with these issues. The field is built around two different sets of technologies. Both are based on prior, more general advances in molecular biology initially achieved by scientists concerned with pure research.

In 1975 Kohler and Milstein discovered that individual immune system cells, which generate antibodies to a specific antigen, could be fused with immortal cancer cells, to create a small "factory" to produce antibodies. They did not take out a patent on their creation. However, their achievement was almost immediately recognized as opening a myriad of commercial possibilities. Hybritech was an early entry in the race to develop applications. It was the first to use monoclonal antibodies in diagnostic kits sold to doctors and hospitals to identify the presence of diseases (for example, AIDS) or heightened hormone levels (for example, pregnancy tests). It received a patent covering this whole open-ended family of diagnostic kits.

Other companies saw exactly the same opportunity, if not so quickly. Monoclonal Antibodies Inc. was one of these, and it created a somewhat different technique, but after Hybritech. Monoclonal Antibodies made and sold these kits, and Hybritech sued. Monoclonal defended by claiming the Hybritech patent invalid, at least in its broad scope, because given the work of Kohler and Milstein, the generic technique was obvious. The trial court recognized the argument, and acknowledged: "The major advance was the invention of Kohler and Milstein in the making of monoclonal antibodies . . . Once the scientific community had the monoclonal antibody it was obvious and logical to those expert in the field to use them in known assays as substitutes for . . . polyclonal antibodies . . . of inferior quality" (*Hybritech v. Monoclonal Antibodies*, 1987).

The appeals court, however, ruled the broad patent claims valid. Granted, the call was not an easy one. Hybritech clearly invented something. The question is, given that it was building on public science, what was the limit of its contribution? The Patent Office allowed Hybritech a broad prospect, and the court concurred. We think that was a mistake. In this case it would have been both fairer and more in line with the objective of preserving competition in inventing to have allowed only the claims on what Hybritech actually created, and obvious equivalents.

The other basic genetic technique was developed earlier by two scientists, Cohen and Boyer. Here, also, the original creators of the procedure—the insertion of a specific gene into a host cell and the subsequent expression of the protein product for which the gene codes—saw it primarily as a contribution to ongoing public science. Their universities urged them to take out a patent, which they did, but the patent is licensed to all comers.

Earlier we noted the broad patent Genentech has been granted on an effective application of this technique. It can be argued, however, that Genentech simply was the first to bring to practice a particular procedure that persons "skilled in the art" knew could be made to work, and that the allowed scope of its patent should be rather small. It is difficult to tell yet whether the breadth implicit in this patent will hold up, but it has created a good deal of trepidation in the industry. According to the head of a rival biotechnology firm, "If interpreted most narrowly, there are certain bacterial [production] systems that wouldn't even be covered. If interpreted most broadly, it could cover all production systems in bacteria, yeast, and cells." In short, if interpreted broadly, Genentech will own the rights to a very large and open-ended prospect, largely created by public science. This strikes us as unfair. And if it happens we would predict that inventing in the field will be less creative and energetic than if the field were open to competition.

Modern biotechnology is a canonical example of a field where technology and science, public knowledge and proprietary intellectual property, are all mixed up together. Semiconductors and computers are other such fields. Superconductivity is another new one. In these fields the advance of public science is continuously illuminating new technological opportunities. Particular inventive efforts in these fields often can yield very large advances in technological capabilities over what had been prior best practice. Yet the contribution, in economist's jargon the value added, of the "first to bring to practice" may be quite small, in that the direction to go was "obvious," and if he or she hadn't achieved success, someone else would have very soon. Nor in many of these cases were the expenses and risks involved in the winning efforts so great, or anticipated to be so, that only the expectation of a giant reward could have induced them. And the granting of a broad patent to the first to bring to practice cannot be justified as likely to lead to more effective and orderly development of the prospect, if history be our guide.

5. Summary and Conclusion

The hallmark of all the histories and cases we have described is the involvement of many generally rivalrous parties in the advance of a technology, sometimes working basically independently of the prior work of others, sometimes taking strong clues and ideas from such prior work and developing significant improvements or variants, with competitors usually making different bets, but sometimes following common routes and leads. Interestingly, the areas where rival inventors seem to have seen opportunities in similar ways are in what we have called "science-based technologies." Here they saw things similarly (which is what the simple neoclassical models presume) because of the strong illumination being provided by recent advances in science which made certain paths "obvious to try."

In the cumulative systems technology cases we considered, broad, prospect-claiming, pioneer patents, when their holder tried to uphold them, caused nothing but trouble. Other parties often were more active or creative than the pioneer patent holder and suits slowed down their ability to put their inventions into practice and undoubtedly damped the interests of other talented people. Bargaining about the terms of individual licenses proved difficult and fractious.

Even aggressive litigation by the holder of a broad patent, however, could not prevent the creation of a wide variety of improvement subservient patents, and patents on components of the system not covered by the claims. Thus the situation soon became one in which no firm could use its own patents in a state of the art system if others refused to license and instead vigorously enforced theirs. Some mechanism that established more or less automatic cross-licensing ultimately provided the solution. Yet clearly in many of these cases the original impasse would have been avoided had patent claims been drawn more narrowly. The fact that the industry eventually learned to deal with, in the sense of running around, the consequences of broad patent grants certainly should not be taken as evidence that such grants are benign.

Nor is there reason to believe that more narrowly drawn patents would have damped the incentives of the pioneers and other early comers to the field. In cumulative systems technologies, superior design, production, and marketing rather than strong patent protection, are the principal source of profit. (See Levin et al., 1987.) And an inventor has a natural lead-time advantage in incorporating his or her own invention into the product or process. The aggressive inventive behavior of individuals and companies in those cases where patents never were enforced, and the rapid development of fields which were blocked initially but later opened up by cross-licensing, support this case.

Our intention here is to flag attention to the question of how patents ought to be defined in cumulative systems technologies, as a general issue. This general question recently has shown up in the sharp debate about the role of patents, or copyright protection that is patentlike, in the particular context of software. Here economists and other analysts increasingly are arguing that the granting of patents or patentlike copyright protection likely will strangle progress in the field, as contrasted with stimulating it, unless there is more-or-less automatic cross-licensing. (See, for example, Mennell, 1987.) We do not want to add here to this particular discussion. And we certainly do not want to be read as arguing against patents in cumulative technologies (although software may be a special case), only about the dangers of wide patents. And this issue is a general one, applying to a wide range of cumulative systems technologies, rather than being specific to software.

A strong patent may be essential, however, if the inventor of a new chemical product is to profit from the invention (Levin et al., 1987). But because product characteristics are very sensitive to the precise chemical formulation, even relatively narrowly defined claims usually can prevent easy "inventing around," and until recently the Patent Office declined to grant roomy prospect-defining claims.

The advent of biotechnology, and the statement of patent claims in terms of a "principle" and all products that can be produced according to it, rather than in terms of the particular product actually produced, has changed all that. Another problem is the tendency of the Patent Office to allow and the courts to uphold a patent defined in terms of a natural product when what the inventor actually achieved was a way of producing that product.

Evidence of "trouble" already is visible. Inventors are coming up with inventions that the broad prospect holder is challenging in court. The danger is that competitors will be harassed out of the field. There is every reason to believe that this would not only diminish the energy devoted to developing the prospect but also cut down on the diversity and creativity of the development.

Where a strong case can be made that an invention basically amounts to following out leads that have been provided by a prior scientific breakthrough, and represents a "first bringing to practice," there are double reasons for limiting the patent to just what the inventor did, and not allowing it to effectively privatize the broad use of that public science. It is bad policy as well as unjust to allow an inventor to claim for private use the fruits of what was largely other people's work. And it is a far better social policy bet to keep inventing in the field pluralistic and rivalrous.

At the present time attempts to gain patent rights on the prospects defined by the identification and purification of particular DNA fragments reveal the problem at its worst. Here the applicant is attempting to claim rights to "whatever useful may come from" use of what is basically a scientific discovery or creation, usually (but not always) financed by public monies. But whether funded by public monies or not, the particular efforts which lead to detailed identification of parts of the genome need to be understood as the work of scientists drawing on public scientific knowledge and trying to achieve goals that everyone knows can be achieved and roughly how. The patent rights that ought to be granted on such achievements, if any should be, ought to reflect that.

We do not think that achieving sounder policy requires any new law or rewriting of existing law. Mostly policy is made by the courts, within the bounds provided by the language of the law. We believe that more consistent strict interpretation of the enablement and equivalents doctrines, together with greater use of reverse equivalents doctrine in cases where the magnitude of improvements over the original calls for release of the hold of the original patent, is much of what is needed. In science-based fields, more consistent recognition is needed that new science as well as prior art delineate and bound what is "novel" and "nonobvious" about an invention, and the allowed claims cut accordingly.

The existing practice at the Patent Office of ceding areas of doubt regarding claims to the applicant also strikes us as warranting serious reconsideration. Threat of litigation and fear of losing the case is a daunting deterrent even for a party that believes strongly that someone else's claims are absurdly broad, and that his or her new ideas are original and outside the proper scope of the other's patent. The present regime leaves too much of the job of reining in scope to litigation and the courts.

The principal basis for our conclusions is the empirical evidence we have presented, and a wider range of cases with which we are familiar but have not the space to recount here. It is important to recognize that the empirical record is just what an evolutionary theory of individual and organizational behavior and cognition, and of technical advance, would predict. Thus the arguments for pluralism and rivalry, and against more centralized control, as the preferred context for invention and innovation are not simply empirical, but are analytically well grounded. In our view they are compelling.

Science and Technical Advance

The three essays in Part III are concerned with the role of science in technical advance. The rise of chemistry, physics, and biology as strong fundamental sciences during the last decade of the nineteenth century was accompanied by several developments that changed the nature of industrial technical innovation. One was the rise of the industrial research laboratory, staffed by university-trained scientists and engineers and dedicated to enhancing the competitive prowess of its mother company through the design and development of new and better products and processes. A second was the greatly increased importance of university training programs in various fields of science and in the engineering disciplines as a source of the personnel who staffed industrial research and development laboratories. As we shall see in Chapter 10, national university systems differed significantly in the extent to which they were able to reorient themselves to this new task. The rise of Germany and the United States in the new chemical and electrical products industries, and the inability of Great Britain to establish itself strongly in them, can be ascribed in considerable degree to the differential performance of the university systems in these countries.

A third important development was the rise of a number of applied sciences and engineering disciplines that drew from the more fundamental sciences but were directly oriented toward solving practical problems, including facilitating the advance of industrial technologies. Metallurgy, for example, grew up as a field of research directed to the technical problems of the rapidly expanding steel industry. Chemical and electrical engineering grew up as fields of research as well as training oriented toward the new chemical products and electrical equipment industries. Research in these fields was undertaken both in universities and in industry, and scientific and technical societies associated with these fields provided a structure for interaction between university and industrial scientists. Thus there was a close interaction in many fields between universities and industry, and an intertwining of science and technology. I proposed in Part II that Schumpeter did not well understand this intertwining of science and technology that had taken place when he wrote *Capitalism, Socialism, and Democracy*. And even today, many otherwise well-informed observers seem to believe that science fortuitously creates understandings that are useful in technology, whereas in fact much of science is consciously and explicitly aimed at that objective.

Chapter 6 is expressly theoretical. Its purpose is to illuminate how the state of understanding influences the focus and productivity of industrial research and development. Science contributes an important part of that understanding, but in times and ways that are not well recognized in lay discussion. Chapter 7 is a detailed study of the research at the Bell Telephone Laboratories that led to the creation of the transistor. The story is fascinating in its own right, but its role here is to illustrate the complex interaction of science and technology. Chapter 8 focuses on the role of U.S. universities in contributing to technical advance in U.S. industry. A portion of the essay is historical, and provides documentation for the "responsiveness" of the American university system to new opportunities opened up by science and industrial needs. The essay is also concerned with the current policy discussion about what kinds of roles American universities should play, given the enhanced concerns in the United States about American industrial competitiveness.

The Role of Knowledge in R&D Efficiency

1. Introduction

Economists and other scholars studying technical advance have had an easier time getting a handle on "demand-side" factors than on "supply-side" ones. It has been relatively easy to comprehend and model how increases in demand for a particular product raise the returns to successful inventions which improve that product or lower its cost of production. Similarly, it is not difficult to understand or model why the increased cost of a particular factor of production should induce inventive efforts to reduce the needs for that input, perhaps by permitting the substitution of other ones that are now relatively cheaper.[1] And most economists studying invention and innovation have a fairly good understanding of why and how the ability of an inventor to appropriate the returns to his or her invention affects the sensitivity of inventive effort to these demand-side factors.

It has proved much more difficult to gain a solid comprehension of factors influencing the "supply" of invention or technical advance. In particular, economists have struggled, and not always effectively, with the proposition that invention proceeds more rapidly and effectively in areas where "technological knowledge" is strong, than in areas where knowledge is weak.[2] Indeed Schmookler (1966), who started his researches on invention with the notion that both demand and supply-side variables were influential in determining the allocation of inventive effort, ultimately moved to a position that market forces and their shifts were much more tightly linked to the magnitude of inventive activities than were variables associated with the strength of knowledge. Rosenberg (1974) and Mowery and Rosenberg

Originally published in the *Quarterly Journal of Economics* 97, no. 3 (August 1982): 453–470. © 1982 by the President and Fellows of Harvard College. Reprinted by permission of The MIT Press Journals.

(1979) have rejoined that the demand for an invention, without the knowledge capability to achieve it, may draw effort but not success. The issue here of course is partly empirical, but it is conceptual as well; serious exploration requires a theory, explicit or implicit, that enables the phrase "the strength of knowledge" to take on some concrete meaning. This is the aim of this essay.

2. A Simple Two-Stage Search Model

It is useful to begin by laying out a very simple model. While almost a "straw man," it does provide a quite sharp and plausible answer to the question "How does knowledge matter?" It also serves as a useful starting point for the development of a more complex analysis.

Consider the following set-up. There is a set of techniques that in principle can be used to produce a particular product. Each has fixed input coefficients and constant returns to scale. Input coefficients differ among the techniques, and certain product attributes may as well, although for expositional simplicity generally I shall assume that product attributes are constant over the set. God knows the input coefficients (and product attributes) of all the techniques, the economic profit associated with each for any set of input (and attribute) prices, and hence the best (most profitable) technique for any market condition. Our R&D decision maker, however, is not blessed with such knowledge. He or she knows about prevailing best practice, and also that prevailing best practice is far from the best possible practice. He or she can list the still unexplored members of the set of technical possibilities, but for openers let us assume our decision maker knows nothing about the economic attributes of any member, save for a probability distribution defined over the set as a whole.

There are two different R&D activities: a "study" or a "test" activity, and a "design" or a "blueprint-drawing" activity. The former makes known the economic characteristics of a technique (for example, its input coefficients). The latter, which can proceed only after the economic characteristics are fully known, develops instructions to make the technique operational for producers or users. There is only a single "round" of R&D, but two decision points. At the start of the round a decision must be made regarding how many and which of the presently unstudied techniques are to be studied.[3] After the studies are completed, the decision maker can proceed to order blueprints drawn up for whatever technique turns out best (assuming that the advantage of that technique over the prevailing one exceeds the costs of the blueprints). The benefits from the R&D are the unit production cost savings associated with the introduction of a better technique, times the quantity of output produced, minus the cost of the studies undertaken and the subsequent design work (if any). The R&D decision maker aims to devise an R&D program that maximizes expected net economic benefits.

Consider the effect of the size of the market upon the R&D to be undertaken. For given factor prices, there is a known probability distribution of possible unit cost savings from techniques that can be explored through R&D. There are positive, but diminishing, returns to increasing the number of unexplored techniques that are tested in the search stage. This is because the expected unit cost saving of the "best" of the techniques studied increases with the number studied, but at a diminishing rate. An increase in the size of the market magnifies the total cost of savings associated with any particular unit cost savings. This means that the larger the market, the more the number of unexplored techniques it pays to explore. Thus the results of this model are fully in the spirit of Schmookler. The larger the market, the more "searching" it pays to do, and the greater the expected technical advance from all that searching.

What about the effects of an increase in the price of a particular factor, for example the wage rate of labor, on the optimal R&D program? A higher wage rate increases the unit cost saving associated with any reduction in labor input per unit of output, and hence, like an increase in the size of the market, "magnifies" the value of any productivity (in this case labor productivity) improvement. Thus a rise in wage rates will, according to this model, induce an increase in "searching."

However, given the assumptions employed thus far, while an increase in the price of the factor of production will induce more searching, it will not induce any change in the orientation of the search. The fact that the wage rate is higher will mean that, of those techniques studied, the one judged best will likely be more labor saving than would have been the case had the wage rate been lower. But given the assumption that the decision maker cannot discriminate ex ante among different alternatives, a higher wage rate cannot influence the "direction" of the search.

Now let me introduce knowledge which can affect the direction of the search. Assume the decision maker knows more than merely the probability distribution of economic payoffs over the entire set of candidate techniques. Assume now that he or she knows the distribution conditional on the values taken on by different known technological attributes of these alternatives. These technological attributes of a technique are obvious ex ante or can be observed without cost. They may be continuous or discrete. Thus expected economic payoff may vary with weight, with a well-defined weight such that expected payoff is maximized. Blue projects may be better than yellow projects. These correlates in general will not be foolproof guides, but they can enable the decision maker to do better than he or she could merely by sampling randomly.

The effect of such information on optimum R&D activity is to enable attention to be focused on certain parts of the set of alternatives, before engagement in the costly part of the endeavor—the actual expensive testing or studying. This characterization seems to capture what is going on when engineers think of designing an engine to operate at a particular temperature and pressure, when chemists look for their compound in a particular class of chemicals rather than in another class, and so on. The portion of the set actually sampled will on average have better projects than the portion of the set ignored.

Let me formalize the idea that stronger knowledge means a better choice set actually explored by defining "better" in terms of stochastic dominance. Stronger knowledge (in this sense) implies a lower expected cost (smaller number sampled) of achieving an advance of given magnitude, or a larger expected advance from a given R&D outlay. It is not surprising, therefore, that, in optimum search models of the sort considered here, the better the choice set, the better the expected outcome (the greater the expected technical advance) from an optimum strategy. However, there is not necessarily any more sampling (R&D input) in the optimum strategy. The result may be regarded as a special case of a general proposition in price theory: an increase in the productivity of an input leads to greater output in the optimum solution but not necessarily to more input.

It should be noted that this proposition puts a different light on the apparent difference between Rosenberg and Schmookler regarding the role of basic knowledge in R&D allocation. There may be no conflict at all. Stronger knowledge within this model, at least, is associated with more rapid progress—Rosenberg's point. However, there is no reason to expect any systematic connection between the strength of the knowledge base and the total amount of R&D input being applied—Schmookler's proposition.

Also, within this model at least, a stronger knowledge base not only enhances the general productivity of search. It increases the sensitivity of search to the fine structure of the market situation. Thus, if the R&D decision maker can discriminate ex ante between techniques likely to save specially on labor input and techniques likely to save specially on materials input, relative factor prices and their changes can influence the direction of the search. Similarly, the search can be guided by the particularities of a consumer demand for different product attributes. Stronger knowledge again means better ability to focus the search.

3. More Complex Search Models

The model sketched in the preceding section has the advantage of being rich enough to contain a plausible characterization of "knowledge," yet simple enough to be analytically tractable and transparent. I propose that the general idea that knowledge is capability to guide R&D activity is robust, and that a number of the insights drawn from the simple model hold when various complications are added. However, the simple characterization of knowledge as understanding of a mapping from technological to economic attributes is too narrow. In this section I explore, qualitatively, several slightly more complicated search models, in which knowledge takes on somewhat different guises. My objective is partly to enrich understanding of the various roles of knowledge in invention, and partly to open analysis of the sources of different kinds of knowledge.

3.1. A Group of Models

First, modify the foregoing model only slightly as follows. The decision maker knows a number of technological attributes that provide powerful guides to the economic attributes of a technique: however, these are not obvious ex ante, nor are they observable without cost. It takes time and resources to identify or observe them. There exist cheap and reliable tests for some but not for others. In this case knowledge of which of the correlates of economic performance can be observed relatively inexpensively, and of the cheap and effective tests for them, are important parts of knowledge.

For a more complex variant on the above theme, consider a situation where the R&D decision maker knows ex ante that there are several technological attributes that need to be present if the technique is to have the desired economic attributes. He knows he wants something that is heavy, blue, and striped, where in pharmaceutical research the first two attributes might refer to physical and chemical characteristics and the last to safety when tested on mice. Not all techniques (pharmaceuticals) that have these characteristics will be efficacious and safe on humans, but lacking these attributes, a technique (pharmaceutical) is certain to be hazardous or worthless. Our R&D decision maker cannot see any of these technological attributes without testing. The screening on candidate techniques can proceed sequentially first by identifying a number of heavy compounds (by weighing), then screening these for color (using a spectroscope), and then testing the heavy blue ones to see whether they give mice stripes. Or, the screening on different variables might proceed to another order. Expected cost may well depend on the order. If one of the desired attributes is rare, but the screening test for it is cheap, one ought to begin by screening on it. Thus, in this case, there are better R&D strategies and poorer ones. Efficient searching is facilitated by knowledge of good R&D strategy.

Relevant knowledge takes on still a different guise in the following example. The set of technological possibilities is defined by the amount of certain ingredients. The R&D decision maker does not know for certain the population statistics about the correlates of good economic performance, but he does know the economic performance of previously explored techniques (compounds), and he has some reason to suspect that the relationship may be continuous. In the past, performance virtually always has been improved as one of the ingredients has been increased. It thus is a sensible strategy to proceed to test the economic attributes of a compound somewhat richer than the prevailing one, if the results are favorable to try an even richer mix, if not cutting back, and so on, in effect hunting for the top of the hill. In general, a good strategy will stop the project short of the top if economic attributes are "good enough," and the further gains from varying the mix one way or another are not expected to be worth the costs of performing another test. However, notice in this case that knowledge has been changed in the course of undertaking the R&D project. The R&D decision maker now knows the economic characteristics of other points in technological space.

As a final example, consider R&D on a system that contains a number of different components—as an aircraft or a television set. Here, as with the chemical mix case, prevailing technology provides a natural starting place for today's R&D. In this case, however, prevailing technology can be viewed as defining a set of available subtechniques or building blocks that can be used, or not. The R&D decision maker has the option of working on one component, or a few, taking the others "off the shelf." A key strategic question is—which directions (in the sense of which components) to push through R&D. As with the pharmaceutical case, in the systems case knowledge of the fruits of past R&D—in this instance awareness of available new component technology—is an important part of knowledge relevant to R&D decision making. And knowledge of the results of today's R&D is important in guiding tomorrow's R&D decision.

Let me bring the analysis of a role of knowledge in R&D back to its earlier characterization in terms of knowledge of technological correlates. A particular problem in R&D on multicomponent systems arises if the appropriate design of one component is sensitive to the design of other components. Such interdependence militates against trying to redesign a number of components at once, unless there is strong knowledge that enables viable designs for each of these to be well predicted ex ante, or there exist reliable tests of cheap models of new systems. If there is such strong knowledge, the R&D decision maker can realistically consider system designs that depart significantly from the status quo in many components; without such strong knowledge of correlates and testing procedures, major departures from prevailing systems are likely to be risky.

3.2. The Effects and Sources of Knowledge

The model examples have grown increasingly complicated. However, while there are interesting differences across the models in the role of knowledge in R&D decision making, to me at least the similarities seem more striking. The basic insights from the simple model are preserved: strong knowledge means ability to guide R&D effectively. Stronger knowledge enables a larger expected advance to be achieved from a given R&D outlay: alternatively, strong knowledge reduces the expected cost of any R&D achievement. Strong knowledge enhances efficiency both by enabling R&D to proceed on a generally better set of candidate projects and by enabling the set worked upon to reflect more accurately particular demands and needs.

Consideration of a number of different models has, however, enabled knowledge to be seen in a variety of different guises. Knowledge relevant to guiding an effective sequential search includes knowledge of correlates, or effective tests and of good R&D strategies, of the outcome of recent R&D projects that have aimed at modifying the technology in particular directions, and of available building blocks for the construction of new structures.

Undoubtedly, the relative importance of these different forms of knowledge differs from industry to industry, and from time to time. However, my reading of technological histories suggests that virtually all of these forms of knowledge are important in guiding the advance of almost all technologies.

Given the diversity of knowledge relevant to R&D, one would not expect a single source of such knowledge. In some fields of technology at some times, scientific understanding won through research in the basic academic sciences has been a tremendous aid to effective prefocusing. Simply under-standing the second law of thermodynamics rules out some proposed de-signs; knowledge of the relationships between electricity and magnetism fur-ther narrows the range of plausible power systems: recent research on superconductivity provides intriguing clues as to promising design avenues to explore. Academic science also has provided knowledge needed to design cheap and powerful tests; the litmus paper test we all used in grade school experiments is perhaps the simplest example of a great range of techniques used in science, which may or may not be understood scientifically, to cheaply and reliably screen properties of materials and systems.

Research in the basic sciences is guided largely by the internal logic of the quest for understanding of a set of fundamental scientific questions. These questions are not generally defined in terms of knowledge needed for the advance of a particular technology. However, there are a number of so-called applied sciences where research priorities are directly tied to technological problems and opportunities. These fields are pursued both in corporate lab-oratories and in universities. The engineering, biomedical, and agricultural sciences are examples. Theoretical exploration may be quite deep, as in Wil-liam Shockley's study of holes and electrons in semiconductors, or as in examination of the character of sound barriers to supersonic flight, or of the causes of particular diseases. I put forth the proposition that in many of the technologies where advance has been very rapid, one important contributing factor has been an institutionalized applied science.

Knowledge is not only won through specialized knowledge-seeking activ-ities; knowledge is also won as a by-product of searching for new technol-ogies. Knowledge of correlates and of effective testing techniques grows through experience. One learns about efficacious R&D strategies through one's successes and failures. What succeeded and failed last time gives clues as to what to try next, and so on. The applied R&D system itself generates new knowledge as well as new techniques.

4. Cumulative Technological Advance and Public and Private Knowledge

The foregoing analysis has relevance to a number of topics of interest to economists. Two will be considered here. One is analysis of continuing pro-ductivity growth fueled by technological advance. The other is the intermix-ture of public and private knowledge in continuing technological advance in competitive industry.

4.1. Cumulative Technological Advance

Several recent models of long-run productivity growth, fueled by technological advance, incorporate the idea of a "knowledge" capital stock. That knowledge capital stock is augmented by present R&D spending, and the stock of knowledge may depreciate as well. See, for example, Griliches (1979) and Mansfield (1980). Exactly what a "knowledge" capital stock might mean and how it might influence productivity are questions not seriously treated, however. The viewpoint on R&D and knowledge developed above casts some light on those questions.

It might be useful to think of continuing R&D expenditure in an industry as buying a continuing sequence of search rounds. If one adopted that viewpoint, the foregoing analysis suggests that one should distinguish between the new techniques won in the course of a round of R&D, and the knowledge gained that serves to guide further R&D, even while recognizing that the former may contribute to the latter. The search models that have been explored suggest several quite different patterns of continuing technological advance associated with different assumptions about the evolution of knowledge. These different models might be appropriate to different industries.

It is possible to explain continuing technological progress with a simple search model of the sort employed in section 2, under the assumption that today's round of R&D projects is independent of what happened during the last round, except for the fact that what was achieved forces the sights to be set higher in this round. If the set of possible technologies is bounded in the space of economic dimensions, if product demand and factor supply curves remain constant over time, and if knowledge guiding a search remains constant, this model will display diminishing expected returns to R&D, and after a point R&D will cease to be profitable. Growth of demand can extend this period, perhaps indefinitely, although the achieved advances will become progressively smaller per unit of R&D input. In short, this search model will display the same diminishing returns to R&D that characterize most of the models where R&D leads to an increased knowledge capital stock.

What if knowledge relevant to R&D is growing over time, say as a result of university research that improves knowledge about "correlates"? An advance of knowledge, by increasing the efficiency of the search, provides an offset to the diminishing returns from search. "Basic research" (if we may call it that) enhances the productivity of applied research and development: again the conclusion here is consistent with that of deterministic models in which basic research and applied research are treated as complements.

However, the logic of the search models suggests that there are two quite different kinds of effects that better knowledge of correlates might have upon applied research and development. Stronger knowledge might lead to ability to focus the search more finely. Thus it might be learned that within the set of "blue" techniques which was already known to be rich relative to the set of "yellow" techniques, the blue striped subset is particularly rich. Applied R&D would continue in the blue region, but would proceed to concentrate on the striped techniques within that region. Alternatively, it might be discovered that, while the set of yellow techniques is a relatively poor one, the small subset of striped yellow techniques is unusually rich. R&D attention then might jump from the blue region to the striped subregion of the yellow region. Transistors are substituted for vacuum tubes, and subsequent R&D on amplifying devices focuses exclusively on semiconductors.

In the model above, technological advance sometimes continues to focus on a particular class of techniques and sometimes is marked by a "revolution" that may, in effect, define a whole new industry. However, the characterization does not capture the *connected* nature of technological advance that seems to mark many technological histories. In many technologies the new is not simply better than the old; in some sense the new evolves from the old.

The models discussed in the preceding subsection provide an interpretation of this phenomenon. In the latter of these models the very business of doing applied R&D leads not only to new techniques but also to enhanced knowledge. There is a quite definite sense in which one round of technological advances lays the foundations for the next round.

In some cases knowledge of correlates has been strengthened and sharpened. Exploring in the set of blue chemicals can continue to yield payoff, and since the last two good ones had stripes, it might make sense to focus the search next time on untested blue striped chemicals. In the last round greater pressures continued to be associated with better performance, and it is possible to try to increase pressures still further. Additional pieces of a puzzle have been found, opening the possibility of building from those pieces. The new availability of a more powerful (higher pressure) engine suggests it might be worthwhile to redesign the air frame to take better advantage of the new engine capabilities. The first of these advances suggests some type of improvement in understanding; the second involves simple knowledge of what has worked and what has not with some simple extrapolation; and the third involves knowledge of available pieces of operative technologies. However, these are all forms of knowledge in the general sense considered above. They all provide clues as to where to search next.

A noteworthy characteristic of this kind of knowledge is that it is won not in basic research in universities where the scientists have strong interests in publishing and making their results public, but within a company that would appear to have a proprietary interest not only in the new technique but also in the knowledge created to guide the next round of R&D.

The fact that techniques are often proprietary means that the above analysis of the evolution of a technology must be modified to recognize that different firms develop and use different techniques. If the knowledge relevant to the next round of R&D also were proprietary, then analysis of the evolution of the frontiers of the technology also would have to take account of who knows what. It is my impression, however, that to a considerable extent knowledge relevant to the next round, even knowledge won through corporate R&D, is made public. If true, this is an interesting phenomenon. I turn now to consider the proprietary, and the public, aspects of technology.

4.2. Public and Proprietary Aspects of Technological Knowledge

Economists clearly are schizophrenic in their treatment of property rights in technological knowledge. In standard microeconomic theory, technological knowledge is assumed available to all. Most of the growth models of the sort discussed above implicitly treat technological knowledge as public. On the other hand, in their analysis of the effect of the patent system, or of technological rivalry among firms, economists treat (at least some aspects of) technological knowledge as proprietary.

I propose that there is both a private and a public aspect to technological knowledge, and that while the lines between these are shady, it is important to recognize both. In part, the distinction stems from differences in the kind of work that leads to public and private knowledge, and from specialization of different institutions in this kind of work. Thus many economists seem to carry around in their heads a model in which science is done by scientists at universities and results in published public knowledge, and inventing is done by inventors in business firms and results in patentable proprietary technology. There is something to this theory. However, as stated earlier, some business firms do "science," and some generally useful knowledge may come as a by-product of inventing. Technology itself is a hybrid term with two roots—one "technique," referring to a way of doing something, and the other "logy," referring to theory. It is interesting that even in rivalrous industries, institutional mechanisms have developed that tend to keep the "logy" public, even though the technique is kept private.

The patent system, which establishes legal property rights on techniques, acts as a vehicle making public the logy associated with that technique; this clearly was intended. The distinction between the private technique and the public logy lies behind, I think, many of the arrangements for patent pooling, or more or less automatic patent licensing. The purpose of firms' freely licensing their inventions certainly is not to give away proprietary techniques to other companies. Rather, it is to enable all firms in the industry to explore in the next round of R&D new things in promising regions without fear that if they come up with something interesting, they may be faced with a lawsuit for infringing on somebody else's patents.

Research and development scientists from rival firms give papers at the meetings of professional societies. They meet together for lunch to exchange information on the evolving frontiers of the "logy," while trying to avoid disclosing details of particular techniques their firms may have under development at the time.[4] This practice of making public the logy while maintaining property rights on the techniques makes considerable sense from a social point of view. While there certainly are some deadweight losses associated with restrictions on the use of particular techniques, and some waste involved in the races to be first to come up with an invention or to invent around somebody else's patent, I suspect these costs are small compared with social costs that would be involved if the background knowledge to facilitate the next round of R&D efforts was kept largely proprietary.

The reasons why firms want to establish proprietary rights on their new inventions are clear enough. The reasons for, and the sources sustaining, treatment of general technological knowledge created by firms as public would appear more complex. Partly the airing of such information in private conversations is a quid pro quo for receiving such information. Partly it is to establish or maintain the reputation of the individual company scientist, or the corporate laboratory within an extended scientific technological community, and thus to facilitate hiring or the holding of scientific personnel, and the raising of capital. But the agreement among firms to keep the logy public may be a fragile one. At least in certain times individual firms may have little to gain, and something considerable to lose, by advertising their new logy.

The dividing lines between public and private knowledge in the evolution of a technology is a topic to which economists have given little attention. Since other disciplines make less of the public-private distinction, the topic has not been explored in any detail by scholars from other disciplines either. I maintain that in industries marked by rapid sustained technological progress a good deal of the logy has been created within the firms themselves, yet made public. Surely this is a phenomenon worth studying.

7

The Link between Science and Invention:
The Case of the Transistor

Introduction

This essay describes the work at the Bell Telephone Laboratories which, in 1948, resulted in the invention of the transistor. It examines how the invention came about, and recounts the complex intertwinings of science and technology that were involved. In addition to presenting the history of one of the twentieth century's most important inventions, the essay also examines the operation of one of the twentieth century's great industrial laboratories in its heyday.

This essay was originally written in 1960, and while at that time some of the promise of the transistor was visible, one could not foresee the subsequent developments—principally the inventions of the integrated circuit and the microprocessor—which have revolutionized microelectronics. That story is left untold here.

The events on which I focus were undertaken at the Bell Telephone Laboratories. At the time of the events, the Laboratories were jointly owned by AT&T and Western Electric—AT&T's production company. The American telephone system was a regulated private utility, and AT&T owned virtually the whole national system, in addition to being integrated vertically, designing and producing virtually all the equipment used in the nation's telephone system. The Bell Telephone Laboratories then involved an extensive basic research operation, out of which came the transistor as well as major operations in applied research and systems design and engineering. Such results make clear the special advantages of linking technology-oriented basic research with applied research and development.

Originally published in *The Rate and Direction of Inventive Activity,* edited by Richard R. Nelson (Princeton: Princeton University Press for the National Bureau of Economic Research, 1962), pp. 549–583.

159

The telephone monopoly of AT&T was the background context for the activities described below. It has since come apart as a result of antitrust proceedings, and AT&T has retreated significantly from the long-run basic research business. But that too is another story.

In the following account, tenses have been left as they were in the original text.

The Bell Telephone Laboratories and the Transistor

Although it is hoped that the analysis presented here has some general applicability, this essay is principally a single case study—a study of the research that led to the invention of the transistor and of the organization responsible for that research—the Bell Telephone Laboratories.

Bell Laboratories are jointly owned by the American Telephone and Telegraph Company and Western Electric, AT&T's production subsidiary. The Laboratories employ about 11,000 people, of whom about one-third are professional scientists and engineers, about one-third are technical aides, and about one-third, clerical and supporting personnel. About 85 percent of the laboratory professionals are engaged in the development of specific devices and systems for use in the telephone system or by the military. About 15 percent of the professional scientists and engineers, about 500 people, constitute the research staff under William O. Baker, vice-president in charge of research. Baker reports directly to James B. Fisk, president of the Laboratories. A large percentage of Baker's budget supports scientific research which is not tied to any specific practical objective. It is on this kind of research that this essay is focused.

The transistor was invented in the course of a research program started in 1946 at the Bell Telephone Laboratories. The transistor has several advantages over the triode vacuum tube, Lee De Forest's invention of half a century ago; it is much smaller than the vacuum tube, it requires much less energy input to do a given job, and in many applications it is much more durable. On the negative side, the performance of the transistor is much more sensitive to varying temperature than is that of the vacuum tube; at present the transistor is not as capable as the vacuum tube at high frequencies and in handling high power, and thus far, problems of quality control have proved quite serious in transistor manufacture.

The transistor has had its most significant impact not as a component replacing vacuum tubes in established products, but as a component of products which were uneconomical before the development of the transistor. There has been an increase in the use of electronic packages where the transistor's strong points are important. Very compact computers are the most striking example. Without transistors, computers of a given capability would have to be much larger both because vacuum tubes are larger than equivalent transistors and because cooling requirements are much greater for vacuum tubes. Almost all of our new airborne navigation, bombing, and fire control systems, for example, are transistorized. So are all of our satellite computers. And without transistors our large computers, which are playing an increasingly important role in science, engineering, and management, undoubtedly would be much more expensive—probably so much so that many of their present uses would not be economically sound.

Thus the transistor has stimulated growth, including the invention and innovation on a considerable scale of products which can profitably use transistors as components. The transistor has also stimulated research and development aimed at reducing the size of complementary electronic circuit elements. Much of the work in printed circuitry, for example, certainly fits this picture. Further, as we shall see, the research which led to the transistor also produced a number of other new and improved semiconductor devices. Thus, if it be argued that one of the indexes of the importance of an invention is the amount of inventive activity it stimulates, then, by this criterion, the transistor is a major invention indeed.

But while the transistor is playing an extremely important role in our more complex electronic equipment and in equipment where size is important, like hearing aids and portable radios, it has not superseded the vacuum tube in all uses. Dollar sales of vacuum tubes are still roughly double dollar sales of transistors. Given existing costs, vacuum tubes are now more economical in the bulk of those jobs in which size and efficiency are not particularly important. And since the birth of the transistor there have been substantial improvements in vacuum tubes, many of these improvements certainly stimulated by the competition of the transistor. Almost no invention eliminates all of its competition overnight, and the transistor is no exception. But there is reason to believe that the transistor may be one of the most important inventions of the twentieth century.

The History of the Transistor

History of Semiconductor Research before the Project at Bell Laboratories

The transistor is a semiconductor device. The research at Bell which resulted in the invention took off from a base of knowledge about semiconductors built by several generations of scientists. Karl Popper has described the state of scientific knowledge at any time as the deposit of observations and conceptual schemes which have stood the test of time and which still are proving useful in explaining and predicting.[1] The current state of knowledge is the result of an evolutionary process operating on ideas. Therefore, in order to understand the post–World War II research at Bell, it is important to sketch the history of prior semiconductor research.[2]

The element germanium is a semiconductor. So are several other elements, including silicon, and a number of compounds, such as copper oxide and zinc oxide. By 1900 many scientists and experimenters with electricity knew that these metals had quite unusual properties. In particular, it was known that these materials conducted electricity although, as the name implies, not as well as conductors like metal. It also was known that the electrical resistance of these materials decreased with temperature. That is, when these materials were warm they conducted current more easily than when they were cold. This puzzling property set semiconductors apart from other conductors, like metals, which conducted more easily when cool than when warm. Also, it was known that these materials sometimes passed current more easily in one direction than in another. In other words, they rectified current.

In this section we shall see how these phenomena, and others, gradually came to be understood. We shall see how research led to a distinction between *n* type and *p* type semiconductors, and how it came to be realized that in a semiconductor there are both electrons and "holes." We shall see how, by the start of World War II, researchers had come to an understanding of semiconductors that was satisfactory in many respects. We shall also see that one important concept, that of "minority" carriers, was being neglected. This will set the stage for analysis of the research at Bell which led to the transistor.

Necessary Terms and Concepts. In order to understand the history of semiconductor research it is necessary to be familiar with a few terms and concepts, so before proceeding with the history let us leap ahead and consider a few aspects of modern-day theory.

Modern theory views a semiconductor as a crystal containing two different types of current carriers—electrons and holes. The electrons are negatively charged and the holes may be considered as positively charged. The number of holes and electrons which are free to carry current is an increasing function of the temperature of the crystal, which explains the negative coefficient of resistivity which had puzzled researchers around the turn of the century.

The proportion of holes and electrons in a semiconductor is a very sensitive function of its purity. By doping a germanium crystal with other elements a very great variation in the hole-electron ratio can be achieved. In some semiconductors there are many more electrons (negative charge carriers) than holes (positive charge carriers). Thus electrons are the "majority" carriers and holes are the "minority" carriers, and this type of crystal is called, conveniently enough, an *n* (for negative) semiconductor. In other crystals, holes are the majority carriers and this sort of semiconductor is called a *p* (for positive) type.

If a *p* and an *n* type crystal are placed end to end they form a "*p-n* junction." Such a *p-n* junction will conduct current much more easily in one direction than in the other, in other words, it is a rectifier. The theoretical explanation of rectification in *p-n* junctions rests on the fact that on one side of the junction (the *n* side) most of the charge carriers are negative, while on the other side of the junction (the *p* side) most of the charge carriers are positive. The explanation makes no use of the concept of minority carriers. However, as we shall see later, in the working of the transistor minority carriers play a key role. Without an understanding of the fact that there are minority carriers as well as majority carriers, the operation of the transistor cannot be comprehended.

Research before World War II.   Returning to our story, though by 1900 many scientists knew that the materials we now call semiconductors had interesting properties, they knew little about why. The birth of the radio industry created a practical demand for good rectifiers and quite early in the game "cat's whisker" rectifiers (semiconductors) became widely used. But, in large part because the vacuum tube rectifier was better understood and hence the direction of possible improvement more clearly indicated, the semiconductor rectifier declined in importance relative to the vacuum tube during the twenties and early thirties.

However, during this period research on semiconductors was far from stagnant. A number of experiments made it quite clear that in some semiconductors the charge carriers behaved as if they had a positive charge, and several scientists were coming to the belief that there were two quite different types of semiconductors.

During the thirties research workers in the field of radio waves and communications turned their interest to higher frequencies. The ordinary vacuum tube performed poorly at these higher frequencies, and attention returned to crystal detectors and hence to research on semiconductors. Improvements came rapidly. Techniques for producing very pure silicon were improved and metallurgists learned how to add very accurately measured quantities of impurities. At the Bell Laboratories it was learned that when silicon ingots were doped with certain elements (arsenic, phosphorous, antimony) the rectifying contact would conduct easily only when the crystal was negative relative to the metal, and that when silicon ingots were doped with certain other elements (aluminum, boron) the rectifying contact would conduct easily only when the crystal was positive relative to the metal. The first type of semiconductor came to be known as the n (for negative) type and the second as the p (for positive) type.[3]

Thus before the war scientists at the Bell Telephone Laboratories and elsewhere were experimenting with p and n crystals and calling them that. Also before the war many scientists were thinking of making a semiconductor amplifier. The reasoning on the prospects for an amplifier was principally in terms of a simple analogy. Vacuum tubes rectified and, with the introduction of a grid, amplified. Semiconductors rectified. Therefore, somehow, they should be able to amplify. Indeed several workers suggested that a grid should be inserted into a semiconductor diode, but due to the extreme thinness of the rectifying area (rectification occurs in a region very close to the surface contact of a cat's whisker rectifier, or at the n-p junction of a junction rectifier) this proved very difficult to do.

Meanwhile the conceptual scheme which we have described earlier and which would permit the workings of the semiconductor to be much better understood was gradually taking shape. Advances in quantum mechanics during the twenties set the stage for A. H. Wilson's quantum mechanical model of a solid semiconductor, which was published in 1931. The Wilson model provided the basis for a theoretical explanation of the difference between n type and p type semiconductors, but, although the model was well known, few scientists saw this until after World War II. Indeed it seems that it was not until the postwar project at Bell Laboratories that the model was extended to apply to doped germanium and silicon. Further, and this is extremely important, though scientists in the field knew, or should have known from their feel for the above theory, that every semiconductor had both positive and negative charge carriers, their attention was focused almost exclusively on majority carriers. Thus n type germanium was pictured as having electrons carrying current, p type as having holes carrying current, and the minority carriers were ignored. The working of the transistor depends on minority carriers as well as majority carriers, and until both types were considered together understanding was sorely hindered.

To one who is not a physical scientist it is interesting that by the mid-1930s a well-known article, Wilson's, contained most of the essential ingredients for a rather complete understanding of semiconductors, but that almost all scientists missed some of the essential points. Similar instances in economic theory are legion. By the start of World War II, then, scientists understood quite well certain aspects of semiconductors, and were well on the road to understanding rectification. The essential theoretical foundations had been laid, but the phenomenon of minority carriers was being neglected. To many scientists doing research in the field the time seemed ripe for major breakthroughs.

The Project at Bell

The Start of the Project. In this section we shall follow the research work at the Bell Telephone Laboratories which led to the transistor. We shall see how difficulties with the first solid state amplifier design which interested Shockley led to a series of experiments which resulted, quite surprisingly, in the discovery of the transistor effect and the invention of the point contact transistor. We shall see how, in attempting to explain the transistor effect, the concept of minority carriers snapped into focus, and how this concept led to the invention of the junction transistor.[4]

The Bell Telephone Laboratories were deep in research in the field of semiconductors long before World War II. Bell's tradition in quantum mechanics was very strong. Several of the experiments which demonstrated the wave nature of electrons were conducted at the Laboratories during the thirties by Clinton J. Davisson; and Davisson and G. P. Thompson of England shared a Nobel Prize for their efforts. William Shockley, Walter Brattain, Dean Wooldridge, and several other top-flight solid-state physicists were brought to the Bell Laboratories during the thirties. People in the Laboratories' metallurgy department were playing a major role in the advances then being made in producing pure crystals, and J. H. Scaff and others at Bell performed the experiment which led to the naming of n and p type crystals. Also, the pre–World War II work of the Laboratories in this area had led to the development of better crystal rectifiers, the thermistor—a circuit element whose resistance decreased with temperature—and other circuit elements.

During World War II research work in semiconductors continued at the Laboratories, but the war work was, of course, device oriented and several of the Bell scientists worked elsewhere. Semiconductor knowledge and technique played an extremely important role in the war-time work on radar. At Bell and at Purdue University research on germanium and silicon was pushed with the aim of developing better rectifiers, and important breakthroughs were made in techniques of producing very pure crystals and doping them to very close specifications.

During the summer of 1945, as it became evident that the war would soon be over, steps were taken to smooth the transition of the Laboratories to a peacetime basis. Shockley, who had been on leave from Bell during the war, believed strongly that the Laboratories should intensify its solid-state work, and in consultation with M. J. Kelly, then director of research, and others was convincing enough so that it was agreed that it would be good research strategy to bring together in one department a number of people who had been working on solid-state physics, and perhaps to draw in some new talent. Within the solid-state research group, to be headed by Shockley and S. O. Morgan, a subgroup, including Shockley, was to work on semi-conductors. It was felt that the greatly increased role of solid-state devices, particularly semiconductors, in communications technology warranted an increase in Bell's effort in this area. It was felt that advances in the under-standing of semiconductors, including a better grasp of the meaning of the quantum mechanical model, had set the stage for major breakthroughs, and that the techniques of making crystals to close specifications promised ma-terials which could be produced to fit the theoretical model. Improvements in rectifiers, and thermo- and photo-electric devices were judged a quite likely result of semiconductor research. Further, Shockley strongly believed that he could make a solid-state amplifier and his enthusiasm was conta-gious.

Shockley and Morgan were given hunting licenses and Brattain and Pearson were talked into joining the semiconductor research group. John Bardeen was hired from the outside. Later R. B. Gibney, a physical chemist, and H. R. Moore, a circuit expert, joined the group. The prime reason for establishing a special solid-state physics research group was the belief that the interaction of physicists, chemists, and metallurgists all interested in re-lated problems would be instrumental in speeding the advance in under-standing, and that the organization of a separate group would facilitate com-munication and mutual help. But it would be a mistake to believe that all the work on semiconductors going on at the Laboratories after 1946 was done by this subgroup. Throughout the period people in the metallurgy de-partment were working on ways to make better crystals and rectifiers and there was considerable interplay between Shockley's group and the metal-lurgists. And scattered throughout the research divisions were people working in this area from time to time. All in all, the people playing a major role at one time or another in the work which led to the transistor discovery may have numbered about thirteen.

We have seen that the motives of the Bell Telephone Laboratories in es-tablishing this new project were reasonably clear. Bell believed that major advances in scientific knowledge in this field were likely to be won and that advances in knowledge were likely to be fruitful in improving communications technology. One possible result was an amplifier. But improvements in rectifiers, thermistors, and other solid-state devices also were judged strong possibilities. It was the wide range of possible useful results which made the project attractive. The motives of the scientists on the project were, of course, much more complex. Several of the scientists involved were not much interested in or concerned with any practical applications their work might lead to. Their intellectual interests were focused almost exclusively on creating more knowledge about semiconductors. Others in the group were concerned with practical applications as well as with the underlying sciences. Shockley's interests were multiple. As a theorist he was fascinated by the prospect of developing a good theory of semiconductors. He also was fascinated with the prospects for a solid-state amplifier. Shockley's work was focused in a direction compatible with both these ends. That a good share of the work of the semiconductor research group was allocated so as to clear the way for an amplifier seems, in large part, to have been the result of Shockley's influence. But it is extremely difficult to say how much of this influence was "authority" and how much was Shockley's ability to interest others in what interested him.

Research Leading to the Discovery of the Transistor Effect.   Stated in broad terms, the general scientific aim of the semiconductor research program was to obtain as complete an understanding as possible of semiconductor phenomena, not in empirical terms, but on the basis of atomic theory. Wilson's work was an important start for, as we have seen, a sound theoretical foundation already was partially built although it had not been fully exploited in thinking about doped germanium and silicon. With the wisdom of hindsight we know that one important roadblock to understanding of doped crystals was failure to consider minority carriers, the flow of electrons in p type germanium and holes in n type germanium. Also (though not to be discussed in this essay), the workers in the field were not adequately treating surface states, that is, the fact that the properties of a solid at the surface can be (and usually are) quite different from the properties in the interior.

During the first few years of the solid-state physics project (the years we are considering here), the Shockley-Morgan group operated on a budget of roughly half a million dollars a year, about enough to support twenty to thirty scientists. Probably less than half of the group worked with Shockley on semiconductors. Both because the developing theory was simpler and better understood for simple crystals, and because the metallurgists at Bell had developed ways to produce very pure germanium crystals and to introduce impurities to close specifications, the work of the semiconductor research group focused on germanium at the start and later broadened to include silicon. During 1945 and 1946 much additional experience was gained in growing crystals, quite a bit was learned about semiconductor impurities, and rectification was studied. During the early years of the project research interest was quite diffuse. Considerable work, however, was focused on a solid-state amplifier.

At the early stages of the effort at Bell, Shockley's ideas on possible ways to make amplifiers shifted from placing a grid in the area of rectification (the strict analog of the vacuum triode) to influencing the number of movable electrons in a semiconductor (and hence the current flow) with an electric field imposed from the outside without actually touching the material. Shockley's calculations, based in large part on his developing extension of the Wilson model, indicated that a device based on the latter idea would amplify. Experiments were devised (in 1946 and 1947) to see if the gadget worked as theory indicated it should. It did not. Sometimes even the sign of the effect was off. When the sign was right the magnitude of the effect was roughly a thousandth of the theoretical effect.

To explain the negative result Bardeen proposed that the electrons affected by the field were not free inside the silicon, but were trapped at the surface in what he called surface states. Thus the application of an electric field would not significantly affect the number of free charge carriers in the semiconductor. Other scientists, including Shockley himself, had previously suggested the possibility of surface states at the free surface of a solid, but no one had realized the importance of this phenomenon to the properties of semiconductors. Bardeen's theory very effectively explained failure of amplification in the field effect experiments and also significantly increased understanding of rectification at the junction of a semiconductor and a metal (cat's whiskers), but for our purposes it is not necessary to describe the theory.

What is important for our purposes is that, to test the Bardeen theory and to attempt to find a way to neutralize the surface states so that a useful field effect amplifier could be built, Shockley, Bardeen, and Brattain, often with the collaboration of others in the group performed a number of experiments. The physical phenomena involved seem to have drawn a great deal of interest.

A set of experiments by Bardeen and Brattain play the key role in our story. These experiments did yield observed amplification from a field effect. But more important, in one of the experiments two contacts were placed quite close together on a germanium crystal (Figure 7.1). It does not matter

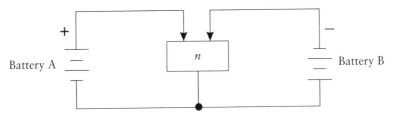

Figure 7.1

here just why this particular experiment was performed. What is significant is that it was not performed with the hope of observing the most important result it yielded. For in the course of the experiment it was observed that connecting up the A battery increased the current flow in the B battery circuit. The device amplified. This was the first indication of the transistor effect.

The research workers were very well aware of the importance of their discovery. Experiments motivated, in part at least, by a desire to make a field effect amplifier work had resulted in the discovery of an amplifier working on quite different principles, an amplifier which, as it was developed and perfected in subsequent work, came to be called a "point contact" transistor.

The most obvious explanation for the current flow increase in the B circuit induced by connecting the A circuit was hole flow from the left top contact to the right top contact. The key concept in the modern explanation is the flow of minority carriers in a crystal, holes in n type germanium. Although the latter was not seen immediately, gradually it came to be accepted.

This description of the discovery of the point contact transistor in late 1947 and very early 1948 is too neat and simple, and the outline of the development of the ideas which explained it is much too orderly to be accurate. Indeed, there still is no really adequate quantitative theory explaining the working of the point contact transistor. But what is important for us is that the experiments were conducted by men who had amplification as their goal, who observed something that they were not looking for or expecting which indicated the possibility of building an amplifier of a design very different from the one they had in mind, and who explained the working of this new amplifier in terms of injected minority carriers.

For the observation that minority carriers are important in semiconductor current flow provided the key which enabled Shockley to propose still another design for an amplifier, a junction transistor. Thus the field effect ex-

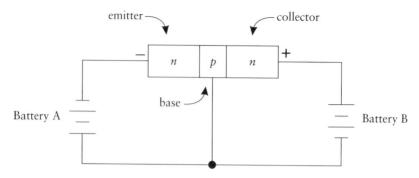

Figure 7.2

periments led to two amplifier designs. They led directly to the point contact transistor and, through theory, to the junction transistor.

The Junction Transistor. Shockley spent most of 1949 writing his *Electrons and Holes in Semiconductors*. Much of the book is a contribution to theoretical physics, but in it he describes the principles of the junction transistor. Unlike the point contact transistor which, as we have seen, was invented partially by accident, the junction transistor was predicted theoretically and then built. Essentially the theory was the invention.

An *n-p-n* junction transistor consists of a germanium or silicon crystal with two *n* regions separated by a thin *p* region (Figure 7.2). The contacts to the *n*, *p*, and *n* layers are referred to as the emitter terminal, the base terminal, and the collector terminal. Shockley showed that an increase in the voltage across the A circuit would lead to an increase in the flow of electrons between the emitter and the collector, the electrons flowing right through the central *p* region. And he showed that, for appropriate battery biases, the resulting change in voltage across the B circuit would exceed the inducing change across the A circuit. Or, the transistor would amplify.

Notice that minority carriers, electrons flowing through the *p* type base region (injected from the *n* type emitter region), are of crucial importance to the working of the junction transistor. If only holes could conduct in *p* type germanium, then the transistor would not work. As we have seen, it took the semiaccidental discovery of the point contact transistor to focus attention on minority carriers. Until the experiments which resulted in the point contact transistor, Shockley did not see clearly that they were important. But once he did, he soon could see that an *n-p-n* junction connected as in Figure 7.2 would amplify.

Research after the Discovery of the Transistor Effect. The discovery of the transistor effect and the consequent invention of the point contact and junction transistors acted to focus much more closely the interests of the semiconductor research group. Funds for this group came from the broader solid-state research group budget, and although the budget of the solid-state group was not dramatically increased for a year or so, it appears that the proportion of the research effort of the Shockley-Morgan group which was directed to semiconductor research definitely increased. Further, a special semiconductor development group under J. A. Morton was organized shortly after the birth of the point contact transistor. And the allocation of research in metallurgy definitely was affected.

Within the semiconductor research group Shockley, as we have seen, directed his attention to working out the theory of holes and electrons in semiconductors. Others directed their experimental and theoretical work to minority carriers. Since an effective amplifier of the junction design requires very pure and orderly crystals, people in Shockley's group, as well as in Morton's group and in metallurgy, intensified their research on this problem. Methods for pulling single crystals from a melt of germanium were developed by G. K. Teal and J. B. Little, and a method known as zone refining was invented by W. G. Pfann. During 1949 and 1950 better and better junction transistors were made, and the construction of a reliable junction transistor is conventionally dated 1951.

It should be stressed here that the breakthrough in knowledge about semiconductors led to the research and development of several other devices in addition to the transistor. The theory led directly to the development of better rectifiers and thermoelectric devices. Parametric amplifiers, amplifiers quite different from the transistors, rest on the principles treated by Shockley's theory. The Bell solar battery, developed a bit later, also rests on the theory. Although many of the new semiconductor devices were invented in laboratories other than Bell, Bell Laboratories has continued to be in the forefront of semiconductor developments. Thus, though the transistor breakthrough tended for a while to draw together the interests of the semiconductor research group, the new theory carried within itself the seeds of subsequent research diversification. The application and value of the theory and the new light it shed on semiconductors far exceeded its specific application to junction transistors.

The years 1948 and 1951 are given as the dates when hand-built point contact and junction transistors were first publicly demonstrated. But generally—and the transistor is no exception—the road is long and difficult between the first demonstrator model of a new invention and a reliable, producible, economic product. In the early days of the transistor, its performance was likely to change if someone slammed a door. All transistors used were laboriously constructed by hand. No one quite knew in what uses the transistor would prove economic.

Much money and talent were spent in improving the operating characteristics of transistors and making them more predictable and reliable, in developing new circuits and designs to take advantage of the transistor's strong points, and in developing an economic production technology. More money has been spent at the Bell Telephone Laboratories on these problems than was spent on the project which was described in the preceding section, but this is beyond our story.

Nature of the Research Activity

Although one case study is insufficient support for confident generalization, in this section I will attempt to sketch certain characteristics of the transistor research history which seem to have relevance to the policy decisions of an organization undertaking basic research.[5] Some implications of these characteristics will be very briefly examined in the introduction to the section treating the actual research policies of the Bell Telephone Laboratories.

Uncertainty and Learning. At the start of the semiconductor research project there was considerable uncertainty whether an amplifier could be achieved at all, and if so, what was the best way of achieving it. Shockley believed he could make a solid-state amplifier but was not quite sure how, and several other people were not so optimistic. Because of the great uncertainties involved, much of the research effort was directed toward learning rather than toward the achievement of a specific and well-defined result. Shockley and others, however, certainly hoped to achieve an amplifier and allocated much of their research time accordingly. And the direction of research changed dramatically in response to what was learned.

To illustrate these points, recall the chronology of the research. At the start of the project much of the semiconductor research was quite generally oriented; only as knowledge accumulated did the amplifier interest tend to predominate. And in the course of the project, three different amplifier designs were considered. In the early stages, almost all amplifier-oriented research was concerned with the field effect amplifier, but this design did not work as hoped and expected. Indeed, the results of the critical experiments in this area were sufficiently unexpected that a new theory had to be formulated to explain them—Bardeen's theory of surface states. The allocation of experimental effort was shifted to check the theory. The second amplifier design, the point contact, was discovered as a more or less surprising result of the surface-state experiments. Further, in order to explain the results of the experiments, attention turned to minority carriers, and once the importance of minority carriers was clearly realized, Shockley was able to design a junction amplifier. Thus only toward the end of the project was the design which has proved most successful clearly perceived.

This last point needs to be stressed. There never seems to have been an attempt to list all research alternatives and to pick the best on the basis of some formal calculation. Rather, the *discovery* of new ideas and alternatives occurred often in the program. It does not seem an adequate representation to say that what was learned from the surface-state experiments made the junction transistor a more promising alternative. Before the experiments, the path to an amplifier by way of junctions and minority carriers just was not clearly perceived.

Interaction. A number of different people with different skills contributed to the research, but the exact nature of the interaction could not have been predicted and planned for in advance. Bardeen's analysis of surface states and Brattain's experimental skill were key factors, but no one at the start of the program could have predicted that these particular experiments would be performed, much less the importance of the results. Throughout the course of the program there seems to have been a great deal of informal exchange of ideas, and quite a bit of cooperation on experimental work.

The major requirements for effective interaction seem to have been easy communication and the ability of individuals to drop what they were doing to help with problems their colleagues brought up, if these problems seemed interesting and important. There is little evidence of closely programmed and directed team work, or of any requirement for it. Unfortunately, I have not been able to uncover much in the way of specific examples to illustrate these points.

Goals. As we have seen, the research program was not justified in its early stages by prospects for the invention of a specific device. Indeed, the early project reports do not even mention amplifiers. Instead the purpose of the project is stated in the early reports as the advancement of knowledge about semiconductors. Of course, this does not mean that the research workers, themselves, had no ideas about possible specific practical results; they certainly did. An amplifier was one. Rectifiers and thermoelectric devices were others. But these devices were listed in the early project reports as "for instances" of the possible practical payoffs. And, as we have seen, the research did in fact lead to a number of technical advances in addition to the transistor.

Research Management at the Bell Telephone Laboratories

The Problems of Research Management

This section will examine the way that basic research decisions are made at the Bell Telephone Laboratories. But first it seems worthwhile to discuss very briefly a few of the implications, with respect to research policy, of the characteristics of basic research sketched in the preceding section.

Given the resources an industrial laboratory intends to allocate to basic research, there are a vast number of projects to which laboratory personnel can be allocated. Clearly somehow some of these projects must be selected and the number of persons working on them decided. The nature of basic research imposes serious constraints on the policies the laboratory can pursue in making these decisions.

Criteria. In order that some projects be selected and others rejected, some criteria must be used. The choice of good criteria must rest on the realization that a successful basic research project promises major advances in scientific understanding and that major advances in scientific understanding are likely to stimulate a wide range of practical inventions, though just what these technical advances will be it is very difficult to specify in advance. A project which is likely to have payoffs in a wide range of applications should not be justified on the basis of any one in particular, especially if it is not at all clear that the specific objective selected will be achieved. Indeed, for many organizations it just does not make very good sense to sponsor basic research at all. The outcomes of most basic research efforts are too unpredictable for a firm with a small range of products and processes to have confidence that the results will be of use to it. But if the range of products and technology is wide, the firm may have some confidence that the results will be of practical value.

Perhaps it can be assumed, as a first approximation, that for a company with a wide technological base there is a high correlation between the value to the company of the technical advances generated by research and the scientific advances achieved by research. Certainly there are major qualifications to this. Probably the criterion should be amended by the requirement that the area of research be one where applications to the technology of the company seem quite possible. But for a company with a wide enough technological base to support basic research at all, the criterion of "scientific promise" is probably better than one that stresses the value of specific predicted practical inventions.

The criterion "scientific promise," subjective though it may be, does seem operational. Recall that before the start of the transistor work a number of scientists agreed that the time was ripe for major advances in knowledge of semiconductors. And the restriction that the research be in fields where applications to company technology seem possible also is operational. Recall that scientists were able to list a number of applications which might result from a major breakthrough in knowledge of semiconductors, and many of their prophecies were fulfilled.

Authority. But who is to apply the criterion? Who is to decide which scientists will work on which projects? For reasons which will be discussed later, that criterion, if adopted, argues for a decentralized decision-making structure. And the nature of the basic research activity, the changing knowledge which is the scientific goal of research, also argues against centralization. Further, the type of interaction we have noted in the transistor project requires that individuals be free to help one another as they see fit. If all allocation decisions were made by a centrally situated executive, the changing allocation of research effort called for as perceived alternatives and knowledge change would place an impossible information processing and decision-making burden on top management. Clearly the research scientists must be given a great deal of freedom, and the type of decision which must be cleared through a central authority must be quite limited.

It is earnestly hoped that the preceding discussion, and the study of Bell Laboratories which follows, is more than a pious restatement of the old saws, "scientific knowledge in itself pays off" and "in research, freedom is good." It is true that I believe the theme generally is valid. However, I trust that this essay sheds a little more light on why it is valid, and what its limitations are. In particular, it is clear that a policy involving decentralized decision making (research freedom), and the acceptance of the criterion of scientific promise must somehow be complemented by policies designed to constrain research to those areas where application to the technology of the company seems promising.

Bell has developed policies which seem to cope with this problem adequately. There is evidence that several other companies noted for their success in basic research management have similar policies.

Research Policy of the Bell Telephone Laboratories

The research philosophy of the Bell Telephone Laboratories has been stated succinctly by James B. Fisk, president of the Laboratories. "Our fundamental belief is that there is no difference between good science and good science relevant to our business. Among a thousand scientific problems, a hundred or so will be interesting, but only one or two will be truly rewarding—both to the world of science and to us. What we try to provide is the atmosphere that will make selecting the one or two in a thousand a matter of individual responsibility and essentially automatic." There are two aspects, then, to Bell's policy toward research. First, scientific worth is assumed to be highly correlated with potential technical value. And second, the individual scientist is to be free to choose the projects he considers of greatest interest. In short, the management philosophy of Bell Laboratories corresponds to the one we have just stated. How does this policy work out in practice? How serious are the problems introduced by the possible divergence of individual scientific interests from the interests of Bell Laboratories? How does Bell cope with the problem? As we shall see, the policy is not quite as simple and clear-cut as it seems. The fact that Bell is in the communications business does play a very major role in determining the type of research that is undertaken.

Freedom of Research Choice.   It is well to dwell a bit here on what is meant by freedom in research. Freedom clearly involves a range of alternatives among which choice can be made but, equally clearly, the range of alternatives in any real situation is constrained in many ways. The training of the research scientist, the equipment available to him, the state of knowledge in the field in which he is interested, all are constraints on his choice. The imagination of the research scientist, of his peers in the laboratory, and of research management also affect the range of his perceived alternatives.

If we use the expression "degree of research freedom" to mean the extent to which constraints are imposed upon the range of choice open to a research scientist as a matter of company policy, then from the point of view of the company it is rational to give the research scientist wide freedom of choice if it is believed that he will tend to do more valuable work, on the average, if he selects his projects as he sees fit than if some higher authority provides him with a much more constrained range of choice. In a way, the arguments for freedom of choice for the research scientist resemble and rest on the same assumptions as the arguments for a free enterprise economic system do.

Let us assume for the moment that institutional arrangements and the system of incentives are such that individual and group aims coincide. This is one of the prerequisites for research freedom, but it is not enough. In addition it must be assumed that the individual has more information about the choices open to him—their relative prospects and their costs—than a central authority has. Usually this assumption is violated in situations where there is strong interdependence among the actions of a large number of different individuals. Where there is such interdependence one person's decision should be made in the light of knowledge about what everyone else is doing. This is the kind of information that a central executive has, but that, if the number of people involved is large, the individual may not have. However, in basic research it seems that the number of persons among whom coordination is required is small at any one time, and the individual scientist is likely to know quite well what his colleagues are doing. In the transistor project this kind of knowledge was facilitated by the policy of bringing most of the scientists doing semiconductor research into one group. And as to the promise of his own line of research, the working scientist is likely to know much more than the laboratory management possibly can know.

Philosophers and Gestalt psychologists have argued convincingly that people do not observe the same things unless those things are in the same context, and at the frontiers of science what is missing is a clear context. A scientist working on a research project often has a "feel" for the promise of his work but is not capable of expressing his intuition, his embryonic theory, in language. Others working in the same area may have the same feel, but often not. Yet one of the marks of a good scientist is that his hunches prove right. The approaches he sees as promising but which he cannot in the beginning describe precisely blossom into useful hypotheses and concept schemes. Often, after the fact, he can state clearly a plausible reason why he thought his work promising when he started it, and why he did things the way he did. But it is more than likely that, if you had queried him ex ante, he would not have given such a good set of reasons for why he was doing what he was doing and why he felt it important. If this point of view is accepted, a research director is likely to be a much poorer judge than the scientist working on a project is of the scientific promise of the project. The scientist has information that the research director cannot have, and much of the information is not in a solid enough form to permit easy communication.

Allocation of Resources.   Given the nature of scientific research, and an organization where individual scientists have a wide degree of freedom, the allocation of the scientific staff among competing alternatives is likely to be accomplished by an evolutionary, or a natural selection, process. We have argued that uncertainty and learning are key aspects of research. Consider a laboratory at a moment of time. Scientists are working on many research projects at many different stages. Some research work has been running for a long time and many of the original objectives have been achieved. Some research work started but a short time ago is looking quite unpromising already. But some research work which has just started is looking extremely promising and interesting, and some research work is producing new answers, new prospects, and new questions. An alert scientist working on a project which is looking increasingly unpromising or on a project which appears to be running into sharply diminishing returns has very strong incentives—his professional reputation, his scientific curiosity, and his future at the laboratories—to phase out his current work and phase in research in a more promising area—a new project or a going project which has exciting prospects.

The above description sounds very much like the economist's model of a changing economy. Some industries are dying and others are thriving. An astute entrepreneur spurred by a higher expected return will leave the dying industry and enter the thriving industry. And, as in the economist's picture of a changing economy, luck plays a great role. The structure of economic demand may change again, and the dull entrepreneur who sticks with the industry his more alert colleague thought declining will ex post have been shown to be the wiser. Meanwhile the alert entrepreneur may find that the skills he applied in the old industry are of little use in the new. And in the laboratory, as in the economy, there are transfer costs. The scientist who jumps from project to project, like the entrepreneur who jumps from industry to industry, may be not very wise.

However, the analogy is weak when incentives and signals are compared. In the economist's model of the market economy, perceived profit opportunities are viewed as the prime motive, and cost and demand are the factors determining profit. Cost and demand are assumed to be clearly signaled by the structure of prices. The incentives of the scientist are much more complex than the incentives of the entrepreneur of economic theory; though perhaps they are no more complex than the incentives of the entrepreneurs of real life. The furthering of a reputation as a scientist among scientists and the satisfaction of intellectual curiosity are certainly as important, perhaps more important, dimensions of the research worker's goals as are financial advance and status within an organization.

Other Advantages of Decentralization. In addition to allocating research scientists among alternative projects, the mechanism described above seems especially well suited for generating new ideas, projects, and alternatives. Even if the performance of the mechanism in allocating men among known alternatives was believed to be far from optimal, this latter attribute would be a strong argument for research freedom. It is quite likely that it is even more important to the success of a laboratory for it to generate good new ideas than it is for it to allocate very efficiently its resources among a given set of alternatives.

Decision making by evolution, in addition to providing greater flexibility and speed than would be possible under a more formal and centralized structure, has another extremely important advantage. The traditions of the scientific community are extremely strong where freedom to pursue research interests is concerned. To be told just what line of research to follow—to have it made clear that the goal of the research is company profit, not increased knowledge or benefit to mankind—to realize all too plainly that a few individual supervisors, not a wide jury of scientific peers, are to evaluate the work—strikes hard at the traditions of science. Since World War II there seems to have been a striking reduction in the intensity with which scientists cling to these traditions. But their force is still strong, and many of the most outstanding scientists feel that to engage in industrial research would prostitute their heritage.

The Bell Telephone Laboratories, perhaps more than any other industrial laboratory, has avoided establishing a decision and control system which would run against the traditions of the scientific community. For this reason the Laboratories have a great advantage, relative to similar institutions, in recruiting people. Many scientists who would work in no other industrial laboratory, will work at Bell. This fact explains the extremely high quality of the laboratory staff that Bell has managed to maintain. Bell salaries are not particularly high by industrial laboratory standards.

Because a scientist at the Laboratories is not forced to abandon the traditions of the scientific community, Bell scientists tend to maintain very strong links with the academic world. Many Bell scientists have taught at universities, and many Bell scientists are actively sought by university faculties. The quantity and quality of Bell's scientific publications is matched only by the best of universities.

In the work which led to the transistor, Shockley, Bardeen, and others were in close touch with members of the university community working in the field of solid-state physics. There were visits and many letters. Clearly, this close link with the mainstream of the scientific community is of major importance to the Laboratories for the flow both of ideas and of men.

Management Controls: Environment and Employment. Although as a broad generalization it may be reasonable to argue that the scientific merit of a project is a good index of potential profit, clearly, from the point of view of the company, advances in some areas of science are likely to be much more profitable than advances in other areas of science. The argument that the results of research are uncertain does not imply that these areas cannot be specified. Thus from the point of view of Bell Laboratories, advances in knowledge of the magnetic properties of material are almost certain to prove more important than advances in botany, and probably more important than advances in organic chemistry. At the start of the semiconductor research project it was clear that if there were significant scientific breakthroughs, the payoffs for communications equipment would be great.

Further, though basic research projects should not be justified in terms of specific practical objectives, we have seen from the case of the transistor that it is sometimes possible to perceive certain practical advances which may result from research. And from the point of view of the company, these objectives should be given some weight in research project selection.

Clearly it is in the interests of the company to have procedures for guiding research so that the most promising areas of science are stressed, and so that practical objectives are not completely suppressed in the research project selection mechanism. The Bell Telephone Laboratories are in the communications industry, and the research work undertaken there reflects this fact, though the research scientists are subject to few, if any, more constraints than their university peers.

Areas of Research.   There are no geneticists working at the Laboratories. There are few organic chemists. At present (though this may be changed shortly) there is no group working in nuclear physics. In 1946 there was but a handful of men at Bell who were working in the field of solid-state physics. Today there are many more. While the choice of the research area of the scientists in the research department is seldom subject to strong executive pressure, formal executive decisions strongly affect the allocation of research effort through the hiring process. The growing promise of the research work in the field of semiconductors definitely strengthened the force of Shockley's requests for more people to work with him. And though "promising" is a difficult word to define in this context, prospects for improving communications equipment certainly do not hurt the promise of an area of research.

The decision to hire or not to hire new researchers certainly does not rest exclusively on evaluation of prospects for advances in different fields applicable to communications technology, but the areas of scientific research which are growing at Bell Laboratories are in general those in which significant advances are expected to have some application to communications technology. And as we have seen, changes in prospects are generated in the course of research activity itself. The striking success of the rather small semiconductor research group led to an expansion in the number of solid-state scientists working at Bell (as well as to an increase in the proportion of the veteran Bell staff interested in and working in solid-state physics). Thus the composition of Bell's scientific staff makes the starting of research work in a field not related to communications technology unusual.

But what happens when a member of the research staff at Bell, hired because at that time he was doing work in a field of interest to the company, becomes interested in a new field (as he sometimes does)? Several factors must be considered here. First, few at the Laboratories will be so rash as to state that research in a particular area of science certainly will not result in knowledge of use in the design of communications systems. Of course, this is not to say that certain areas are not considered much more promising than others. Second, the best way to find out whether a new area of science looks promising is to do some work in the area. Third, a policy of applying strong formal pressure to dissuade a scientist from working in a certain area would, if used as a matter of course, undermine the general philosophy of research direction at Bell which has proved so successful in the past, and further, would tend to make the Laboratories a much less attractive place to top-flight scientists. Therefore laboratory policy is to avoid pressuring someone not to work in an area of interest to him.

If the new work of an individual proves of significant interest, both scientifically and in possible communications applications, then it is likely that others in the laboratory will also initiate work in the field, and that people from the outside will be brought in. Thus a new area of laboratory research will be started. If the work does not prove of interest to the Laboratories, eventually the individual in question will be requested to return to the fold, or leave. It is hoped that pressure can be informal. There seems to be no consensus about how long to let someone wander, but it is clear that young and newly hired scientists are kept under closer rein than the more senior scientists. However even top-flight people, like Jansky, have been asked to change their line of research. But, in general, the experience has been that informal pressures together with the hiring policy are sufficient to keep AT&T and Western Electric more than satisfied with the output of research.

Interest in Devices. The hiring process is also an important mechanism for keeping the laboratory alert to the possibilities for new devices. The Bell Telephone Laboratories tend to attract scientists who are also interested in devices. Shockley is a case in point. Further, problems relating to practical devices are often very interesting ones. Bardeen and Brattain found the problem of why Shockley's field effect amplifier did not work extremely exciting as a scientific one. And results worthwhile from the purest scientific point of view came from their efforts to explain the failure of the amplifier. The fact that the research department is housed in the same building with the development and systems engineering departments also seems important in keeping the research people alert to the device needs of the Telephone Company. There are many interdepartmental seminars and formal talks. But perhaps informal contact is the most important link.

Device consciousness on the part of the research staff can lead to a serious misallocation of research effort if device-oriented work is permitted to cut back sharply the effort directed toward advancing scientific knowledge. For this reason, though the research scientists are encouraged to be device conscious, laboratory policy discourages research people from working on a device beyond the building of a simple working model.

Thus, early in 1948, very shortly after the discovery of the point contact transistor, a development group under the direction of J. A. Morton was established. By 1950 there were more people engaged in development work than in research. The ultimate role of Morton's group was to create new devices for the systems development groups to use in creating new systems for Bell Telephone and for the military. The early objectives of the development group were to improve the point contact amplifier, to examine and test a wide range of possible applications, and to produce a number of transistors to achieve these purposes. Later the development group began to concern itself with problems of cost.

But the research group that created the transistor did not participate in this work. The history of the solid-state research group after the transistor experiments is a good illustration of the evolutionary allocation mechanism which has been described. In 1951, with the advances achieved in junction transistors, the solid-state physics group began to grow rapidly, and in addition to the work on the junction transistor and underlying physics, work in other areas was intensified. As germanium and silicon were better understood, research in that area ran into diminishing returns and research on more complex semiconductors grew more promising. Similarly, research on magnetics and dielectrics was increased. In 1952 a separate transistor physics department was organized, headed by Shockley. Semiconductors research, once a subsection headed by Shockley under the solid-state physics group of Shockley and Morgan, which in turn was under physical research, is now a separate major department.

There is a limit to what can be learned from one case study. Generalizations are hazardous. But it seems worthwhile to speculate on aspects of industrial research that have been the subject of much public interest.

"Teamwork" in Research

Much of the recent literature on industrial research has stressed the "team" aspect of this activity.[6] Many writers have expressed sharp discomfort with the idea of the research team, and have argued that industrial research which stresses teamwork is likely to be scientifically arid. As I have emphasized before, the transistor is just one case, but nonetheless it seems worthwhile to examine what teamwork meant in the case of the transistor.

First of all, we have seen that it meant interaction and mutual stimulation and help. Shared intense interest in the general field, ease of communication, differences in the viewpoints and experience of different scientists—these elements naturally call for interaction and make interaction fruitful for scientific advance. The purpose of bringing together the people doing work in solid-state physics was to achieve this end, and from the history of the project it seems that the close interaction of several people definitely contributed to the advance achieved. But several people outside the team also interacted in an important way. In particular, the metallurgists' work in developing ways to produce pure crystals was both an important link at many places in the chain of research and an activity in large part stimulated by the solid-state research effort of the team.

Second, we have seen that teamwork in the case of the transistor did not mean a closely directed project with an assigned division of labor in the form of tasks and schedules for each of the team members. There were no closely defined goals shared by all members of the group. All were interested in understanding semiconductors, but, at least at the start, all were not excited by amplifiers. The project was marked by flexibility—by the ability to shift directions and by the rather rapid focusing of attention by several people on problems and phenomena unearthed by others.

Third, we have seen that teamwork in the case of the transistor did mean a more concentrated effort than probably would have developed had the individuals involved not been brought together in one group. Shockley's interest in amplifiers definitely tended to draw the research interests of the group toward his focus. The research work of the transistor team, despite its very loose formal structure, was definitely affected by the fact that the members were working very closely together. In the case of the transistor this pulling together of interests proved extremely fruitful. Yet in many cases a more diversified attack might prove rewarding.

One wonders whether an invention like the transistor, which came about as a direct result of an advance in scientific theory, ever can be a team effort, if invention refers to a basic idea, and team refers to a group of people whose work is closely coordinated and planned by a team leader. It appears that the type of coordination required in an organization emphasizing fundamental science and the practical devices that might be created from advances in fundamental science is achieved quite effectively without planned coordination of effort and central control. Indeed it seems unlikely that a more formal control structure would be flexible enough to achieve anything like the type of coordination that marked the work of the research group on semiconductors. No one could have predicted the course of new knowledge or planned ahead to ensure the right type of help at the right time. The informality of the decision structure played a very important role in permitting speedy cooperative response to changing ideas and knowledge. Thus the transistor was a team invention, but not in the sense of the term which has grown fashionable in recent years.

The Role of the Large Corporation

In contrast to the public dismay about "teamwork" in research, many people have argued that the research laboratories of the large corporation are the only possible source of such inventions as the transistor. To what extent is an invention like the transistor dependent upon a sponsoring organization like the Bell Telephone Laboratories? How did the size of the Laboratories and the size of the corporations owning the Laboratories affect the project? Could the transistor have been developed at a significantly different institution, say, a laboratory owned by a much smaller company? My feeling is that devices like the transistor, based on fundamental new scientific knowledge, can come from small industrial laboratories or from universities, but that a large industrial laboratory like Bell does have a comparative advantage in this business.

The ingredients which seem to have played such an important role in the success of the semiconductor research project include the close interaction of a group of top-flight scientists, a great deal of freedom in the course of research, and an extremely strong interest on the part of at least one member of the group in inventing a practical device. This is high-priced talent at work, and when the project was initiated no guarantees were given as to the profits which would result. And for about two years before the transistor was invented, the group was kept free from pressure to produce practical results. This is not the type of project a small industrial laboratory is likely to be able to afford.

On the other hand, a university with strong science departments would have the resources to support work like the semiconductor research project. During World War II, and for a time after the war, work was going on at Purdue University under Lark-Horowitz which might have led to the transistor. The idea that an amplifier could be constructed from semiconductors was quite widely held by people working in the field. But, if my interpretation of the Bell project is correct, device-minded scientists are essential if a laboratory is to develop devices such as the transistor. Shockley's theory, on which rests the design of the junction transistor, was in large part motivated by the desire to design a transistor. Further, it seems likely that if the identical theory had been developed by someone not interested in amplification, it would have taken some time for another worker to see that an amplifier could be designed on the basis of the theory. The popular image of the university scientist is that of a pure scholar, not interested in practical devices. If all university scientists were so, universities could hardly be the source of inventions like the transistor. For better or for worse, many university scientists do not fit that image, but are quite interested in devices. It is my feeling that the university with strong science departments, including scientists with a major interest in devices—not the laboratory of the small industrial corporation—is the major alternative source to the large industrial laboratory for inventions like the transistor.

Economic Factors Affecting the Direction of Scientific Research

It has often been argued that the rate and direction of advance in pure science must be considered as an autonomous factor in any theory of the factors affecting the rate and direction of inventive activity. And it is likely that any analysis describing the motives of the scientists who played the key roles in advancing quantum mechanics (Bohr, de Broglie, Schrödinger, Heisenberg, Pauli, Dirac, and others) as involving, in an important way, prospects for advancing practical technology, would be farfetched. But this case study has shown that the laboratories of large corporations may be effective institutions for drawing scientific research to areas where the importance of practical advances is great. And recall that the science of thermodynamics was, in large part, called forth by the development of steam engines, not vice versa. Advances in technology itself certainly affect the direction of scientific research.

The tremendous increase in the number of students taking undergraduate and graduate training in solid-state physics clearly has been strongly influenced by improved income prospects resulting from the increased use of solid-state physicists in industry and government sponsored research and development. This is not the whole explanation. Solid-state physics is much more scientifically fashionable now than it was. But even what is "fashionable" is strongly affected by applications. Since the birth of the transistor the proportion of articles relating to solid-state physics has significantly increased, and many scientists believe that the correlated change in the allocation of research effort was, in considerable part, due to the invention of the transistor and the consequence spotlighting of the field. Of course the same statements could be made about nuclear physics and the bomb. The direction of scientific advance is not independent of economic and practical factors.

What Is Basic Research?

One of the most important things which can be learned from the history of the transistor is that the distinction between basic research and applied research is fuzzy. In the transistor project the results included both an advance in fundamental physical knowledge and the invention and improvement of practical devices. The scientists involved, though many of them were not interested in devices, were able to predict roughly the nature of the practical advances; indeed in some instances they were able to predict quite closely. And several of the scientists were motivated by the hope both of scientific advance and of practical advance. Thus the project was marked by duality of results and of motives. Yet by the standards of the National Science Foundation the Bell semiconductor research work most certainly would be considered basic research.

I have a feeling that duality of interests and results is far from unusual. I wonder how many scientists—university scientists—doing basic research do not think now and then about the possible practical applications of their work. I wonder how many are completely uninfluenced in their choice of research by consideration of possible practical benefit to mankind? By posing these questions I am not implying that the answer to both is "none." But the answer may be "only a small proportion."

I have the feeling that many scientists in industrial research laboratories, including—perhaps, particularly including—those with considerable executive authority, are defensive and internally torn about the dual nature of the research work. Unlike the management of most other industrial laboratories, the administration at the Bell Telephone Laboratories is strongly imbued with a belief in the value of fundamental research to the telephone company and with the understanding that people doing fundamental research, to be effective, must be kept free from day-to-day practical problems. Since the telephone laboratories were among the first industrial laboratories to undertake fundamental research, and since Bell's record has been so outstanding, the organization likes to toot its horn now and then. People in the Laboratories like to stress the extent to which much of their research is fundamental, and how fundamental research yields big payoffs. When it is suggested that much of the fundamental research is not conducted with "pure" motives, there is a tendency to get defensive, for the scientific community has long been accustomed to separate fundamental research from applied research on the basis of purity of motive. If research is conducted solely to advance man's knowledge it is fundamental; if it is conducted to help achieve a practical objective, it is applied, and somehow less intellectually respectable. And many people at Bell who are defenders of the fundamental research program are cut on this intellectual saw.

Shockley, however, suffers from no such intellectual split. In his Nobel lecture he states, "Frequently, I have been asked if an experiment I have planned is pure or applied science; to me it is more important to know if the experiment will yield new and probably enduring knowledge about nature. If it is likely to yield such knowledge, it is, in my opinion, good fundamental research; and this is more important than whether the motivation is purely esthetic satisfaction on the part of the experimenter on the one hand or the improvement of the stability of a high-power transistor on the other." Much of the history of science bears out Shockley's view. Some of the greatest scientific advances resulted from the research of men who were much concerned with the practical implications of their work, and their work was in large part motivated by the desire to benefit mankind.

The fuzzy nature of the boundary between basic and applied research does not imply, however, that some projects are not clearly more basic than others. Nor does it imply that there are no important distinctions between the industrial research laboratory and the university laboratory. Basic research undertaken at industrial laboratories must somehow be related to expected company profit. And many of the greatest scientists have taken pride in the "purity" of their research motives and in the apracticality of fundamental science. Much of the foundation of modern physics was laid by individuals who chose science as a career in part because it offered an escape from the materialistic world. Although they were often able to predict roughly the practical implications of their research, such practical aspects were unimportant, or even repugnant, to them. For these scientists the industrial research laboratory would seem a poor home. An industrial laboratory is not and probably should not be the equivalent of a university science department. It is risky to speculate how much of the "pure" research conducted at universities is "purer" than the "pure" research conducted at the Telephone Laboratories, but I believe that Einstein would have been unhappy at Bell, and Bell would be most unhappy if most of their research scientists were as intellectually pure as Einstein. It is probably best for all that this is so.

Epilogue

The Bell Telephone Laboratories, as described above as of 1960, are no more. One can argue that the breaking up of the AT&T monopoly has had a positive effect over the last fifteen years on telephone service and prices in the United States. At the same time, one can look at the old Bell Telephone Laboratories as they operated in their heyday, and posit that society is the worse off for their loss.

American Universities and Technical Advance in Industry

1. Introduction

Over the last decade, debate over the role of American universities in fostering technical advance has intensified. On the one side are those who argue that universities can and should play a larger and more direct role in assisting industry. Such enterprises as Stanford's Center for Integrated Systems, and hundreds of centers like it around the country, show a cluster of firms and a university attempting to make their connections more intimate and more effective (Government-University-Industry-Research Roundtable, 1986). The percentage of academic research funded by industry was estimated to be about 6.9 percent in 1990, up considerably from 3.9 percent a decade earlier (National Science Foundation, 1991). In a recent study Cohen, Florida, and Goe [1993] estimate that 19 percent of university research is now carried out in programs that involve linkages with industry in a fundamental way. The federal government, through such programs as the Engineering Research Centers sponsored by the National Science Foundation, and a large number of state-supported programs have strongly supported these developments. Much of the discrepancy between 6.9 percent and 19 percent in the figures reported above is accounted for by governmental support of these programs.

On the other side, many academics and others see these developments as a threat to the integrity of academic research. They despair that greater involvement with industry and commerce will corrupt academic research and teaching, divert attention away from fundamental research, and potentially destroy the openness of communication among university scientists that is such an essential component of academic research.

By Nathan Rosenberg and Richard R. Nelson; originally published in *Research Policy* 23 (1994): 323–348.

It is striking, however, that the present discussion focuses so closely on the here and now; there is very little examination of the roles traditionally played by American universities or of how these roles have evolved. Nor is there even much probing into the nature of the academic research enterprise as we know it today, or of the differences between academic and industrial R&D, or of the connections between universities and industry that are in place. Thus the current debate is proceeding with surprisingly little grounding in what actually is going on now, and why and how we arrived at our present predicament.

A principal purpose of this essay, therefore, is to lay out the history of involvement of American universities in research that has been germane to industry, and the different kinds of connections that have existed between university and industry. Section 2 undertakes a historical discussion of these connections through World War II. A very important development that occurred during that period was the rise of engineering disciplines and certain other "applied sciences" as fields of academic research and teaching. This is the topic of section 3. World War II was a watershed for American universities. Before that time the federal government provided little research funding. After the war the federal government became the universities' principal source of research funding. Section 4 discusses this development and its effect on the research efforts of universities and the connections between university research and technological advance. Section 5 considers the division of labor between industrial researchers and academics as it exists today, and the concluding section addresses the current debate.

2. Historical Perspective

Today approximately two-thirds of the research done at American universities is labeled "basic research" (Table 8.5). We shall argue in section 4 that this does *not* mean what many people think it does, that is, that the bulk of university research today proceeds with no ties to nonacademic objectives. In fact, the preponderance of university research today is in fields that, by their nature, are oriented toward facilitating practical problem solving in health, agriculture, defense, and various areas of civil industrial technology. On the other hand, the large fraction of university research that is classified as basic does indicate a certain distancing of much of university research from immediate, "hands-on" practical problem solving.

In this and the following section we will argue that this distancing is a relatively recent phenomenon, although it developed in stages. Several recent historical studies have documented that, until the 1920s or so, for better or for worse, a large share of American university research was very much "hands-on" problem solving (Bruce, 1987; Geiger, 1986).

This is not a new understanding. Over 160 years ago Alexis de Tocqueville commented, not specifically on this, but on the broader issue of the role of science and the attitudes toward science, in the young republic that he visited in the 1830s:

> In America the purely practical part of science is admirably understood and careful attention is paid to the theoretical portion, which is immediately requisite to application. On this head, the Americans always display a clear, free, original, and inventive power of mind. But hardly any one in the United States devotes himself to the essentially theoretical and abstract portion of human knowledge ... every new method which leads by a shorter road to wealth, every machine which spares labor, every instrument which diminishes the cost of production, every discovery which facilitates pleasure or augments them, seems [to such people] to be the grandest effort of the human intellect. It is chiefly from these motives that a democratic people addicts itself to scientific pursuits ... In a community thus organized, it may easily be conceived that the human mind may be led insensibly to the neglect of theory; and that it is urged, on the contrary, with unparalleled energy, to the applications of science, or at least to that portion of theoretical science which is necessary to those who make such applications. (Tocqueville, 1876).

This general orientation to science clearly molded what went on in American universities. Thus Ezra Cornell, founder of Cornell University, stated as his intention: "I would found an institution where any person can find instruction in any study." The quotation still appears on the official seal of his distinguished university.[1] British visitors long sneered at what they perceived as the "vocationalism" of the nineteenth- and early twentieth-century American higher educational system. These educational institutions assumed responsibility for teaching and research in fields such as agriculture and mining, commercial subjects such as accounting, finance, marketing and management, and an ever-widening swath of engineering subjects, civil, mechanical, electrical, chemical, aeronautical, and so on, long before their British counterparts and, in most cases, long before their other European counterparts as well.

There were a number of reasons for this more "practical" orientation. American universities, it has been often observed, emerged in a new country with a culture strongly influenced by the need to vanquish a large, untamed geographic frontier. But there was much more to it than that.

One important additional factor was that the American university system has always been decentralized. There has never been centralized control, as developed in France after Napoleon. Nor, until quite recently, did "scholars" come to dominate the universities, as they did in many European countries. While some "finishing" and religious preparatory schools such as Harvard and Yale were clearly modeled after European institutions, a very large number of schools chose their missions, styles, and focus on the basis of the idiosyncratic needs of the provincial environment. The consequence of this approach was that the funding and enrollment of these schools became heavily dependent on the mores and needs of the local community. And, as Tocqueville indicated, these mores tended strongly to the practical. Further, American higher education has been noticeably more accessible to a wider portion of the population when compared with more class-rigid Europe (see Table 8.1).[2] Where the aristocracy in Europe expressed disdain for "commercial affairs" (and this was reflected in their university curricula), American universities were perceived as a path to commercial as well as personal success, and university research and teaching were focused more clearly on these goals.

The passage of the Morrill Act in 1862 reflected and supported American views about the appropriate roles of university research and teaching. The purpose of the act was eminently practical; it was dedicated to the support of agriculture and the mechanic arts. Moreover, control of universities was left to the states. The long-term prosperity and success of these state institutions was generally understood to depend upon their responsiveness to the demands of the local community. Thus the leadership of state universities was heavily beholden to the needs of local industries and to the priorities established by state legislatures. This responsiveness was particularly apparent in the contributions to the needs of agriculture that were provided by the land-grant colleges and, somewhat later, by the agricultural experiment stations. In general, intellectual innovations were likely to be quickly seized upon and introduced into university curricula, especially at those universities that were publicly supported, as soon as their practical utility was established.

Thus a primary activity of early American universities was the provision of vocational skills for a wide range of professions important to local economies. In many cases the training activities and research concerned with the problems of local industry went together. Not only did the University of Akron supply skilled personnel for the local rubber industry, but it in fact became well known for its research in the processing of rubber. (Later on it achieved distinction in the field of polymer chemistry.) The land-grant colleges (and later the agricultural experiment stations) are rightly praised for fostering the high productivity of the American farm through the teaching

Table 8.1 Average years of formal educational experience of the population aged 15–64

Country	Year	Total	Higher
France	1913	6.18	0.10
	1950	8.18	0.18
	1973	9.58	0.47
	1984	10.79	0.90
Germany	1913	6.94	0.09
	1950	8.51	0.14
	1973	9.31	0.20
	1984	9.48	0.31
Netherlands	1913	6.05	0.11
	1950	7.41	0.24
	1973	8.88	0.39
	1984	9.92	0.58
U.K.	1913	7.28	0.08
	1950	9.40	0.13
	1973	10.24	0.25
	1984	10.92	0.42
U.S.	1913	6.93	0.20
	1950	9.46	0.45
	1973	11.31	0.89
	1984	12.52	1.62

Source: Reprinted from Maddison (1987).

of food production skills. And along with the training went research aimed to meet the needs of the local agricultural community. The Babcock test, developed by an agricultural research chemist at the University of Wisconsin and introduced in 1890, provided a cheap and simple method for measuring the butterfat content of milk, and thus an easy way to determine the adulteration of milk, a matter of no small consequence in a state of dairy farms.

State universities, in general, were likely to have programs addressing a diverse range of needs. After World War I, a college of engineering might offer undergraduate degrees in a bewildering array of specialized engineering subjects. In the case of the University of Illinois, this included architectural engineering, ceramic engineering, mining engineering, municipal and sanitary engineering, railway civil engineering, railway electrical engineering, and railway mechanical engineering. An observer has noted, "Nearly every industry and government agency in Illinois had its own department at the state university in Urbana-Champaign" (Levine, 1986).

While usually connected with training, university research programs aimed to meet the needs of local industry often took on a life of their own, and became institutionalized. We have already mentioned rubber research at the University of Akron. The University of Oklahoma has long distinguished itself for its research in the field of petroleum, and the universities of Kentucky and North Carolina have worked extensively on developing technologies that have been employed in the post-harvest processing of tobacco. For many years the universities of Illinois and Purdue did work on railroad technologies, ranging from the design of locomotive boilers to their maintenance and repair. To this day the Purdue football team is called the "Boilermakers."

The tradition of universities doing generic industrial research continues to the present. In the early 1980s, for example, there were no fewer than thirty-seven universities in the United States that were performing research for local and regional forest products industries. In 1982 they spent approximately $12 million on such research, financed primarily by state governments.

On occasions, university research on problems of industry involved large-scale, long-run commitments to the solution of a particular problem. One of the most important such projects was conducted at the University of Minnesota's Mines Experiment Station over the course of many years, ranging from just before World War I until technical success was achieved in the early 1960s. The problem arose in connection with the gradual exhaustion of the high-yielding iron ores in the Mesabi Range. As the supply of these ores declined, attention focused increasingly upon ores of lower iron content, specifically the taconite ores containing impurities to the amount of 50 to 70 percent, but available in gigantic quantities. Although no new scientific knowledge was required, the solution to innumerable engineering and processing problems turned out to require decades of tedious experimentation. The financing of this experimentation was provided primarily by the Minnesota state government and channeled through the university to its Mines Experiment Station, which operated its own blast furnace in these experiments (Davis, 1964).

3. The Institutionalization of Engineering and Applied Sciences

In the nature of the case, much of research to help local industry is highly specific. Also, until the late nineteenth century, there was little in the way of a systematic disciplinary basis for such research and training that tied together intellectually the individuals and universities engaged in such activities. One of the major accomplishments of the American universities during the first half of the twentieth century was to effect the institutionalization of the new engineering and applied science disciplines. Thus in the years after the turn of the century, fields like chemical engineering, electrical engineering, and aeronautical engineering became established in American universities. In each of these fields, programs of graduate studies with certified professional credentials grew up, along with professional organizations and associated journals. These new disciplines and professions both reflected and solidified new kinds of close connections between American universities and a variety of American industries. The rise of these new disciplines and training programs in American universities was induced by and made possible the growing use of university-trained engineers and scientists in industry, and in particular the rise of the industrial research laboratory in the chemical industry and the new electrical equipment industries, and later throughout industry (see Hounshell and Smith, 1988; Mowery, 1981; Noble, 1977; Reich 1985).

Engineering education hardly existed in the United States before the Civil War. Obviously many schools offered vocational education, but the systematic training of professional engineers was nearly unknown until the latter part of the century. Although Rensselaer Polytechnic Institute (RPI) was founded in 1824, the first engineering school was in fact the U.S. Military Academy at West Point, founded in 1802. The civil engineering skills of graduates of West Point made a major contribution to the vast construction enterprises associated with the building of an extensive, ultimately transcontinental, railroad system beginning in the 1830s. The needs of the railroad, the telegraph and, later, an expanding succession of new products and industries brought a multiplication in the demand for engineers with specific skills. The response involved the establishment of new schools, such as MIT (1865) and Stevens Institute of Technology (1871), as well as the introduction of engineering courses into older universities. Here again the American experience in higher education was distinctly different from that of the European scene. Whereas in Great Britain, France, and Germany, engineering subjects tended to be taught at separate institutions, in the United States such subjects were introduced at an early date into the elite institutions. Yale introduced courses in mechanical engineering in 1863, and Columbia University opened its School of Mines in 1864 (Grayson, 1977).

The introduction of highly varied engineering subjects highlights certain broad regularities in the focus of American universities. Not only did they tend to be intensely practical, and intensely specific to the needs of emerging

American industries, but American engineering institutions fostered this practical approach in the very foundations of the teaching methodology.

Electrical Engineering

The emergence of electrical engineering marked a distinct development among the engineering disciplines. It represented a discipline that was based entirely upon recent experimental and theoretical breakthroughs in science. Not surprisingly, physicists dominated the intellectual leadership in this new field (McMahon, 1984).

The response of the American higher education system to the emerging electricity-based industries was swift. It is common among historians to date the beginning of the electrical industries in 1882, the year in which Edison's Pearl Street Station, in New York City, went into operation. In fact, by that year crude versions of the telephone and electric light were already in existence, and the demand for well-trained electrical engineers was beginning to grow rapidly. Electricity-based firms such as General Electric and Westinghouse were trying, with only limited success, to train their own employees in this new and burgeoning field.

The response of the universities was essentially instantaneous. In the same year that the Pearl Street Station opened, 1882, MIT introduced its first course in electrical engineering (courses in electrical engineering at MIT were taught in the Physics Department for twenty years, 1882–1902). Cornell introduced a course in electrical engineering in 1883 and awarded the first doctorate in the subject as early as 1885. By the 1890s "schools like MIT had become the chief suppliers of electrical engineers" (Wildes and Lindgren, 1985).

Throughout the twentieth century the American schools of engineering have provided the leadership in engineering and applied science research upon which the electrical industries have been based. Problems requiring research in such areas as high voltage, network analysis, or insulating properties were routinely undertaken at these schools. Equipment for the generation and transmission of electricity was designed by professors of electrical engineering, working within university labs.[3] The qualitative difference between this research and research conducted earlier was that the emergence of the discipline of electrical engineering defined a community of technically trained professionals with connections across universities, as well as between universities and industry. The relationships were systematic and cumulative, rather than ad hoc and sporadic.

Although the establishment of new companies by university professors, intent upon commercializing their research findings, has been regarded as a peculiar development of the post–World War II years, the practice has ample earlier precedent. The Federal Company, of Palo Alto, California, was founded by Stanford University faculty and became an important supplier of radio equipment during World War I (Bryson, 1984). The klystron, a thermionic tube for generating and amplifying microwave signals for high-frequency communication systems, was the product of an agreement, in 1937, between Hal and Sigurd Varian and the Stanford Physics Department. Stanford University provided the Varians with access to laboratory space and faculty, and a $100 annual allowance for materials. In exchange, Stanford was to receive a one-half interest in any resulting patents. This proved to be an excellent investment for Stanford.[4]

Thus the development of electrical engineering as a discipline, and also as a profession, clearly has its roots in American higher education. The development of this discipline was in response to a national need, the emerging electricity-based industries, rather than the more provincial needs that motivated other research referred to earlier. Training electrical engineers became the province of universities, and the interface between universities and technical advance was fostered through the adoption of this role. Further, university research was influential in technical change, often through consulting relationships with industry and occasionally through the establishment of firms that were headed by academics.

Chemical Engineering

The critical economic role of university research in engineering may be further observed in the emergence of the discipline of chemical engineering in the United States in the early years of the twentieth century. This discipline was associated, to a striking degree, with a single institution: MIT (see the excellent article by John W. Servos, 1980).

The discipline of chemical engineering emerged precisely because the knowledge generated by major scientific breakthroughs frequently terminates far from the kinds of knowledge necessary to produce a new product on a commercial scale. This is particularly true in the chemical sector. Perkin's accidental synthesis of mauveine, the first of the synthetic aniline dyes, in 1856, was the initial, critical step in the creation of a synthetic dyestuffs industry, in addition to exercising a powerful impact upon research in organic chemistry. At the same time, however, the breakthroughs at the scientific bench did not disclose how the new product might be produced on a commercial scale, nor was it possible to deduce such information from the scientific knowledge itself. It proved necessary to invent the discipline of chemical engineering around the turn of the twentieth century in order to devise process technologies for producing new chemical products on a commercial basis.

The essential point to understand here is that chemical engineering is not applied chemistry. It cannot be adequately characterized as the industrial application of scientific knowledge generated in the chemical laboratory. Rather, it involves a merger of chemistry and mechanical engineering, that is, the application of mechanical engineering to the large-scale production of chemical products (see Furter, 1980). Chemical engineers acquire an idiosyncratic methodology for decision making that allows them to become efficient at what might seem, at first blush, to be a quite straightforward calculus, translating laboratory results into commercially viable chemical processing plants. However, process plants are not merely scaled-up versions of the laboratory glass tubes and retorts in which discoveries were initially made. Chemical engineering is not properly understood as merely a scaling-up process, that is, doing something on a very large scale that had originally been done on a small scale in the laboratory. That kind of enlargement is not economically feasible and often not even technically possible. Typically, entirely different processes have to be invented, and then put through exhaustive tests at the pilot plant stage, a stage that reduces the uncertainties in the designing of a large-scale, highly expensive commercial plant.

Thus the design and construction of plants devoted to large-scale chemical processing activities involves an entirely different set of activities and capabilities than those that generated the new chemical entities. The problems of mixing, heating, and contaminant control, which can be undertaken with great precision in the lab, are immensely more difficult to handle in large-scale operations, especially if a high degree of precision and quality control are required.

It has been true of many of the most important new chemical entities that have been produced in the twentieth century that a gap of several or even many years has separated their discovery under laboratory conditions from the industrial capability to manufacture them on a commercial basis. Eventually, to manage the transition from test tubes to manufacture, where output had to be measured in tons rather than ounces, an entirely new methodology, totally distinct from the science of chemistry, had to be devised. This new methodology involved exploiting the central concept of "unit operations." This term, coined by Arthur D. Little at MIT in 1915, provided the essential basis for a rigorous, quantitative approach to large-scale chemical manufacturing, and thus may be taken to mark the emergence of chemical engineering as a unique discipline. It was a methodology that could also provide the basis for the systematic, quantitative instruction of future practitioners. It was, in other words, a form of generic knowledge that could be taught at universities.

In Arthur D. Little's words:

> Any chemical process, on whatever scale conducted, may be resolved into a coordinated series of what may be termed "unit actions," as pulverizing, mixing, heating, roasting, absorbing, condensing, lixiviating, precipitating, crystallizing, filtering, dissolving, electrolyzing and so on. The number of these basic unit operations is not very large and relatively few of them are involved in any particular process. Chemical engineering research . . . is directed toward the improvement, control and better coordination of these unit operations and the selection or development of the equipment in which they are carried out. It is obviously concerned with the testing and the provision of materials of construction which shall function safely, resist corrosion, and withstand the indicated conditions of temperature and pressure. (Little, 1933)

Aeronautical Engineering

The contribution of American higher educational institutions to the progress of aircraft design before World War II is an impressive additional instance of how universities produced information of great economic value to the development of a new industry. It is doubly interesting, for present purposes, because scientific leadership in the realm of aerodynamics was generally agreed to have been located in Germany, where Ludwig Prandtl was undoubtedly the central intellectual figure in providing the necessary analytical framework for understanding the fluid mechanics that underlies the flight performance of aircraft. Research in aeronautical engineering in the United States, at the California Institute of Technology, Stanford, and MIT, all drew heavily upon Prandtl's fundamental researches.[5] Research in aeronautical engineering, at a number of American universities, but primarily at the three mentioned, was of decisive importance to technical progress in aircraft design in the United States in the interwar years.

An excellent illustration of university engineering research that yielded valuable design data, and also knowledge of how to *acquire* new knowledge, was the propeller tests conducted at Stanford University by W. F. Durand and E. P. Lesley from 1916 to 1926 (Vincenti, 1990, chap. 1 and p. 137). Extensive experimental testing was necessary because of the absence of a body of scientific knowledge that would permit a more direct determination

of the optimal design of a propeller, given the fact that "the propeller op-
erates in combination with both engine and airframe ... and it must be
compatible with the power-output characteristics of the former and the flight
requirements of the latter" (Vincenti, 1990, p. 141). Thus designing a propeller is not independent of the design of the entire airplane, and the ten-
year research project not only expanded the understanding of airplane design
but also increased confidence in the reliability of certain techniques utilized
in aircraft design. An important consequence of the experiments, which re-
lied heavily upon wind tunnel testing, was not so much the ability to improve
the design of propellers as to improve the ability of the designer to achieve
an appropriate match between the propeller, the engine, and the airframe.[6]

As was eventually appreciated, what was essential to the successful design
of aircraft was not just the experimental equipment or the requisite scientific
knowledge. Indeed, the central point with respect to aircraft is precisely the
complexity of the process of aircraft design because of the *absence* of such
a body of scientific knowledge. The method of experimental parameter variation was necessary because a useful quantitative theory did not exist. The
Stanford experiments led to a better understanding of how to approach the
whole problem of aircraft design. In this sense, a critical output of these
experiments was a form of generic knowledge that lies at the heart of the
modern discipline of aeronautical engineering. As Vincenti has astutely observed:

> In formulating the concept of propulsive efficiency, Durand and Lesley were
> learning how to think about the use of propeller data in airplane design. This
> development of ways of thinking is evident throughout the Stanford work; for
> example, in the improvement of data presentation to facilitate the work of the
> designer and in the discussion of the solution of design problems. Though less
> tangible than design data, such understanding of how to think about a problem
> also constitutes engineering knowledge. This knowledge was communicated
> both explicitly and implicitly by the Durand-Lesley reports. (Vincenti, 1990,
> p. 158)[7]

The greater degree of sophistication in aeronautical research methods that
resulted from the Stanford experiments made an important contribution to
the maturing of the American aircraft industry in the 1930s, a maturity
crowned by the emergence of the DC-3 in the second half of that decade.
But the success of the DC-3, the most popular commercial transport plane
ever built, owed an enormous debt to another educational institution, the
California Institute of Technology. Cal Tech's Guggenheim Aeronautical
Laboratory, funded by the Guggenheim Foundation, performed research

that was decisive to the success of Douglas Aircraft, located in nearby Santa Monica. Both technical features, such as durability and reliability of components, and economically important features, such as passenger carrying capacity, were largely the product of the Cal Tech research program, highlighted by their use of multicellular construction and the exhaustive wind tunnel testing of the DC-1 and DC-2.[8]

One final point of general significance to aeronautical engineering research is worth noting. As Vincenti points out, what the Stanford experiments eventually accomplished was something more than just data collection and, at the same time, something other than science. It represented, rather, the development of a specialized methodology that could not be directly deduced from scientific principles, although it was obviously not inconsistent with those principles. One cannot therefore adequately characterize these experiments as applied science.

> [T]o say that work like that of Durand and Lesley goes beyond empirical data gathering does not mean that it should be subsumed under applied science . . . [I]t includes elements peculiarly important in engineering, and it produces knowledge of a peculiarly engineering character and intent. Some of the elements of the methodology appear in scientific activity, but the methodology as a whole does not. (Vincenti, 1990, p. 166)

Computer Science and Engineering

Computers have been probably the most remarkable contribution of American universities to the last half of the twentieth century. Important work on computers had of course been performed elsewhere (one thinks of Alan Turing in Great Britain and Konrad Zuse in Germany), but for reasons closely connected with the impact of World War II, the emergence of a practical, electronic, digital computer was largely the product of research and development activities conducted at American universities. More precisely, this research was overwhelmingly concentrated in schools of engineering. Further, these schools were decisive in transforming a logical possibility into a technical reality. In the process, a new discipline emerged, computer science, that was strongly influenced by the historical development of disciplines such as electrical engineering and physics, yet has nurtured its own particular research methodology.

The first fully operational electronic digital computer, the Electronic Numerical Integrator and Computer (ENIAC) was built at the Moore School of Electrical Engineering at the University of Pennsylvania over the period

1943–1946 (Howard Aiken, working at Harvard in conjunction with IBM, completed his Mark I in 1944; but his device, which had powerful computational capabilities, was still electromechanical, not electronic). The work conducted at the University of Pennsylvania owed a great deal to earlier research at other American universities, particularly to research at electrical engineering departments, or research on the part of people who had very close ties to engineering departments. Of special importance was work by John Atanasoff, a mathematician and physicist, at Iowa State, and Vannevar Bush, an electrical engineer at MIT.

John Mauchly, who was to play a critical role in the development of the ENIAC at the University of Pennsylvania, visited Atanasoff in Ames in 1941, a visit that was to figure prominently in a later lawsuit challenging the validity of the ENIAC patent *(Honeywell v. Sperry Rand)*. Atanasoff's device was designed for a single, specific purpose, the solution of systems of linear equations, although he appears to have given a good deal of thought to the possibility of a general purpose electronic digital computer. However, Atanasoff's machine never became operational and existed only in crude prototype form (see Stern, 1981).

Another important predecessor of the ENIAC was the differential analyzer that had been developed at MIT by Vannevar Bush and his associates during the interwar years. The differential analyzer was especially important for the practical reason that the Moore School's visibility in the field of computation had been considerably enhanced by its construction, in 1939, of a differential analyzer that was directly modeled after the MIT device. In fact, the Moore School's analyzer was really a more powerful version of that analyzer (Stern, 1981, pp. 9–10). Bush's work grew out of problems arising in electric power transmission, especially problems associated with transient stability as electric power systems became increasingly interconnected. His device was used for solving differential equations that could not readily be solved in other ways. "Though others had attempted such machines before, the MIT differential analyzer was the first practical and useful computational machine; though an analog (not digital) machine, it marked the beginning of the 'Second Industrial Revolution,' the Information Revolution" (Wildes and Lindgren, 1985).

As a result of the construction of a differential analyzer at the Moore School, based on Bush's work at MIT, the University of Pennsylvania developed a close relationship with the Ballistics Research Laboratory, belonging to the Army Ordnance Department, at the Aberdeen Proving Ground in Aberdeen, Maryland. The construction of the ENIAC was financed by an Army contract over the years 1943–1946 as part of the Army's determination to accelerate the speed with which it could calculate solutions to ballistics problems.[9] As it happened, by the time the ENIAC was ready for testing, in the fall of 1945, the war had just ended, and the need for firing tables was vastly diminished. As a result of the intercession of John Von Neumann, the ENIAC's first major task consisted of extensive calculations to establish the feasibility of a hydrogen bomb (Stern, 1981, p. 62). From these rather apocalyptic beginnings, the computer has become a ubiquitous feature of modern life, and computer science has come to be respected as one of the most important and energetic fields in academia today.

How should the university research that led to the postwar emergence of the digital electronic computer be categorized? What of the discipline of computer science today? What of artificial intelligence? The early participants were trained in engineering, mathematics, and physics. Mauchly and Bush taught and performed their research in schools of engineering. Atanasoff taught physics and mathematics at Iowa State. Howard Aiken was a mathematician who had, earlier, worked in engineering. But it is the peculiarity of the *object* of their research that it is difficult to categorize in the conventional R&D boxes of "basic research," "applied research," and "development." Although the term "computer science" is common enough in university curricula today, the discipline, if it is indeed a science, is a distinctly different kind of science. It is certainly not a *natural* science. Nor does it qualify as basic research if one employs the NSF definition as research that has as its objective "a fuller knowledge or understanding of the subject under study, rather than a practical application thereof." It may, however, be appropriately regarded, in Herbert Simon's apt phrase, as a "science of the artificial." Research activities in computer science, however classified, are directed toward the design and construction of an artifact, or machine.

The Applied and Engineering Sciences More Generally

Indeed, the same may be said of the other engineering disciplines. Designing is precisely what the domain of the engineer is primarily about. Sciences of the artificial, a subset of which have been outlined above, consist of purposive, goal-directed activities. Their explicit design orientation seems to exclude them from the usual definition of basic research. Basic research involves the quest for fundamental understanding and, in the traditional natural sciences, such a quest has often been identified with research that was significantly distanced from any immediate concerns with practical applications. However, a widely accepted definition of basic research has come to focus on the absence of a concern with practical applications rather than the search for a fundamental understanding of natural phenomena. This is unfortunate, indeed bizarre. In the applied sciences, and in engineering, some of the research is in fact quite basic in the sense of a search for understanding at a very fundamental level. Most of the research in the medical sciences is undertaken with specific practical applications in view. Medical studies of carcinogenic processes necessarily involve research into fundamental aspects of cell biology.

The definition of basic research should not be made to turn upon the absence of a useful goal in the motivation of the individuals performing the research. By such a construction, research oriented toward the design and improved performance of computers, airplanes, or plants, involving such activities as massive parallel processing or extensive parametric variation, would have to be excluded from the category of basic research.

However, research directed toward such practical goals has made important contributions to areas that are unhesitatingly categorized as basic. Consider computer science, which has emerged as an interdisciplinary subject lying between engineering and mathematics. In an effort to develop organizing principles for computer architecture, computer science had to branch out to explore deep questions of logic, linguistics, perception, cognition and, ultimately, intelligence itself. Similarly, aeronautical and chemical engineers have posed important questions for their colleagues in physics, materials science and chemistry, while focusing on the development of practical design tools. In some cases, the questions have been pursued by members of the engineering disciplines; in other cases, the questions have been passed along to other members of the academic research community. In aircraft design early in the century, a standard problem involved calculations of the flow over wings. In solving these problems, Ludwig Prandtl devised what has come to be essentially a new branch of mathematics, now known as asymptotic perturbation theory. That theory, in turn, eventually found applications in radar design, the study of combustion processes, astronomy, meteorology, biology, and pharmaceuticals. More recently, the field of turbulence research, which involves some quite fundamental issues, is being studied by researchers trained in aeronautical engineering, physics, and mathematics.

If we review the history of the development of a number of important engineering disciplines, it seems apparent that engineering education in the United States has consistently attempted to provide reference points for inquiry into the details of very practical problems. At the same time, university research has been instrumental in providing an appropriate intellectual framework for training efficient professional decision makers. Once again,

Herbert Simon reminds us of an often insufficiently recognized aspect of modern university education:

> The intellectual activity that produces material artifacts is no different fundamentally from the one that prescribes remedies for a sick patient or the one that devises a new sales plan for a company or a social welfare policy for a state. Design, so construed, is the core of all professional training; it is the principal mark that distinguishes the professions from the sciences. Schools of engineering, as well as schools of architecture, business, education, law, and medicine, are all centrally concerned with the process of design. (Simon, 1969)

There are a large number of academic disciplines that, like engineering, are consciously and deliberately oriented toward specific useful goals. This would include research directed toward improving human nutrition through the enlargement of the food supply, an explicit goal of the life sciences as they are utilized in schools of agriculture. It would include statistics, certainly one of the most useful of disciplines. And statistics, it should be noted, achieved curricular and department status in the United States long before such developments occurred in Europe.[10]

By the start of World War II the applied sciences and engineering disciplines, that is, the sciences of the artificial, had established firm places in the American university system. A few of the old ivy institutions, like Harvard and Yale, tended to resist or to isolate them, but they were strong at most of the land-grant universities, which, after all, accounted for a very large share of American university research. The presence of the engineering disciplines and the applied sciences came on top of, and significantly molded, but did not replace, the longer-standing tradition in American universities of research in the service of local industry and agriculture, and the training of people to go out into industry.

Of course, American academic research strength was not solely in the engineering disciplines and applied sciences. During the interwar period, American universities came into their own in astronomy, as well as in certain areas of fundamental physics and chemistry. This was the outcome of a long struggle by American academic scientists against what they regarded as an excessively practical orientation to American university research and teaching, and a weakness in the fundamental sciences, as compared with the United Kingdom and, particularly, Germany. Ben-David (1971), Geiger (1986), and Bruce (1987) tell this story well. Nevertheless, prior to World War II, as I. B. Cohen has stressed, the bulk of the frontier research in theoretical physics and chemistry was being carried out in Europe. American students who wanted advanced training continued to get it on the other side of the Atlantic, if they could arrange to do so.

4. The Post–World War II Era and the Emergence of the Federal Funding Commitment

World War II was a watershed in the history of American science and technology and, in particular, led to a dramatic change in the roles played by American universities in scientific and technical enterprises. During the war the lion's share of the country's scientific and technical capabilities was mobilized to work on projects aimed at hastening the successful termination of the war. The nation's university scientists and engineers played a central role in these endeavors. Academic researchers, often working closely with scientists and engineers from industry, achieved advances in electronics which greatly advanced the Allied defensive and offensive causes, in military medicine which made possible the saving of thousands of lives, and in many other areas (Baxter, 1946). Of course the Manhattan Project, which successfully developed the atomic bomb, was the most dramatic of these research endeavors, and the one that most caught the imagination of the American people.

As a result of all this, the prestige of American academic science was lifted enormously among those in government, and among the American electorate. While large-scale public support of university research was unthinkable prior to World War II, the wartime successes completely changed that picture. Vannevar Bush, whom we have met in another context, was the director of the wartime Office of Scientific Research and Development, which was responsible for mobilizing much of this effort. Bush wrote an influential document, *Science, The Endless Frontier*, which put forth the case for large-scale postwar support by the federal government of the American scientific enterprise (Bush, 1945). There were three major parts to the Bush proposal.

First, the U.S. government should not let the capability for military R&D, assembled during the war, atrophy but, rather, should continue to sustain a level and mix of funding adequate to preserve those capabilities. With the rise of the cold war in the late 1940s and early 1950s this policy became manifest in large-scale funding of military R&D. While the bulk of that funding went to support work on military systems and components carried out in industry, a sizable amount of money flowed to universities to support work on computers, electronics more generally, materials, and the applied

Table 8.2 Support for academic R&D, by sector, 1935, and 1960–1990 (millions of current dollars)

Year	Total academic R&D ($)	Federally supported R&D ($)	Federal percentage of total
1935	50	12	24
1960	646	405	63
1965	1,474	1,073	73
1970	2,335	1,647	71
1975	3,409	2,288	67
1980	6,077	4,104	68
1985	9,686	6,056	63
1990 (est.)	16,000	9,250	58

Sources: Data for 1935, National Resources Committee (1938); data for 1960 on, National Science Foundation (1991).

sciences and engineering disciplines that were relevant to military technologies.

The second part of the proposal was for significant public support of medical R&D. Here the universities from the beginning have been the largest recipient of government funding, with the National Institutes of Health the principal funder.

The third part of the postwar strategy articulated in *Science, The Endless Frontier* was for the federal government to assume responsibility for supporting basic research at the universities in a broader sense. After several false starts, this responsibility became manifest in the establishment, in 1950, of the National Science Foundation.

Federal funding of academic research, which probably amounted to about a quarter of total academic research support in the mid-1930s, increased enormously, and by 1960 was accounting for over 60 percent of the total. The total academic research enterprise increased more than tenfold in nominal terms between 1935 and 1960, and more than doubled again by 1965 (see Table 8.2). Over this same period the Consumer Price Index (CPI) increased more than twofold from 1935 to 1960 (from 41.1 in 1935 to 88.7 in 1960, where prices in 1967 = 100) and more than 6 percent between 1960 and 1965. While the CPI is not fully adequate as a research expense deflator, it is quite plausible that by 1965 real resources going into academic research were more than twelve times what they were in the mid-1930s. Rapid growth continued from 1965 until 1980 or so. It is estimated that real academic research funding grew at a rate of about 3 percent a year over this period.

With the vast expansion of resources employed in the university enterprise, and the very great expansion in the funding role of the federal government, there came about an equally dramatic transformation in the character of university research.

We shall argue shortly that solutions to practical problems continue to dominate the articulated rationale for most university research. However, there was a major shift in the nature of university research toward the basic end of the spectrum. In contrast with the pre–World War II era, when proponents of basic research had to fight hard against a dominant applications orientation, in the environment after World War II "basic research" became not only respectable but widely perceived as what the universities ought to be doing. By the mid-1960s the American system was clearly providing world leadership in most fields of science. Statistics of Nobel Prizes tell part of the story, but the best indicator is the flow of students from Europe to the United States for their graduate training, a reversal of the situation prior to the war.

But while American universities became the preeminent centers of basic research and graduate education, the dominant rationale for most of the research funding continued to be the expectation that the research would yield practical benefits. The National Science Foundation is indeed committed to the support of basic research for its own sake, with the broad rationale that the research sooner or later will yield social benefits, but the NSF has accounted for less than one-fifth of federal support for university research over the postwar period. The Department of Defense and two other government agencies that are allied with Defense in many ways, NASA and the Department of Energy (earlier the Atomic Energy Commission), have accounted for much more, roughly one-third in total (see Table 8.3). This share has remained virtually constant since 1960, but is likely to fall significantly in the coming years. In the years through 1960 the National Institutes of Health provided roughly comparable funds, about a third of the federal total. After 1960 NIH funding of university research increased greatly, and the NIH presently is by far the largest federal supporter of academic research, now accounting for almost half of total federal support.

The mission orientation of the biggest funders of academic research, and their particular fields of interest, is reflected in the distribution of research funding by field. Funded research in the engineering disciplines exceeds funded research in the physical sciences (see Table 8.4). The interests and money of the DoD and kindred organizations thus show through very

Table 8.3   Agency funding of academic research

Year	Percentage of federal research funds originating within particular agencies						
	NIH	NSF	DoD	NASA	DoE	USDA	Other
1971	36.7	16.2	12.8	8.2	5.7	4.4	16.0
1976	46.4	17.1	9.4	4.7	5.7	4.7	12.0
1981	44.4	15.7	12.8	3.8	6.7	5.4	11.0
1986	46.4	15.1	16.7	3.9	5.3	4.2	8.4
1991	47.2	16.1	11.6	5.8	4.7	4.0	10.7

Source: National Science Foundation (1991).

clearly. We should note, however, that research in academic engineering now tends to be quite basic, as suggested by the frequency with which the term "engineering sciences" has been employed in recent years.

The interests of NIH (and to a lesser extent the Department of Agriculture) can be seen in the fact that more than one-half of academic research is in the life sciences, and most of that is in the medical and agricultural science areas. While it is officially called "basic research," the research is motivated by practical problems, the helplessness of doctors and hospitals in dealing with various kinds of cancers, or AIDS, and is aimed at providing a better understanding and framework for arriving at solutions to these very real problems and priorities.

This orientation is of course consistent with the intentions of the funders of the research, and it is further reflected in the research funding mechanisms. Thus proposals sent to the National Institutes of Health are rated in terms of both their intrinsic scientific merit *and* their possible contribution to dealing with various health problems. Similarly, the departments of Defense and Energy choose the academic projects that they finance with a strong sense of their own practical, mission-oriented priorities. Put another way, while the fact that a research project is called "basic" indicates a certain distance from immediate particular practical applications, it should not be interpreted to mean that the research project has been selected without an explicit concern for eventual usefulness.[11] Indeed, in the applied sciences and engineering disciplines research seldom proceeds without some attention to potential practical payoffs.

It should also be noted that, even when basic research is defined this broadly, except for the period between the mid-1960s and the mid-1970s, over 30 percent of university research has been on projects that are explicitly labelled as "applied research" or even "development" (see Table 8.5). Here

Table 8.4   Federal and nonfederal R&D expenditures at universities and colleges, by field and source of funds, 1989

Field	Thousands of dollars	Percentage
Total science and engineering	14,987,279	100.0
Total sciences	12,599,686	84.1
Life sciences	8,079,851	53.9
Physical sciences	1,643,377	11.0
Environmental sciences	982,937	6.6
Social sciences	636,372	4.2
Computer sciences	467,729	3.1
Psychology	237,945	1.6
Mathematical sciences	214,248	1.4
Other sciences	337,227	2.3
Total engineering	2,387,593	15.9
Electrical/electronic	600,016	4.0
Mechanical	340,280	2.3
Civil	249,552	1.7
Chemical	185,087	1.2
Aero/astronautical	146,548	1.0
Other	866,110	5.8

Sources: National Science Foundation (1991) and unpublished tabulations.

the Department of Defense and related agencies would appear to be the principal clients.

The changing composition of funding sources is additionally reflected in the changing output of university research. In view of the fact that more than half of the university research funding since the 1960s has come from DoD, DoE, NASA, and the NIH, one would expect that this would be reflected in an increase in the role played by university research in defense and space technology and in health and medicine. Indeed, the role of universities in these areas has been very substantial since 1945.

In fact, a large part of university defense-related research funding in the postwar years built directly upon an earlier military research program that has already received brief attention: the development of the electronic digital computer. MIT, which had done important earlier work on techniques of electronic computation in the late 1930s (work with which Vannevar Bush had been closely associated), played an even more prominent role in the postwar years. MIT's research in this field had been supported by the Rockefeller Foundation and then, on a substantially larger scale, as part of Project Whirlwind. Project Whirlwind, supported by the Office of Naval Research

Table 8.5   Expenditures for academic basic research, applied research, and development, 1960–1990 (millions of current dollars)

Year	Total academic R&D ($)	Basic research ($)	%	Applied research ($)	%	Development ($)	%
1960	646	433	67	179	28	34	5
1965	1,474	1,138	77	279	19	57	4
1970	2,335	1,796	77	427	18	112	5
1975	3,409	2,410	71	851	25	148	4
1980	6,077	4,041	67	1,698	28	338	6
1985	9,686	6,559	68	2,673	28	454	5
1990 (est.)	16,000	10,350	65	4,845	30	805	5

Source: National Science Foundation (1991), p. 347.

for the development of general-purpose computer programming capabilities, had achieved some important successes. These included Jay Forrester's invention of a magnetic storage system in 1949. After the Soviets detonated an atomic bomb in August 1949, the Air Force proposed that Whirlwind be incorporated in a highly ambitious national air defense system, called SAGE (Semi-Automatic Ground Environment). The first portion of the SAGE system went into operation in June 1958 (see Wildes and Lindgren, 1985, chap. 17).

MIT, whose postwar prominence owed a great deal to DoD research support, also served as the location for another military-supported project that led to a major improvement in machining capability. One of the most important advances in machine techniques for shaping metal originated with an Air Force contract for MIT to design and build a numerically controlled milling machine. This resulted in the emergence of numerically controlled machines that were capable of performing highly complex machining operations of a kind that were critical to the manufacture of aircraft components, especially wings. The technology essentially consisted of attaching a digital computer to the machine tool. The computer was capable of being programmed to "instruct" the machine tool to conduct a sequence of complex operations with a minimum of human intervention.

MIT provided the first demonstration of the numerical control of machine tools in 1952. While the technology successfully met the needs of the military sponsor, its complexity and cost hampered the diffusion of numerical control for about two decades.[12] It was only in the early 1970s that the advances in the field of solid-state technologies favored the widespread development of commercial applications of numerical control.[13] In the era of microcomputers, the basic technology is being joined to improvements in robotics, automated handling, and transfer systems into what are called flexible manufacturing systems.

The link between federal research priorities and university research's contribution to technical advance is further strengthened by an examination of the biotechnology revolution. Since World War II, the federal government has devoted substantial resources toward medical research and the life sciences. The genetic engineering revolution that began in the mid-1970s represents a clear payoff from this investment. However, over twenty years passed before university researchers were able to synthesize the first human genes, a synthesis based upon the identification of the double helix structure of the DNA molecule in the early 1950s. Research at Stanford, the University of California at San Francisco, and Harvard was critical in the development of the methods for this pathbreaking innovation. In fact, a share of the revenue from the primary patent for the genetic cloning process, the Cohen-Boyer patent, is currently received by Stanford University. The scientific research that went into the creation of biotechnology products, such as human insulin or human growth hormone, required close links between university research and industrial development. For example, Herbert Boyer, a university researcher, was a founding partner in Genentech, the first private biotechnology firm. Other early firms, such as Cetus, were (and are) heavily reliant on access to university research results and have developed intimate consulting relationships with prominent molecular biologists.

However, numerous "start-up" firms with close connections to universities have operated on the assumption that the performance of good science was a sufficient condition for the achievement of financial success. Biogen, whose CEO in the early 1980s was a Harvard Nobel Prize–winning biologist, is symptomatic of biotech firms that concentrated on good science with little financial discipline or attention to "downstream" product development. It survived after its stock fell from $23 in 1983, when it first went public, to around $5 by the end of 1984, only as a result of drastic managerial reorganization. As will be explored further below, biotechnology represents an important industrial sector with a strong contemporary reliance on university research. Not surprisingly, the links between university research and industry are closer in this field than in many others.

As a result of the changes we have been describing, research aimed at helping local civilian industry and agriculture, which was the hallmark of the American university research enterprise prior to World War II, became a much smaller part of the total picture in the postwar era. American university research that was aimed at solving practical problems for local economic needs dwindled (at least relatively) because defense and health-related problems became the dominant foci and the rationale for university research funding. Large parts of the earlier traditional enterprise were, as we have noted, very much hands-on, dirt-under-the-nails work, and the post–World War II notion that the proper role for academic research was to make scientific and technical breakthroughs militated against this kind of work.

Deborah Shapley and Rustum Roy (1985) comment critically on this change in orientation of university research and also on the low prestige of engineering relative to pure natural science that they saw prevalent in academia. But we believe that they overstate their case. As we noted, whatever its standing in terms of prestige, engineering is receiving more resources than physical science. Research at medical schools receives far more resources than research in arts and sciences biology departments.

And while the relative share of university research directly aimed to help civilian industry declined greatly from what it was before World War II, many universities did remain in the role of helping local industry. Engineering schools like RPI and Georgia Tech continued to serve local industry, even if MIT and, even more so, Cal Tech drew away from that function. Federal and state funding for agricultural research actually increased over the postwar period, even if it became a relatively very small part of total university research funding.

The rise of concerns about the competitiveness of American industry that marked the 1980s rekindled notions that a major explicit objective of American universities ought to be to service civilian industry. The end of the cold war and the erosion of the credibility of national security as a rationale for public support of universities has also led to a rethinking of old missions. Before offering our commentary, however, it is important to look more directly at the roles American universities are currently playing in technical advance.

5. The Contributions of University Research to Technical Advance in Industry

In the preceding sections we have followed the American university research enterprise over the past century and a half and called attention to two major structural transitions that have occurred. The first, which began to occur toward the end of the nineteenth century, was the rise and institutionalization of the engineering disciplines and applied sciences as accepted areas of academic teaching and research. This development regularized and brought into the mainline academic structure the programs of research and training for industry which earlier had been proceeding on a more or less ad hoc basis with each university being a special case. The second major change occurred after World War II, which saw massive increases in federal funding of academic research. One consequence was a shifting of emphasis of university research from the needs of local civilian industry to problems associated with health and defense. Another result was a shift of academic research toward the basic end of the spectrum, and the development of a strong belief, at least in academia, that basic research is the proper role of the university.

Over the last half century there has developed a relatively clear division of labor between academic and industrial research. R&D to improve existing products and processes became almost exclusively the province of industry, in fields where firms had strong R&D capabilities. So too the work directly aimed at bringing into practice and commercial use the next generation of products and processes. Industrial R&D is almost totally concentrated on this kind of work. In a few industries, some industrial firms may engage in longer-run research more broadly oriented toward advancing understanding. But basic research in industry, although it accounts for more than one-fifth of all U.S. basic research, constitutes only 5 percent of industrial R&D.

Basic research became increasingly viewed as the task of universities. The policies of the DoD and the NIH, as well as the NSF, supported this view of the universities' appropriate roles. Today, except for those fields where, in effect, university work is substituting for industrial R&D, as in forest products, university research is "basic" research.

However, by this we do not mean that such research is not guided by practical concerns. As our discussion in the preceding section showed, it is a gross misconception to think that if research is "basic" this means the work is not motivated by or funded because of its promise to deal with a class of practical problems. Nor does it mean that university scientists and engineers are not building and working with prototypes of applicable industrial technology. Indeed this is a central part of academic research in many engineering fields. Academic medical scientists are centrally involved in exploring the efficacy of new treatments. However, cases like the taconite project of the interwar period, and SAGE, where university work brought new industrial processes and products fully to practice, are rare and so too are cases where academic medical scientists carry their work close to the point of operational practice.

What university research most often does today is to stimulate and enhance the power of R&D done in industry, as contrasted with providing a substitute for it. By far the largest share of the work involved in creating and bringing to practice new industrial technology is carried out in industry, not in universities.

One good way of seeing what it is that universities do not do is to recognize that in most technologies the bulk of the effort that goes into R&D is D, not R. If we consider total R&D spending for the American economy, D has constituted approximately two-thirds of that total for many years. Except when special institutions or projects are established (as in the Ag schools, and in certain special DoD projects) academic institutions are not motivated by or likely to be good at D.

Usually, moreover, most of the science employed in achieving the objective of a marketable new technology is rather old science (Rosenberg, 1985). This is not the kind of work that naturally excites academics, and its successful completion generally does not lead to publication and tenure. Moreover, the understandings that are most important in guiding the R&D efforts are often those associated with detailed familiarity with prevailing technology, and of user needs, rather than familiarity with the most recent research findings. Universities are not set up to do this kind of work. The exceptions are where university projects or laboratories have been established to perform an industry service function, as in the case of the University of Minnesota's Mines Experiment Station, and in a number of the university-affiliated agricultural experiment stations, and in places like Georgia Tech and RPI which have set up industry-servicing engineering facilities.

As we described in the previous section, over the post–World War II period the Department of Defense and the National Institutes of Health energetically built up the academic research enterprise in fields of particular interest to them. Academics in these fields have developed many prototypes of new technology which were subsequently developed in industry, and on some occasions have been involved in development work as well. This shows up in the patent statistics, where academics account for a significant share in several areas of medical science and electronics (see Table 8.6).

Patents, of course, provide only a partial and necessarily biased picture of the contributions of university research. Many of the kinds of contributions discussed earlier do not generally result in patents.

A survey of industrial R&D managers, undertaken in the mid-1980s by one of the authors of this essay (RRN) and several of his colleagues at Yale, provides a wealth of data that make it possible to see more clearly into how university research contributes to the advance of industrial technology, and

Table 8.6   Percentage of patents by universities by patent classes ranked by university share of total

Class title	Rank	Class	Univ. patents	Total patents	1990 share (%)
Genetic engineering, recombinant DNA	1	935	58	321	18.1
Chemistry: natural resins; peptides or proteins	2	530	91	583	15.6
Chemistry: molecular biol. and microbiol.	3	435	171	1,417	12.1
Surgery	4	600	12	105	11.4
Organic compounds	5	536	66	615	10.7
Superconductor technology	6	505	25	233	10.7
Drug, bio-affecting and body treating comp'n	7	424	147	1,490	9.9
Chemistry: analytical and immunological testing	8	436	67	688	9.7
Prosthesis (artificial body parts)	9	623	25	399	6.3
Drug, bio-affecting and body treating comp'n	10	514	181	3,003	6.0
Coherent light generators	11	372	27	531	5.1
Robots	12	901	12	251	4.8
Surgery	13	128	90	2,149	4.2
Plant patents	14	PLT	13	317	4.1
Organic compounds	15	556	13	326	4.0
Compositions: ceramics	16	501	18	462	3.9
X-ray/gamma ray systems/devices	17	378	13	343	3.8
Optics: measuring and testing	18	356	36	1,012	3.6
Organic compounds	19	549	26	715	3.6
Chemistry, inorganic	20	423	33	965	3.4
Chemistry: electrical and wave energy	21	204	41	1,263	3.2
Electricity: measuring and testing	22	324	40	1,259	3.2
Organic compounds	23	558	14	433	3.2
Surgery	24	604	38	1,223	3.1
Organic compounds	25	540	16	518	3.1
Radiant energy	26	250	60	1,987	3.0
Organic compounds	27	548	34	1,141	3.0
Semiconductor device manufacturing	28	437	23	755	3.0
Surgery	29	606	18	621	2.9
Organic compounds	30	544	27	1,037	2.6
Organic compounds	31	546	28	1,128	2.5
Coating processes	32	427	43	1,801	2.4
Process disinfecting, deodorizing, preserving	33	422	23	953	2.4

Table 8.6   *(Continued)*

Class title	Rank	Class	Univ. patents	Total patents	1990 share (%)
Organic compounds	34	564	13	546	2.4
Synthetic resins or natural rubbers	35	528	28	1,230	2.3
Organic compounds	36	560	15	640	2.3
Measuring and testing	37	73	46	2,056	2.2
Active solid state devices (e.g., transistors)	38	357	34	1,535	2.2
Metal treatment	39	148	17	765	2.2
Liquid purification or separation	40	210	28	1,499	1.9
Catalyst, solid sorbent or support	41	502	13	699	1.9
Organic compounds	42	568	12	628	1.9
Optics: systems and elements	43	350	41	2,280	1.8
Food or edible materials	44	426	18	1,008	1.8
Plastic/nonmetallic article shaping/treating	45	264	32	1,946	1.6
Synthetic resins	46	525	22	1,495	1.5
Adhesive bonding and miscellaneous chem. mfg.	47	156	28	1,982	1.4
Compositions, miscellaneous	48	252	26	1,844	1.4
Stock material or miscellaneous articles	49	428	40	3,196	1.3
Gas separation	50	55	14	1,606	0.9
Electrical transmission/ interconnection	51	307	11	1,288	0.9
Electrical computers and data processing	52	364	53	6,474	0.8
Electric heating	53	219	10	1,268	0.8
Communications, electrical	54	340	14	2,026	0.7

Source: Unpublished data gathered by Jonathan Putnam and Richard Nelson.

into the industrial fields where this role is most important. The respondents to the questionnaire were asked to rate the importance of research done at universities to technical advance in their lines of business. Table 8.7 lists the industries (for which there were three or more responses) that rated the contributions of university research as very important or important.

There are several particularly interesting features displayed by this table. First, a striking number of the industries are related to agriculture or forestry. This clearly reflects the long-standing "service" research role of universities for the industries that provide key inputs for agriculture or which process

Table 8.7   Industries rating university research as "important" or "very important"

Fluid milk
Dairy products except milk
Canned specialties
Logging and sawmills
Semiconductors and related devices
Pulp, paper and paperboard mills
Farm machinery and equipment
Grain mill products
Pesticides and agricultural chemicals
Processed fruits and vegetables
Engineering and scientific instruments
Millwork, veneer and plywood
Synthetic rubber
Drugs
Animal feed

Source: Previously unpublished data from the Yale Survey on Appropriability and Technological Opportunity. For a description of the survey, see Levin et al. (1987).

agriculture or forest products. While in the postwar era such service R&D has been dwarfed by university research funded by agencies like the DoD and NIH, it is apparent that for the agriculture-related industries, university research efforts aimed to help them continue to be critical. This shows up, among other places, in the significant university role in such fields as plant patents.

The presence of drugs was to be expected, in view of the prominence of NIH funding of university research. The major electronics industries are also on the list, as well as the scientific and measurement instrument industries. In these broad areas the university contributions apparently are often patentable.

What fields of university science are important to these industries? Table 8.8 shows the number of industries giving various fields of university research a high relevance score.

It is striking what a large fraction of the fields of university research rated as important by a number of industries are applied sciences or engineering disciplines. Very few of the more basic sciences are much mentioned. An exception is chemistry. However, those knowledgeable about academic chemistry know that a significant fraction of such work is done in appreciation of practical industrial problems. In some cases, as in the research on catalysis, such work may win a Nobel Prize, as well as contributing impor-

Table 8.8   The relevance of university science to industrial technology

Science	No. of industries with scores		Selected industries in which the relevance of university science was large
	≥ 5	≥ 6	
Biology	12	3	Animal feed, drugs, processed fruits/vegetables
Chemistry	19	3	Animal feed, meat products, drugs
Geology	0	0	None
Mathematics	5	1	Optical instruments
Physics	4	2	Optical instruments, electron tubes
Agricultural science	17	7	Pesticides, animal feed, fertilizers, food products
Applied math/operations research	16	2	Meat products, logging/sawmills
Computer science	34	10	Optical instruments, logging/ sawmills, paper machinery
Materials science	29	8	Synthetic rubber, nonferrous metals
Medical science	7	3	Surgical/medical instruments, drugs, coffee
Metallurgy	21	6	Nonferrous metals, fabricated metal products
Chemical engineering	19	6	Canned foods, fertilizers, malt beverages
Electrical engineering	22	2	Semiconductors, scientific instruments
Mechanical engineering	28	9	Hand tools, specialized industrial machinery

Source: Previously unpublished data from the Yale Survey on Appropriability and Technological Opportunity. For a description of the survey, see Levin et al. (1987).

tantly to the ability of chemical companies to produce products more effectively. That is to say, among the basic sciences on which there is extensive university research, chemistry appears to be closest to certain ongoing needs of the industrial community.

The fact that university research in fields such as physics and mathematics shows up so little in Table 8.8 should not be interpreted as indicating that academic research in these fields makes little contribution to technical advance. Rather, Table 8.8 should be interpreted as attesting that it takes a long time before fundamental advances in physics, mathematics, and kindred

Table 8.9   The relevance of science to industrial technology

Science	No. of industries with scores		Selected industries in which the relevance of science was large
	≥ 5	≥ 6	
Biology	14	8	Drugs, pesticides, meat products, animal feed
Chemistry	74	43	Pesticides, fertilizers, glass, plastics
Geology	4	3	Fertilizers, pottery, nonferrous metals
Mathematics	30	9	Optical instruments, machine tools, motor vehicles
Physics	44	18	Semiconductors, computers, guided missiles
Agricultural science	16	9	Pesticides, animal feed, fertilizers, food products
Applied math/operations research	32	6	Guided missiles, aluminum smelting, motor vehicles
Computer science	79	35	Guided missiles, semiconductors, motor vehicles
Materials science	99	46	Primary metals, ball bearings, aircraft engines
Medical science	8	5	Asbestos, drugs, surgical/medical instruments
Metallurgy	60	35	Primary metals, aircraft engines, ball bearings

Source: Previously unpublished data from the Yale Survey on Appropriability and Technological Opportunity. For a description of the survey, see Levin et al. (1987).

fundamental sciences have an impact on industrial technology. In our view, that impact also tends to be indirect. Thus advances in physics and mathematics are picked up and used in fields like chemistry, electrical engineering, and materials science, and through these applied fields they ultimately work their way into influencing industrial technology.

Some evidence for this interpretation is provided in Table 8.9. The responses reported in the table are not to questions about the importance of academic research in a field, but rather simply about the importance of the field itself. Note that many more respondents tended to give physics and mathematics a high importance rating as a field of science than gave university research in those fields a high importance rating. In our view this is a crucial distinction which reflects two things. First, the fundamental science learned by industrial scientists and engineers when they attended university plays a very important role in their problem solving in industrial R&D, even though recent publications in those fields may find little direct use in those endeavors. Second, the respondents understood very well that, while the academic research findings that were of direct use to them were in fields like electrical engineering and medical science, those disciplines were, in turn, drawing from, and enriched by, the more basic sciences such as physics and molecular biology.

It is useful and valuable to compare the findings discussed above, drawn from the Yale questionnaire, with those of two other recent studies that have probed the connection between university research and technical advance in industry. One of these was a series of interviews conducted by the Government-University-Industry-Research Roundtable (1991) in which the present authors participated. The other is a study by Edwin Mansfield.

The GUIR Roundtable study was carried out through discussions with seventeen senior industrial research managers, mostly from large successful industrial companies. A few of the companies were heavily involved in bio-technology. There was reasonable representation from the pharmaceutical and electronics industries. A number of the respondents were from compa-nies that designed and put together large "systems," and some were from companies that produced commodities like metals or household products.

Once one sorts through the interviews, biotechnology stands out almost uniquely as an area where corporate managers look to university research as a source of "inventions." Here the respondents stated that this was largely because the technology was very new, and that they believed that, as the industry matured, the direct role played by university research in inventing would diminish. We would add that the technology itself was born in a university setting, which actually is quite unusual. The respondents from the electronics companies tended to make a distinction between what they called "breakthrough inventions" and normal incremental inventions. They took the position that, in the field of electronics, academic research is often the source of radically new designs and concepts. However, they argued that the bulk of the total inventive effort in their field, and the bulk of the practical payoffs, came from incremental advances, and that this was almost exclu-sively the domain of industrial research, design, problem solving, and de-velopment.

Respondents discussing drugs other than those emanating from biotech-nology stated that university research was almost never the direct source of

Table 8.10   Percentage of new products and processes based on recent academic research, seven industries, United States, 1975–1985

Industry	Percentage that could not have been developed (without substantial delay) in the absence of recent academic research		Percentage that was developed with very substantial aid from recent academic research	
	Products	Processes	Products	Processes
Information processing	11	11	17	16
Electronics	6	3	3	4
Chemical	4	2	4	4
Instruments	16	2	5	1
Pharmaceuticals	27	22	17	8
Metals	13	12	9	9
Petroleum	1	1	1	1
Average	11	9	8	6

Source: Mansfield (1991).

a new drug; in virtually all cases the key work was in industry. However, they also noted that, in a number of cases, academic research had illuminated the kinds of biochemical reactions the pharmaceutical companies should look for in their search for new drugs, or permitted the companies to make a more effective assessment of the possible uses for drugs that they were testing. Respondents from the pharmaceutical and several other industries observed that a major function of academic research was to improve understanding of technologies, particularly new technologies, so that industry could more effectively go about improving them.

It should be noted that only one of the executives interviewed was from a company with products based in agriculture or forestry; and that person did stress the important role of university research to his company. The kind of local company that state universities and regional engineering schools traditionally have served was not represented at all.

Mansfield's study (1991) provides still another window into the role of university research in technical advances in industry. Mansfield asked respondents in seventy-six large American firms the percentage of new products and processes introduced and commercialized by that firm over the period 1975–1985 that could not have been developed without substantial delay in the absence of recent academic research. Then he asked about the percentage whose development was substantially aided by recent academic research. His findings are summarized in Table 8.10.

Executives in the pharmaceutical industry reported strong dependence on academic research. They stated that over one-quarter of the new drugs commercialized by the companies could not have been developed, or only with substantial delay, absent academic research. Close to another 20 percent were acknowledged to have had their development substantially aided by academic research. The discussions reported above with the pharmaceutical executives interviewed by the GUIR project almost surely accurately characterizes the nature of the dependence. Academic researchers are seldom directly involved in the development of new drugs. Rather, they are primarily creating knowledge that enables drug companies to search for and develop new drugs more expeditiously.

After pharmaceuticals, the reported fraction of new products that were heavily dependent upon academic research for their introduction drops off dramatically. The executives from the companies producing information-processing equipment, and from those producing instruments, report a 10 to 15 percent figure. In the information-processing field, in all likelihood, a good share of university contributions are in the form of the prototype "radical breakthroughs" discussed by the GUIR respondents. For instrumentation, the likely mechanism was that university scientists created new or improved old instrumentation for their own research uses. The respondents from the metals industry also report that over 10 percent of the new products and processes could not have been developed in the absence of recent academic research.

While Mansfield did not stress the matter, a striking finding was that three of the industries in his set, electrical equipment, chemical products, and oil products, report that only a small percentage of their new products (6 percent or under) were significantly dependent upon recent academic research. This is not to say that technical advance in these fields is not science based. Rather, the implication is that the science used is not particularly new, or is not the stuff that academics are now doing.

Let us summarize. Several recent studies provide a broad picture of the role academic research is presently playing in technical advance in industry. While the coverage and methodology are different, by and large the studies provide a coherent picture.

The old service role to local industry, and in particular industry tied to agriculture and forest products, clearly is much smaller as a part of the total than was the case before the war, and these industries themselves have dwindled in importance. But the evidence shows a continuing dependency of these industries on research done at universities.

The massive funding by DoD and kindred agencies shows up clearly in various measures of the contributions of university research to technical advance in electronics; similarly the funding of the NIH in health-related fields. However, in these fields the university contribution is largely R, with industry doing almost all of the D.

And there are a large number of industries that seem to be relatively untouched by university research. These include such basic industries as steel, autos, and textiles.

6. Conclusion

We began this essay by remarking on the significant increase in the fraction of academic research funded by industry over the past two decades, and the rapid growth in the number and size of university-industry research centers. Many in universities clearly see all this as just the beginning, and anticipate a significant further increase of industry funding of academic research. Many of those concerned with government policies toward universities also foresee this development, anticipating that in the coming years industry funding will reduce the need of government funds to support the academic research enterprise. But while at first this sounds like a harmony of consistent anticipations and expectations, there are strong reasons for skepticism.

In the first place, many of the academics hoping for a significant further increase in industrial funding also hope for this to occur without much change in what academics actually do or in how their research is oriented. Many academics clearly have a firm belief in what has been called the "linear model" of technological advance, seeing unfettered research by academics as providing the basis for technological innovations in industry, with the process not calling for strong industry influence over what the academics actually do. The new government programs buy into some of this, but increasingly are insisting upon significant industry involvement in the processes by which research funds get allocated, and therefore influence over the composition and nature of academic research, as well as strong links to ensure "technology transfer."

While many academics believe, as noted above, that business as usual should be the order of the day, other academics clearly welcome the notion that there should be close ties to industry, along with more industry funding. They are quite eager to reorient their work to make it more commercially relevant and rewarding. Indeed among some there seems to be a belief that, if they put their minds to it, with financial support from industry, academic researchers can provide industry with a cornucopia of new product and process prototypes and restore the lost competitiveness of American industry.

The industry views drawn forth by the Roundtable interviews suggest, on the other hand, considerable industry skepticism over the ability of academics to contribute directly to industrial innovation, which probably reflects a drawing back from more hopeful and less realistic beliefs held earlier in the 1980s. To a considerable extent the industry views expressed to the Roundtable were that the academics should stick with the basic research they are doing, and heed their training functions, and stop thinking of themselves as the source of technology. These views also suggest that it is highly unlikely that industry funding of academic research is going to increase much in the coming years.

We believe that expectations held by some about what university research, if suitably reoriented, can contribute directly to industrial innovation, are quite unrealistic, and so also are beliefs about how much funding of academic research private industry is likely to shoulder. At the same time we disagree with those academics and others who argue for a simple continuation of the status quo. We do think that the times call for a major rethinking about what Americans ought to expect of their university research system and in particular about how university research ought to relate to industry. We believe the issue of competitiveness is a serious one. We also believe that American universities can help restore competitiveness in those technologies that their research illuminates. However, it is important to sort out when universities are capable of helping and where, while there may be problems, university research does not seem to be an appropriate answer.

While much of the attention recently has been on the weakness of American industry in product and process development, we think it a mistake to see universities as a likely source of solution here. Less attention has been given to the erosion of industrial research, as contrasted with design and development, in a number of industries where industrial research traditionally has been very strong, particularly in electronics. Here university research can be of more help (Rosenbloom, 1993).

Actually, as we have noted, the present danger is that the university contribution may decline. The end of the Cold War has eroded the rationale that has served over the past forty years to provide the justification for government support of university research in a number of fields of vital importance to American industry. The first order of business, in our view, is to ensure that government support of university research in the engineering disciplines and applied sciences, such as materials and computer science, not be orphaned by sharp cutbacks in military R&D that are almost certain to occur over the coming years. One element that is essential is to articulate clearly that a major purpose of government funding of university research in these fields is to assist American industry.

But we also believe that more is needed than a mere change in rhetoric. We need to establish university research support programs that have that objective expressly, and that also have allocation machinery that can achieve a sensible allocation of funds, given that objective. This would require advisory committees knowledgeable about industry needs, and decision criteria and proposal evaluation systems that are sensitive to those needs.

And probably more than that. As the experience over the past quarter century with industrial research clearly indicates, if such research is to be fruitful there must be close communication and interaction between those who do research and those who are responsible for product and process design and development. If university research is to pick up more of the role that industrial research has been serving, this would seem to mean that there needs to be close links between university researchers doing the research and their scientific and technical colleagues in industry. These exist in important areas of defense technology, and in technologies relating to agriculture and health. The new university-industry research centers extend the range of such connections. If university research is to play a more helpful role in industrial innovation, the connections need to be further extended and strengthened.

Does this mean, as some people seem to argue, that universities should get much more into the business of helping industry develop particular new products and processes? As a general rule, we don't think so. There are several reasons.

First, as we have stressed, the development over the past century of the applied sciences and engineering disciplines has, in many fields of technology at least, led to the establishment of a fruitful division of labor between universities and industry. Universities have taken the responsibility for training young professionals, most of whom will go on to work in industry. And they have performed much of the research that has led to theories, concepts, methods, and data that are useful to industry in the development of new products and processes. In some fields this has involved developing and experimenting with pilot versions of radically new products and processes, as well as research into fundamental scientific questions relating to what is going on inside some particular industrial technology. But by and large it has not involved putting academics in the position of having to make commercial judgments.

Industry has also undertaken some quite fundamental research, and in some fields a good deal. Corporate research laboratories such as Bell Labs,

IBM Yorktown, Du Pont Central Lab, and others have performed at or sometimes even above the level of top universities. But the returns from such research are hard to make proprietary and reserved for the funder. As we have noted, many companies have been cutting back on their research. While corporate research may recover from its recent slump, in many fields universities will remain the dominant site of such research.

Sustained strong public support of university research in fields such as electrical engineering, computer science, and materials science will continue to benefit mostly the "high-tech" industries, whether the funding be civilian or military. Although the shifting of objectives certainly should be associated with changed mechanisms for setting priorities, and a changed pattern of university-industry interactions in these fields, it does not seem to us that the change would involve breaking new institutional ground.

Based on the surveys and interviews reported in section 5 it is evident, however, that university research in the engineering and applied sciences is strongly servicing only a limited range of industries, specifically those connected with electronics, chemical products, health, and agriculture. This ought not to come as a great surprise. By and large these are the fields where government agencies have been supporting the underlying sciences for a long time. A policy of consciously broadening the range of industries under which there is university research is quite reasonable to contemplate. However, if that is to be a policy, it must be policy that looks to practical returns in the long run, not the short. It must, in brief, be a patient policy.

Except under special circumstances, we think it ill-advised to try to get university researchers to work on specific practical problems of industry, or on particular product or process development efforts. In general, university researchers are poorly equipped for judging what is likely to be an acceptable solution to a problem and what is not. University researchers are almost always insufficiently versed in the particulars of specific product markets to make good decisions about appropriate tradeoffs. Equally important, such work provides few results that are respected or rewarded in academic circles, unlike research that pushes forward conceptual knowledge in an applied science or engineering discipline.

What of the practical problem solving that marked earlier days of American university research, the research on boilers or the processing of ores, that used to be quite common on university campuses? That kind of work is still there, often associated with education programs for engineers who will go out into local industry, or in business "incubator" programs at places such as Georgia Tech. It is there in larger scale and more systematic form in institutions affiliated with universities, but not an integral part of them, where research is undertaken to serve the needs of particular national industries (for example, Carnegie-Mellon's Center for Iron and Steelmaking Research, or the Forest Products Laboratory at the University of Wisconsin).

By and large, these programs have grown up in fields where industrial research is not strong. They are a substitute for industrial R&D, or represent a locus for it outside of industry itself. The industries in question tend to be, although not always, made up of small firms without R&D facilities, and often the technologies in question lack a sound underlying scientific base. As our earlier discussion indicated, university involvement in this kind of research often has its historical origins, and much of its current basis, in training programs. Larger-scale research organizations, such as the agricultural experiment stations affiliated with many universities, tend not to be central integral parts of the university, but partially detached. Often many of the researchers are not university faculty members, although some may teach courses. Their interactions with their industrial clients, on the other hand, may be very close.

These kinds of programs can be very valuable to industries whose firms do little R&D of their own. They are an important part of the activities of many universities. However, after a certain size is surpassed, their locus at universities becomes more a matter of historical happenstance or convenience than a particular source of strength. They could exist just as well as separate organizations.[14]

In any case, we do not think that the emphasis of university research ought to be here, or that a revamped policy of federal support of university research which places the emphasis on contributions to industrial technical advance ought to be oriented to this kind of work. It is in research, not commercial design and development, that universities excel. While many of the problems of American industry may reside in product and process development and improvement, this is the kind of work they have to do largely themselves, or in specialized industry-linked institutions, which may or may not be associated with universities.

A shift in emphasis of university research toward more extensive connections with the needs of civilian industry can benefit industry and the universities if it is done in the right way. That way, in our view, is to respect the division of labor between universities and industry that has grown up with the development of the engineering disciplines and applied sciences, rather than one that attempts to draw universities deeply into a world in which decisions need to be made with respect to commercial criteria. There is no reason to believe that universities will function well in such an environment, and good reason to believe that such an environment will do damage to the legitimate functions of universities. On the other hand, binding university research closer to industry, while respecting the condition that research be "basic" in the sense of aiming for understanding rather than short-run practical payoff, can be to the enduring benefit of both.

International Differences
and International Convergence

The concluding essay of Part III highlighted two themes. One is the complex institutional structures, including universities and involving government support and programs of a considerable variety, that have evolved to support technical advance in industry. The other is the historical uniqueness of the American experience. These subjects are examined further in Part IV, which focuses on the significant convergence of technological capabilities and of the systems supporting technical advance that has occurred among the advanced industrial nations over the past quarter century.

The years following World War II were marked by American technological dominance across a broad front of industries. Since the late 1960s this dominance has eroded and in some cases completely disappeared. Chapter 9 first explores the sources of the United States' postwar technological superiority. How did the technological leadership that Americans and citizens of other countries once took for granted come into existence in the first place? To what extent did this leadership result from particular characteristics of U.S. firms and industries and supporting institutions? The essay presents a variegated answer to these questions. The second phenomenon it seeks to explain is the disappearance of the American lead. The central argument is that the key factors that made the American environment for industrial innovation significantly different from the European—the fact that American firms faced a far larger market than firms abroad and (after World War II) the fact that American investments in science and technology vastly exceeded those of other countries—have lost their bite. Since World War II the world has increasingly been a common market, and since the 1960s other nations have emulated U.S. investment in science and technology.

The erosion of the American technological lead and the rapid rise of Japan as a major technological power have stimulated a considerable amount of research on differences across countries in "national innovation systems." Chapter 10 summarizes a large-scale comparative study, stressing the complex of institutions that support technical advance in industry and interindustry and intercountry differences. The study suggests that differences in national innovation systems among advanced industrial nations can largely be explained by examining variations in size, industry mix, and the nature and size of defense procurement activities. Nonetheless, nations differ significantly in broad philosophical views regarding the appropriate role of government in the support of industrial innovation, and the systems reflect these differences. Over the last decade national policies in support of technical advance have been the subject of acrimonious disputes between nations, with complaints about "unfairness." The essay concludes by examining this controversy.

The Rise and Fall of
American Technological Leadership:
The Postwar Era in Historical Perspective

1. Introduction

During the quarter century following World War II, the United States was the world's most productive economy by virtually any measure. U.S. output per worker was higher by margins of 30 to 50 percent over the other leading industrial nations, and the gap in total factor productivity was nearly as large (Denison, 1967). These differences held not just in the aggregate but in almost all industries (Dollar and Wolff, 1988). Many factors lay behind the U.S. edge, but it seems evident that the country's position of world leadership in advanced technology was an important one. The U.S. technology lead was partly reflected in the productivity statistics but is not the same thing. On the one hand, measured total factor productivity is affected by many elements, command over technology being only one of them. On the other hand, the productivity measures fail to reflect the fact that American output included sophisticated goods that could not be produced abroad. While in this essay we sometimes use productivity data as part of the evidence about technological leadership, our concern is with the latter rather than with the former. A wide variety of measures, backed by the commentary of informed observers, provides solid evidence that during the period in question the U.S. technological lead was real. U.S. firms were significantly ahead in developing and employing the leading edge technologies, their exports accounted for the largest share of world trade in their product fields, and their overseas branches often were dominant firms in their host countries.

No longer. The U.S. technological lead has been eroded in many industries, and in some the U.S. is now a laggard. A growing volume of studies,

By Richard R. Nelson and Gavin Wright; originally published in the *Journal of Economic Literature* (December 1992): 1931–1964.

Log Scale

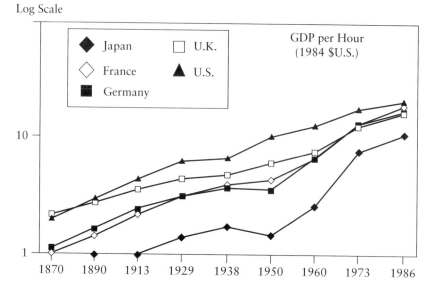

Figure 9.1   Gross domestic product per hour, 1870–1986. *(Source: Maddison, 1987, 1989.)*

books, commission reports, and popular media accounts bemoans this loss of leadership and looks for causes and cures (for example, Dertouzos, Lester, and Solow, 1989; Womack, Jones, and Roos, 1991). This essay is motivated by the apparent weakening, perhaps loss of American technological leadership, but more basically by the observation that relatively little of the current discussion is informed by an understanding of the sources of America's unique position in the mid-twentieth-century economic world. How can policies respond appropriately to "what we have lost" without a clear knowledge of what it was that we had and how we got it?

However, the questions of how the postwar American lead came about, and how and why it has eroded, pose deeper questions in turn. There has in recent decades been a striking convergence among the most advanced industrial nations in per capita income and in output per man hour, both in the aggregate and in a wide spectrum of industries (Figure 9.1). This phenomenon has spawned a thriving new literature on "convergence" (Abramovitz, 1986; Baumol, 1986; De Long, 1988; Dollar and Wolff, 1988; Baumol, Blackman, and Wolff, 1989; Barro, 1991). While a portion of the analytic apparatus and a few of the ideas in this recent literature are new, the general questions being explored have been around for a long time. Historical economists have long been interested in why Britain forged ahead of the Continent in the new technologies of the first industrial revolution, and the process through which other economies later caught up (Elbaum and Lazonick, 1986). More generally, how can one explain why certain countries take a significant technological lead in key industries in certain eras, and maintain it for some time? How do other countries catch on? Is convergence really the dominant process over long epochs, with history punctuated from time to time by new leadership surges from formerly backward nations? If so, why the "punctuations"?

But these questions pose still deeper ones. In what sense can one talk about "national" technological capabilities? In what ways do borders and citizenship matter? What is the role of the nation-state in technological development, and has this role changed historically? Is the recent trend to convergence mainly an equilibration process among nations, or is it a sign of decline in the importance of nationalities and borders?

As we see it, the recent literature on these topics contains three broad perspectives, often implicit. One, associated with the convergence literature, sees the U.S. postwar lead as inherently transient, attributable partly to the late start of many of our present rivals and partly to the destruction of our major industrial rivals during the war; convergence was therefore relatively automatic and inevitable. A second view sees not convergence but rather U.S. industry losing out in a competitive struggle with other national industries. In this view, the United States is now falling below the pack of leading countries as England did a century ago, with Japan and perhaps Germany taking on new leadership roles. The authors of this school vary in the reasons they stress. For Paul Kennedy (1987) it is the burden of defense spending. For Christopher Freeman (1987), Michael Piore and Charles Sabel (1984), James Womack, Daniel Jones, and Daniel Roos (1991), and Lazonick (1990), relative U.S. decline reflects the rise in other nations of new and better ways of organizing aspects of economic activity, with the U.S. stuck in its old ruts. A third interpretation posits a more fundamental decline in the role of national borders and nationally based industrial centers. Convergence has occurred, in this view, but not simply as a result of postwar recovery or international technological diffusion and imitation, or the rise of superior new national systems. Rather, the argument is that just as markets and business have become more global, the network of individuals and organizations generating and improving new science-based technologies has become less national and more transnational, so that convergence reflects a diminution of the saliency of nation-states as technological and economic entities.

We do not claim that these three frameworks are neatly distinguishable,

and we certainly do not claim to have answered our own questions definitively. But we believe there is value in posing these questions carefully and
clearly, and we attempt to marshal analysis and evidence bearing on them.
This we have tried to do in the context of the U.S. experience, within the
limits of our own competence and the space available.

Let us tip our hand by stating where we come out on some of the critical
issues. First, the U.S. lead of the early postwar era was not merely a temporary result of the war but stemmed from two relatively distinct sources.
Part of the lead reflected long-standing American dominance in mass production industries, which in turn derived from uniquely favorable historical
access to natural resources and to the world's largest domestic market. The
other part of the American lead, in high-technology industries, was new, and
reflected the massive private and public investments in R&D and scientific
and technical education that the United States made after World War II.
Though these investments built on older institutional foundations, broadly
based world leadership by the United States in basic science and in technologies drawing on new scientific frontiers was largely a postwar development.
Thus there were two components to U.S. leadership, and they have weakened
for conceptually different but institutionally connected reasons. Growing
domestic markets outside the United States, and the opening of the world as
a common market in resource commodities as well as consumer and producer goods have virtually eliminated the advantages American firms used
to have in mass production. And as the networks of technological development and communication have become more oriented to professional peer-
group communities, which have themselves become increasingly international, technology has become more accessible to companies that make the
requisite investments in research and development, regardless of their na-
tionality. Increasingly, such investments have been made by firms based in
other countries. These developments are associated with the fact that large
industrial firms are increasingly transnational. Where national industries become tradition-bound and fall behind, international convergence is still advanced by the migration of capital, management, and personnel across international borders. The net result of these developments is a world in which
national borders and citizenship mean significantly less technologically than
they used to.

Our discussion is organized as follows. We begin by examining the rise
of American strength in the mass production industries during the nineteenth
century, considering especially the reasons why American technology came
to differ from, and in an important sense to surpass, that of the Europeans.
We also describe the rise during the early twentieth century of the American

chemical and electrical products industries. Then we turn to the interwar period when the U.S. consolidated its lead in mass production and laid the basis for its advances in "high tech" after World War II, by establishing a solid base in organized research and by providing the experience of post-secondary education to a broad segment of the population. Then we consider the early postwar era, focusing particularly on how U.S. primacy was achieved in such fields as microelectronics. Finally, in light of our analysis of the nature of U.S. leads in mass production and high tech, and the factors that maintained the U.S. advantages, we present our diagnosis of how and why the twin leads have declined since the late 1950s, and our views of what might lie ahead.

2. Long-Standing American Strengths

In this section we deal with that part of the American postwar lead in manufacturing that had been there for a long time: mass production industries. We shall distinguish the reasons for the U.S. advantage in these industries rather sharply from the factors behind U.S. dominance after World War II in fields like semiconductors and computers. But before we get into the discussion of American leadership in mass production, it is important to consider the senses in which we can talk at all about national technological capabilities. What does it mean to say that (firms in) one country has a technological lead over (firms in) other countries?

2.1. National Technologies and Technological Leadership

If technology were a pure public good, as economists are wont to assume in elementary versions of microeconomic theory, then the proposition that firms in certain countries are able to employ technologies that lie beyond the ken of firms elsewhere would make no sense. The input and output mixes of firms located in different countries might be different, but such divergence would merely reflect differences in market or other environmental conditions that influence what firms choose to do. Thus during the nineteenth century the special U.S. conditions of cheap resources, high wage rates, and large markets could be understood to induce the high labor productivity, large-scale, capital-intensive production methods that became known as characteristically American. But the contrast with European practice would be ascribable entirely to economic choices rather than to differences in the technology choice set.

Of course economists have long recognized that firms are sometimes able to bar others from using their technology through threats of a patent infringement suit or by tightly held trade secrets. But there is little evidence that patent suits were effective barriers to technological transfer in the metalworking and mass production industries where nineteenth-century American firms achieved their greatest advantage. Some American firms certainly tried to guard key trade secrets, but high interfirm mobility among technically informed personnel made firms into relatively leaky institutions for technical information that could be carried in the heads of knowledgeable individuals. Just as British restrictions in an earlier era did not stop Samuel Slater and a host of followers from carrying their understanding of textile technology across the Atlantic (Jeremy, 1981), American firms of the late nineteenth and early twentieth centuries were seldom able to block technological secrets from international dissemination.

Nonetheless we argue that the concept of a "national technology" is a useful and defensible analytical abstraction, appropriate for much of modern history if decreasingly so in recent times. Our proposition rests on three intertwined arguments. First, the technologies in question were complex, involving different kinds of machines and a variety of learned skills, and often requiring relatively sophisticated coordination and management. While certain features of these complex operations were described in writing or, more generally, were familiar to the experts in the field, to get the technologies under control and operating well typically required a lot of learning-by-doing on the part of many interacting people, from engineers to managers to machine operators, as well as investment in plant and equipment. Thus "technology transfer" involved much more than what one or a few men could carry away in their heads, or in a few drawings or models. These could provide a start on technology transfer, but real command of the technology required a considerable amount of trial-and-error organizational learning. Thus the technology was not really a public good in the standard sense. American firms had a command of it that others did not, and could not master without significant time and effort.

Second, to a considerable extent technical advance in these fields was local and incremental, building from and improving on prevailing practice. The knowledge useful for advancing technology included, prominently, experience with the existing technology so as to be aware of its strengths and weaknesses, and to know how it actually worked. Thus those at the forefront of the technology were in the best position to further advance it. Economic historians have long been aware of this kind of technological learning.

Nathan Rosenberg (1963) recounts the evolution of American machine-tool technology in the nineteenth century as a sequence of problem-solving challenges. At any given point, progress was constrained by a particular bottleneck known mainly by those experiencing it, yet each new solution shifted the focus to another technical constraint or phase of production. With frontier technology rapidly changing and new applications being spun off, physical presence in the active area was virtually indispensable for anyone who hoped to improve on the prevailing best-practice.

Third, sustained technological advance was not the result of one person or firm pushing things ahead, but involved many interacting people and firms. One learned from another's invention and went a step further. Robert C. Allen (1983) describes this process of "collective invention" in some detail in his study of British Bessemer steel producers in the Cleveland district, and Elting Morison (1974) describes a similar process among American Bessemer producers. The interdependencies went well beyond mere aggregation of achievements over time. As demonstrated in Ross Thomson's account of the origins and diffusion of the sewing machine (Thomson 1989), the success of new technical breakthroughs required that they mesh with prevailing complementary technologies, and that they fit into a complex chain of contingent production and exchange activities, from raw material to final distribution. Any number of technically successful mechanical stitchers had been invented in the sixty years prior to Elias Howe's officially recognized invention of 1846, but none succeeded commercially. Howe's machine did succeed, because it fit in with complementary technologies and skills, and because it initiated a process in which new firms formed nodes in a communication network linked to other innovators. In turn, the principles and the networks of interdependence that came out of sewing machine development became applicable to a host of related industries.

In short, technological progress is a network phenomenon replete with "network externalities" of the sort that have now come in for intensive theoretical scrutiny (Katz and Shapiro, 1985), by *path dependence,* that is, dependence of successive developments on prior events (David, 1975, 1988; Nelson and Winter, 1982), and a tendency for particular systems to become "locked in" beyond a certain point (Arthur, 1988, 1989). A striking historical feature of these networks of cumulative technological learning is that down to recent times their scope has been largely defined by national borders. Why should this have been so?

In the first place, for reasons of geographical proximity. The networks described by Allen, Morison, and Thomson all involved inventors and tinkerers living in the same general area and having intimate contact with one another's inventions if not one another. Second, to the extent that technological communications networks follow in the tracks of previously established linguistic and cultural communities, it would be entirely natural for technologies to have something of a national character. Such a primary basis might well be reinforced by the existence of centralized or uniform national institutions for technical training, though this was a less striking feature of American development than it was in European countries like France and Germany. Even in the absence of officially mandated uniformity, however, American scientists and engineers displayed early signs of national identity, rooted in the distinctness and commonality of their problem-solving environment: the resource base, the product market, and the legal/institutional conditions were markedly different from those in European countries. The key elements of such networks are common terms and reference points, methods of measurement, and standards of technical performance. A Scottish visitor during 1849–50 complained that American mineralogists disdained to label their formations with the names of European localities, but insisted on an independent national terminology. Nathan Rosenberg (1985) points out that most of what we now call science-based progress did not deploy "frontier" scientific concepts, but involved largely mundane and elementary tasks, such as grading and testing of materials, for which scientific training was needed but where the learning was specific to the materials at hand. Standardizing such measurements, and physically embodying them in instruments and apparatus (as well as procedures) were among the main tasks of the distinctly American scientific and engineering associations which emerged in this country at the end of the nineteenth century (Constant, 1983). Critics of American capitalism complain that by the 1920s, American engineers themselves had become standardized commodities, through the close links between corporations and institutions of higher education (Noble, 1977). As the American technology was by that time the envy of the industrial world, however, aspiring young engineers could hardly have done better than to gain the training that would give them access to the national technological network.

Of course not all countries had such indigenous national technological communities, for reasons of scale, political stability, or historical accident. We do not address ultimate questions of historical economic development in this essay, but focus instead on the narrower task of describing the emergence of a distinctive American technology from the end of the nineteenth century onward, and tracing the course of that national characteristic in the twentieth century.

2.2. The Rise of Mass Production in the Nineteenth Century

American technology began to make a splash in the world at least as early as the mid-nineteenth century. Mechanical reapers, mass-produced firearms, and many other American novelties created a noticeable stir at the Crystal Palace Exhibition in London in 1851. In this early period, however, the impressive technical achievements of the "American System of Manufactures" pertained only to a small subset of industries, while in other major areas (such as iron making) the United States was clearly behind European countries (James and Skinner, 1985).

Nonetheless, across the nineteenth century the country did develop the sine qua non for advanced technological status, an indigenous technological community able to adapt European techniques to American conditions. Though the process of technological search was decentralized and competitive, flows of information through trade channels, printed media, and informal contacts served to establish a distinctive American problem solving network. An important early institutional manifestation was the emergence of a specialized machine-tool industry, which evolved from machine shops linked to New England textile mills in the 1820s and 1830s and became a "machinery industry" generating and diffusing new technologies for a wide range of consumer goods industries (Rosenberg, 1963). Economic historians have traced remarkable threads of continuity in the histories of firms and individual machinists, as steady improvements in machine speeds, power transmission, lubrication, gearing mechanisms, precision metal cutting, and many other dimensions of performance were applied in one industrial setting after another: textiles, sewing machines, farm machinery, locks, clocks, firearms, boots and shoes, locomotives, bicycles, cigarettes, sewing machines, and so on (Hounshell, 1984; Thomson, 1989). This distinctively American development represented a type of collective learning, which fed into the twentieth-century technologies that formed the basis of U.S. world leadership.

By the end of the nineteenth century, American industry assumed a qualitatively different place in the world. A number of important innovations concentrated in the 1880s took advantage of the opportunities for mass production and mass marketing offered by the national rail and telegraph networks. These included new branded and packaged consumer products (cigarettes, canned goods, flour and grain products, beer, dairy products, soaps and drugs); mass-produced light machinery (sewing machines, typewriters, cameras); electrical equipment; and standardized industrial machinery such as boilers, pumps, and printing presses (Chandler, 1990, pp. 62–71). Although most of these products were developed for the domestic market, many of them became exports as well. The first wave of alarmist European books on "Americanization" dates from 1901 and 1902, with titles and themes about an "American invasion" which would again become familiar in the 1920s and 1960s (for example, MacKenzie, 1901). Particularly noteworthy were growing American exports of industrial machinery, farm equipment, hardware and other engineering goods, producers' goods which embodied mass-production principles and which in many cases posed a new competitive challenge abroad. In addition, by 1900 the American steel industry had become a world leader, and the country was exporting an extensive array of iron and steel products (Allen, 1977). This international standing was new. Prior to the 1890s, American steel rails would not have survived in the domestic market without tariff protection (Allen, 1981).

These new turn-of-the-century achievements may be thought of as the confluence of two technological streams: the ongoing advance of mechanical and metalworking skills and performance, focused on high-volume production of standardized commodities; and the process of exploring, developing, and utilizing the mineral resource base of the national economy. As surprising as it may seem from a modern perspective, the rise of American industry to world leadership was intimately connected with the rise of the country to world leadership in the production of coal, iron ore, copper, petroleum, and virtually every other major industrial raw material of that era. To cite one important example, the breakthrough in the steel industry coincided with the opening of the rich Mesabi iron range in the 1890s and to concomitant adaptations in technology and transportation (Allen 1977). Analysis of trade in manufactures reveals that intensity in nonreproducible resources was one of the most robust characteristics of American goods, and this relative intensity was in fact increasing across the critical period from 1880 to 1930 (Wright, 1990). Louis Cain and Donald Paterson (1986) find that material-using technological biases were significant in nine of twenty American sectors, including those with the strongest export performance.

It would be a mistake to imply that the country's industrial performance rested on resource abundance and scale economies *as opposed to* technology, because mineral discovery, extraction, and metallurgy drew upon, stimulated, and focused some of the most advanced engineering developments of the time, as did mass production. The U.S. Geological Survey was the most ambitious and successful government science project of the nineteenth century, and the country quickly rose to world leadership in the training of mining engineers (David and Wright, 1991). New processes of electrolytic smelting and refining had a dramatic impact on the industrial potential of copper, nickel, zinc, and aluminum. The oft-noted complementarity between capital and natural resources in that era was not merely an exogenous technological relationship, but may be viewed as a measure of the successful accomplishment of a technology in which Americans pioneered. Mass production industries were also intensive in their use of fuels and materials. Not only did the capital stock itself embody domestic materials, but "high-throughput" methods, to maximize the sustainable rate of capacity utilization, imply high ratios of physical materials and fuels to labor. For these reasons, although they were highly profitable given the economic conditions in the United States, American technologies were often not well adapted to other localities. Robert Allen (1979, p. 919) estimates that in 1907–1909 the ratio of horsepower to workers was twice as large in America as in either Germany or Great Britain. On the other hand, American total factor productivity in this industry was only about 15 percent ahead of Great Britain, and approximately equal to that in Germany. This statistic does not imply that German steel makers could have matched American labor productivity levels "simply" by operating at the American level of capital and resource intensity. Our central point is that there is nothing "simple" about the processes through which firms come to adopt and learn to control technologies that have been in use elsewhere for some time. Rather, the numbers illustrate the particular kinds of new technological developments that the Americans developed. Accounts of the course of technological progress in Germany suggest an entirely different orientation governed by "the desire to find substitutes for expensive and uncertain imports" (Hayes, 1987, p. 1).

American manufacturing firms and their technologies not only were resource and capital intensive, but operated at much greater scale than did their counterparts in the United Kingdom and on the Continent. Large-scale operation was well tuned to the particularities of the large affluent American market. By 1900 total national income in the United States was twice as large as that of the United Kingdom, about four times as large as France or Germany. Per capita income had also surpassed that of Great Britain and was well ahead of continental Europe. American language and culture were reasonably homogeneous, and internal transportation and communications systems were well developed. Perhaps because of their relative freedom from traditional class standards, American consumers readily took to standardized products, a development which came much later in Europe. Further, this large American market was effectively off limits to European producers because of high prevailing levels of tariff protection. Although the size of the U.S. domestic market may have been partially offset by the greater relative importance of exports for the European countries, foreign markets were highly diverse and much less receptive to standardized goods than they later became. Oriented mainly toward the domestic market, American firms tended to produce a narrow range of product specifications. In the steel industry, for example, though the U.S. was dominant in mass-produced products, in specialty steels the U.S. performance was "a story of false starts, technological backwardness, commercial failures, and continued dependence on foreign steel" (Tweedale, 1986, p. 221). American harvesting machinery and locomotives (like automobiles at a later point) were technically impressive but inappropriate for most of the world's markets. Many European engineers held a low opinion of their American counterparts, for emphasizing production and speed over quality and durability (Headrick, 1988, pp. 75, 84).

It has often been argued that the distinctive strength of American corporations lay less in technology per se than in organizational efficiencies associated with mass production and mass distribution. The success abroad of the Singer Sewing Machine Company, for example, was based not on highly sophisticated product design or factory technology, but in the efficiency of its production, sales, and service organization (Carstensen, 1984, p. 26). Singer's ventures abroad came relatively early; but in general, the interest of American firms in foreign markets emerged belatedly, only after they had established national distribution networks (Wilkins, 1970). Here again, we should not think of organizational strength as an alternative but as a complement to advanced technology. As Alfred Chandler has argued, modern corporate enterprise tended to arise in sectors which had undergone prior technological transformation, and the new organizational form served to make more effective use of these new technological possibilities (Chandler, 1977). Chandler's comparative work, *Scale and Scope,* emphasizes that the United States had far more of these new technically and managerially advanced corporate institutions much earlier than any other country. Chandler's account of the "organizational capabilities" within large American firms is compelling and persuasive, but we would place more emphasis than he does on systemwide features of the economy and on the ongoing development of the technology itself. The large American companies were not just efficiently streamlined organizations; they were part and parcel of an emerging technological and managerial network, engaged in a collective learning process with a strongly national character. By the late nineteenth century the management style in American manufacturing companies had become very different from that in Great Britain and continental Europe.

The concept and practice of "professional management" first arose in the

United States, and by 1900 it was common for a large American firm to be staffed by a cadre of professional, educated middle managers, a phenomenon that seems to have been almost exclusively American. Lazonick (1990) argues that American management increasingly took control of the job floor at this time, in contrast to Britain, where management had little control over the details of work. The "scientific management" movement was singularly American, and closely associated with the professionalization of management. In a fascinating paper, Kogut (1992) stresses the importance of basic principles of management and organization, which he argues take on a strikingly national character, or at least used to. He proposes that it was the style of management and organization, far more than the simple economies of scale and scope, that led to the preeminence of American corporations in the early years of the twentieth century, although the former was essential to the latter. In his empirical examination of American corporations that established overseas branches, Kogut found many large companies, but also some middle-sized ones. Almost all of them, however, were marked by strong adherence to the management and organizational principles described above, which formed a distinctly American style.

We note here that relatively little of the American performance during this era was based in science, nor even on advanced technical education. American technology was practical, shop-floor oriented, built on experience. The level of advanced training in German industry was substantially higher (Kocka, 1980, pp. 95–96). As prominent an American engineer as Frederick W. Taylor, who played a major role in developing high-speed tool steel years before he invented "scientific management," had only an undergraduate degree and was deeply skeptical of the practical value of university training. The search for valuable petroleum by-products was carried out by people with only a smattering of chemical education (Rosenberg, 1985, p. 43). Many of the industries in which American strength was clearest and strongest, such as nonelectrical machinery, steel, and vehicles, were distinguished well into the twentieth century by an aversion to organized science-based research. American universities did have areas of strength in certain applied fields, but an aspiring student who sought the best available academic education in scientific disciplines like physics and chemistry would have been advised to study in Germany, Britain, or France. As Figure 9.2 shows, the United States did not surpass these countries in scientific Nobel Prizes until long after World War II.

These observations are intended to delineate rather than to downplay the magnitude of what American industry had achieved by the early twentieth century. American firms were the clear leaders in productivity across the

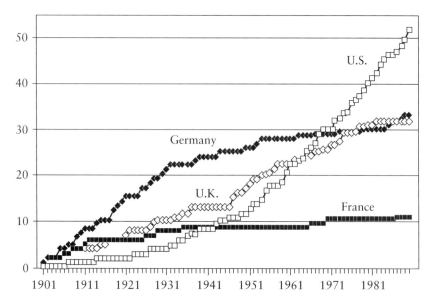

Figure 9.2   Cumulative Nobel Prizes in physics and chemistry, 1901–1990.

range of mass production industries. This lead in manufacturing combined with highly productive American agriculture to support wage rates and living standards higher than those in England, and higher still than on the Continent (Phelps-Brown, 1973). In turn, high wage rates and living standards induced and supported large-scale, capital- and resource-intensive production. And while the particular technologies and structures adopted by U.S. manufacturing firms reflected these unique aspects of the American scene, by and large where American industry went, Europe followed, if often with a pronounced lag.

2.3. Building the Infrastructure for Science-Based Industry

By the start of World War I, the United States had established a position of leadership in mass production and mass distribution industries, a technology characterized by scale economies, capital intensity, standardization, and the intensive use of natural resources. Though the United States was not the world leader in science or in the use of science-based technologies at that time, the country had developed much of the private organization and public infrastructure needed to operate effectively in the science-based industries that were coming into prominence.

Federal government support for university programs in agriculture and the practical arts dates from the Morrill Land Grant College Act of 1862. Though this act led directly to the founding of several major state universities and the strengthening of others, little significant research could be credited to it prior to the Hatch Act of 1887, which provided each state with funding for an agricultural experiment station. The level of support for research was doubled by the Adams Act of 1906, and unique institutions for the dissemination of knowledge among farmers were in place with the establishment of the cooperative extension service in 1914. At this juncture the United States was well behind Europe in the deployment of "scientific agriculture"—soil chemistry, plant biology, animal husbandry. But a generation later these investments in infrastructure had unprecedented payoffs in agricultural productivity.

The Morrill Act also provided a federal stimulus to engineering education; within a decade after its passage, the number of engineering schools increased from 6 to 70, growing further to 126 in 1917. The number of graduates from engineering colleges grew from 100 in 1870 to 4,300 at the outbreak of World War I (Noble, 1977, p. 24). Like their agricultural counterparts, engineers and scientists at American universities were under continuing pressure to demonstrate the practical benefits of their efforts. "Merely theoretical" research was openly belittled, and the areas of applied science which did show some strength in the nineteenth century were mainly those linked to state-specific economic interests, such as geology and industrial chemistry (Bruce, 1987). Nonetheless, by the turn of the century a network of research universities had come into being, striking an institutional balance between the demand for immediate usefulness and the ethos of academic independence espoused by the emerging scientific disciplines. According to Roger Geiger (1986), the main elements in this balance were the provision of large-scale undergraduate teaching as a means of financing research and graduate training; and the successful mobilization of nationalistic sentiments in support of science. A watershed of sorts was passed with the founding of the American Association of Universities in 1900, to bolster academic standards, establish uniformity in requirements for the Ph.D., and achieve foreign recognition for U.S. doctorates. Although business-university cooperation has continued to be an important part of American technological history, the prospect of world-class research universities came only after a certain social distance from industry had been established.

At the same time, American industry was building its own technological infrastructure. In the wake of the great merger wave in American business

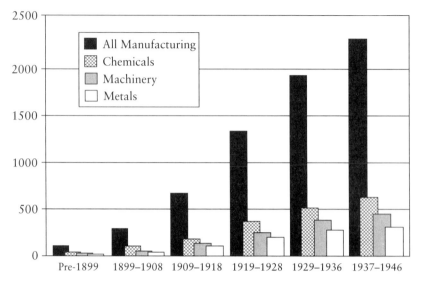

Figure 9.3   Laboratory foundations in U.S. manufacturing. *(Source: Mowery and Rosenberg, 1989, table 4.1.)*

(1897–1902), which established many of today's well-known corporations in positions of national market power for the first time, an unprecedented expansion of private-sector research laboratories occurred, a trend that accelerated over the next half century (Figure 9.3). General Electric, Du Pont, AT&T, and Kodak all set up formal research laboratories before World War I. Here, too, the lasting institutional implications may have been very different from the original motivations of the founders. Business historians have argued that these early firms were looking not to do pioneering research in new technologies, but to control innovation and protect an established patent position (Reich, 1985; Smith, 1990). Once established, however, a science-based research tradition evolved, often with considerable autonomy from the immediate objectives of the employer.

Only in chemistry had there been any substantial use of scientifically trained personnel prior to 1900. In 1875 the Pennsylvania Railroad hired a Yale Ph.D. chemist to organize a laboratory for testing and analysis of materials brought from suppliers. As Nathan Rosenberg argues, much of the early use of science by industry was of just this sort, a relatively mundane application of laboratory procedures for testing materials, well within the frontiers of existing science. Institutionalizing such procedures, however, often led to unexpected results. The Pennsylvania Railroad laboratory, for example, went on to develop an improved lubrication composition for lo-comotives. A Ph.D. chemist hired by the Carnegie Steel Company not only helped to identify high-quality ores, but found ways to make better iron and steel. Increasingly, chemists came to play an important part in technological innovation in iron and steel making, in traditional inorganic chemicals like soda, and in new organic chemical substances like dyes and later plastics.

The German chemical industry unquestionably was the leader in dye-stuffs, plastics, and other new products based on organic chemistry. Christopher Freeman's data show that through 1945, I. G. Farben was by far the largest patentor in plastics. By 1910 or so, however, the leading American companies like Du Pont, Dow, and Kodak had established R&D laboratories and had developed the capacity to produce a full range of industrial chemicals and a wide range of fine chemicals (Noble, 1977; Hounshell and Smith, 1988). These companies were able to draw upon the newly emerging specialty of chemical engineering, an American professional hybrid. They were thus organizationally well positioned to take advantage of the cutoff of trade with the Germans during World War I, and to respond to the need to provide a variety of products for the military. The abrogation of German patents brought the American companies close to technological parity with the Germans by the 1920s.

The story in the new electrical industry is similar, except that here American strength was apparent somewhat earlier. As in chemistry, performance was clearly not rooted in any American advantage in fundamental science; U.S. universities were significantly behind those in Germany and other continental countries in teaching and research in physics. But American industry had early access to trained personnel in electrical *engineering*. By the last decades of the nineteenth century in universities like MIT and Cornell, physics and mechanical engineering had been self-consciously combined as a field of training (Rosenberg, 1984). Thomas Hughes has argued that in the new electrical industries, the Americans excelled in the conception, design, development, and implementation of large-scale systems (Hughes, 1987). In addition, the U.S. industry benefited from scientifically educated European émigrés like Thomson, Tesla, Steinmetz, and Alexanderson.

Here again one may see the influence of the large, affluent American market, not as an alternative to technology, but as an influence on the directions taken by American technology and a source of unique advantages in international comparisons. There are numerous examples of innovations which were European in origin, but whose development progressed most rapidly in the United States because of the scale economies accessible in the American market (Braun, 1983).

3. The Interwar Period

In the 1920s and 1930s, American industry consolidated its position of leadership in mass production industries, while joining these longer-term strengths to organized research and advanced training in important new industries such as chemical and electrical engineering. Some of the circumstances were historically fortuitous. The United States escaped damage and even enjoyed industrial stimulation from World War I. After the war, the institutions of international trade and finance remained in disarray, stumbling toward their complete collapse in the 1930s. Industrial countries that depended on foreign markets had a hard time of it (though Japan managed to continue its industrial growth despite these obstacles). American industries were largely insulated from these problems. The country was highly protectionist from the time of the Civil War. In the 1920s, despite the emerging strength of American industry, import barriers were increased, first by the Fordney-McCumber Tariff of 1922, and then by the notorious Hawley-Smoot Tariff of 1930. But the domestic market was more than sufficient to support rapid productivity growth and the ongoing development and diffusion of new technologies and new products.

3.1. The Marriage of Old and New Industrial Strengths

The automobile industry was the most spectacular American success story of the interwar period, a striking blend of mass production methods, cheap materials, and fuels. The distinct lead of American producers over French and British rivals really dates only from the advent of the assembly line at Ford between 1908 and 1913, but the ascendancy was rapid thereafter. Though the historical origins of this performance may be traced back to characteristics of the domestic market, the extent of American leadership is clearly indicated by the high volume of exports, notwithstanding the fact that the size and fuel requirements of American cars were poorly suited to foreign demand. Despite barriers to trade and weak world demand, U.S. cars dominated world trade during the 1920s, and motor vehicles dominated American manufacturing exports (Figure 9.4). Henry Ford's books were best sellers abroad, and "Fordism" developed a cult technocratic following in both Germany and the Soviet Union (Hughes, 1989). The components of the U.S. cost advantage are difficult to measure with precision, however, because the large-scale auto firm came as a package: organizational, managerial, financial, and technological. The branch plants of American firms were also dominant abroad, though during the interwar period they were

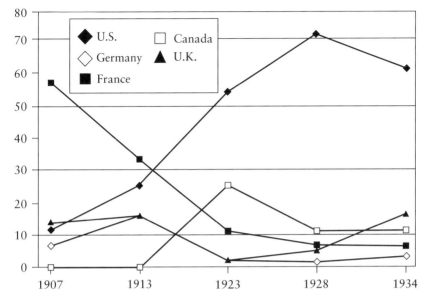

Figure 9.4   Shares of world motor vehicle exports, 1907–1934. *(Source: Foreman-Peck, 1982, p. 868.)*

not fully able to replicate performance at home (Foreman-Peck, 1982). The process of global diffusion and adaptation of American methods would surely have continued, however, either by imitation or by direct foreign investment, if it had not been interrupted by World War II.

In many ways a more lasting and significant basis for technological leadership was established in those industries that were able to marry mass production methods to organized science-based research, such as the electrical industries and chemical engineering. Though the fundamental scientific breakthroughs in electricity had come earlier, the interwar period saw the realization of this potential through full electrification of factories and households. Paul David (1989) has called attention to electrification as an example of an innovation whose productivity impact was delayed for a full generation because of the need to disseminate and adapt the underlying knowledge and to restructure physical plants and work routines. The percentage of factories using electric power grew from 25 in 1910 to 75 in 1930 (Devine, 1983), a development essential for the acceleration of productivity growth at this time. A similar infusion occurred in the household, where the use of electric lighting rose from 33 percent of urban families in 1909 to 96 percent in 1939 (Lebergott, 1976). Large firms like GE, Westinghouse, and AT&T established advanced research organizations that generated an ongoing flow of innovative new electrical products, sometimes advancing the frontiers of science in the process.

The rise of chemical engineering was also a marriage of old and new strengths. Ralph Landau and Nathan Rosenberg (1990) point out that this professional category was an American innovation, combining chemistry with training in industrial processes. It was also relatively new, emerging as a course of study at MIT in the first two decades of the twentieth century, becoming a separate department only in 1920. The American surge was also closely associated with a shift in the basic feedstock for chemical plants from coal to petroleum, a primary product in which the United States dominated world production. As technology developed, the production of organic chemicals was carried on most effectively as a by-product of general petroleum refining, hence closely connected with the location of petroleum supplies. Prior to the 1920s, there was little contact between petroleum companies and the chemical industry. In that decade, however, important connections emerged, through mergers, research establishments, and industry-university associations. Working in close partnership with MIT, New Jersey Standard's research organization in Baton Rouge, Louisiana, produced such important process innovations as hydroforming, fluid flex coking, and fluid catalytic cracking (Landau, 1990a). Here we have a remarkable blend of mass production, advanced science, and American resources. The chemical engineer Peter Spitz notes: "Regardless of the fact that Europe's chemical industry was for a long time more advanced than that in the United States, the future of organic chemicals was going to be related to petroleum, not coal, as soon as companies such as Union Carbide, Standard Oil (New Jersey), Shell, and Dow turned their attention to the production of petrochemicals" (Spitz, 1988, p. xiii). Petroleum led the way in the use of scientifically trained personnel in the first half of the century (Figure 9.5).

3.2. Education and Technology

Sooner or later, discussions of American industrial and technological performance generally come around to the educational system. Americans seem to believe in a golden age during which the country led the world in mass public schooling, and that this enlightened leadership in education was also closely associated with leadership in technology. There is some truth in this account, but the story is less straightforward than commonly imagined. It is true that the United States was an early leader in literacy and primary education, achieving close to universal elementary enrollment before the Civil War (outside of the South), well ahead of France and Britain (Easterlin,

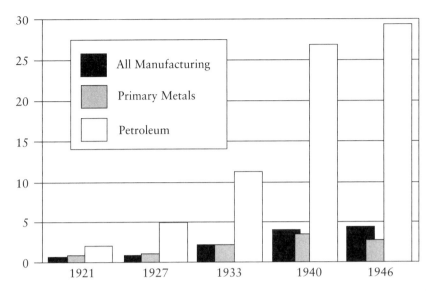

Figure 9.5   Scientists and engineers per thousand wage earners. *(Source: Mowery and Rosenberg, 1989, tables 4.2–4.6.)*

1981). Only Germany (where in Prussia compulsory education dated from 1763) approached these levels. Because basic education has a clear effect on the capacity to conduct commercial operations and process written information (Schultz, 1975), the diffusion of schooling among the American farming population undoubtedly had a positive influence on its responsiveness to new opportunities and its receptivity to innovations. But these benefits pertained largely to a population of farm proprietors, which for the most part was not the source of the labor for American factories during the country's surge to world industrial leadership. From the time of the Irish influx in the 1840s, the bulk of the industrial labor force came from immigration, mostly from non-English-speaking countries with far lower educational standards than those prevailing among the native born. In 1910 the foreign born and the sons of the foreign born were more than 60 percent of the machine operatives in the country, and more than two-thirds of the laborers in mining and manufacturing. There is no reason to believe that this labor force was particularly well educated by world standards. This may not have been a drawback. It has been argued that the workpace in American factories was uniquely high (Clark, 1987), an intensity of effort that one might well associate with "high-throughput" production strategy, but not necessarily with high levels of education on the part of workers. To be sure, the educational background of overhead and administrative personnel un-

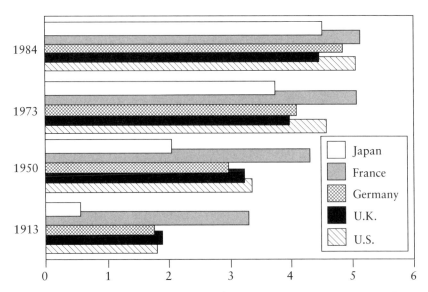

Figure 9.6 Average years of secondary education, 1913–1984 (pop. 15–64). *(Source: Maddison, 1987, table A-12.)*

doubtedly contributed to rising productivity; but the combination of a well-educated staff at the top and hard-driving workers at the bottom is very different from the success formulas of today's world. The upgrading of educational standards for production workers came largely after the cutoff of immigration in the early 1920s.

Educational attainment did indeed increase rapidly, as much of the country moved toward the norm of a high school degree. As job qualifications were raised and mechanization tended to eliminate jobs requiring mere brute strength and exertion, it is reasonable to hold that higher educational standards contributed to the remarkable rates of productivity growth maintained by American industry between 1920 and 1960, though we have no detailed understanding of this process. It is appropriate to note, however, that the expansion of secondary education in the twentieth century was not particularly unique to the United States. Similar trends were recorded in virtually all of the "advanced" countries of the world, and as of 1950 there was no marked difference in average years of secondary education among the United States, France, and Britain, all of them still well behind Germany (Figure 9.6). This does not gainsay the contribution of secondary education to American performance, but it underscores the point that broadly based education contributes to technological leadership only as these skills are effectively utilized by industrial employers. The disrupted conditions of

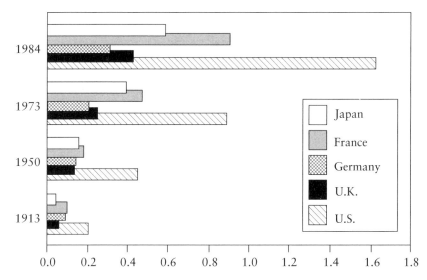

Figure 9.7 Average years of higher education, 1913–1984 (pop. 15–64). *(Source: Maddison, 1987, table A-12.)*

world trade between 1914 and 1950 very likely constrained many countries from exploiting their educational potential.

The respect in which the United States was distinct among the nations of the world was the percentage of the population gaining access to a college education (Figure 9.7). As early as 1890, the ratio of university students per 1,000 primary students in America was two to three times that of any other country, and this gap was maintained and increased through the period of American industrial ascendancy. After 1900, the surge in enrollment was particularly robust in applied sciences and engineering (Geiger, 1986, p. 14); in new specialties like electrical engineering, American institutions such as MIT were reputed to be the best in the world by World War I. Advanced training in business management also experienced rapid post-1900 growth (Chandler, 1990, p. 83). Though university-trained engineers, scientists, and managers were no more than a small percentage of those employed in American industry, here if anywhere is a specific institutional basis for American technological leadership. Utilization of such personnel grew steadily through the twentieth century (Mowery and Rosenberg, 1989).

So also did employment of college-trained people in a wide range of activities ancillary to R&D and production. Employment in marketing, accounting, legal service, finance, insurance, and communications grew rapidly over the interwar period, some of it in manufacturing firms, some of it in other sectors. By and large American organizations were able to tap a more highly educated population for these jobs than their European counterparts.

There are reasons to believe that the numbers somewhat exaggerate the American educational advantage "at the top." The elite grammar schools of the United Kingdom, the gymnasium of Germany, and the lycée of France tended to teach subjects beyond what was taught in all but the best American high schools, and Americans graduating from high school tended to be younger and to have fewer years of education than their European counterparts coming out of the secondary institutions listed above. A number of commentators (for example, Geiger) have noted that American university faculty often complained that their students were far less educated when they came to university than were students entering university in Europe. However, particularly with the advantage of hindsight, it is clear that long before the Europeans, Americans developed a tradition in which a significant fraction of the sons (and later the daughters) of middle-class families went on to education beyond high school. And the American middle class wanted "practical education."

Though the significance of university education for technology may seem self-evident, we have to acknowledge that we lack a clear understanding of the specific linkages. As with education more generally, what is important is not the sheer number of students or the quantity of their training, but the effectiveness with which that training is integrated into the process of improving the technology of operating firms. In interwar America that coordination was advanced to a high state of refinement, as the curricula of educational institutions came to be closely adapted to the requirements of the "positions" that graduates would be taking; and vice versa (Lazonick, 1990, pp. 230–32). A 1921 survey made note of the "progressive dependence [of corporations] upon higher education institutions as sources of employee supply . . . the prejudice of many businessmen to higher education as a factor in employment is being rapidly overcome" (quoted in Noble, 1977, p. 243). Political critics have complained that the process of national standardization in the specifications for products and processes came to be extended to personnel, as engineers "automatically integrated professional requirements with industrial and corporate requirements" (Noble, 1977, p. 168). In 1919, for example, MIT launched its Cooperative Course in electrical engineering, a program that divided the students' time between courses at the Institute and at General Electric, which hired half of the students after graduation. The program was later joined by AT&T, Bell Labs, Western Electric, and other firms (Noble, 1977, p. 192). Whatever the merits of

Noble's reservation about the close links between universities and private firms, what he describes is an effective network of training and utilization, operating efficiently at a national level because it was self-contained, internalizing the resource base and market demands of the national economy.

We have noted that in recent years a sizable literature on economic "convergence" has emerged, oriented around the proposition that large technological gaps between countries, and the associated gaps in productivity and income, are not sustainable if the lagging countries have the requisite "social capabilities." Abramovitz (1986) has suggested that these include, prominently, a well-educated work force including competence at the top in the major sciences and technologies of the era, adequate firm management and organization, and financial institutions and governments capable of keeping their fiscal and monetary houses in order. It is arguable that during the interwar period the major European economies were not significantly outmatched by the United States in these dimensions, although we have highlighted some important differences. It is noteworthy, however, that there was little if any tendency toward systematic convergence in command of mass production technologies during this period, nor in levels of labor productivity and per capita income relative to the United States. Although general dispersion narrowed, the mean productivity of Maddison's fifteen successful countries was no higher in 1938 as a percentage of the U.S. level than it had been in 1929, 1913, or 1890 (Abramovitz, 1986, p. 391).

There are a number of reasons. One was the chaotic economic climate that affected most economies over this interval. Indeed Maddison's data show a sharp drop in the growth of world exports from nearly 4.0 percent per year between 1870 and 1913 to about 1.0 percent per year on average between 1913 and 1950. The average ratio of merchandise exports to GDP in the countries he examined fell from 11.2 percent in 1913 to 8.3 percent in 1950, and the number was almost certainly even lower during the 1930s. Thus during the interwar period nations were even more self-contained than they had been in the thirty years or so before World War I, and far more so than they became after World War II. This meant that the mass production methods used by American producers, which were highly productive and efficient on the American scene, were less attractive to European firms facing their own home markets. Convergence is far from an automatic phenomenon. It requires not only that the lagging nations have requisite social capabilities, but also that their firms face an economic and political environment conducive to adopting technology used in the leading country. Rather than refining procedures for testing the "convergence hypothesis" as a universal tendency, it seems more fruitful to examine the new features of the postwar era that have encouraged and facilitated convergence among the world's leading countries.

4. The Postwar Era: The American Breakaway at the Technological Frontiers

Just as after World War I, the United States came out of World War II buoyant, with technological capabilities extended by wartime production experience, while Europe came out prostrate. In contrast to the 1920s, after World War II Japan too was a demolished economy and nation. By the mid-1950s, most of the war-devastated countries had regained and surpassed prewar productivity and income levels, but as Figure 9.1 shows, the U.S. productivity and income edge remained enormous. While some Europeans seemed surprised at the lead of the Americans even after European recovery, they should not have been. The U.S. productivity lead in general, and in mass production industries in particular, had been around since the turn of the century. What was new was U.S. dominance in the "high-technology" industries of the postwar era. Several intertwined but distinguishable reasons lay behind this development.

4.1. National Technology and National Leadership in Science-Based Fields

Like the mass production technologies, newer "science-based" technologies are advanced through community efforts. But to a far greater extent, chemical and electrical technologies, and nowadays fields like aircraft and semiconductors, require university-trained scientists and engineers, engaged in teamwork aimed to achieve new and better production process designs, through activities that have come to be called research and development. As a result, possession of university training, and involvement in organized R&D define the relevant technological communities.

Put another way, in science-based technologies the skills and experience needed to advance a technology include much more than can be acquired simply by working with that technology and learning from experience. In some cases the two components are completely disjoined. A chemist working on a new drug in a laboratory owned by a pharmaceutical company may know little about how pharmaceuticals are produced or even how the drug works on the human body. In other cases both kinds of understanding are needed. Thus a chemical engineer working on a way to produce a new plastic must know both standard production practice and a lot of formal chemistry. If the two types of understanding are separated too widely, problems of execution can easily result. But whatever the optimal mixture or practice, the industries in which the United States forged ahead after World War II required experience, specialized training, and organized research and development for effective advancement of the technology.

How then did the United States achieve its new lead in high-technology industry? By investing more than other nations in training scientists and engineers and in R&D in these technologies. The groundwork for these massive investments had been well laid earlier. We have described the rise of industrial R&D, and the rise of higher education. By World War II the United States had a number of world-class firms in science-based industries, and several universities doing world-class research. But the United States was not dominant in high-technology industries.

4.2. The Surge of Investment in R&D

World War II changed the context. Victory brought a new sense of confidence and pride in America's strength, an awe for the power of science and technology engendered by their role in winning the war, and a burning belief in their capabilities for opening new horizons for the future. The write-ups of wartime science clearly were designed to kindle this appreciation on the part of the public (for example, Baxter, 1946). Vannevar Bush's *Science, The Endless Frontier* (1945) gave the trumpet call, and the United States was off to levels of investment in science and technology that were historically unprecedented.

Before the war Americans had on average roughly double the years of postsecondary education as did the Europeans, although as we have noted the statistics may exaggerate the actual size of the educational gap. Between 1950 and 1973 the average number of years of American postsecondary education again doubled, further widening the gap. In part this was a simple consequence of affluence and a belief in the value of education. But the trend was also strongly encouraged by government policies. The G.I. bill of rights, which guaranteed educational funding to all qualified veterans, was both emblematic and an important factor in its own right. College fellowships became available through a number of other public programs. The state-supported part of the American higher education system provided significant additional funding and subsidy. Only a relatively small share of the new wave of university students went into natural science and engineering. But the sheer numbers meant that there was a large increase in the supply of trained scientists and engineers.

The expansion of supply was also supported, and in part propelled, by major increases in demand from several sources. A small but important fraction was employed by the rapidly expanding U.S. university research system. The scientists and engineers who had engaged in the war effort had striking success in their argument that university science warranted public support, and during the half decade after the war the government put into place machinery to provide that support. The new research support programs of the National Science Foundation and the National Institutes of Health provided public funding of university basic research across a wide spectrum of fields. However, the bulk of government support for university research came not from these agencies but from agencies pursuing particular missions and using university research as an instrument in that endeavor. Thus the Department of Defense and the Atomic Energy Commission provided large-scale research funding in fields of particular interest to them. And the support was not just for basic research. These agencies funded research that involved applied science and engineering departments in work at the forefront of technologies in materials and electronics. By the mid-1950s the American research universities clearly were ahead of those in the rest of the world in most fields. Just as young American scholars flocked to German universities to learn science during the late nineteenth century, so young students from Europe, Japan, and other parts of the world came to the United States for their training.

The largest share of the increased demand for engineers and scientists, however, came from a vast expansion in the number of American companies doing R&D and in the size of their R&D programs (Mowery and Rosenberg, 1989). Figure 9.8 displays estimates of the number of scientists and engineers engaged in R&D (including corporate, university, and other organizations) as a fraction of the work force. Figure 9.9 shows the same phenomenon in terms of R&D as a fraction of GNP. Between 1953 and 1960 total R&D expenditures (in constant dollars) more than doubled, and the ratio to GNP nearly doubled. Employment of scientists and engineers in industrial research grew from fewer than 50,000 in 1946 to roughly 300,000 in 1962. Other countries lagged in increasing these kinds of investments. As late as 1969, total U.S. expenditure on R&D was more than double that of the U.K., Germany, France, and Japan combined. But by then the slowdown in U.S. productivity growth had already begun.

The R&D figures exaggerate somewhat the increase in investments in

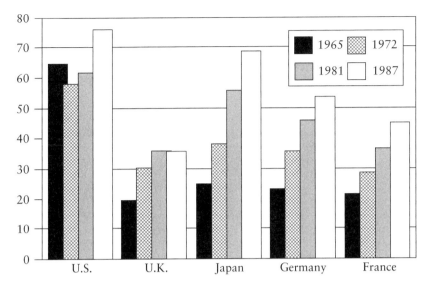

Figure 9.8 Scientists and engineers engaged in R&D per 10,000 workers. *(Source: U.S. National Science Board, 1989, 1991, app. table 3-19.)*

technical progress (Soete et al., 1989). While formal R&D is the principal vehicle for technological advance in the science-based industries, a good share of the work of improving manufacturing processes goes on outside formal R&D organizations, and often is not included in the R&D statistics. For example, a major part of improvement is often in design, usually done in an engineering department and often not counted as R&D despite the fact that it involves comparable activities. Many small firms engage in inventing, design, and development work without a formal R&D department and often without reporting any R&D. During the period in question the term R&D was becoming fashionable, and it is likely that a growing fraction of that work was so labeled. With all of these qualifications, however, it is clear that the increase in resources allocated to advancing technology was massive, and not matched in other countries.

The rise of corporate R&D in the United States had two sources. Partly it was the result of major increases in private corporate R&D funding, based on optimistic beliefs in the profitability of such investments, a belief which by and large was well founded. Partly the rise came from large DoD, and later NASA, investments in new systems. In the mid-1960s private funds accounted for about half of corporate R&D, government funds the other half. In some industries, such as pharmaceuticals and other chemical industries, corporate funds provided almost all the support. In others, such as

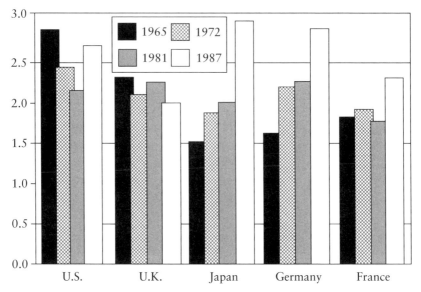

Figure 9.9   Expenditures for R&D as percentage of GNP. *(Source: U.S. National Science Board, 1989, app. table 4-19; 1991, app. table 4-26.)*

electronics, there was both strong private effort in such firms as AT&T and IBM, and large-scale DoD funding. In industries like jet engines and space systems almost all the funding was DoD or NASA.

American dominance in computer and semiconductor technologies gained the most European attention and concern during the 1950s and 1960s. These were considered the leading-edge technologies of the era, and many foreign observers attributed the American advantage to defense support. Military and to a lesser extent space R&D support certainly was important. But military demands and money were going into an R&D system that was well endowed with trained scientists and engineers, had a strong university research base, and was populated with companies that were technically capable.

During the 1930s those concerned with the capabilities of the armed forces, both in Europe and in the United States, were sharply aware of the advantages that could be gained by an enhanced ability to solve complex equation systems rapidly. Ballistics calculations were perhaps the dominant concern, but there were others as well (Flamm, 1987; Katz and Phillips in Nelson, 1982). Prior to and during World War II the Germans and British as well as the Americans funded research aimed at developing a rapid computer. It is clear enough that during and shortly after the war, by which time the feasibility of electronic computers had been established, the United States vastly outspent other governments in bringing this embryonic technology into a form that was operational in terms of military needs. Several major research universities were involved in the effort, notably MIT. IBM and AT&T participated actively. Early assessments were that the nonmilitary demand for computers would be small. It was apparent by 1960, however, that nonmilitary demand would be large, and it also turned out that the design experience that the major U.S. companies had had in their work on military systems was directly relevant to civilian systems.

The story regarding semiconductors is somewhat different (Malerba, 1985; Levin in Nelson, 1982). Although military funds had gone into semiconductor devices during World War II, it was the Bell Telephone Laboratories that came up with the critical discoveries and inventions, using their own money, and motivated by the perceived technological needs of the telephone system. Once the potential had been demonstrated, however, the armed services, and later NASA, quickly recognized the relevance of the technology to their needs. Significant government R&D went into supporting technical advance in semiconductors and, perhaps more important as it turned out, the DoD and NASA signaled themselves as large potential purchasers of transistors. The evidence is clear that major amounts of private R&D money went into trying to advance semiconductor technology, in anticipation of a large government market. And in the field of semiconductor technology, as well as computer technology, design experiences with the transistors and later the integrated circuits that were of high value to the military set companies up to produce items for civilian products.

By the mid-1960s the American lead in the new high-technology industries, like the old lead in mass production industries, was widely taken as a fact of life, a source of pride for Americans, and a concern to Europeans, but not readily subject to change. Jean Jacques Servan-Schreiber pointed to the U.S. lead with alarm, arguing that if Europeans did not act quickly to catch up, they would be permanently subservient to the Americans. His diagnosis of the sources of American strength was rich and complex, if in places ironically amusing in the face of subsequent developments. He pointed not only to American investments in R&D and in science and engineering education, but to the overall quality of the American work force, its willingness to cooperate with management, and the skill, energy, and willingness to take risks that he believed characterized American management.

In its famous "technology gap" studies, the OECD provided a more systematic, nuanced, and variegated diagnosis. The OECD argued that there

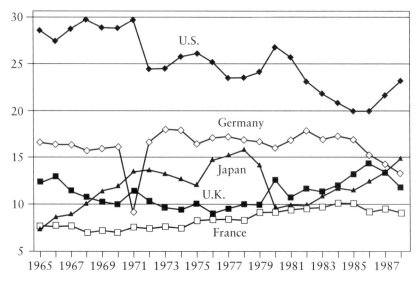

Figure 9.10   Country shares of world high-technology exports, 1965–1988. *(Source: U.S. National Science Board, 1987, app. table 7-10; 1989, app. table 7-10; 1991, app. table 6-7. Note that decline for Japan in 1980 corresponds to shift in basis of calculation.)*

was little that American scientists and engineers knew that good Europeans did not know also. The "gaps" stemmed mainly from management and organization, and experience, just as we have stressed. Technology is partly in books and mind, partly in the fingers and organization. The information part is largely a public good for those with the requisite training and experience. But the latter part involves significant firm specific investment and learning. Ironically, just at the time when American dominance was most visible, conditions were changing to undermine its sources. By the 1960s the U.S. lead was shrinking, both in the areas of long-standing strength, and in the new high-technology fields.

5. The Closing Gaps

The period since the mid-1950s has seen a dramatic narrowing of the economic and technological gaps among the major industrial powers, largely ending a leadership position nearly a century old. The U.S. lead in high-technology industries was a more recent phenomenon. Interestingly, it appears to have held up better than the general U.S. economic lead. Figure 9.10 shows the share of the major industrial nations in exports of high-technology products over the period since 1965. Contrary to popular belief, the U.S.

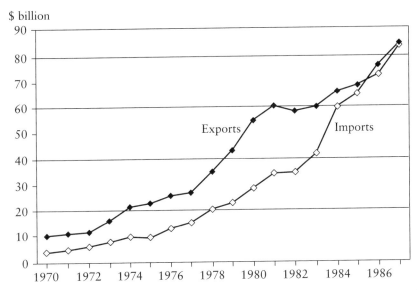

Figure 9.11   U.S. trade in high-technology products, 1970–1987. *(Source: U.S. National Science Board, 1989, app. table 7-14.)*

share has diminished only slightly. The major change has been in the position of Japan relative to Europe, although the latest revised figures soften the picture. Figure 9.11 shows U.S. exports and imports of high-technology products since 1970. It has been the growth of U.S. imports, particularly since 1983, not a decline of export performance, that has been the principal source of the erosion of the U.S. high-technology trade balance.

The data on patents reflect the same pattern. Since 1970 there has been a significant decline in the share of patents taken out in the United States assigned to Americans. However, a large part of this decline reflects a rise in the fraction of inventions originating in other countries that are patented in the United States. From the mid-1960s to the mid-1980s the share of all world patents given to Americans has been relatively constant. Japan's share has risen dramatically, mainly at the expense of Europe. Many analysts have noted that U.S. patenting has shown an absolute decline since the late 1960s. That is so, but it is also true of the major European countries, and the U.S. rate has partially recovered since 1980. We do not know what forces may account for these trends, but of the major industrial nations only Japan has experienced an increase in patenting (U.S. National Science Board, 1991).

Within the group of industries in question, more fine-grained analysis displays a more variegated picture regarding U.S. performance. Between the mid-1960s and the mid-1980s, the U.S. export share held up well in aircraft, aircraft engines and turbines, computing and other office machinery, and in several classes of chemical products. The U.S. export share declined significantly in professional and scientific instruments and in telecommunications. U.S. firms were routed in consumer electronics. The data on national patenting show a similar pattern. By and large U.S. export shares have persisted in industries where U.S. patenting has held up, and declined where patents by nationals elsewhere have risen relative to American patenting.

The definition of high-technology industries is somewhat arbitrary in that it is tied to R&D intensity exceeding a particular level. A number of industries are excluded from the definition, whose product and process technologies are complex and sophisticated, and where technical advance has been significant. Automobiles, machine tools, and other kinds of machinery are examples. By and large U.S. export share and patenting have fallen significantly in these industries. Europe has done rather well. In contrast, the United States continues to be the export and patenting leader in many industries connected with agricultural products and others based on natural resources.

Thus beneath the surface of general productivity convergence, there is a much more variegated picture. U.S. performance continues to be strong in several of the most R&D-intensive industries and those connected to natural resources. It has declined in many of the industries—like automobiles, consumer electrical products, and steel making—where the United States has had a dominant world position since the late nineteenth century. The interesting question, of course, is how this broad convergence came about. What were the forces behind it?

We would highlight four different developments. First, the decline in transportation costs and trade barriers has greatly expanded the flow of world trade, eroding the advantages in market size and raw material costs that U.S.-based firms used to have. Second, technology has become much more generally accessible to those with the requisite skills and willing to make the required investments, and hence much less respecting of firm and national boundaries than had been the case earlier. Third, the other major industrial powers significantly increased the fraction of their work forces trained in science and engineering and the fraction of their GNP allocated to research and development, thus establishing strong indigenous competence to exploit technologies from abroad as well as to create new technology. Indeed, by 1980 a number of countries were outspending the United States in nonmilitary R&D as a fraction of GNP. This is important, because the fourth major factor behind convergence was, in our view, a decline in the importance of spillover from military R&D into civilian technology.

The period since 1960 has seen a significant rise in the percentage of manufactured products exported and imported in virtually all major industrial countries. Between 1960 and 1980, U.S. imports roughly doubled as a fraction of GNP. In France, Germany, and the United Kingdom taken as a group, the ratio of imports to GNP increased by about 50 percent. It grew by a quarter in Japan. All of these ratios were substantially higher for manufacturing alone. Thus, over this period, efficient companies producing attractive products increasingly faced a world rather than a national market. At the same time, trade in natural resources greatly expanded, and countries became less dependent on local materials. Postwar resource discoveries were far more dispersed around the globe than previously. Although the United States continued to be a large contributor to world mineral production, the country became a net importer of most major minerals, implying that the cost to industrial users was essentially the same as that in other countries. Thus the twin advantages long possessed by American mass producers— cheap raw materials and more-or-less exclusive access to the world's largest market—both have dissolved. Despite continuing fears of a return to protectionism, by the 1980s much of the world had largely become a common market.

At the same time, business has become increasingly international. Technologically progressive American companies had established European branches even in the nineteenth century, but the scale of overseas direct investment surged dramatically during the 1950s and 1960s. In *The American Challenge*, Servan-Schreiber expressed concern that American companies were taking over the European economy at least as much by investing there as by exporting. By the late 1960s Europe was beginning to return the favor by establishing branches or buying plants in the United States. Recently Japanese companies have done the same, on a larger scale.

The internationalization of business has greatly complicated the interpretation of international trade statistics. For example, a nontrivial share of the rising U.S. imports in high-technology industries mentioned above originate in foreign subsidiaries of U.S.-owned companies (Langlois, 1987, chap. 4). While the U.S. share of world manufacturing exports (low and middle tech as well as high tech) fell somewhat from the mid-1960s to the mid-1980s, the export share of U.S.-*owned* firms held up, with gains in exports from foreign branches matching declines in exports from U.S.-based plants (Lipsey and Kravis, 1986).

The internationalization of trade and business has been part and parcel of the second postwar development that we want to highlight—the erosion of firm and national borders as barriers obstructing or channeling access to technology. Modern science has, from its beginnings, been an international activity. The ethos of science has for centuries stressed the public and international nature of scientific knowledge. British and French scientists continued to communicate during the Napoleonic wars, and attempts by national governments to define and keep separate a particular national science have often been condemned by the scientific community. Despite this ancient tradition, the real world of practical science has also displayed strong national elements, explicitly so in wartime, implicitly at other times in language, terminology, institutional structures, and objects of study.

In contrast to the universalist ethos of science, the notion that individuals and firms have proprietary rights to their inventions has been accepted for many centuries, and so too the idea that it is appropriate for a nation to gain advantage from the inventive work of its nationals. Nations have often tried to keep national technologies within their borders, however futile these efforts may often have been in many cases. Though technologists from different countries have communicated and formed something of an international community, until recently the notion that best-practice technology was approachable by any nation with requisite resources was probably not correct. The technological advantage of the American mass market firms in industries like steel and automobiles did not derive from patents or well-protected secrets, but largely from experience gained well ahead of foreigners because of differences in the economic environment. With firms all over the world facing a common market for products and inputs, the forces that used to provide U.S. companies with incentives to get into certain technologies first have been largely eroded.

While the increasing similarity of economic environments may be the immediate reason for the convergence of technological capabilities, another important underlying development in the post–World War II era is that many technologies became more like sciences than before. Earlier we described the particular characteristics of science-based industries like chemical products and electronics. It is noteworthy that patents in these industries (and recently in bio-technology) have tended to cite scientific literature to a far greater extent than do patents in fields like steel and automobiles. Since 1960, however, the number of citations to scientific literature in patents has increased significantly in almost all technological fields, including steel and autos (Narin and Noma, 1985). In contrast to an earlier era, a larger proportion of the generic knowledge relevant to a technology now is written down, published in journals, discussed at national and international meetings, and taught in schools of engineering and applied science.

Internationalization of business is an important part of this story. It is not just that foreigners can learn what American engineers can learn by going to American universities. European engineers can observe American technology in operation in their home countries, and purchase operating American firms. Companies like IBM have industrial research laboratories in a number of different countries, each employing a mix of nationals. In turn, scientists from IBM, Phillips, and Fujitsu meet at conferences and exchange papers. Employees often move across national borders, within a firm or between firms. These are truly international networks, involving highly trained scientists and engineers, employed in universities and in industry, undertaking significant R&D efforts. The technologies emerging from such networks no longer have geographic roots, because horizons have become global and because material resource inputs more generally have declined in importance, relative to processing.

Generic technological knowledge, of the sort taught in graduate school, written down in books and articles, and exchanged among high-level professionals, does have strong public good attributes. However, access is limited to those with the requisite training, and in many cases only someone who is actually doing research in a particular field can understand the significance of publications in that field. To take industrial advantage of generic knowledge, or technology that is licensed from another company, or more generally to understand what another company has done and how, generally requires significant inputs of trained scientists and engineers, plus research and development expenditure aimed to tailor what has been learned to the specific relevant uses (Pavitt, 1987; Nelson and Winter, 1982; Nelson, 1988).

The other major industrial nations have, with a lag, followed the United States in making those big investments in education and training, and R&D. The convergence in scientists and engineers in R&D as a fraction of the work force, and in R&D as a fraction of GNP, shown in Figures 9.8 and 9.9, is an essential part of, and a complement to, the internationalization of technology. Definitions of these concepts are subject to continuing debate and change, and the most recent revisions by the National Science Board put the current U.S. position in a more favorable light. By any definitions, however, the direction of change is clear. The U.S. lead in the early 1960s is striking. Convergence has occurred among those nations with modern educational systems, strong internal scientific and engineering communities, and sophisticated industrial enterprises. Nations without these attributes have tended to fall farther and farther behind the frontiers. There are now few important technological secrets, but it takes major investments of many kinds to command a technology.

Military technology has had a somewhat different history. The major military powers, prominently the United States, continue to bend strong efforts to prevent military technology from leaking away to potentially hostile nations or to nations who might serve as a conduit to hostile nations. But just as the political context of world conflict has changed with the end of the cold war, the economic context has altered completely. While American dominance of the frontiers of military technology gave us significant civilian technology advantages during the 1950s and 1960s, today it buys us little outside the military sphere. In terms of access to technology that affects productivity in industry broadly defined, it does not hurt the Europeans or the Japanese that American companies are engaged in military R&D to a much greater extent than they are, and that access to that technology is difficult if not closed.

There are several reasons for the diminished importance of military R&D as a source of technological advantage outside the military field. First, while initially civilian demands for computers, semiconductors, and jet aircraft had lagged behind military demands, by the mid-1960s the civilian market for these products was as large or larger than the military; and in many dimensions, the performance demanded by the civilian market was actually higher. Companies responded by mounting their own R&D projects to meet these demands. Indeed, a strong case can be made that from the late 1960s the major direction of "spillover" was from the civil to the military. Thus the military bought the KC10 as its tanker of choice, a plane that grew out of the McDonnel-Douglas DC-10, designed by the company for use by commercial airlines.

At the same time, military R&D increasingly focused on areas where its needs were specialized, engaging in specific product development efforts as contrasted with broadly applicable research. The percentage of military R&D that went into research and experimental development has diminished significantly. With the end of the cold war, the outlook is for further decline in military R&D along with military spending more generally, but at this point we do not foresee dire consequences for American technology as a result.

6. Conclusion

Let us recapitulate. We have argued that the postwar American techno-logical lead had two conceptually distinct components. There was, first of all, the long-standing strength in mass production industries that grew out of unique conditions of resource abundance and large market size. There was, second, a lead in "high-technology" industries that was new and stemmed from investments in higher education and in research and devel-opment, far surpassing the levels of other countries at that time. Several factors lay behind the erosion of these twin leads. The most basic of these is that over the post–World War II era, commodity and resource trade, busi-ness and finance, and technological communities have all become increas-ingly transnational rather than national.

In his now classic 1986 article on convergence, Abramovitz distinguished between two variables influencing the extent to which (firms in) countries that are technologically behind a leader are able to catch up. One of these was "opportunity." The other was "social capabilities." Abramovitz noted that while the United States was the clear productivity leader from before World War II, there is little evidence of other countries doing much "catching up" prior to the post–World War II era. Our arguments above attempt to flesh out the reasons for this delay. Other countries with the requisite social capabilities, principally then in Europe, lacked the market size and resource availabilities that lay behind the U.S. advantage in mass production industries, and barriers to external trade foreclosed the possi-bility of replicating the U.S. path on an international basis. Until trade bar-riers came down after World War II, the "opportunities" really were not there. The reason for persistence of the U.S. lead in "high-tech" industry was somewhat different. Until the European nations and Japan made the requisite massive investments in scientific and engineering education and in R&D, they lacked the "social capability" to catch up in these industries.

It is not our intention here to resolve the full range of issues raised in the convergence literature. We do have two related observations. First, much of the literature treats technology as if it were a "public good," allowing only that there may be some friction in moving it around. Instead, as we have argued, much of what is involved in mastering a technology is organization-specific investment and learning. Hands-on technological capability is more like a private good than a public good. For that reason, if the economic conditions and incentives facing firms in different countries differ signifi-cantly, then firms in one country will require technological capabilities very different from those in another country. This argument is far removed from the conventional distinction according to which firms simply "choose" to employ different techniques (for example, factor mixes) within a common underlying technology. To the extent that our interpretation holds, there is nothing automatic about convergence.

Second, however, since the 1950s the world has been changing so that, as a reduced form, the convergence model looks more and more plausible. In our view, it is the internationalization of trade, business, and generic technology and the growing commonality of the economic environments of firms in different nations that have made it so.

We believe that the internationalization of trade, business, and technology is here to stay. This means that national borders mean much less than they used to regarding the flow of technology, at least among the nations that have made the now needed social investments in education and research facilities. National governments have been slow to recognize these new facts of life. Indeed, the last decade has seen a sharp increase in what has been called "techno-nationalism," policies launched by governments with the objective of giving their national firms a particular edge in an area of technology. Our argument is that these policies do not work very well anymore. It is increasingly difficult to create new technology that will stay contained within national borders for very long in a world where technological sophistication is widespread and firms of many nationalities are ready to make the investment needed to exploit new generic technology.

A closely related observation is that a well-educated labor force, with a strong cadre of university-trained engineers and scientists at the top, is now a requirement for membership in the "convergence club." This is not to denigrate the continued importance of hands-on learning by doing and using, but in modern technologies this is not sufficient. It is no accident that countries like Korea and Taiwan, which have been gaining so rapidly on the world leaders, now have populations where secondary education is close to universal for new entrants to the work force, and where a significant fraction of the secondary school graduates go on to university training (Baumol, Blackman, and Wolff, 1989; Barro, 1991).

In our introduction we acknowledged another interpretation of convergence—that the trends reflect a growing incapacity of the American economy, and foreshadow the United States falling behind Japan, and perhaps Germany, as Great Britain fell behind the new leading economies at the turn of the last century. While we argue that the principal factor driving convergence over the last quarter century has been internationalization, we do not dismiss the possibility that the United States may be in the process of slipping into second, third, or fifth rank in productivity and per capita income and in terms of mastering the application of several important technologies. Although the forces that now bind together nations with sufficient "social capabilities" are far stronger than they were in the past, there is certainly room for variance within that group. If the notion of social capability includes not merely the educational levels at leading universities and research laboratories but the social and political processes affecting the educational system, transportation and communications networks, and the legal and regulatory apparatus of federal and state governments, then it is entirely possible that a once-dominant nation may slip into social paralysis and decline. The distressing examples of Britain and Argentina are often cited, and Robert Reich (1991) argues that the United States is in danger of a similar fate.

To enter this question would require us to survey several additional bodies of literature, and we cannot do that here. There is, first, the puzzle of the extraordinarily slow growth rate of U.S. per worker productivity, per capita income, and total factor productivity, since the early 1970s. There is, second, the question of the national rate of savings and its link to investment: despite the increased flows of financial and direct foreign investment, it is still true to a considerable extent that a nation's volume of investment is closely related to its own flow of savings (Hatsopoulos, Krugman, and Summers, 1988), and that the growth of productivity is linked to capital investment (Landau 1990). Third, there is the literature proposing that the U.S. has lagged *because* it was the pioneer of older forms of corporate organization, which have now been made obsolete by radically different ways of organizing companies and political economies (for example, Freeman, 1987; Dertouzos et al., 1989; Lazonick, 1990). These and other vital issues are beyond the scope of this essay. But none of them impinges upon our basic argument that the advanced nations of the world have come to share a common technology.

National Innovation Systems:
A Retrospective on a Study

1. What Is the Study About?

In this essay I will describe a large comparative study of national innovation systems (Nelson 1993) that has recently been completed, tell something of what motivated the study and how it was organized and undertaken, and highlight some of the more interesting findings. This is a difficult task, for the project was not only large but also complex.

The heart of the project consisted of studies of fifteen countries, including all of the prominent large market-oriented industrialized ones, several smaller high-income countries, and a number of newly industrializing states. The studies were carefully designed, developed, and written to illuminate the institutions and mechanisms supporting technical innovation in the various countries, the similarities and differences across countries and how these came to be, and to permit at least preliminary discussion of how the differences seemed to matter. No other project has come remotely close to treating the range of countries considered here. Moreover, many of the individual studies stand as major contributions in their own right to the understanding of the innovation systems of particular countries, going far beyond anything written on those countries before. To describe and summarize in compact form what came out of the project simply is impossible. I must pick and choose and hint.

The project was undertaken to try to throw some light on a very complicated and important set of issues. The slowdown of growth since the early 1970s in all of the advanced industrial nations, the rise of Japan as a major economic and technological power, the relative decline of the United States, and widespread concerns in Europe about being behind both have led to a rash of writing and new policy departures concerned with supporting the

Originally published in *Industrial and Corporate Change* (1992): 347–374.

technical innovative powers of national firms. At the same time the enhanced technical sophistication of Korea, Taiwan, and other newly industrializing countries (NICs) has broadened the range of nations whose firms are competitive players in fields which used to be the preserve of only a few, and led other nations who today have a weak manufacturing sector to wonder how they might emulate the performance of the successful NICs. There clearly is a new spirit of what might be called "techno-nationalism" in the air, combining a strong belief that the technological capabilities of a nation's firms are a key source of their competitive performance with the belief that these capabilities are in a sense national, and can be built by national action.

It is this climate that has given rise to the current strong interest in national innovation systems, their similarities and differences, and in the extent and manner that these differences explain variation in national economic performance. There now may be more awareness and research about such national differences than on any other area where comparative institutional analysis would seem interesting and illuminating.

The project on which I report here was born of this intellectual climate, and came out of a belief on the part of the participants that much of the writing and argument were somewhat hyped, and rather haphazard. Moreover, many of the allegedly comparative studies in fact had concentrated on one country—in recent times usually Japan—with the comparison with other countries largely implicit. The actual comparative studies tended to be of two or a very small group of countries. This limitation struck the project participants as particularly serious in view of the absence of a well-articulated and verified analytic framework linking institutional arrangements to technological and economic performance. In the absence of such a framework there were (and are) only weak constraints on the inclinations of analysts to draw possibly spurious causal links between differences in institutional structures that clearly are there, and differences in performance which clearly are there also. Different authors have focused on different things and made different kinds of arguments about why this feature or that was an important factor behind strong or weak performance. A broadening of a set of countries considered simultaneously seemed to us an important way to tighten these constraints by enlarging the number of "points" that a causal theory had to "fit."

The way I have been putting the matter clearly signals that the orientation of this project has been to carefully describe and compare, and try to understand, rather than to theorize first and then attempt to prove or calibrate the theory. However, a comparative study like this requires, at the least, some agreement on basic terms and concepts.

There is, first of all, the concept of a national innovation system itself. Each of the terms can be interpreted in a variety of ways, and there is the question of whether, in a world where technology and business are increasingly transnational, the concept as a whole makes much sense.

Consider the term "innovation." In this study we, the participants, interpret the term rather broadly, to encompass the processes by which firms master and get into practice product designs and manufacturing processes that are new to them, whether or not they are new to the universe, or even to the nation. We do so for several reasons. First, the activities and investments associated with becoming the leader in the introduction of a new product or process, and those associated with staying near the head of the pack, or catching up, are much less sharply distinguishable than commonly is presumed. Second, much of the interest in innovative capability is tied to concern about economic performance, and here it is certainly the broader concept rather than the narrower one (the determinants of being first) that matters. This means that our orientation is not limited to the behavior of firms at the world's technology forefront, or to institutions doing the most advanced scientific research, although in some countries the focus is here, but is more broadly on the factors influencing national technological capabilities.

Then there is the term "system." While to some the word connotes something that is consciously designed and built, this is far from the orientation here. Rather the concept here is of a set of institutions whose interactions determine the innovative performance, in the sense above, of national firms. There is no presumption that the system was, in some sense, consciously designed, or even that the set of institutions involved works together smoothly and coherently. Rather, the "systems" concept is that of a set of institutional actors that, together, play the major role in influencing innovative performance. The broad concept of innovation that we have adopted has forced us to consider much more than simply the actors doing research and development. Indeed, a problem with the broader definition of innovation is that it provides no sharp guide to just what should be included in the innovation system, and what can be left out. More on this later.

Finally, there is the concept of "national" system. On the one hand, the concept may be too broad. The system of institutions supporting technical innovation in one field, say pharmaceuticals, may have very little overlap with the system of institutions supporting innovations in another field, say aircraft. On the other hand, in many fields of technology, including both pharmaceuticals and aircraft, a number of the institutions are or act transnational. Indeed, for many of the participants in this study, one of the key interests was in exploring whether, and if so in what ways, the concept of a "national" system made any sense nowadays. National governments act as if it did. However, that presumption and the reality may not be aligned.

The studies in this project are unified by at least broad agreement on the definitional and conceptual issues discussed above. They also were guided by certain common understandings of the way technical advance proceeds, and the key processes and institutional actors involved, that are now widely shared among scholars of technical advance. In a way these understandings do provide a common analytic framework, not wide enough to encompass all of the variables and relationships that are likely to be important, not sharp enough to tightly guide empirical work, but broad enough and pointed enough to provide a common structure in which one can have some confidence.

In particular, our inquiry was strongly shaped by our shared understandings about the complex intertwining of science and technology that marks the modern world. In the first place, we take the position that technology at any time needs to be recognized as consisting of both a set of specific designs and practices and a body of generic knowledge that surrounds these and provides an understanding of how things work, key variables affecting performance, the nature of currently binding constraints, and promising approaches to pushing these back. In most fields of technology a considerable portion of generic understanding stems from operating and design experience with products and machines and their components, and generalizations reflecting on these. Thus, consider a mechanic's guide, or the general knowledge of potters, or steel makers.

However, over the last century science has played an increasing role in the understandings related to technology. Indeed most modern fields of technology today have associated with them formal scientific or engineering disciplines like metallurgy, computer science, and chemical engineering. These kinds of disciplines are basically about technological understanding, and reflect attempts to make that understanding more scientific. An important consequence has been that, nowadays, formal academic training in the various applied sciences and engineering disciplines has become virtually a prerequisite for understanding a technology.

The intertwining of science and technology which began to occur a century ago led to the rise of the industrial research laboratory as the dominant locus of technological innovation, first in the chemical and electrical industries, and then more broadly. These facilities, dedicated to advancing technology and staffed by academically trained scientists and engineers, were closely tied to individual business enterprises.

It is important to understand that not all of the activities and investments made by firms in innovating are conducted in R&D laboratories or get counted as R&D. The extent to which they do varies from industry to industry. Where firms are small, or where firms are engaged in designing products to order for individual customers, much of innovative work may not be counted as R&D. Nonetheless, while not always counted as R&D, and while often drawing extensively on external sources like universities and government labs, in most industries the lion's share of innovative effort is made by the firms themselves.

There are several reasons. First, after technology has been around for a period of time, in order to orient innovative work fruitfully one needs detailed knowledge of its strengths and weaknesses and areas where improvements would yield high payoffs, and this knowledge tends to reside with those who use the technology, generally firms and their customers and suppliers. Second, profiting from innovation in many cases requires the coordination of R&D, production, and marketing, which tends to proceed much more effectively within an organization that itself does all of these. These arguments hold whether one defines the innovation concept narrowly, as the introduction of a product or process that is truly new, or whether one defines it broadly as we do in the study, as the introduction of something that is new to the firm. Thus all of the country studies paid a considerable amount of attention to the activities and investments being undertaken by firms.

The other two institutional actors with which all of the country studies were concerned are universities (and scientific and technical educational structures more generally) and governments and their policies as these influence industrial innovation. University and kindred institutions play two different kinds of roles in modern industrial innovation systems. They are the place where scientists and engineers who go into industry get their formal training. And in most (but not all) countries they are the locus of a considerable amount of research in the disciplines that are associated with particular technologies. To a much greater extent than commonly realized, university research programs are not undifferentiated parts of a national innovation system broadly defined, but rather are keyed into particular technologies and particular industries. University training and research that support technical innovation in farming and the food processing industries simply are very different from university teaching and research that supports the electronic industries. Thus a major question in this study was how the research and teaching orientation of a nation's universities reflected or molded the industries where technological innovation was important in the nation.

And, of course, the individual country studies looked closely at the range of government programs and policies bearing on industrial innovation. As is the case with the activities of universities, many government programs are focused specifically on particular technologies or industries, and these obviously were of central interest. However, as noted in my earlier discussion of the meaning of an "innovation system," given the broad way we are using the term innovation, innovative performance cannot be cleanly separated from economic performance and competitiveness more broadly. Thus in many cases the examination of government policies bearing on industrial innovation had to get into things like monetary and trade policies.

In designing the study the participants faced a quandary. From the discussion above it is obvious that a very wide range of factors influence the innovative performance of a nation's industries. The desire for comparability across the studies seemed to call for a rather elaborate list of things all country studies would cover. Yet it was apparent that the most interesting feature of a country's innovation system varied significantly across countries, and we wanted to illuminate these. Limits on resources and space foreclosed doing both. Our compromise involved two strategic decisions. First, we agreed on the limited list of features all country studies were to cover, for example, the allocation of R&D activity and the sources of its funding, the characteristics of firms and the important industries, the roles of universities, and the government policies expressly aimed to spur and mold industrial innovation. Beyond these the authors were encouraged to pick out and highlight what they thought were the most important and interesting characteristics of their country. But second, considerable effort was put into identifying the kinds of comparisons—similarities or differences—that seemed most interesting and important to make. In general these did not involve comparisons across all countries, but rather among a small group where for various reasons comparison was apt.

The overall project covered three sets of countries where we thought ingroup comparisons would be most interesting. The first group consisted of six large high-income countries—the United States, Japan, Germany, France, Italy, and the United Kingdom. The second group consisted of four small high-income countries, with a strong agricultural or resource base—Denmark, Sweden, Canada, and Australia. Finally, included in the set were five lower-income countries—Korea, Taiwan, Argentina, Brazil, and Israel. While we were interested in the similarities and differences across groups, a considerable amount of thought and effort went into laying out within-group comparisons.

As I said at the offset, it is impossible to summarize what came out of this study; I can only give some highlights and a flavor. In the following section I highlight some of the key similarities and differences across countries, and our assessments about what lies behind the differences. Then I report our tentative judgments on what distinguishes systems where firms are strong and innovative from systems where they are not; most of us believe that this has somewhat less to do with aggressive "technology policies" than current fashion might have one believe. Indeed, many of us believe that the current focus of discussion on "high-tech" industries may exaggerate the importance to a nation of having strong national firms in those fields. An important reason is that firms in these industries increasingly are going transnational, which brings me to my next topic: what remains of national systems in a world where business and technology increasingly are transnational? I conclude by reflecting on the acrimonious aspects of national technology policies.

2. Country Differences and What Lies behind Them

To compare means to identify similarities as well as differences. Certainly the broad view of technical innovation which I laid out above and which guided this study implies certain commonalities. That view applies to economies in which profit-oriented firms are the principal providers of goods and services, and where central planning and control is weak. These conditions hold in all of the countries in our set, although in some a certain portion of industry is nationalized, and in some governments do try to mold the shape of industrial development in at least a few economic sectors. In all of the countries in our set, the bulk of education, including university education, is conducted in public institutions. In all, the government is presumed to have major responsibility for the funding of basic research, although there are major differences across countries regarding how much of that they do and where basic research is mostly carried out. From one point of view, what is most striking about the country comparisons is the amount of basic similarity. Had the old Soviet Union been included in the set, or China, or Nigeria, the matter would have been different. But as it is, the differences across our set of countries must be understood as differences of individuals of the same species.

Within our group of countries, it would appear that to a considerable extent the differences in the innovation systems reflect differences in economic and political circumstances and priorities. First of all, size and the degree of affluence matter a lot. Countries with large affluent populations can provide a market for a wide range of manufacturing industries and may engage in other activities that "small" countries cannot pursue, at least with any chance of success, and their innovation systems will reflect this. Low-income countries tend to differ from high-income ones in the kinds of economic activities in which they can have comparative advantage, and in internal demand patterns, and these differences profoundly shape the nature of technical innovation that is relevant.

The threefold division of our countries into large high-income industrial nations, small high-income countries, and low-income countries thus turned out to be a useful first-cut analytic separation. By and large the economies in the first group had a significantly larger fraction of their economies in R&D-intensive industry, like aerospace, electronics, and chemical products, which require large sales to be economic, than economies in the second and third groups. There are some anomalies, at the surface at least. Thus, Sweden in the second group and Israel and Korea in the third have higher R&D to GNP ratios than several of the countries in the first group. Some of the mystery disappears when Israel's ambitious military R&D is recognized, and Sweden's and Korea's strong presence in several R&D-intensive industries that live largely through export. Both of the latter two countries also have strong defense programs and this also undoubtedly affected their R&D intensities. There are certain interesting similarities of countries in different groups—Japan and Korea, for example. However, by and large there were strong intragroup similarities and strong intergroup differences. Thus the United States and Japan look much less different than advertised, once one brings Australia and Israel into the comparison set. And much of the U.S.-Japan difference can be seen to reside in differences in their resource bases and defense policies.

Whether or not a country had rich natural resources or ample farming land clearly is another important variable influencing the shape of its innovation system. It turns out that all our "small" high-income countries also were well endowed in this respect. Among the large high-income countries the United States was far and away the best endowed here. Countries that possess resources and good farmland face a different set of opportunities and constraints than countries without these assets.

Countries that lack them must import resources and farm products, which forces their economies toward export-oriented manufacturing and an innovation system that supports this. One sees this strikingly in the cases of Germany, Japan, and Korea. On the other hand, countries with a rich resource base can support relatively high living standards with farm products and resources and the affiliated industries providing exports to pay for imported manufactured goods. The countries that have been able to do this—

Denmark, Canada, and Australia stand out in our set—have developed significant publicly supported R&D programs to back these industries. So also has the United States. While effective agriculture and resource exploitation does require R&D, compared with high-tech industry the R&D intensity here is low.

The discussion above suggests that, to some extent at least, a nation's innovation system is shaped by factors like size and resource endowments that affect comparative advantage at a basic level. But it also is true that a nation's innovation system tends to reflect conscious decisions to develop and sustain economic strength in certain areas, that is, it builds and shapes comparative advantage.

Some of the project members were surprised to find in how many of our countries national security concerns had been important in shaping innovation systems.

In the first place, among high-income countries defense R&D accounts for the lion's share of the differences among the countries in government funding of industrial R&D, and the presence of large military programs thus explains why government industrial R&D spending in the United States, and the United Kingdom and France, is so much greater than in Japan and Germany. In the second place, the industries from which the military procures tend to be R&D intensive, whether the firms are selling to the military or to civilians. The study of Japan shows clearly that the present industrial structure was largely put in place during an era when national security concerns were strong. This structure, now oriented to civilian products, is one of the reasons for Japan's high R&D intensity. It is possible that, to some extent, this argument also holds for Germany.

Interestingly, every one of the low-income countries in our study has been influenced by national security concerns or a military government, or both. Thus much of high-tech industry in Israel is largely oriented toward the military. The broad economic policies, industrial structures, and innovation systems of Korea and Taiwan were molded in good part by their felt need to have a capable military establishment. The pockets of high tech atop the basically backward Brazilian and Argentine economies clearly reflect the ambitions of their military elites.

As noted, all of the countries in our set are, basically, ones in which firms are mostly expected to fend for themselves in markets that are, to a considerable extent, competitive. However, all are marked by significant pockets of government overview, funding, and protection. In our countries with big military procurement programs, the defense industries are the largest such pocket. However, in many of our countries government support and protection extends into space, electric power, telecommunications, and other areas of civilian high tech. While by and large these extensions are most significant in the big high-income countries, Canada has large public programs in electric power and telecommunications, and so does Sweden.

There clearly are significant differences across the nations regarding beliefs about which kind of a role government should play in shaping industrial development. The role of military concerns is a powerful variable influencing this. But a relatively active government also is associated with "late" development, along the lines put forth by Alexander Gerschenkron (1962). Aside from the arena of national security and related areas, Britain and the United States are marked by restrained government. In contrast, all of our low-income late-developing countries have quite active governments. However, there certainly are exceptions to this rule. France's Étatism goes far back in history, and while Italy is a late developer except during the Fascist era, its government has been weak.

The above discussion suggests that one ought to see considerable continuity in a nation's innovation system, at least to the extent that the basic national objectives and conditions have a continuity. Although this proposition clearly has only limited bearing on the countries in our set that were formed or gained independence in recent years—Israel, Taiwan, Korea—even here one can see a certain consistency within these nations' short histories. All of these countries have experienced dramatic improvements in living standards since the 1950s, and their industrial structure has changed markedly. Their innovation systems have changed as well, but as our authors tell the story, in all of these countries today's institutional structures supporting innovation clearly show their origins in those of several decades ago.

For countries with longer histories, the institutional continuity is striking, at least to the study authors. Thus one can see many of the same things in 1990 in France, Germany, and Japan that were there in 1890, and this despite the enormous advances in living standards and shifts in industrial structure all have experienced, and the total defeat of the latter two nations in World War II and the stripping away of their military. Britain of 1990 continues many of the institutional characteristics of Britain in 1890, although they seemed to work better then than now.

Indeed, in this author's eyes, of the countries with long histories the one that has changed most institutionally is the United States. The governmental roles in funding university research and defense R&D that came into place only after World War II had little precedent prior to the war, and profoundly changed the nature of the innovation system.

3. What Is Required for Effective Innovative Performance?

We have defined innovation broadly so that the term basically stands for what is required of firms if they are to stay competitive in industries where technological advance is important. Such industries span a large share of manufacturing, many service sectors such as air transport, telecommunications, and medical care, and important areas of agriculture and mining. Staying competitive means different things in different national contexts. For firms located in high-wage countries, being competitive may require having a significantly more attractive product or a better production process than firms in low-wage countries. For the latter, being competitive may not require being at the forefront. Indeed much of innovation in low-income countries involves the learning of foreign technology, its diffusion, and perhaps its adaption to local circumstances of demand or production. But in either kind of country, if technological advance in the industry is significant, staying competitive requires continuing innovation.

We, the group that has produced the country studies, think we can discern several basic features that are common to effective innovative performance, and which are lacking or attenuated in countries where innovation arguably has been weak. First, the firms in the industry were highly competent in what mattered to be competitive in their lines of business. Generally this involved competence in product design and production, but usually also effective overall management, ability to assess consumer needs, links into upstream and downstream markets, and so on. In most cases significant investments lay behind these firm capabilities. All this enabled firms to master the relevant technologies and other practices needed to compete and to stay up with or lead with new developments.

This observation does contain a hint of tautology, but is better regarded as confirmation of a point stressed above, that the bulk of the effort in innovation needs to be done by the firms themselves. While they may draw on outside developments, significant internal effort and skill is needed to complement and implement these. One cannot read the studies of Japan, Germany, Italy, Korea, and Taiwan, all arguably countries where firms have displayed strong performance in certain industries, without being impressed by the authors' description of the firms. In contrast, one is impressed the other way by the authors' commentary on the weaknesses of firms in certain industries in Britain, France, Australia, Argentina, and Israel.

Being strong did not necessarily mean that firms were large. Economists long have understood that while in some industries a firm has to be large in order to be a capable innovator, in other industries this is not the case. Many of the strong Italian, Taiwanese, and Danish firms are relatively small. Nor does it mean that the firms spend heavily on formal R&D. In some fields like electronics generally it did, at least for firms in our first two groups of countries; however, in Korea and Taiwan electronics firms often were doing well with technical efforts mostly oriented toward "reverse engineering." The Italian textile industry is strong on fashion and design, and highly innovative in these respects, but little of that work is accounted as R&D. Nor does it imply that the firms were not benefiting from publicly funded R&D programs or favored procurement status. However, as our authors describe it, the bulk of the inputs and direction for innovative activity was coming from the firms themselves.

While our concept of a strong firm entails ability to compete, in all of our cases becoming strong involved actually being exposed to strong competition and being forced to compete. As Michael Porter (1990) has noted, in a number of cases the firms faced strong rivals in their own country. Thus the Japanese auto and electronics companies compete strongly with each other, American pharmaceutical companies compete, and so do Italian clothing producers. However, it is not at all clear that this generalization holds for small countries, where there may be only one or a few national firms, such as Ericson in Sweden and Northern Telecom in Canada. For these firms most of their competition is with foreign rivals.

Porter (1990) and Bengt-Ake Lundvall (1988) have proposed that firms in industries where a country is strong tend to have strong interactive linkages with their upstream suppliers, which also are national firms. Our studies show many cases where this proposition is verified. The supplier networks of Japanese automobile firms, and the upstream-downstream connections in Danish agricultural product processing, are good examples. The cooperation of Italian textile producers with one another and with their equipment suppliers is another. However, there are a number of examples where the proposition does not seem to hold. Pharmaceutical companies, strong in Germany and the United States, do not seem generally to have any particularly strong supplier connections, international or national. In aircraft production, the producers of components and subcomponents increasingly are located in countries other than that of the system designer and assembler.

A similar observation is obtained regarding the proposed importance of a demanding set of home market customers. In many cases this holds. But in small countries or for industries that from their start have been export oriented, the main customer discipline may come from foreign customers.

While "strong firms" are the key, that only pushes the question back a stage. Under what conditions do strong firms arise? As the discussion above suggests, to some extent the answer is "spontaneously." However, our studies do indicate strongly that aspects of the national background in which firms operate matter greatly.

One important feature distinguishing countries that were sustaining competitive and innovative firms was education and training systems that provide these firms with a flow of people with the requisite knowledge and skills. For industries where university-trained engineers and scientists were needed, this does not simply mean that the universities provide training in these fields, but also that they consciously train their students with an eye to industry needs. The contrast here between the United States and Germany on the one hand and Britain and France on the other is quite sharp, at least as the authors of our studies draw the picture. Indeed these studies suggest strongly that a principal reason why the former two countries surged ahead of the latter two around the turn of the century in the science-based industries then emerging is that their university systems were much more responsive to the training needs of industry.

While strength in high tech depends on the availability of university-trained people, industry more generally requires a supply of literate, numerically competent people in a wide range of functions outside of R&D, who are trained to industry demands either by the firms themselves (as in Japan) or in external training systems linked to firms (as in several German and Swedish industries). Countries differed in the extext to which their public education and training systems combined with private training to provide this supply, and the differences mattered. Thus among high-income countries Germany, Japan, and Sweden came through much stronger in this respect than Britain and Australia. Among developing countries the contrast is equally sharp between Korea and Taiwan on the one hand, and Brazil on the other.

The examples of Korea and Taiwan, and the other Asian "tigers," can be read as remarkably successful cases of education-led growth. As the authors tell the story, the ability of firms in these countries to move quickly from the relatively simple products they produced in the 1950s and 1960s to the much more complex and technologically sophisticated products they produced successfully in the 1980s was made possible by the availability of a young domestic work force that had received the schooling necessary for the new jobs. The cases of Argentina and Israel, however, suggest that the availability of an educated work force is not enough by itself. The economic incentives facing firms must be such as to compel them to mind the market and to take

advantage of the presence of a skilled work force to compete effectively with
their rivals.

Another factor that seems to differentiate countries where firms were effectively innovative from those where they were not is the package of fiscal,
monetary, and trade policies. By and large where these combined to make
exporting attractive for firms, firms have been drawn to innovate and compete. Where they have made exporting difficult or unattractive, firms have
hunkered down in their home markets, and when in trouble called for protection. As I shall indicate later, in some cases at the same time as firms were
competing abroad, they were working within a rather protected home
market, so the argument is not a simple one for "free trade." Rather, it is
that export incentives matter significantly because for most countries if firms
do not compete on world markets they do not compete strongly. Up until
recently the United States possibly was an exception to this rule. The U.S.
market was large enough to support considerable competition among domestic firms, which kept them on their toes and innovative. No other country
could afford the luxury of not forcing its firms to compete on world markets:
now the United States cannot either.

Of course much of the current interest in national systems of innovation
reflects a belief that the innovative prowess of national firms is determined
to a considerable extent by government policies. Above I have identified two
features of the national environment in which firms live that seem to affect
their ability and incentives to innovate profoundly, and which are central
responsibilities of government in all of the countries in our sample: the education of the work force and the macroeconomic climate. But what of
government policies and programs more directly targeted at technological
advance? This is where much of the contemporary interest is focused. How
effective have been these kinds of policies?

In assessing this question in the light of the fifteen country systems studied
in this project, one strong impression is the wide range of policies targeted
at technological advance. Thus, in recent years government policies toward
industrial mergers and acquisitions, interfirm agreements and joint ventures,
and allowable industrywide activities often have been strongly influenced by
beliefs about the effects of such policies on innovative performance. Many
countries (and the EC) now are encouraging firms to cooperate in R&D of
various sorts. Similarly, in recent years a number of governments have
worked to restructure or augment financial institutions with the goal of fostering industrial innovation; thus several have tried to establish their ana-
logue to the "venture capital" market that exists in the United States. As

suggested, these policies are a very diverse lot and differ from country to country. Our case studies do provide scattered evidence on them, but, simply because they are so diverse, I cannot see any strong generalizations that can be drawn.

Of course our country study authors were primed to look at government programs directly supporting R&D, and here I think the evidence collected is more systematic. It seems useful to distinguish between government programs that largely provide funds for university research or for research in government or other laboratories not tied to particular business firms, and government programs that directly support R&D done in firms. I consider each in turn.

Scholars of innovation now understood that, in many sectors, publicly supported research at universities and in public laboratories is an important part of the sectoral innovation system. A substantial share of the funding of such institutions goes into fields directly connected with technological or industrial needs—fields like agronomy, pathology, computer science, materials science, and chemical and electrical engineering.

Do our country studies support the proposition that strong research at universities or public laboratories aids a country's firms in innovation, defining that term broadly as we have? Not surprisingly, the answer seems to differ from field to field, and to be sensitive to the mechanisms in place to mold and facilitate interactions with industry. All the countries that are strong and innovative in fine chemicals and pharmaceuticals have strong university research in chemistry and the biomedical sciences. A strong agriculture, and a strong farm product processing industry, is associated in all of our cases with significant research going on relevant to these fields in national universities, or other types of public research institutions dedicated to these industries. In contrast, Argentine agriculture is surprisingly weak, despite favorable natural endowments. The author of the study of Argentina lays the blame on Argentina's failure to develop an adequate agricultural research system.

Where countries have strong electronics firms, for the most part there is some strong research in university departments of electrical engineering, and this would appear to include Japan. Government laboratories have been important sources of new electronic product designs later taken over by firms in Taiwan. On the other hand, university research does not seem of much importance to technical advance in automobiles and aerospace.

Where universities or public laboratories do seem to be helping national firms, one tends to see either direct interactions between particular firms and particular faculty members or research teams, as through consulting arrangements, or mechanisms that tie university or public laboratory programs to groups of firms. Thus in the U.S. agricultural experimentation stations do research of relevance to farmers and seed producers and have close inter-actions with them. Various German universities have programs designed to help machinery producers. Taiwan's electronics industry is closely linked to government laboratories. In all of these cases, the relationships between the university or government labs and the industry are not appropriately de-scribed as the universities or public laboratories simply doing research of relevance to the industry in question. The connections were much broader and closer than that, involving information dissemination and problem solving. Universities and industry were co-partners in a technological com-munity. Although not important in all industries, such technology- and in-dustry-oriented public programs have made a big difference in many fields.

These programs are far less politically visible than government programs that directly support industrial R&D, and the latter also tend to involve far more money. Countries differ significantly in the extent to which the gov-ernment directly funds industrial R&D. And while most of such programs tend to be concentrated on a narrow range of high-tech industries, programs of this sort vary significantly and have been put in place for different reasons.

I noted above that, in most of our countries, military R&D accounts for by far the largest portion of government funding of industrial R&D. Ana-lysts have been divided as to whether military R&D and procurement has been a help or a hindrance to the commercial competitiveness of national industry. Of the major industrial nations, the United States spends by far the largest share of industrial R&D on military projects. A strong case can be made that in the 1960s this helped the American electronics and aircraft industries to come to dominate commercial markets, but that since the late 1960s there has been little "spillover." Britain has the second largest of the defense R&D budgets among our set of nations, but most of the companies receiving R&D contracts have shown little capability to break into nonmi-litary markets. The same can be said for most of the French companies. While until recently civilian commercial spillover seldom has been a central objective of military R&D, except in the sense that it was recognized that selling on civilian markets could reduce the public costs of sustaining a strong military procurement base, it is interesting to try to understand where military R&D did lend civilian market strength and where it did not.

Analysis of the U.S. experience suggests that civilian strength is lent when military R&D programs are opening up a broad new generic technology, as contrasted with focusing virtually exclusively on procuring particular new pieces of fancy hardware wanted by the military. Increasingly the U.S. military effort has shifted from the former to the latter. A much smaller share of military R&D now goes into research and exploratory development than during the 1960s, and a larger share into highly specialized systems development. And the efforts of the other countries in our set who have invested significantly in military R&D—Britain, France, and Israel—have from the beginning focused largely on the latter.

Space programs and nuclear power programs have much in common with military R&D and procurement. They tend to involve the same kind of government agency leadership in determining what is done. They too tend to be concentrated on large-scale systems developments. Spillover outside the field has been quite limited.

Government programs in support of company R&D in telecommunications, other civilian electronics, and aircraft may overlap the technical fields supported by military and space programs, and in some cases the support may go to the same companies. These programs also tend to involve the same blend of industrial R&D support, and protection from foreign competition. However, there are several important differences. One is that, compared with military R&D, the public funds almost invariably are much smaller. Indeed programs like Eureka, Esprit, Jessi, Fifth Generation, and Sematech are small relative to industry funding in the targeted areas. Second, the firms themselves usually have a major say regarding the way the public monies are spent, and the projects are subject to far less detailed public management and overview than are defense projects. Third, these programs are targeted to firms and products in civilian markets, and while their home base may be protected through import restriction or preferential procurement, the hope is that the firms ultimately will be able to stand on their own.

Thus, while they involve a commitment to high R&D spending, otherwise these programs have much in common with other "infant industry" protection programs, many of which have grown up for reasons with no particular connections with national security, or a belief in the importance of high tech but simply because of the desire of a government to preserve or create a "national" industry. Infant industry protection, subsidy, and government guidance are policies that have been around for a long long time. They mark French policy since Colbert. During the nineteenth century and through World War II the United States was protectionist. The Japanese and Korean steel and auto industries, which were highly protected up until the 1980s, are more contemporary examples.

Do the infants ever grow up? Some do and some do not. The Japanese auto and electronics companies and the Korean Chaebol-based enterprises are well-known examples of presently strong firms that grew up in a protected market, but it also should be recognized that the American computer and semiconductor industries grew up with their market shielded from foreign competition and with their R&D funded to a considerable extent by the Department of Defense. After a period of such shelter and support, these firms came to dominate the world's commercial markets. Airbus may be another successful example. On the other hand, the country studies in this project give many examples of protected and subsidized industries which have never gotten to a stage where the firms can compete on their own. France's electronics industry is a striking example, but so also are the import-substituting industries of Argentina and Brazil.

What lies behind the differences? If I were to make a bet it is that the differences reside in two things: first, the education and training systems which in some cases did and in others did not provide the protected firms with the strong skills they needed to make it on their own; second, at least in today's world, the extent to which economic conditions, including government policies, provide strong incentives for the firms to quickly start trying to compete on world markets, as contrasted with hunkering down in their protected enclave.

The picture of government policies supporting industrial innovation that I have been presenting highlights the diversity of such policies and programs, and their generally fragmented nature—some supporting research and other activities aimed to help industry in universities or public labs, others connected with defense or space or nuclear power, still others aimed directly at supporting or protecting certain industries or industry groups. This is the picture I draw from the country studies of this project. These studies play down the existence of active coherent industrial policies more broadly. The interpretation they present of the industrial policies of nations widely believed to have them is closer to that of modern-day infant industry protection with some R&D subsidy, than to a well-structured and thought-through general policy.

Some readers will dispute this conclusion, arguing that the failure of the studies in this project of countries well known to have active coherent industrial policies to highlight them and their successes reflects a serious misjudgment of the authors. The authors of those studies respond by arguing that in fact government policies in their countries are highly decentralized, and by pointing, the case of Airbus an exception, to the very small fraction of industry R&D accounted for by government programs.

The skeptics rejoin that, while the policies did not involve massive public monies, they had a lot of leverage on private decisions and investments. The authors respond that government leverage has been exaggerated and that where strong policies have been executed, they as often lead to failure as to success. This clearly is the position taken by our Japanese authors on MITI. Without a more fine-grained understanding of technological innovation than we now have, there is no way of resolving this debate in a way that will persuade all people.

4. The Dispute over High-Tech Policies

Above I stressed that the bulk of government R&D support, particularly support of industrial R&D, goes into high tech, a portion of it through programs expressly designed to lend their firms a commercial edge. Where these latter programs exist, they tend to be complemented by various forms of protection and, sometimes, export subsidy. They are motivated and justified by the argument that if an economy does not have considerable strength in high tech it will be disadvantaged relative to countries that do.

But does this seem to be the case? The logic of the case and the evidence supporting it are not totally compelling.

For a firm or industry to be competitive in a high-wage country certainly requires that it make effective use of skills and technological and managerial sophistication that are not readily available in low-wage countries. The high-tech, high R&D intensity industries are of this sort, but there are many others as well. The definition of "high" tech used by statistical agencies is directly tied to R&D intensity. However, we have stressed that an industry can be characterized by considerable innovation and not have a high R&D intensity. If firms are relatively small, or if there is significant design work aimed at particular customers or market niches, while considerable innovation may be going on, the firms may not report much R&D.

Further, while national programs have tended to focus on areas like semiconductors, computers, and new materials, where technical advance clearly is dramatic, much of the economic value created by these advances occurs downstream, in the industries and activities that incorporate these new products into their own processes and products—automobiles, industrial machinery, financial services, shipping. To do this effectively often involves significant innovation and creative innovation here may generate major competitive advantage, but not much in the way of large-scale formal R&D may be involved. On the other hand, it can be argued that active government policies often can be more effective when aimed to help an industry take advantage of new upstream technologies than when oriented toward subsidizing major breakthroughs. A large portion of the clearly effective public programs discussed in the various country studies of this project were or are focused on bringing an industry up to world practice (this certainly characterizes many of the successful Japanese programs) or to spread knowledge about new developments (American agriculture and several of the government programs in Germany, Denmark, and Sweden).

Of course, the lure of high tech to countries that know they must be highly innovative if they are to compete with lower-wage countries is not based solely on statistical illusion. The discussion above acknowledges the special place of innovation in semiconductors, computers, new materials, and the like in the contemporary pattern of industrial innovation more broadly. Advances in these fields provide the building blocks, the key opportunities, for technical innovation in a wide range of downstream industries from high-speed trains to cellular telephones to commercial banking. Many observers noting this have proposed that a nation that wants its firms to be strong over the coming years in the downstream industries had better not let foreign firms control the key upstream technologies. This argument is prevalent in some newly developing countries, like Brazil, Korea, and Taiwan, as well as in today's high-income ones.

Another argument seems to square the circle. It is that a nation needs to have strength in the downstream industries in order to provide a market for the key component industries. Thus nations are supporting firms working on high-definition television and telecommunications, partly on the argument that in the absence of a home market a nation's semiconductor and computer firms will be disadvantaged. Similarly, public support of aerospace is justified partly on alleged stimulation to upstream technology.

Put more generally, the argument is that high-tech industries generate unusually large "externalities," which flow to national downstream firms. This possibility is one of those modeled in what has come to be called the "new trade theory" (see, for example, Krugman, 1987) which has developed a collection of arguments which support subsidy or protection as a means of gaining real national advantage. The fact that these industries are natural oligopolies who, in equilibrium, likely will support higher than average profits or wages, is another "new trade theory" argument sometimes used to rationalize protection or subsidy, on the grounds that subsidy now will yield high returns later.

The authors of our country studies clearly have different, and perhaps mixed, minds about this matter. There is a certain plaintiveness expressed in the studies of the major European countries that, while doing well in some other areas, national firms are not doing well in these critical high-tech fields. The authors of the studies of Australia and Canada, on the other hand, seem to regard electronics envy as silly and expensive faddism.

While our country studies cannot resolve the issues, they can at least bring to attention three matters that ought to give pause to the zealots. In the first place, there does not seem to be strong empirical support for the proposition that national economies are broadly advantaged if their firms are especially strong in high tech and disadvantaged if they are not. Thus the United States continues to be strong (and a major net exporter) in a wide range of high-technology R&D-intensive industries, but its economic growth has been lagging badly for nearly twenty years. Italy has very limited capacity in these industries, but its overall productivity and income levels have been growing briskly for many years. One can argue that France has had broad economic success more despite its efforts to nurture and subsidize its high-technology industries than because of them. Japan is strong in DRAMS, but also in automobile production, which accounts for much more employment and export value, and its efficiency in producing cars seems to have little to do with high tech. And Canada, Australia, Denmark, and the United States all continue to be strongly competitive in industries based on agriculture or natural resources.

Also, as we have noted, the record of national policies expressly aimed to help high-tech industries through support of industrial R&D and protection is very uneven. Indeed, the strongest positive examples occurred long ago, when the U.S. government provided broad support for advances in electronics and aircraft, and the American edge here has not proved to be durable. Other successful cases are largely "infant industry" cases (for example, Japanese electronics during the 1960s and 1970s, and Korea during the early 1980s) where, as the companies became strong, the active and protective role of government diminished. Airbus may (or may not) be a contemporary success story. However, by and large the success record is not very good.

Moreover, and of crucial importance, firms and projects in the aircraft and electronics industries are rapidly becoming transnational. Partly this is because of a need to share very high up-front R&D costs, which can be met by joining with other firms. Traditional intranational rivalries tend to make firms look for foreign partners. And this tendency, of course, is increased to the extent that governments try to keep the products of foreign firms out of domestic markets and to channel subsidy to national firms. Unless the home market is very rich and the subsidies very high, firms have strong incentives to somehow form links with other firms so that they have a chance at other markets.

Today, there probably is no other matter which so forces one to step back, and consider the contemporary meaning of a "national innovation system."

To what extent are there really "innovation systems," and to the extent that there are, in what ways are they defined by nation states?

5. What Remains National about Innovation Systems?

There obviously are a number of difficulties with the concept of a "national innovation system." In the first place, unless one defines innovation very narrowly and cuts the institutional fabric to that narrow definition, and we did neither, it is inevitable that analysis of innovation in a country sometimes would get drawn into discussion of labor markets, financial systems, monetary fiscal and trade policies, and so on. One cannot draw a line neatly around those aspects of a nation's institutional structure that are concerned predominantly with innovation in a narrow sense excluding everything else, and still tell a coherent story about innovation in a broad sense. Nonetheless, most of our authors were able to tell a coherent story about innovation in their country focusing largely on institutions and mechanisms that fit the narrow definition, with discussion of country institutions more broadly serving largely as a frame.

Second, the term suggests much more uniformity and connectedness within a nation than is the case. Thus one can for the most part discuss Canadian agriculture independently of Canadian telecommunications. R&D and innovation in the American pharmaceutical industry and R&D in aircraft by American companies have little in common. And yet one cannot read the studies of Japan, Germany, France, Korea, Argentina, and Israel, to name just a few, without coming away with the strong feeling that nationhood matters and has a persuasive influence. In all these cases, a distinctive national character pervades the firms, the educational system, the law, the politics, and the government, all of which have been shaped by a shared historical experience and culture.

I believe that most of us would square these somewhat divergent observations as follows. If one focuses narrowly on what we have defined as "innovation systems," these tend to be sectorally specific. However, if one broadens the focus, the factors that make for commonality across sections within a country, the wider set of institutions referred to above, come into view and these largely define the factors that make for commonality across sectors within a country.

From the start of this project we recognized that borders around nations are porous, and increasingly so. Indeed, one of the questions that motivated this study was whether or not the concept of *national* innovation systems made sense anymore. I suspect that many of us come out on this as follows.

It is a safe bet that there will be increasing internationalization of those aspects of technology that are reasonably well understood scientifically. Efforts on the part of nations, and firms, to keep new understandings won in R&D privy increasingly will be futile. Among firms with the requisite scientific and technical people, the competitive edge will depend on the details of design, of production process, of firm strategy and organization, upstream-downstream connections, and so on. Today this is quite clearly the case in fields like semiconductors, aircraft, computers, and automobiles. In these fields, there are no broad technological secrets possessed by individual countries or particular firms. On the other hand, strong firms have a good deal of firm specific know-how and capability.

It is also a good bet that differences across firms stamped into them by national policies, histories, and cultures will diminish in importance. Partly that will be because the world is becoming much more unified culturally, for better or for worse. Partly it will be because firm managers and scholars of management increasingly are paying attention to how firms in other countries are organized and managed. And cross-country interfirm connections are likely to grow in importance. Firms in industries where there are large up-front R&D design and production engineering costs increasingly are forging alliances with firms in other countries, to share some of the costs and to get over government-made market barriers. The establishment of branch plants in protected countries or regions is another mechanism. Thus, increasingly, the attempts of national governments to define and support a national industry will be frustrated because of internationalization.

What will remain of "national systems"? The firms that reside in the country, for one thing, but people and governments will have to get used to dealing with plants whose headquarters are abroad. The countries of Europe have been struggling with this matter for some time, and many of the Latin American countries, too. The United States is now having to try to deal with this, and Japan and Korea are beginning to. As yet, no large country seems to have made its peace with the problem, however. While in most countries resident firms will be largely national, the presence of "foreign" firms in important industries is something that nations will have to learn to cope with better.

We noted earlier the striking continuity of a nation's basic institutions bearing on industrial innovation. A good example is national education systems, which sometimes seem never to change in their basics. While top-level scientists and engineers may be highly mobile, and some high-level students will continue to take training abroad, below the Ph.D. level, by and large, countries will be stuck with their nationals who are trained at home.

The nation's system of university research and public laboratories will continue to be, largely, national, particularly the programs that are specifically keyed to advancing technology or otherwise facilitating technical progress in industry, and with built-in mechanisms for interacting with industry. These programs will have to work with foreign branch firms as well as domestic ones in certain fields. But the notion that universities and public laboratories basically provide "public goods" and that therefore there are no advantages to firms that have close formal links simply does not fit the facts in many industries.

The nation's other public infrastructure, and laws, its financial institutions, its fiscal, monetary, and trade policies, and its general economic ambiance, still will be a major influence on economic activity, including innovating, and these are very durable. For large high-income countries at least, the lion's share of private investment will continue to be domestic, and constrained by domestic savings. Moreover, nations will continue to have their own distinctive views of the appropriate relationships between government and business.

And these will strongly influence a nation's policies bearing explicitly on science and technology. From the evidence in this study, these must be understood as an agglomeration of policies directed toward different national objectives, each with a somewhat special domain in terms of the fields and the institutions most affected, rather than as a coherent package.

All can hope that there will be a significant diminution of defense programs, but it is a safe bet that military R&D will continue to account for the lion's share of government industrial R&D spending in the United States, France, Britain, and Israel. It is likely, however, that there will be little commercial "spillover."

Outside of defense and space, a nation's programs of R&D support will in all likelihood continue to reflect both the needs of industry and broad attitudes toward what government should be doing and how. While there will be exceptions, particularly when a defense connection is argued, the United States will continue to resist programs that directly fund industrial R&D, but will use the universities as the base for a variety of programs including some directly targeted at certain technologies and industries. European countries are likely to make much more use of programs that directly support civil industrial R&D, either in individual firms or in industrywide research organizations. And in Japan, France, and various other countries, government agencies and high-tech firms will continue to be quite close.

6. The Diversity of National Systems: Do We Need Some Standards Regarding What Is Fair?

At the present time nations seem to be conscious as never before of their "innovation systems" and how they differ from those of their peers. This consciousness of differences is leading in two very different directions.

On the one hand, it is leading to attempts on the part of nations to adopt aspects of other systems that they see as lending them strength. However, the experimentation is far from systematic, and it is highly influenced by perceptions that may have little contact with reality. Thus, the United States and the European countries (and the EC) have been loosening laws that restrict interfirm R&D cooperation, and establishing programs to encourage and subsidize it in some areas. If the chapter on Japan has got it right, this may be somewhat ironic in view of the argument that the role in Japan's rapid postwar growth of cooperative R&D among firms in the same line of business probably has been exaggerated, and in any case is diminishing.

The less-developed countries are looking, with good reason, to Korea and Taiwan for models. But, aside from their strong support of education, high levels of investment in plant and equipment, and their pressure on firms to go for exports, these two countries have quite different innovation systems. In one, Taiwan, government research laboratories have been an important source of industrial technology; in the other, Korea, apparently they have not, at least until recently. Korea has encouraged the growth of large industrial conglomerates, and resisted foreign ownership; Taiwan has not especially encouraged the growth of large firms and has admitted foreign firms selectively. But both have been successful in building innovative competitive manufacturing industry based on foreign-created technologies and other low-income countries are trying to learn from their experience.

While today attempts at emulation are at a peak, they are nothing new. The study of Japan shows how earlier in the century the Japanese tried to pick and choose from European and American experience, and came out with something quite different. The Americans earlier tried to adopt the German university system, and actually built a very different one.

On the other hand, perceptions of differences are leading nations to declare certain aspects of their rivals' systems illegitimate. Prominent Americans have expressed the opinion that MITI support and guidance of key Japanese industries, together with the special connections between Japanese firms and their customers and their sources of finance, amount to an unfair system, involving subsidy and dumping as well as protection. Similar complaints have been lodged against Eureka and Airbus. The Europeans complain about Japan and about U.S. programs like the SDI, claiming that such large-scale government R&D support, while aimed at a military target, is sure to build commercial advantages, and that this requires response on their part. The Japanese make similar complaints, but particularly about the import barriers being imposed by other countries. Some have gone so far as to argue that presently there is a war between competing national innovation systems that only can be resolved if there are new accepted standards regarding what is fair and what is not (see, for example, Ostry, 1990). Otherwise, nations will have to adopt the norm of managed trade in high-technology products.

These two aspects of the current concern about differences in national innovation systems—attempts at emulation, and expressions of hostility—are opposite sides of the same coin. They reflect a combination of beliefs that a nation's performance in high tech is vital to its broader economic performance and security, real uncertainty regarding just how to achieve high performance, and lack of agreed-upon criteria for judging what are legitimate and illegitimate government policies.

In my view, which may not be shared by all of my colleagues, the current brouhaha seems somewhat hysterical. There is little more reason to get upset over intercountry differences in the government's role in the support and protection of high tech than about other areas where government policies differ sharply. For one thing, governments' anguish that their economies are fated to be surely disadvantaged if they do not have a high-tech industry of their own probably is unwarranted. For another, beliefs that strength in high tech is due largely to promotional government policies seem grossly exaggerated.

At the same time, the studies in this project show that the institutional structures supporting technical innovation are complex and variegated. Technology and science interact in intricate ways. Both private for-profit and public institutions play roles in virtually all arenas of technological advance and the efficient division of labor is not obvious. Simple-minded arguments that private enterprise is what does industrial innovation and public institutions have little useful role in it are simple minded indeed.

In this area it is not totally clear what one should call subsidy or protection, as contrasted with legitimate public spending or coordination or regulation.

Economists are wont to draw the line in terms of whether or not government spending or regulation or guidance can be justified by market failure arguments. If so, while public action may give advantage to a particular national industry, such support can be argued to increase economic efficiency. If not, it is considered naked subsidy or protection, and is not to be condoned. Thus while international trade theorists long have known that a nation could enhance the well-being of its own citizens vis-à-vis those in other countries by selected naked subsidy or protection, the argument was that, under the theory then in vogue, for nations taken as a group, this was a negative sum game.

But the problem with this line of argument here is that "market failure" is ubiquitous in the activities associated with industrial innovation, and thus subsidy or protection or guidance could be efficiency enhancing; hence the game of active industrial policy need not be negative sum. What has come to be called the "new trade theory" recognizes some of this, nervously. If there are large up-front R&D costs, or significant learning through doing or using, or major externalities in certain activities like research and training, the simple arguments that free trade is "Pareto Optimal" (in the parlance of economists) falls apart.

Of course "market failure" is greater in certain activities than in others. Also, government competence and incentives are more likely to lead to productive programs in certain arenas than in others. Further, it is apparent that competitive protection and subsidy among nations can get beyond any level conceivably justified on grounds of "efficiency." It is in the interest of all nations to rein in such tendencies.

However, it seems unlikely that simple rules—for example, that government support of R&D on public sector needs and for "basic" research is efficient and fair, and that direct support of industrial R&D aimed to develop products for a civilian market is both inefficient and unfair—will carry the discussion very far. This argument certainly can be used to attack Airbus. But Europeans rejoin that government help was needed to overcome the huge headstart American companies had won in large part as a spillover from military R&D, and can be justified economically both on infant industry grounds and as a policy to avoid the development of a one-company world monopoly. And what of government support for telecommunications R&D where telecommunications is a government service? Americans are prone to argue that telecommunications should be privatized, but there surely is limited agreement on that. One can try, and with some hope of success, to open government procurement to bids from foreign firms. However, what to one eye is blockage to competition in public procurement to another is a valuable close relationship between customer and steady supplier.

Nor are there clean lines separating "basic research" from applied. No one seems to object to government support for research on the causes of cancer (although a breakthrough here may give the firms with close contact with the research a major advantage in coming up with a proprietary product). But what about research to advance agricultural productivity? To improve crops growing in a particular national soil and climate? Research on superconductivity, or on surface phenomena in semiconductors, conducted in universities? Conducted in an industry cooperative research organization? In a particular firm?

The argument about whether government funding of certain kinds of R&D is appropriate and efficient or unfair subsidy of course gets intertwined with arguments about protection and about constraints in direct foreign investments. Here countries clearly disagree on what they regard as appropriate. The disagreements can be discussed, and agreements negotiated. However, it does not seem to me that the question of whether or not a protected industry is high tech changes the nature of the discussion, or the stakes, that much.

All this is no argument against trying to establish some norms and rules regarding government policies bearing on industrial innovation, and in certain areas aiming for uniform or at least comparable policies. However, it is an argument against one nation or another believing self-righteously that its ways are efficient, fair, and quite justified, and the policies of other nations are not. And it is an argument against the belief that agreeing on ground rules will be simple, if only the advice of economists is heeded.

And finally, it is an argument against trying to impose too much uniformity. Countries differ in their traditions, ideologies, and beliefs about appropriate roles for government, and they will guard the differences they think matter. A central reason for undertaking this project was, by expanding the set of countries considered, and by trying to enable comparisons where these seemed most interesting, to try to tease out what features of national systems seemed systematically to enhance innovation performance, and what features seemed useless or worse. My colleagues and I like to believe that we have learned a good deal. But there still is a lot of room for informed differences of opinion.

Given that there is, it is not simply inappropriate for one group or another to argue for its preferred uniformity. While (as this project testifies) it is not easy to tease out signal from noise, potentially we all can learn from one another about what seems to be effective and what is not.

Notes

Chapter 2   CAPITALISM AS AN ENGINE OF PROGRESS

1. For a survey of the vast empirical literature, see Cohen and Levin (1989).
2. Each of the following contains an important collection of studies or summarizes large aspects of this literature: Dosi et al. (1988), Freeman (1982), Rosenberg (1985), Mansfield (1968, 1971, 1981), Griliches (1984), Nelson (1962), and Nelson and Winter (1982). Cohen and Levin (1989) summarize the portions of this literature concerned with the connections between technical advance and market structure.
3. I refer here of course to the demonstration, beloved by many economists, that given a set of assumptions of great stringency the allocation of resources generated by a competitive system is "Pareto optimal." See, for example, Arrow and Hahn (1971).
4. While many scholars have stressed the importance of uncertainty in R&D, Klein (1977) has developed the point with special force. See also the studies conducted under his direction at RAND and published in Nelson (1962) and the modeling in Marschak et al. (1967).
5. See, for example, Arthur (1984) on competing technologies when there are economies associated with the number of users of each, and David (1985) on how the contemporary typewriter keyboard came into being.
6. For semiconductors see, for example, Braun and MacDonald (1978), Dosi (1984), Malerba (1985), or Levin in Nelson (1982). For computers see, for example, Katz and Phillips in Nelson (1982) or Flam (1988). Miller and Sawers (1968) and Mowery and Rosenberg in Nelson (1982) are good on aircraft. Freeman (1982) provides a good summary of technical advance in synthetic materials. See Schwartzman (1975) for pharmaceuticals.
7. Dosi (1982) calls these technological paradigms.
8. There are several recent accounts of how the engineering fields came into being. See Noble (1977) and Kranzberg (1986).
9. There have been several good studies of the cost of technology transfer. See, for example, Teece (1977) and Mansfield (1981).

10. See, for example, the studies of publications by scientists working for pharmaceutical companies by Narin and Rozek (1988) and Koenig (1983).

11. Actually, the question of how close to on-line problems and capabilities a lab should work is a central one in R&D management. For a discussion of the history of the issue at Du Pont, see Hounshell and Smith (1988).

12. The study by Wyatt et al. (1985), while directed more narrowly at multinational corporations, covered some of the same ground and came up with similar findings.

13. These technologies are what Winter and I have called cumulative. For good studies of cumulative technologies, see Sahal (1981), Enos (1962), and of course Gilfillan (1935).

14. Our findings regarding where patents are important are similar to those of Scherer et al. (1959), Mansfield et al. (1981), and Wyatt et al. (1985).

15. The topic being discussed here is akin to that often called the "diffusion" of innovations. However, in writings under that rubric there often is a failure to distinguish between the spread of an innovation created upstream among customers, and the imitation of a rival's innovation by competitors. The focus here is the spread of technology among rivals.

16. The well-known patent pools in aircraft design and manufacture, automobiles and radio reflect all of these factors. In addition, prior to the pooling firms were engaged in litigation that clearly hurt all or most of the participants.

17. T. Allen (1966, 1970) has described networks among engineers. See also R. Allen (1983) on the phenomenon of open access to competitors of new technological developments in steel making.

18. Freeman (1982) provides a nice analysis of the relationships between chemical plant designers and chemical companies. See Lundvall in Dosi et al. (1988) for a discussion of long-run vertical cooperation in design.

19. There are a number of recent studies on joint ventures. See, for example, Mowery (1988) and Harrigan (1987).

20. Among the many good studies of the correlation of academic and industrial research in chemistry and electricity are Rosenberg (1985), Nobel (1977), and Thackray (1982).

21. The basic distinction is whether industrial R&D workers use the findings and techniques of academic research in going about their problem solving, or whether what comes out of academic research directly invokes particular industrial R&D efforts to exploit those findings. Our conclusions, that the former is common but the latter is not, is quite consistent with Gibbons and Johnston (1974).

22. This section draws extensively on Nelson (1982).

23. For a discussion of Schumpeter's sometimes schizophrenic views, see Langlois (1987). For the more radical stance, see Veblen (1921).

24. For an especially perceptive analysis, see Freeman (1987).

Chapter 6   THE ROLE OF KNOWLEDGE IN R&D EFFICIENCY

1. For a good survey of induced-innovation models, deterministic and stochastic, see Binswanger and Ruttan (1978).
2. Gibbons and Johnston (1974) give a balanced review of earlier studies, and present a view on the links between science and invention similar to my own. Salhal's book (1981) develops the argument that the knowledge relevant to advancing a technology is won largely in either such effects, a theme I shall develop later in this essay.
3. Thus it is assumed that studies must be undertaken in parallel, in the spirit of my earlier model (Nelson, 1961). Other models of R&D as search assume sequential drawing. See, for example, Evenson and Kisler (1976) and Dasgupta and Stiglitz (1980). For my purposes here, the differences between the approaches are not of consequence.
4. Rogers (1981) presents a fascinating study of communication among R&D scientists and engineers working for different firms in the Silicon Valley.

Chapter 7   THE LINK BETWEEN SCIENCE AND INVENTION

1. See Popper (1959). The history that follows is primarily taken from Pierson and Brattain (1955).
2. The semiconductor types were named before theoretical understanding of the differences was achieved. Note that for the first type of semiconductor the rectifying contact conducts when the metal is positive relative to the crystal, so it could have been called *p* type, and similarly the second could have been called *n* type. Had they been, language use would have worked against the understanding of semiconductors. The situation would have been much like that in the early nineteenth-century electrical theory, where Franklin's convention of defining current flow direction as from plus to minus hindered understanding of electron flow.
3. The material in this section is taken from several sources, the most important of which are the Shockley and Bardeen Nobel Prize lectures.
4. Several other studies of basic research show much the same pattern as the transistor history. See, for example, Cohen (1948), Conant (1951), and Smyth (1948). Many other references could be cited, though few deal in any detail with specific research projects.
5. For an extension and elaboration of this line of argument, see Nelson (1959).
6. "Team" is used here in the popular sense, not in the sense of the theory of teams.

Chapter 8   AMERICAN UNIVERSITIES AND TECHNICAL ADVANCE
           IN INDUSTRY

1. Cornell's founder and benefactor also expected students at his university to perform manual labor, including janitorial labor, while undergraduates.

2. Of course, offsetting the high American enrollment figures in higher education has been the often inferior quality of teaching in its secondary schools. A distinguished French biologist who visited the United States in 1916 observed, "Secondary teaching seems to me to be the weakest of the American system of education. The student who comes out of the high school at eighteen has not a sufficient intellectual training. A good part of his university studies consists in finishing his secondary studies" (Caullery, 1922). To which one can only add, Plus ça change, plus c'est la même chose.

3. For a detailed description of the contributions of MIT, see Wildes and Lindgren (1985).

4. See Leslie and Hardy (1985). Over the years Stanford University received the equivalent of $10 million 1978 US dollars.

5. See Vincenti (1990) for a penetrating analysis of the production and utilization of engineering knowledge in the case of aircraft. See also Hanle (1982).

6. Durand and Lesley actually began their experiments by designing and constructing the necessary wind tunnel equipment, since American capabilities with respect to wind tunnels were well behind European capabilities at the time.

7. Durand himself eventually prepared a six-volume aeronautical encyclopedia with the encouragement of the Guggenheim Fund, which had financed much of the Stanford research (1934–1936).

8. "Cal Tech ran more than three hundred wind tunnel tests on the airplane before test pilot Carl Cover, on December 17, 1935, the thirty-second anniversary of the Wright brothers' flight, completed the first flight of the DST. The DST, later designated DC-3, first went into service with American Airlines on June 7, 1936" (Hallion, 1977). Details of Cal Tech's contribution to the aircraft industry and to aeronautical development appear in Appendix I of Hallion's book.

9. "The ENIAC was to be designed with a special application in view. That is, it would be designed expressly for the solution of ballistics problems and for the printing of range tables, though, as originally envisioned by Mauchly, the device could have had wider applicability" (Stern, 1981, p. 15).

10. "Nor is it an accident that the pioneering roles in the introduction of techniques of statistical analysis were carried out far from the elite universities, at places such as Iowa State University and the University of North Carolina. Both of these universities had strong agricultural experiment stations where sophisticated statistical techniques were indispensable in evaluating the results of agricultural field research" (Ben-David, 1971).

11. It would be interesting to know what percentage of federal funds in support of basic research are awarded solely on the basis of peer review, and with no consideration of potential usefulness. We suspect that, outside of the NSF, that percentage is very small.

12. See Noble (1984) for a critical treatment of MIT's role in the development of this technology.

13. During the later period, however, America's historical eminence in the machine

tool industry declined drastically, as Japan, Germany and other countries emerged as leading producers. The coordination of development efforts and a closer interaction between producers and users seem to be most important among the reasons for such a shift in the comparative advantage of industry.

14. Harvey Brooks (1993), who takes a position on these issues similar to our own, suggests that, when universities are associated with such work, it should go on in somewhat separated institutions. In fact, this is mostly the case.

References

Abernathy, William J. 1978. *The Productivity Dilemma: Roadblock to Innovation in the Automobile Industry.* Baltimore: Johns Hopkins University Press.

Abramovitz, Moses. 1952. "Economics of Growth." In *A Survey of Contemporary Economics,* vol. 2, ed. Bernard Haley. Homewood, Ill.: Richard D. Irwin, pp. 132–178.

—— 1956. "Resource and Output Trends in the United States since 1870." *American Economic Review,* May, 46: 5–23.

—— 1979. "Rapid Growth Potential and Its Realization: The Experience of Capitalist Economics in the Postwar Period." *Economic Growth and Resources: The Major Issues,* vol. 1, ed. Edmond Malinvaud. London: Macmillan Press, pp. 1–30. Reprinted in Abramovitz (1989).

—— 1986. "Catching Up, Forging Ahead, and Falling Behind." *Journal of Economic History,* June, 46(2): 386–406; reprinted in Abramovitz (1989).

—— 1989. *Thinking about Growth.* Cambridge: Cambridge University Press.

Albu, Austin. 1980. "British Attitudes to Engineering Education: A Historical Perspective." *Technical Innovation and British Economic Performance,* ed. Keith Pavitt. London: Macmillan Press, pp. 67–87.

Alchian, Armen A. 1950. "Uncertainty, Evolution, and Economic Theory." *Journal of Political Economy,* June, 58: 211–221.

Allen, Robert C. 1977. "The Peculiar Productivity History of American Blast Furnaces, 1840–1913." *Journal of Economic History,* September, 37(3): 605–633.

—— 1979. "International Competition in Iron and Steel, 1850–1913." *Journal of Economic History,* December, 39(3): 911–937.

—— 1981. "Accounting for Price Changes: American Steel Rails, 1879–1910." *Journal of Political Economy,* June, 89(3): 512–528.

—— 1983. "Collective Invention." *Journal of Economic Behavior and Organization,* 4: 1–24.

Allen, Thomas J. 1966. "Studies of the Problem Solving Process in Engineering Design." *IEEE Transactions in Engineering Management,* vol. EM-13, June: 72–83.

———— 1970. "Roles in Technical Communications Networks." *Communications among Scientists and Engineers,* ed. C. Nelson and D. Pollock. Lexington, Mass.: Heath Lexington Press.

Ames, Edward, and Nathan Rosenberg. 1968. "The Enfield Arsenal in Theory and History." *Economic Journal,* December, 78: 827–842.

Argyris, Christopher. 1962. *Interpersonal Competence and Organizational Effectiveness.* Homewood, Ill.: Dorsey Press.

Arrow, Kenneth J., and F. Hahn. 1971. *General Competitive Analysis.* San Francisco: Holden-Day.

Arthur, W. Brian. 1988. "Self-Reinforcing Mechanisms in Economics." In *The Economy as an Evolving Complex System,* ed. Philip W. Anderson, Kenneth J. Arrow, and David Pines. Reading, Mass.: Addison-Wesley, pp. 9–31.

———— 1989. "Competing Technologies, Increasing Returns, and Lock-in by Historical Events." *Economic Journal,* March, 99(394): 116–131.

Asher, Harold. 1956. *Cost Quantity Relationships in the Airframe Industry.* Santa Monica, Calif.: RAND Corporation, R291.

Bacon, Robert William, and Walter Alfred Eltis. 1976. *Britain's Economic Problem: Too Few Producers.* London: Macmillan.

Barnard, Chester Irving. 1938. *The Functions of the Executive.* Cambridge, Mass.: Harvard University Press.

Barro, Robert J. 1991. "Economic Growth in a Cross Section of Countries." *Quarterly Journal of Economics,* May, 106(2): 407–443.

Barzel, Y. 1968. "Optimal Timing of Innovations." *Review of Economics and Statistics,* 1348–1355.

Baumol, William J. 1968. "Entrepreneurship and Economic Theory." *American Economic Review,* May, 58: 64–71.

Baumol, William J., Sue Anne Batey Blackman, and Edward N. Wolff. 1989. *Productivity and American Leadership: The Long View.* Cambridge, Mass.: MIT Press.

Baumol, William J., and M. Stewart. 1971. "On the Behavioral Theory of the Firm." In *The Corporate Economy: Growth, Competition and Innovation Potential,* ed. R. Marris and A. Wood. Cambridge, Mass.: Harvard University Press.

Baxter, James P. 1946. *Scientists against Time.* Boston: Little, Brown.

Ben-David, Joseph. 1971. *The Scientist's Role in Society.* Englewood Cliffs, N.J.: Prentice-Hall.

Binswanger, Hans, and Vernon Ruttan. 1978. *Induced Innovation: Technology, Institutions, and Development.* Baltimore: Johns Hopkins University Press.

Braun, E., and S. MacDonald. 1978. *Revolution in Miniature.* Cambridge: Cambridge University Press.

Braun, Hans-Joachim. 1983. "The National Association of German-American Technologists and Technological Transfer between Germany and the United States, 1884–1930." *History of Technology,* 8: 15–35.

Bright, Arthur A. 1949. *The Electric Lamp Industry: Technological Change and Economic Development from 1800 to 1947.* New York: Macmillan.

Brock, Gerald. 1975. *The U.S. Computer Industry: A Study of Market Power.* Cambridge, Mass.: Ballinger.

Brooks, Harvey. 1993. "Research Universities and the Social Contract for Science." *Empowering Technology,* ed. Lewis M. Branscomb. Cambridge, Mass.: MIT Press, chap. 7.

Bruce, Robert V. 1987. *The Launching of Modern American Science, 1846–1876.* New York: Alfred A. Knopf.

Bryson, Effie. 1984. "Frederick E. Terman: Educator and Mentor." *IEEE Spectrum,* March: 71–73.

Bureau of Labor Statistics, Misc. Series. 1923. "Time and Labor Costs of Manufacturing 100 Pairs of Shoes." No. 360. Washington, D.C.: Government Printing Office.

———— 1933. "Labor Productivity in the Automobile Industry." No. 585. Washington, D.C.: Government Printing Office.

———— 1939. "Productivity of Labor in the Cotton Garment Industry." No. 662. Washington, D.C.: Government Printing Office.

———— 1979. "Productivity of Labor in Merchant Blast Furnaces." No. 474. Washington, D.C.: Government Printing Office.

Burgelman, Robert, and Richard Rosenbloom. 1989. "Technology Strategy: An Evolutionary Process Perspective." In *Research on Technological Innovation, Management, and Policy,* vol. 4, ed. R. Burgelman and R. Rosenbloom. Greenwich, Conn.: JAI Press, pp. 1–23.

Bush, Vannevar. 1945. *Science, The Endless Frontier.* Washington, D.C.: Government Printing Office.

Cain, Louis P., and Donald G. Paterson. 1986. "Biased Technical Change, Scale, and Factor Substitution in American Industry, 1850–1919." *Journal of Economic History,* March, 46(1): 153–164.

Cantwell, John. 1989. *Technological Innovation and Multinational Corporations.* London: Basil Blackwell.

———— 1993. "Corporate Technological Specialization in International Industries." Casson, M., and J. Creedy, eds., *Industrial Concentration and Economic Inequality.* Cambridge: Edward Elgar.

Carstensen, Fred. 1984. *American Enterprise in Foreign Markets.* Chapel Hill: University of North Carolina Press.

Carter, Charles F., and B. R. Williams. 1957. *Industry and Technical Progress: Factors Governing the Speed Application of Science.* London and New York: Oxford University Press.

Caullery, Maurice. 1922. *Universities and Scientific Life in the United States.* Cambridge, Mass.: Harvard University Press, p. 138.

Caves, Richard E. 1980. "Productivity Differences among Industries." *Britain's Eco-*

nomic Performance, ed. Richard E. Caves and Lawrence B. Krause. Washington, D.C.: Brookings Institution, pp. 135–198.

Caves, Richard E., H. Crookell, and P. Killing. 1983. "The Imperfect Market for Technology Licenses." *Oxford Bulletin of Economics and Statistics,* 45: 249–267.

Chandler, Alfred D. 1962. *Strategy and Structure: Chapters in the History of the Industrial Enterprise.* Cambridge, Mass.: MIT Press.

—— 1977. *The Visible Hand: The Managerial Revolution in American Business.* Cambridge, Mass.: Harvard University Press.

—— 1990. *Scale and Scope: The Dynamics of Industrial Capitalism.* Cambridge, Mass.: Harvard University Press.

Charles River Associates. 1980. *Innovation, Competition, and Government Policy in the Semi-Conductor Industry.* Lexington, Mass.: Lexington Books.

Christensen, L., and D. Jorgenson. 1971. "Conjugate Duality and the Transcendental Logarithmic Function." *Econometrica,* July, 39: 255–256.

Clark, Gregory. 1987. "Why Isn't the Whole World Developed? Lessons from the Cotton Mills." *Journal of Economic History,* March, 47(1): 141–173.

Clark, K., and T. Fujimoto. 1991. *Product Development Performance: Strategy Management and Organization in the World Auto Industry.* Cambridge, Mass.: Harvard Business School Press.

Cohen, Wesley, and Stephan Klepper. 1991. "Firm Size versus Diversity in the Achievement of Technological Advance." In *Innovation and Technological Change: An International Comparison,* ed. Z. Acs and D. Audretsch. New York: Harvester Wheatsheaf.

Cohen, Wesley, and Richard Levin. 1989. "Empirical Studies of Innovation and Market Structure." In *Handbook of Industrial Organization,* ed. R. Schmalensee and R. Willig. New York: North Holland, pp. 1059–1107.

Cohen, Wesley, and Daniel Levinthal. 1989. "Innovation and Learning: The Two Faces of R&D." *Economic Journal,* September: 569–596.

Cohen, Wesley, Richard Florida, and Richard Goe. 1993. "University-Industry Research Centers in the United States." Report to the Ford Foundation.

Coleman, James, Elihu Katz, and Herbert Menzei. 1957. "The Diffusion of an Innovation among Physicians." *Sociometry,* December, 20: 253–270.

Constant, Edward. 1983. "Scientific Theory and Technological Testability." *Technology and Culture,* April, 24: 183–198.

Cornwall, John. 1977. *Modern Capitalism: Its Growth and Transformation.* London: Martin Robertson.

Cyert, Richard M., and James G. March. 1963. *A Behavioral Theory of the Firm.* Englewood Cliffs, N.J.: Prentice-Hall.

Dahlman, Carl J. 1979. "A Macroeconomic Approach to Technical Change: The Evolution of the Usiminas Steel Firm in Brazil." Ph.D. diss., Yale University.

Dasgupta, Partha, and Paul David. 1988. "Priority, Secrecy, Patents, and the Socio-Economics of Science and Technology." Center for Economic Policy Research, Stanford University, March.

Dasgupta, Partha, and Joseph Stiglitz. 1980a. "Uncertainty, Industrial Structure, and the Speed of R and D." *Bell Journal of Economics*, 11, no. 1: 1–28.

—— 1980b. "Industrial Structure and the Nature of Innovative Activity." *Economic Journal*, 90: 266–293.

David, Paul A. 1975. *Technical Choice, Innovation, and Economic Growth: Essays on American and British Experience in the Nineteenth Century*. London: Cambridge University Press.

—— 1985. "Clio and the Economics of QWERTY." *American Economic Review*, 75: 332–39.

—— 1988. "Path-dependence: Putting the Past into the Future of Economics." IMSSS Technical Report No. 533. Stanford University, November.

—— 1991. "Computer and Dynamo: The Modern Productivity Paradox in a Not-Too-Distant Mirror." OECD, Paris, July.

—— 1992. "Heros, Herds, and Hysteresis in Technological History: Thomas Edison and the Battle of the Systems Reconsidered." *Industrial and Corporate Change*, 129–180.

David, Paul A., and Gavin Wright. 1991. "Resource Abundance and American Economic Leadership." CEPR Publication No. 267, Stanford University.

Davis, E. W. 1964. *Pioneering with Taconite*. St. Paul: Minnesota Historical Society.

Davis, Lance E., and Douglass C. North. 1971. *Institutional Change and American Economic Growth*. London: Cambridge University Press.

Day, Richard, and Theodore Groves, eds. 1975. *Adaptive Economic Models: Proceedings of a Symposium Conducted by the Mathematic Research Center*. New York: Academic Press.

Day, Richard, and Inderjit Singh. 1977. *Economic Development as an Adaptive Process: The Green Revolution in Indian Punjab*. Cambridge and New York: Cambridge University Press.

De Long, J. Bradford. 1988. "Productivity Growth, Convergence, and Welfare: Comment." *American Economic Review*, December, 78(5): 1138–1159.

Denison, Edward F. 1962. "The Sources of Economic Growth in the United States and the Alternatives before Us." Supplementary Paper No. 13. Committee on Economic Development, New York.

—— 1964. "The Unimportance of the Embodied Question." *American Economic Review*, March, 54: 90–94.

—— 1967. *Why Growth Rates Differ: Postwar Experience in Nine Western Countries*. Washington, D.C.: Brookings Institution.

—— 1974. *Accounting for United States Economic Growth, 1929–1969*. Washington, D.C.: Brookings Institution.

—— 1979. *Accounting for Slower Economic Growth: The United States in the 1970s*. Washington, D.C.: Brookings Institution.

Dertouzos, Michael, Richard Lester, and Robert Solow. 1989. *Made in America*. Cambridge, Mass.: MIT Press.

Devine, Warren D., Jr. 1983. "From Shafts to Wires: Historical Perspective on Electrification." *Journal of Economic History*, June, 43(2): 347–372.

Doeringer, Peter B., and Michael J. Piore. 1971. *Internal Labor Markets and Manpower Analysis.* Lexington, Mass.: D. C. Heath.

Dollar, David, and Edward N. Wolf. 1988. "Convergence of Industry Labor Productivity among Advanced Economies, 1963–1982." *Review of Economics and Statistics,* November, 70(4): 549–558.

Domar, Evsey, et al. 1964. "Economic Growth and Productivity in the United States, Canada, United Kingdom, Germany and Japan, in the Postwar Period." *Review of Economics and Statistics,* February, 46: 33–40.

Dore, Ronald. 1973. *British Factory, Japanese Factory: The Origins of National Diversity in Industrial Relations.* Berkeley: University of California Press.

Dosi, Giovanni. 1982. "Technological Paradigms and Technological Trajectories." *Research Policy,* 11: 147–162.

———— 1984. *Technical Change and Industrial Transformation.* New York: St. Martin's Press.

Dosi, Giovanni, Christopher Freeman, Richard Nelson, Gerald Silverberg, and Luc Soete, eds. 1988. *Technical Change and Economic Theory.* London: Pinter Publishers.

Dosi, Giovanni, David J. Teece, and Sidney Winter. 1992. "Toward a Theory of Corporate Coherence: Preliminary Remarks." In *Technology and the Enterprise in Historical Perspectives,* ed. G. Dosi, R. Gianetti, and A. Toninelli. Oxford: Oxford University Press.

Durand, W. F. 1934–36. *Aerodynamic Theory: A General Review of Progress under a Grant of The Guggenheim Fund for the Promotion of Aeronautics.* Berlin: Julius Springer Verlag.

Easterlin, Richard A. 1981. "Why Isn't the Whole World Developed?" *Journal of Economic History,* March, 47(1): 1–19.

Elbaum, Bernard, and William Lazonick, eds. 1986. *The Decline of the British Economy.* Oxford: Oxford University Press.

Eliasson, Gunnar. 1977. "Competition and Market Processes in a Simulation Model of the Swedish Economy." *American Economic Review,* February, 67(1): 277–281.

Enos, John. 1962. *Petroleum Progress and Profits: A History of Process Innovation.* Cambridge, Mass.: MIT Press.

Etzkowitz, H. 1983. "Entrepreneurial Scientists and Entrepreneurial Universities in American Academic Science." *Minerva,* Autumn, 31: 326–360.

Evenson, Robert, and Yoav Kislev. 1976. "A Stochastic Model of Applied R&D." *Journal of Political Economy,* 84: 265–282.

Fabricant, Solomon. 1954. *Economic Progress and Economic Change.* 34th Annual Report of the NBER. New York: NBER.

Farrell, Michael J. 1970. "Some Elementary Selection Processes in Economics." *Review of Economic Studies,* July, 37(3): 305–319.

Field, Alexander J. 1983. "Land Abundance, Interest/Profit Rates and Nineteenth-Century American and British Technology." *Journal of Economic History,* June, 43(9): 405–431.

Flamm, Kenneth. 1987. *Targeting the Computer: Government Support and International Competition.* Washington, D.C.: Brookings Institution.

——— 1988. *Creating the Computer.* Washington, D.C.: Brookings Institution.

Flink, J. 1978. *America Adopts the Automobile.* Cambridge, Mass.: MIT Press.

Florida, Richard, and Martin Kenney. 1991. "Transplanted Organizations: The Transfer of Japanese Industrial Organization to the United States." *American Sociological Review,* June: 381–398.

Foreman-Peck, James. 1982. "The American Challenge of the Twenties: Multinationals and the European Motor Industry." *Journal of Economic History,* December, 42(4): 865–881.

Freeman, Christopher. 1982. *The Economics of Industrial Innovation.* London: Penguin.

——— 1987. *Technology Policy and Economic Performance: Lessons from Japan.* London: Francis Pinter.

——— 1991. "The Nature of Innovation and the Evolution of the Production System." OECD, Paris.

Freeman, Richard B., and James L. Medoff. 1979. "The Two Faces of Unionism." *Public Interest,* Fall, 57: 69–93.

Furter, William F., ed. 1980. *History of Chemical Engineering.* Washington, D.C.: American Chemical Society, chap. 2.

Fusfeld, Herbert. 1986. *The Technical Enterprise.* Cambridge, Mass.: Ballinger.

Geiger, Roger L. 1986. *To Advance Knowledge.* New York: Oxford University Press.

Gerschenkron, A. 1962. *Economic Development in Historical Perspectives.* Cambridge, Mass.: Harvard University Press.

Gibbons, Michael, and Ronald Johnston. 1974. "The Role of Science in Technological Innovation." *Research Policy,* 4: 220–242.

Gilbert, Richard. 1989. "Mobility Barriers and the Value of Incumbency." In *Handbook of Industrial Organization,* ed. R. Schmalensee and R. Willig. New York: North Holland, pp. 475–535.

Gilbert, Richard, and Carl Shapiro. 1990. "Optimal Patent Length and Breadth." *Rand Journal of Economics,* Spring, 21: 106–112.

Gilfillan, S. 1935. *Inventing the Ship.* Chicago: Follett.

Gillette Safety Razor Co. v. Clark Blade & Razor Co., 187 Federal Reports 149 (C.C.D.N.J. 1911). *Affirmed* 194 Federal Reports 421 (3d cis. 1912).

Goldmann, R. 1975. "Work Values: Six Americans in a Swedish Plant." Yale Social Science Library, March. Mimeo.

Gouldner, Alvin W. 1954. *Patterns of Industrial Bureaucracy.* Glencoe, Ill.: Free Press.

Government-University-Industry-Research Roundtable. 1986. *New Alliances and Partnerships in American Science and Engineering.* Washington, D.C.: National Academy Press.

——— 1991. *Industrial Perspectives on Innovation and Interactions with Universities.* Washington, D.C.: National Academy Press.

Graver Tank & Mfg. Co. v. Linde Air Products Co., 339 United States Reports 685 (1950).

Grayson, Lawrence. 1977. "A Brief History of Engineering Education in the United States." *Engineering Education*, December: 246–264.

Gregory, Robert G., and Denis W. James. 1973. "Do New Factories Embody Best Practice Technology?" *Economic Journal*, December, 83(332): 1133–1155.

Griliches, Zvi. 1957. "Hybrid Corn: An Exploration in the Economics of Technological Change." *Econometrica*, October, 25: 501–522.

———— 1960. "Measuring Inputs in Agriculture: A Critical Survey." *Journal of Farm Economics*, December, 42: 1411–1427.

———— 1979. "Issues in Assessing the Contribution of Research and Development to Productivity Growth." *Bell Journal of Economics*, 10: 92–116.

———— 1980. "R&D and the Productivity Slowdown." *American Economic Review*, May, 70: 343–348.

————, ed. 1984. *R&D Patents and Productivity*. Chicago: University of Chicago Press.

Griliches, Zvi, and Vidar Ringstadt. 1971. *Economics of Scale and the Form of the Production Function: An Econometric Study of Norwegian Manufacturing Establishment Data*. Amsterdam: North Holland.

Gruber, William H., and Donald G. Marquis, eds. 1969. *Factors in the Transfer of Technology*. Cambridge, Mass.: MIT Press.

Gulick, Luther H., and Lyndall Urwick, eds. 1937. *Papers on the Science of Administration*. New York: Institute of Public Administration, Columbia University.

Habakkuk, H. John. 1962. *American and British Technology in the Nineteenth Century*. New York: Cambridge University Press.

Hackman, J. Richard, and Greg R. Oldham. 1980. *Work Redesign*. Reading, Mass.: Addison-Wesley.

Hahn, F. H., and Matthews, R. C. O. 1967. "The Theory of Economic Growth." *Surveys of Economic Theory*, vol. 2: *Growth and Development*, ed. American Economic Association and the Royal Economic Society. New York: St. Martin's Press, pp. 1–124.

Haklisch, C. S., H. I. Fusfeld, and A. D. Levenson. 1984. *Trends in Collective Industrial Research*. New York: Center for Science and Technology Policy.

Hall, G. R., and R. E. Johnson. 1970. "Transfers of United States Aerospace Technology to Japan." In *The Technology Factor in International Trade*, ed. Raymond Vernon. Universities-National Bureau Conference Series, No. 22. New York: NBER; distributed by Columbia University Press, pp. 305–358.

Hallion, Richard P. 1977. *Legacy of Flight: The Guggenheim Contribution to American Aviation*. Seattle, Wash.: University of Washington Press.

Hanle, Paul A. 1982. *Bringing Aerodynamics to America*. Cambridge, Mass.: MIT Press.

Hanson, Paul, and Keith Pavitt. 1987. *The Comparative Economics of Research, Development, and Innovation in East and West: A Survey*. London: Harwood.

Harrigan, Katherine. 1987. *Strategies for Joint Ventures.* Lexington, Mass.: Lexington Books.

Hatsopoulos, George, Paul Krugman, and Lawrence Summers. 1988. "United States Competitiveness: Beyond the Trade Deficit." *Science,* July 15.

Hayes, Peter. 1987. *Industry and Ideology: IG Farben in the Nazi Era.* Cambridge: Cambridge University Press.

Hayes, Robert H., and William J. Abernathy. 1980. "Managing Our Way to Economic Decline." *Harvard Business Review,* July/August, 58(4): 67–77.

Headrick, Daniel R. 1988. *The Tentacles of Progress: Technology Transfer in the Age of Imperialism, 1850–1940.* New York: Oxford University Press.

Henderson, Rebecca, and Kim Clark. 1990. "Architectural Innovation." *Administrative Science Quarterly,* March, 35: 9–30.

Hirsch, Werner Z. 1952. "Manufacturing Progress Functions." *Review of Economics and Statistics,* May, 34: 143–155.

Hodgson, Geoffrey. 1993. *Economics and Evolution: Bringing Life back into Economics.* Cambridge: Polity Press.

Hollander, Samuel. 1965. *The Sources of Increased Efficiency: A Study of Du Pont's Rayon Plants.* Cambridge, Mass.: MIT Press.

Holmstrom, Bengt, and Jean Tirole. 1989. "The Theory of the Firm." *Handbook of Industrial Organization,* ed. R. Schmalensee and R. Willig. New York: North Holland, pp. 61–133.

Homans, George. 1950. *The Human Group.* New York: Harcourt Brace.

Hounshell, David A., and John K. Smith, Jr. 1988. *Science and Corporate Strategy: Du Pont R and D, 1902–1980.* New York: Cambridge University Press.

Hughes, Thomas P. 1983. *Networks of Power: Electrical Supply Systems in the United States, England, and Germany.* Baltimore: Johns Hopkins Press.

——— 1987. "The Evolution of Large Technological Systems." *The Social Construction of Technological Systems,* ed. Wiebe E. Bijker, Thomas P. Hughes, and Trevor J. Pinch. Cambridge, Mass.: MIT Press.

——— 1989. *American Genesis.* New York: Penguin Books.

Hughes, William R. 1971. "Scale Frontiers in Electric Power." In *Technological Change in Regulated Industries,* ed. W. Capron. Washington, D.C.: Brookings Institution.

Hybritech, Inc. v. Monoclonal Antibodies, Inc., 623 Federal Supplement 1344 (N.D. Cal. 1985), reversed 802 Federal Reports 2d 1367 (1986).

International Nickel Co., Inc. v. Ford Motor Co., 166 Federal Supplement 551 (1958).

James, John A., and Jonathan S. Skinner. 1985. "The Resolution of the Labor-Scarcity Paradox." *Journal of Economic History,* September, 45(3): 513–540.

Jeremy, David. 1981. *Transatlantic Industrial Revolution.* Cambridge, Mass.: MIT Press.

Jewkes, John, David Sawers, and Richard Stillerman. 1969. *The Sources of Invention.* New York: W. W. Norton.

Jones, David T., and S. J. Prais. 1978. "Plant-Size and Productivity in the Motor

Industry: Some International Comparisons." *Oxford Bulletin of Economics and Statistics,* May, 40: 131–152.

Jorgenson, Dale W., and Zvi Griliches. 1967. "The Explanation of Productivity Growth." *Review of Economic Studies,* July, 34: 249–283.

Jorgenson, Dale W., and Barbara Fraumeni. 1980. *Substitution and Technical Change in Production.* Cambridge, Mass.: Harvard Institute of Economic Research Discussion Paper No. 752, March.

Kamien, Morton I., and Nancy L. Schwartz. 1975. "Market Structure and Innovation: A Survey." *Journal of Economic Literature,* March, 13(1): 1–37.

Katz, Barbara Goody, and Almarin Phillips. 1982. "The Computer Industry." *Government and Technical Progress,* ed. Richard Nelson. New York: Pergamon Press, pp. 162–232.

Katz, Michael, and Carl Shapiro. 1985. "Network Externalities, Competition, and Compatibility." *American Economic Review,* June, 75: 424–440.

Kendrick, John W. 1956. "Productivity Trends: Capital and Labor." *Review of Economics and Statistics,* August, 38: 248–257.

——— 1961. *Productivity Trends in the United States.* New York: NBER; Princeton: Princeton University Press.

——— 1973. *Postwar Productivity Trends in the United States, 1948–1969.* New York: NBER, Columbia University Press.

Kendrick, John W., and E. Grossman. 1980. *Productivity in the United States: Trends and Cycles.* Baltimore: Johns Hopkins Press.

Kennedy, Paul. 1987. *The Rise and Fall of the Great Powers.* New York: Random House.

Kindleberger, Charles. 1964. *Economic Growth in France and Britain, 1851–1950.* Cambridge, Mass.: Harvard University Press.

Kitch, Edward. 1977. "The Nature and Function of the Patent System." *Journal of Law and Economics,* 20: 265–290.

Klein, Burton H. 1962. "The Decision Making Problem in Development." In *The Rate and Direction of Inventive Activity: Economic and Social Factors: A Conference of the Universities-National Bureau Committee for Economic Research.* Princeton: Princeton University Press for the NBER, pp. 477–497.

——— 1977. *Dynamic Economics.* Cambridge, Mass.: Harvard University Press.

Klemperer, Paul. 1990. "How Broad Should the Scope of Patent Protection Be?" *Rand Journal of Economics,* Spring, 21: 113–130.

Kocka, Jürgen. 1980. "The Rise of the Modern Industrial Enterprise in Germany." *Managerial Hierarchies,* ed. Alfred D. Chandler and Herman Daems. Cambridge, Mass.: Harvard University Press, pp. 77–116.

Koenig, E. 1983. "A Bibliometric Analysis of Pharmaceutical Research." *Research Policy,* 12: 15–36.

Kogut, Bruce. 1987. "Country Patterns in International Competition: Appropriability and Oligopolistic Agreement." *Strategies in Global Competition,* ed. N. Hood and J. Vahlne. London: Croom-Helm, pp. 315–340.

——— 1992. "National Organizing Principles of Work, and the Erstwhile Dominance of the American Multinational Corporation." *Industrial and Corporate Change,* 285–326.

Koopmans, Tjalling C. 1957. *Three Essays on the State of Economic Science.* New York: McGraw-Hill.

Kranzberg, M., ed. 1986. *Technological Education—Technological Style.* San Francisco: San Francisco Press.

Krugman, Paul, ed. 1987. *Strategic Trade Policy and the New International Economics.* Cambridge, Mass.: MIT Press.

Kuznets, Simon. 1966. *Modern Economic Growth: Rate, Structure, and Spread.* New Haven, Conn.: Yale University Press.

Landau, Ralph. 1990a. "Chemical Engineering: Key to the Growth of the Chemical Process Industries." In *Competitiveness of the U.S. Chemical Industry in International Markets,* ed. Jaromir J. Ulbrecht. American Institute of Chemical Engineers, Symposium Series No. 274.

———— 1990b. "Capital Investment: Key to Competitiveness and Growth." *Brookings Review,* Summer, 8: 52–56.

Landau, Ralph, and Nathan Rosenberg. 1992. "Successful Commercialization in the Chemical Process Industries." In *Technology and the Wealth of Nations,* ed. Ralph Landau, David Mowery, and Nathan Rosenberg. Stanford: Stanford University Press.

Landes, D. 1970. *The Unbound Prometheus.* Cambridge: Cambridge University Press.

Langlois, Richard N. 1987. "Schumpeter and the Obsolescence of the Entrepreneur." Paper presented at the History of Economics Society Meeting, Boston.

———— 1988. *Microeconomics: An Industry in Transition.* Boston: Unwin Hyman.

———— 1991. "Transaction Cost Economics in Real Time." *Industrial and Corporate Change,* June: 99–127.

Lazonick, William. 1990. *Competitive Advantage on the Shop Floor.* Cambridge, Mass.: Harvard University Press.

Lebergott, Stanley. 1976. *The American Economy: Income, Wealth, and Want.* Princeton: Princeton University Press.

Leder, P., and T. Stewart. 1988. U.S. Patent 4,736,866.

Leibenstein, Harvey. 1966. "Allocative Efficiency vs. X-Efficiency." *American Economic Review,* June, 56: 392–415.

———— 1976. *Beyond Economic Man: A New Foundation for Microeconomics.* Cambridge, Mass.: Harvard University Press.

———— 1979. "A Branch of Economics Is Missing: Micro-Micro Theory?" *Journal of Economic Literature,* June, 17(2): 477–502.

Leslie, Stuart, and Bruce Hardy. 1985. "Steeple Building at Stanford: Electrical Engineering, Physics, and Microwave Research." *Proceedings of the IEEE,* July: 1168–1179.

Levin, Richard C. 1982. "The Semiconductor Industry." *Government and Technical Progress,* ed. R. R. Nelson. New York: Pergamon Press, pp. 9–100.

Levin, Richard C., A. Klevorich, Richard Nelson, and Sidney Winter. 1987. "Appropriating the Returns to Industrial R&D." *Brookings Papers on Economic Activity,* No. 3: 783–820.

Levine, David O. 1986. *The American College and the Culture of Aspiration, 1915–1940.* Ithaca, N.Y.: Cornell University Press, p. 52.

Lindbeck, Assar. 1974. *Swedish Economic Policy.* Berkeley, Calif.: University of California Press.

Lipsey, Robert E., and Irving J. Kravis. 1987. "The Competitiveness and Comparative Advantage of U.S. Multinationals, 1957–1984." *Banca Nazionale Lavoro Quarterly Rev.,* June, 161: 147–65.

Little, Arthur D. 1933. *Twenty-Five Years of Chemical Engineering Progress,* Silver Anniversary Volume. New York: American Institute of Chemical Engineers, D. Van Nostrand Company, pp. 7–8.

Lundberg, Erik. 1968. *Instability and Economic Growth.* New Haven, Conn.: Yale University Press.

Lundvall, B. A. 1988. "Innovation as an Interactive Process: From User-Producer Interaction to the National System of Innovation." In *Technical Change and Economic Theory,* ed. G. Dosi et al. London: Pinter Publishers.

Lupton, T. 1963. *On the Shop Floor: Two Studies of Workshop Organization and Output.* New York: Macmillan.

MacAvoy, Paul W. 1979. *The Regulated Industries and the Economy.* New York: W. W. Norton.

MacKenzie, Frederick A. 1976 [1901]. *The American Invaders.* New York: Arno Press.

Maddison, Angus. 1967. *Economic Growth in the West: Comparative Experience in Europe and North America.* New York: W. W. Norton.

——— 1979. "Long-Run Dynamics of Productivity Growth." *Banca Nazionale Lavoro Quarterly Review,* March: 3–44.

——— 1980. "Western Economic Performance in the 1970s: A Perspective." *Banca Naz. Lavoro Quart. Rev.,* September: 247–288.

——— 1987. "Growth and Slowdown in Advanced Capitalist Economies: Techniques of Quantitative Assessment." *Journal of Economic Literature,* June, 25(2): 649–698.

——— 1989. *The World Economy in the Twentieth Century.* Paris: OECD.

——— 1991. *Dynamic Forces in Capitalist Development.* New York: Oxford University Press.

Malerba, Franco. 1985. *The Semiconductor Business.* Madison, Wisc.: University of Wisconsin Press.

Mansfield, Edwin. 1962. "Entry, Gilbrat's Law, Innovation, and the Growth of Firms." *American Economic Review,* 53, December.

——— 1968. *Industrial Research and Technological Innovation: An Econometric Analysis.* New York: W. W. Norton.

———— 1972. "Contribution of R and D to Economic Growth in the United States." *Science,* 175, February.

———— 1980. "Basic Research and Productivity Increase in Manufacturing." *American Economic Review,* 70: 863–873.

———— 1991. "Academic Research and Industrial Innovation." *Research Policy,* 20: 1–12.

Mansfield, Edwin, J. Rapoport, J. Schnee, S. Wagner, and M. Hamburger. 1971. *Research and Development in the Modern Corporation.* New York: W. W. Norton.

Mansfield, Edwin, J. Rapoport, A. Romeo, E. Villani, S. Wagner, and F. Husic. 1977. *The Production and Application of New Industrial Technology.* New York: W. W. Norton.

Mansfield, Edwin, Mark Schwartz, and Samuel Wagner. 1980. "Imitation Costs and Patents: An Empirical Analysis." Mimeo.

March, James G., and Herbert A. Simon. 1958. *Organizations.* New York: John Wiley and Sons.

Marschak, Jakob, and Roy Radner. 1972. *Economic Theory of Teams.* New Haven, Conn.: Yale University Press.

Marschak, T., T. Glennan, and R. Summers. 1967. *Strategy for R&D.* New York: Springer Verlag.

Marshall, A. 1948 [1920]. *Principles of Economics,* 8th ed. New York: Macmillan.

Marx, Karl. 1932. *Capital.* New York: Random House.

McFetridge, D., and R. Rafiguizzaman. 1986. "The Scope of Duration of Patent Right and the Nature of Research Rivalry." *Research in Law and Economics,* 8: 91–120.

McMahon, A. M. 1984. *The Making of a Profession: A Century of Electrical Engineering in America.* New York: Institute of Electrical and Electronic Engineers.

Mennell, Peter. 1987. "Tailoring Legal Protection to Computer Software." *Stanford Law Review,* July: 1329–1372.

Merges, Robert, and Richard Nelson. 1990. "The Complex Economies of Patent Scope." *Columbia Law Review,* 90: 839–916.

Miller, Ronald, and David Sawers. 1968. *The Technical Development of Modern Aviation.* London: Routledge and Kegan Paul.

Morison, Elting E. 1974. *From Know-How to Nowhere.* New York: Basic Books.

Mowery, David C. 1981. "The Emergence and Growth of Industrial Research in American Manufacturing, 1899–1945." Ph.D. diss., Stanford University.

———— 1983. "The Relationship between Intrafirm and Contractual Forms of Industrial Research in American Manufacturing, 1900–1940." *Explorations in Economic History,* 20, no. 4: 351–374.

———— 1988. *International Collaborative Ventures in U.S. Manufacturing.* Cambridge, Mass.: Ballinger Press.

Mowery, David C., and Nathan Rosenberg. 1979. "The Influence of Market Demand upon Innovation: A Critical Survey of Several Recent Empirical Studies." *Research Policy,* 6: 102–153.

—— 1989. *Economic Growth*. New York: Cambridge University Press.

Mueller, Dennis, and John Tilton. 1970. "Research and Development as a Barrier to Entry." *Canadian Journal of Economics*, February, 2: 570–579.

Murrell, Peter. 1990. *The Nature of Socialist Economics: Lessons from Eastern European Foreign Trade*. Princeton: Princeton University Press.

Nadiri, M. Ishaq. 1970. "Some Approaches to the Theory and Measurement of Total Factor Productivity: A Survey." *Journal of Economic Literature*, December, 85(4): 1137–1177.

—— 1980. "Sectoral Productivity Slowdown." *American Economic Review*, May, 70: 349–352.

Narin, F., and F. Noma. 1985. "Is Technology Becoming Science?" *Scienceometrics*, 7: 369–381.

Narin, F., and R. Rozek. 1988. "Bibliometric Analysis of U.S. Pharmaceutical Industry Research Performance." *Research Policy*, 17: 139–154.

National Resources Committee. 1938. *Research: A National Resource*. Vol. 1. Washington, D.C.: Government Printing Office, p. 178.

National Science Foundation. 1991. *Science and Engineering Indicators, 1991*. Washington, D.C.: Government Printing Office.

National Science Foundation, Science Resources Studies Division. 1991. "Academic Science/Engineering: R&D Expenditures, Fiscal Year 1989, NSF 90-321, Detailed Statistical Tables." National Science Foundation, Washington, D.C.

Nelson, Richard R. 1959. "The Simple Economics of Basic Scientific Research." *Journal of Political Economy*, 67(3): 297–306.

—— 1961. "Uncertainty, Learning, and the Economics of Parallel Research and Development Efforts." *Review of Economics and Statistics*, 43: 351–364.

——, ed. 1962. *The Rate and Direction of Inventive Activity*. Princeton: Princeton University Press.

—— 1973. "Recent Exercises in Growth Accounting: New Understanding or Dead End?" *American Economic Review*, June, 63(3): 462–468.

—— 1980. "R&D, Knowledge, and Externalities." In *Economic Growth and Resources*. Vol. 3, *Natural Resources*, ed. C. Bliss and M. Boserup. London: Macmillan, pp. 146–151.

——, ed. 1982. *Government and Technical Progress: A Cross-Industry Analysis*. New York: Pergamon Press.

—— 1984. *High Technology Policies: A Five Country Comparison*. Washington, D.C.: American Enterprise Institute.

—— 1988. "Institutions Supporting Technical Change in U.S. Industry." In *Technical Change and Economic Theory*, ed. Giovanni Dosi et al. London: Pinter Publishers, pp. 312–329.

—— 1990. "The U.S. Technological Lead: Where Did It Come From and Where Did It Go?" *Research Policy*, August, 19: 117–132.

——, ed. 1993. *National Innovation Systems: A Comparative Analysis*. New York: Oxford University Press.

Nelson, Richard R., and Edmund Phelps. 1966. "Investment in Humans, Technological Diffusion, and Economic Growth." *American Economic Review*, May, 56: 69–75.

Nelson, Richard R., Merton J. Peck, and Edward D. Kalachek. 1967. *Technology, Economic Growth, and Public Policy.* Washington, D.C.: Brookings Institution.

Nelson, Richard R., T. Paul Schultz, and Robert L. Slighton. 1971. *Structural Change in a Developing Economy: Colombia's Problems and Prospects.* Princeton: Princeton University Press.

Nelson, Richard R., and Sidney Winter. 1977. "In Search of Useful Theory of Innovation." *Research Policy*, Summer, 6: 36–76.

———— 1982. *An Evolutionary Theory of Economic Change.* Cambridge, Mass.: Harvard University Press.

New York Times. 1991. "AIDS Drug Patent Challenged in Suit." March 20, p. 19, col. 1.

Noble, David. 1977. *America by Design.* New York: Alfred A. Knopf.

———— 1984. *Forces of Production.* New York: Alfred A. Knopf.

Nordhaus, William D. 1969. *Invention, Growth, and Welfare: A Theoretical Treatment of Technological Change.* Cambridge, Mass.: MIT Press.

Ordover, J., and G. Saloner. 1989. "Predation, Monopolization, and Antitrust." In *Handbook of Industrial Organization*, ed. R. Schmalensee and R. Willig. New York: North Holland, pp. 537–596.

Ostry, Sylvia. 1990. *Governments and Corporations in a Shrinking World.* New York: Council on Foreign Relations Press.

Pavitt, Keith, ed. 1980. *Technical Innovation and British Economic Performance.* London: Macmillan.

———— 1984. "Sectoral Patterns of Technical Change: Towards a Taxonomy and a Theory." *Research Policy*, 13: 343–373.

———— 1987a. "On the Nature of Technology." Inaugural lecture delivered at the University of Sussex, 23 June.

———— 1987b. "The Objectives of Technology Policy." *Science and Public Policy*, 4: 182–188.

———— 1990. "The Nature and Determinants of Innovation: A Major Factor in Firms' (and Countries') Competitiveness." Paper prepared for the conference on "Fundamental Issues in Strategy: A Research Agenda for the 1990s."

Pavitt, Keith, and R. Patel. 1987. "Is Western Europe Losing the Technological Race?" *Research Policy*, 16: 59–85.

Peck, Merton J. 1986. "Joint R&D: The Case of Microelectronics and Computer Technology Corporation." *Research Policy*, 15: 219–231.

Penrose, Edith. 1959. *The Theory of the Growth of the Firm.* London: Basil Blackwell.

Perrow, Charles. 1979. *Complex Organization: A Critical Essay.* 2nd ed. Glenview, Ill.: Scott Foresman.

Peters, L., and H. Fusfeld. 1982. *Current U.S. University-Industry Research Connections in University-Industry Research Relationships.* Washington, D.C.: National Science Board.

Phelps-Brown, H. E. 1973. "Levels and Movements of Industrial Productivity and Real Wages Internationally Compared, 1860–1970." *Economic Journal*, March, 83(329): 58–71.

Phillips, Almarin. 1971. *Technology and Market Structure: A Study of the Aircraft Industry*. Lexington, Mass.: Heath Lexington.

Pigou, A. 1932. *Economics of Welfare*. London: Cambridge University Press.

Piore, Michael J., and Charles F. Sabel. 1984. *The Second Industrial Divide*. New York: Basic Books.

Popper, Karl R. 1959. *The Logic of Scientific Discovery*. New York: Basic Books.

Porter, Michael E. 1990. *The Competitive Advantage of Nations*. New York: Free Press.

Prahalad, C. K., and G. Hamel. 1990. "The Core Competence of the Corporation." *Harvard Business Review*, 68(3): 79–91.

Pratten, Clifford F. 1976. *A Comparison of the Performance of Swedish and U.K. Companies*. Cambridge: Cambridge University Press.

——— 1976. *Labour Productivity Differentials within International Companies*. Cambridge: Cambridge University Press.

Price, Don K. 1962. *Government and Science: Their Dynamic Relation in American Democracy*. New York: Oxford University Press.

Ray, G. F. 1974. "Introduction" and "Summary of Interim Report." In *The Diffusion of New Industrial Processes: An International Study,* by L. Nasbeth and G. F. Ray. Cambridge: Cambridge University Press, pp. 1–21.

Reich, Leonard S. 1985. *The Making of American Industrial Research: Science and Business at G.E. and Bell*. New York: Cambridge University Press.

Reich, Robert. 1991. *The Work of Nations*. New York: Knopf.

Reinganum, J. 1989. "The Timing of Innovation: Research, Development, and Diffusion." In *Handbook of Industrial Organization*, ed. R. Schmalensee and R. Willig. New York: North Holland.

Richter, M. 1966. "Invariance Axioms and Economic Indexes." *Econometrica*, October, 34: 739–755.

Roethlisberger, Fritz, and William Dickson. 1939. *Management and the Worker: An Account of a Research Project Conducted by the Western Electric Company*. Cambridge, Mass.: Harvard University Press.

Rogers, Everit. 1981. "Technological Information-Exchange in High-Technology Industry in the Silicon Valley." In *The Transfer and Utilization of Technological Knowledge*. Lexington, Mass.: D. C. Heath.

Rosenberg, Nathan. 1963. "Technological Change in the Machine Tool Industry, 1840–1910." *Journal of Economic History*, December, 23: 414–443.

——— 1969. "The Direction of Technological Change: Inducement Mechanisms and Focusing Devices." *Economic Development and Cultural Change*, part I, 18(1): 1–24.

——— 1974. "Science, Invention, and Economic Growth." *Economic Journal*, 84: 90–108.

——— 1976. *Perspectives on Technology*. Cambridge: Cambridge University Press.

—— 1982. *Inside the Black Box: Technology and Economics*. Cambridge: Cambridge University Press.

—— 1985. "The Commercial Exploitation of Science by American Industry." In *The Uneasy Alliance: Managing the Productivity-Technology Dilemma*, ed. K. Clark, R. Hayes, and C. Lorenz. Boston: Harvard Business School Press.

—— 1986. "Schumpeter and Marx: How Common a Vision." In *Technology and the Human Prospect*, ed. Roy MacLeod. London: Francis Pinter.

—— 1988. "Why Do Firms Do Basic Research (with Their Own Money)?" *Research Policy*, 19: 165–174.

Rosenberg, Nathan, and C. Frischtak. 1984. "Technological Innovation and Long Waves." In *Design, Innovation, and Long Cycles*, ed. C. Freeman. London: Thetford Press.

Rosenberg, Robert. 1984. "The Origins of Electrical Engineering Education: A Matter of Degree." IEEE Spectrum, July.

Rosenbloom, Richard, ed. 1993. "The Future of Industrial Research," papers presented at the Harvard Business School Conference, 10–12 February.

Ross, Stephen A. 1973. "The Economic Theory of Agency: The Principal's Problem." *American Economic Review*, May, 63(2): 134–139.

Rostas, László. 1948. *Comparative Productivity in British and American Industry*. Cambridge: Cambridge University Press.

Rumelt, R. P. 1984. "Towards a Strategic Theory of the Firm." In *Competitive Strategic Management*, ed. R. B. Lamb. Englewood Cliffs, N.J.: Prentice-Hall, pp. 556–570.

Ryan, Bryce, and Neal Gross. 1943. "The Diffusion of Hybrid Seed Corn in Two Iowa Communities." *Rural Sociology*, March, 8(1): 15–24.

Sahal, Devendra. 1981. *Patterns of Technological Innovation*. Reading, Mass.: Addison-Wesley.

Salter, W. E. G. 1960 [1966, 2nd ed.]. *Productivity and Technical Change*. Cambridge: Cambridge University Press.

Scherer, F. M., et al. 1959. *Patents and the Corporation*. Boston: Privately printed.

Schmalensee, Richard, and Robert Willig, eds. 1989. *Handbook of Industrial Organization*. New York: North Holland.

Schmookler, Jacob. 1952. "The Changing Efficiency of the American Economy." *Review of Economics and Statistics*, August, 34: 214–231.

—— 1962. "Determinants of Industrial Invention." In *The Rate and Direction of Inventive Activities*, ed. Richard R. Nelson. Princeton: NBER.

—— 1966. *Invention and Economic Growth*. Cambridge, Mass.: Harvard University Press.

Schonfield, Andrew. 1965. *Modern Capitalism*. New York: Oxford University Press.

Schultz, Theodore William. 1953. *The Economic Organization of Agriculture*. New York: McGraw-Hill.

—— 1975. "The Value of the Ability to Deal with Disequilibria." *Journal of Economic Literature*, September, 13(3): 827–846.

Schumpeter, Joseph A. 1939. *Business Cycles.* New York: McGraw-Hill.

——— 1950 [1942]. *Capitalism, Socialism, and Democracy.* New York: Harper and Row.

——— 1954. *History of Economic Analysis.* New York: Oxford University Press.

——— 1961 [1911]. *The Theory of Economic Development.* New York: Oxford University Press.

Schwartzman, David. 1975. *Innovation in the Pharmaceutical Industry.* Baltimore: Johns Hopkins University Press.

Scotchmer, Susan. 1991. "Standing on the Shoulders of Giants." *Journal of Economic Perspectives,* Winter: 29–42.

Scotchmer, Susan, and J. Green. 1990. "Novelty and Disclosure in Patent Law." *Rand Journal of Economics,* Spring: 131–146.

Servan-Schreiber, Jean Jacques. 1968. *The American Challenge.* New York: Atheneum Press.

Servos, John W. 1980. "The Industrial Relations of Science: Chemical Engineering at MIT, 1900–1939." *Isis,* 71, December: 531–549.

Shapley, Deborah, and Rustum Roy. 1985. *Lost at the Frontier.* Philadelphia: ISI Press.

Shockley, William, and John Bardeen. 1956. Nobel Prize (for Physics) Lectures.

Simon, Herbert A. 1957. *Administrative Behavior: A Study of Decision-Making Processes in Administrative Organization.* 3rd ed. New York: Free Press.

——— 1969. *The Sciences of the Artificial.* Cambridge, Mass.: MIT Press.

Smith, John Kenly, Jr. 1990. "The Scientific Tradition in American Industrial Research." *Technology and Culture,* January, 31.

Smyth, H. D. 1946. *Atomic Energy for Military Purposes.* Princeton: Princeton University Press.

Soete, Luc. 1981. "A General Test of Technological Gap Grade Theory." *Weltwirsch. Arch.,* 117(4): 638–660.

Soete, Luc, et al. 1989. *Recent Comparative Trends in Technological Indicators in the OECD Area.* The Netherlands: Maastricht Economic Research Institute on Innovation and Technology.

Solow, Robert M. 1956. "A Contribution to the Theory of Economic Growth." *Quarterly Journal of Economics,* February, 70: 65–94.

——— 1957. "Technical Change and the Aggregate Production Function." *Review of Economics and Statistics,* August, 39: 214–231.

——— 1970. *Growth Theory: An Exposition.* Oxford: Oxford University Press.

Solow, Robert M., et al. 1966. "Neoclassical Growth with Fixed Factor Propositions." *Review of Economic Studies,* April, 33: 79–115.

Spitz, Peter H. 1988. *Petrochemicals: The Rise of an Industry.* New York: John Wiley and Sons.

Stein, John P., and Allen Lee. 1977. *Productivity Growth in Industrial Countries at the Sectoral Level, 1963–1974.* Santa Monica, Calif.: RAND Corporation, R-2203-CIEP, June.

Stern, Nancy. 1981. *From ENIAC to Univac.* Bedford, Mass.: Digital Press, chap. 2.

Stoneman, Paul. 1987. *The Economic Analysis of Technology Policy.* Oxford: Oxford University Press.

Swan, T. W. 1956. "Economic Growth and Capital Accumulation." *Economic Record,* November, 32: 334–361.

Swords-Isherwood, Nuala. 1980. "British Management Compared." In *Technical Innovation and British Economic Performance,* ed. Keith Pavitt. London: Macmillan Press, pp. 88–99.

Taylor, Frederick W. 1911. *The Principles of Scientific Management.* New York: Harper.

Teece, David J. 1976. *The Multinational Corporation and the Resource Cost of Technology Transfer.* Cambridge: Ballinger.

―――― 1977. "Technology Transfer by Multinational Firms: The Resource Cost of Transferring Technological Know-How." *Economic Journal,* June, 87 (346): 242–261.

―――― 1980. "Economies of Scope and the Scope of the Enterprise." *Journal of Economic Behavior and Organization,* 1: 223–247.

―――― 1982. "Towards an Economic Theory of the Multiproduct Firm." *Journal of Economic Behavior and Organization,* March: 39–63.

―――― 1986. "Profiting from Technological Innovation." *Research Policy,* 15: 285–305.

Teece, David J., G. Pisano, and A. Shuen. 1990. "Firm Capabilities, Resources, and the Concept of Strategy." CCC Working Paper 90-8, Center for Research on Management, University of California at Berkeley.

Texas Instruments, Inc. v. United States International Trade Commission, 805 Federal Reports 2d 1558 (Federal Circuit 1986).

Thackray, Arnold. 1982. "University-Industry Connections and Chemical Research: An Historical Perspective." In *University-Industry Research Relationships.* Washington, D.C.: National Science Board.

The Incandescent Lamp Patent, 159 United States Reports 465 (1895).

Thomson, Ross. 1989. *The Path to Mechanized Shoe Production in the United States.* Chapel Hill: University of North Carolina Press.

Tobin, James. 1980. "Stabilization Policy Ten Years After." *Brookings Papers in Economic Activity,* January: 19–90.

Tocqueville, Alexis de. 1876. *Democracy in America.* Vol. 2. Boston: John Allyn Publisher, pp. 48, 52, 53.

Tushman, Michael, and P. Anderson. 1986. "Technological Discontinuities and Organizational Environments." *Administrative Science Quarterly,* September: 439–465.

Tweedale, Geoffrey. 1986. "Metallurgy and Technological Change: A Case Study of Sheffield Specialty Steel and America, 1830–1930." *Technology and Culture,* April, 27.

U.S. National Science Board. 1987, 1989, 1991. *Science and Engineering Indicators.* Washington, D.C.

Veblen, Thorstein. 1921. *The Engineers and the Price System.* New York: Viking Press.

Vernon, Raymond. 1966. "International Investment and International Trade in Product Cycles." *Quarterly Journal of Economics,* May, 80: 190–207.

Vincenti, Walter. 1990. *What Engineers Know and How They Know It.* Baltimore: Johns Hopkins Press, chaps. 4 and 5.

Vogel, Ezra F. 1979. *Japan as Number One: Lessons for America.* Cambridge, Mass.: Harvard University Press.

Von Hippel, Eric. 1976. "The Dominant Role of Users in the Scientific Instruments Innovation Process." *Research Policy,* 5: 212–239.

——— 1982. "Appropriability of Innovation Benefit as a Predictor of Source of Innovation." *Research Policy,* 11: 95.

——— 1988. *The Source of Innovation.* Oxford: Oxford University Press.

Vroom, Victor. 1976. "Leadership." In *Handbook of Industrial and Organizational Psychology,* ed. Marvin D. Dunnette. Chicago: Rand McNally, pp. 1527–1552.

Weber, Max. 1947. *The Theory of Social and Economic Organization.* Trans. A. M. Henderson and Talcott Parsons. Glencoe, Ill.: Free Press.

Welch, Finis. 1970. "Education in Production." *Journal of Political Economy,* January/February, 78(1): 34–59.

Wildes, Karl L., and Nilo A. Lindgren. 1985. *A Century of Electrical Engineering and Computer Science at MIT, 1882–1982.* Cambridge, Mass.: MIT Press.

Wilkins, Mira. 1970. *The Emergence of Multinational Enterprise: American Business Abroad from the Colonial Era to 1914.* Cambridge, Mass.: Harvard University Press.

Williamson, Oliver E. 1970. *Corporate Control and Business Behavior: An Inquiry into the Effects of Organization Form on Enterprise Behavior.* Englewood Cliffs, N.J.: Prentice-Hall.

——— 1975. *Markets and Hierarchies: Analysis and Antitrust Implications.* New York: Free Press.

——— 1981. "The Modern Corporation: Origins, Evolution, Attributes." *Journal of Economic Literature,* December, 19: 1537–1564.

——— 1985. *The Economic Institutions of Capitalism.* New York: Free Press.

Winter, Sidney G. 1964. "Economic 'Natural Selection' and the Theory of the Firm." *Yale Economic Essays,* Spring, 4: 225–272.

Wohlin, Lars. 1970. "Structural Change on the Forest Industries." *Skandinavian Banken Quarterly Review,* May, 4(51): 110–115.

Womack, James, Daniel T. Jones, and Daniel Roos. 1991. *The Machine That Changed the World.* Cambridge, Mass.: MIT Press.

Woodward, Joan. 1965. *Industrial Organization: Theory and Practice.* London: Oxford University Press.

Wright, Gavin. 1990. "The Origins of American Industrial Success, 1879–1940." *American Economic Review*, September, 80(4): 651–668.

Wyatt, S., G. Bertin, and K. Pavitt. 1985. "Patents and Multinational Corporations: Results from Questionnaires." *World Patent Information*, Fall.